Anyone Can Be An Expert Skier 2

Powder, Bumps, and Carving

Harald R. Harb

Anyone Can Be An Expert Skier 2–Powder, Bumps and Carving
A Getfitnow.com Book

Hatherleigh Press/Getfitnow.com Books
An Affiliate of W.W. Norton and Company, Inc.
5-22 46th Avenue, Suite 200
Long Island CIty, NY 11101
Toll Free 1-800-528-2550
Visit our websites getfitnow.com and hatherleighpress.com

DISCLAIMER:

Anyone Can Be An Expert Skier books are available for bulk purchase, special promotions and premiums. For more information on reselling and special purchase opportunities, please call us at 1-800-528-2550 and ask for the Special Sales Manager.

LIBRARY OF CONGRESS CATALOGING AND PUBLICATION DATA TO COME
ISBN: 1-57826-074-4

Interior Layout and Design, Photomontages, and Illustrations by Diana Rogers

Cover Design by Peter Gunther

Photos by Byron Hetzler

VISIT THE HARB SKI SYSTEMS WEB SITE
www.harbskisystems.com
NEW RELEASES • INSTRUCTION • CAMPS • RESORT INFORMATION

---

10 9 8 7 6 5 4 3 2 1
Printed in Canada on acid-free paper.

Contents

About the Author

Harald Harb is president of Harb Ski Systems. An Austrian by birth, he moved to Eastern Canada shortly thereafter. He followed his desire to become a skier from an early age, winning his first regional race in the Laurentain Mountains of Quebec at eight. Harald raced in his first World Cup race at 18 with the Canadian National Ski Team and later was the Overall Pro Ski Champion on the US Eastern Regional Circuit. He then started to coach racers and became a director of racing programs. Harald's understanding of skiing movement developed through study of anatomy and kinesiology, as well as his coaching experience. Harald directed and coached programs that produced some of the USA's most successful National Team members and Olympic medalists. He has been a master coach in the USSCA organization since 1985. He was the program director for Glacier Creek Academy in Alaska, the program that developed Tommy Moe, Olympic gold medalist.

After coaching for 20 years, Harald spent four years on the US National Demonstration Team. He was a Rocky Mt. PSIA Examiner and Trainer. Working with recreational skiers, he was convinced that current teaching systems needed improvement. Harald developed and established the Alignment Performance center concept at Aspen and Telluride. Now he operates his own centers. Harald created the Primary Movements Teaching System™ and the Harb Skier Alignment System™ so that skiers could learn movements and choose equipment to become expert quickly. He is the author of four books on skiing and skiing-related subjects. Over 100,000 lessons have been taught with his system. PMTS Direct Parallel, as it is called, currently is the only teaching system in use that makes a clean break from the traditional wedge, wedge christie progressions.

Harald also writes for *Skiing* magazine and several skiing Web sites. Harald and Robert Hintermeister, Ph. D., co-author of the *PMTS Instructor Manual*, presented the PMTS Direct Parallel System and Harb Skier Alignment System to the 2nd International Congress of Skiing and Science in St. Christoph, Austria, in January 2000. The Association of PMTS Direct Parallel Instructors is a new not-for-profit organization formed for the further education of ski instructors worldwide. Harald is the Technical Director of the PMTS Instructor Association.

You can keep up to date with Harald and Harb Ski Systems on the Web site,

www.harbskisystems.com

Acknowledgments

I just come up with the ideas, ski for the photographs and write the thing, then pass it on to the editors. Presto, that's all it takes for a new book. I only wish it were that easy. This book has been in the works for the past three years. It was conceived right after the first *Anyone can be an Expert Skier*. The ideas came from developing skiers of all kinds. I started with racers. Racers need to learn to ski just like anyone else and they need to learn to ski well before they can ski fast. Too many racers ski poorly and stagnate during their racing careers. I see it all the time at the start of races: coaches and racers rubbing and brushing expensive wax to gain that extra tenth of a second. I watch them ski the first few gates where they lose two seconds because of poor technique. The wax isn't the problem. As long as they are having fun, that's okay, but with a half a day of good ski instruction they could make up tenfold what they try to gain with waxing.

I thank the racers whom I coached over the years; I learned from them as they learned. I learned what worked and what didn't. I've coached 12- and 13-year-old kids who achieved more then I ever dreamed. Some grew up to compete in the National Championships, NCAA, Olympics and World Championships, and some won medals.

I'd also like to thank the skiers who bought my first book and attend my camps and private lessons. I have watched them exceed their expectations, becoming expert skiers in all conditions. They are dedicated skiers and they have drive. They believe in themselves, they know they can do it, but for some reason had never found the answers. These are the skiers who motivated me to develop the ideas for this book. I thank you for giving me the opportunity to work with your skiing, and I thank you for trusting me.

Encouragement and having people believe in what you are doing is as important as personal drive and perseverance. PMTS is developing a huge following. Its not because thousands of people are skiing with me or with the best PMTS instructors, it's because they are reading my books and the methods work.

My greatest supporter as well as critic is my partner, Diana Rogers. Diana is an aerospace engineer, and just as importantly, she is a great skier and coach. I don't know anyone better. She is a graduate of the University of Colorado and has a master's degree from Stanford. Skiers love to ski with her and learn from her. There is no one I know who wouldn't learn and benefit from her coaching. She is so clear and easy to understand. Diana is a deserving member of the small but elite PMTS Training, Teaching and Skiing Team. She takes rocket science and turns it into cooking soup, simple and easy. Diana is also the master of book layout, photo organizing and montage construction. This is her third book and she gets better with each one.

Bob Hintermeister is a friend and colleague. He holds a Ph.D. in Biomechanics as well as an accreditation in PMTS. These credentials make him a valuable instructor and PMTS trainer. Bob is a rock, so solid in his understanding of mechanics and the human body that I feel relaxed and confident with our programs because of his scrutiny. Bob accompanied me to Austria last winter to present PMTS to the International Congress on Skiing and Science. It was one of the highlights of my coaching career. The most prominent scientists and researchers from universities all over the world attended to present skiing research and learn the latest innovations. To that group we introduced PMTS with overwhelming acceptance. Bob is a respected member of this highly regarded academic group. The respectability that PMTS is developing in the scientific community is due largely to Bob's help in developing the system.

Bob Emery is a friend and PMTS instructor and trainer. PMTS, Harb Ski Systems and this book would not be here if it weren't for Bob's dedication and belief in the system. Bob is an attorney, has his own legal practice and is a professor of law. His guidance has been invaluable in shaping, mentoring and guiding our efforts. Bob is the president of The Association of PMTS Direct Parallel Instructors.

Rich Messer is a skiing icon and has been a friend for over 30 years. He has a degree in education and began his official skiing career as the technical director at Stratton Mountain, where I met him. He was a PSIA examiner in the Eastern Division and former Ski School Director at Glen Ellen, Vermont, before it became Sugarbush. Rich has certified in three different national teaching systems and is a trainer and examiner in three systems. He currently is a trainer and examiner for the Association of PMTS Direct Parallel Instructors. He is the ski school director at Silver Creek, Colorado, and builder of the paper bale house, in Fraser, Colorado. Rich is one of the best skiing evaluators I know. He never misses a detail about skiing movements or teaching methodology. He has been a contributor to PMTS and our books since the beginning.

Kim Peterson holds an MA and is currently completing his dissertation for his Ph.D. in education. He is a PMTS trainer and consultant, and is a co-author of the *PMTS Instructor Manual*. He has been of invaluable assistance with editing and content for this book. Kim introduced me to his methods of Student Directed Ski Instruction when I was training director at Winter Park ski school. I immediately enrolled Kim as a trainer in the ski school and we have worked together ever since.

Craig McNeil, friend and ski buddy, black level PMTS instructor and ski writer for the *Rocky Mountain News*. Craig has been writing the only ski information fit to print for the last six years. John Clendenin is former two-time world freestyle champion, PMTS black level instructor and advisor. Thanks to Descente for providing Harb Ski Systems with its uniforms.

There are hundreds of instructors and skiers who have supported us and lent a helping hand through this process of developing PMTS and this most recent book. I acknowledge them here for what they have done for skiing and ski teaching.

Still more thanks to…

Scott Fortner and Loveland Ski Area for the great powder and overall skiing and for providing the locations for photos in this book.

Byron Hetzler, our skiing photographer, for all the great photos.

Mary and Rod Rogers, for their help with editing the book.

Andrew Flach, president of Hatherleigh Press, for his assistance with producing our books.

Foreword

The fact that you have this book in your hands (and are reading the foreword) suggests that you are a serious student of skiing. Even if this is only your second book on skiing (supposing that *Anyone Can Be An Expert Skier* was your first), you may recognize that you are holding a powerful tool. This book does not skirt the issues of physics or ignore the impact of anatomical concerns. Instead, it will guide you right through them.

Skiing has oft been labeled as a simple sport. Many teachers of skiing appeal to the minimization of complex ideas, the simplification of intricate concepts and the reduction of various unrelated notions by retorting, "Keep It Simple, Stupid (KISS)." While this axiom may prove useful to limit jargon or to focus the ramblings of careless instructors, it certainly does not minimize, simplify or reduce the laws of physics. Truly, the anatomy of a skier does not change because someone teaching skiing wants learning to be easy. Similarly, the laws of physics don't change because a skier struggles to understand them.

During the course of reading this book, you can expect to understand more about the common elements of skiing. You can expect to identify movements and patterns that are common to all skiers in all conditions. After reading this book, you can expect to be able to apply those movements to any skiing terrain, under any snow condition, at any time. Truly, this book defines how to become a versatile skier by introducing new vocabulary and innovative exercises.

Harald's vast experience and genuine concern with the issues of skiing have qualified him to identify movements that mediate the successful negotiation of "any time, anywhere" skiing. You may already know that these are called the "primary movements of skiing." The foundation of PMTS is in the "P". Primary means just that: the foundation or basis from which everything else proceeds. Movements that are primary on your first day are also primary on your best day, your most exciting day and your breakthrough day.

Learning to ski has been plagued with clichés. By definition, a cliché is an overused (hackneyed) phrase. Some of these clichés have ceased to communicate any sort of serious meaning. Consider what is meant by the phrase "point your skis in the direction you want to travel." Any instructor of first-day skiers knows that many first-timers possess the uncanny ability to point their wedge across the hill while picking up speed sliding down the hill. How about the suggestion that as you increase pressure on your downhill ski, your skis will come together? It is clear that some skiers' bodies don't allow that to happen.

Exercises can become cliché also. How many "bicycle turns" does it take to become an expert skier? How many steps are really in "thousand steps" turns? While these exercises can produce good movements in some skiers, they are obviously not the answer to every skier's needs. In fact, these overused skiing exercises have become nothing more than calisthenics. No wonder that many skiers are tired of exercises. Jumping jacks were never that exciting either. You will find that the exercises presented here target specific outcomes and produce observable changes in your skiing.

This book represents years of experience, careful analysis, multiple iterations, and volumes of feedback. The descriptions contained herein promise to be concise and accurate. You will discover that these descriptions are reliable. Not only will you understand the descriptions, you will be able to share them with your friends and those who try to describe skiing to you. Skiers finally have a common language that communicates accurate meaning and is applicable across all situations. As you might expect, these descriptions are not always simple…but they are always accurate.

In addition to the vocabulary of expert skiing, Harald has developed the exercises that produce primary movements. Like the words, the exercises are also not always easy. These exercises identify the components of primary movements and provide a way to make the movements habitual. Mastering the exercises will increase your ability to recall the movement any time and anywhere. This versatility is a coveted ability and distinguishes the expert from the recreational skier. The exercises contained in this book would cost hundreds of dollars to accumulate from intermittent ski lessons. You have them now at your fingertips.

Versatility increases freedom. Can you imagine an airplane that is able to fly only in fair weather? What if an airplane were capable of beautiful take-offs but had little capacity to land? Surely, you'd never board those planes. Some skiers pick and choose the runs and conditions to ski based on a limited ability to comfortably ski any time or anywhere. Maybe you've noticed that you shy away from some terrain or some snow conditions. Once mastered, the vocabulary and movements described in this book will increase your freedom. Imagine standing above the run that has always intimidated you, knowing that when you need to, you'll be able to turn, absorb, create balance, or stop. This kind of confidence can be learned only through accurate descriptions and relevant exercises. Now you can ski the hill instead of having the hill ski you.

The "T" in PMTS is also significant. Primary movements can't be communicated in secondary or tertiary generalities. The precision and accuracy of primary movements demand precision and accuracy in the delivery system. For this reason, an experiential approach has been adopted to form the Teaching System for Primary Movements. As you discover primary movements you also access past experiences by creating situations in which you can discover new meaning. By combining new vocabulary with new experiences, your ability to recall those experiences also will increase.

The forces involved in skiing haven't changed; the body parts involved in skiing haven't changed. Since these things have been common from the first pioneers who sought to slide on snow, some ski teachers have concluded that the Primary Movements Teaching System is another description of what skiers have always done. These naïve criticisms resemble the conclusion that since skiing and fishing both use poles, they must be the same. While neither the parts of the body or the laws of physics have changed, your understanding and application of those principles makes you unique in the skiing world. Interestingly enough, many of these "assimilators" who are anxious to reduce PMTS to a reiteration of old ideas were vehemently opposed to PMTS just months ago. We have to salute the dexterity with which ski philosophers adopt, generalize, and accommodate the things they can't mimic or copy. The vocabulary, exercises, precision, and accuracy described in this book distinguish it from previous skiing fads. Like the width of collars, size of pant cuffs, vogue colors and hairstyles, the trendy descriptions of skiing come and go and come again. Like the fact that pants will always have two legs and collars will always be somewhere around the neck, primary movements are reliable, accurate and dependable.

Some teachers of skiing have attempted to disbelieve the success and importance of primary movements. Their disbelief didn't change the force of gravity, the role of velocity, or the impact of friction. The shape of the earth didn't change because Columbus's peers didn't believe it was round. Beliefs and belief systems belong in the realms of philosophy and religion. Ski preachers who promote a system based on belief assume the right to require some sort of charismatic commitment to emotions that can change from skier to skier and from situation to situation. Beliefs influence motivation but don't reduce the importance of movements.

Gravity, momentum, inertia and velocity combined with muscles, ligaments and bones create a common ground for describing skiing. These realities don't change because of beliefs or opinions. The science of skiing is the same today and tomorrow. While the descriptions of skiing vary and the preachers of skiing beliefs impose their charisma on innocent listeners, the realities stay the same. In the end, we have to conclude: it **is** rocket science.

Kim Peterson
October 2000

Chapter 1:

Better Technique, Faster Learning

Shaped Skis Open the Door to The New Way to Ski

The opportunity to improve your skiing immediately has been available for the last four years. PMTS Direct Parallel is providing marvelous, innovative approaches to help skiers improve more quickly and easily. Simply put, by learning PMTS Direct Parallel, you gain a biomechanical advantage.

In my first book, *Anyone Can be an Expert Skier*, I showed how this new method is applied with shaped skis, progressing from the beginning skier to the expert level. Readers of that book responded enthusiastically. Here are some of the typical comments I received:

- "I learned to ski better and improved faster reading your book than from any ski lesson."
- "As soon as I tried your 'Phantom Move' my skiing improved."
- "This is the only technique that should be taught."
- "I am a beginner. Where do I take lessons in your system?"

This book expands on the use of the PMTS methods for advanced skiers and intermediate skiers who want to move up to expert level in all conditions. I show the techniques that I use in my skiing and have developed for the PMTS system. At age 51, I feel I am skiing better than at any time of my life. With the assistance of this new technology, all skiers now have the potential to improve their skiing, as age no longer should be a limitation. Even prior injuries or poor technique need not be obstacles to skiing improvement.

All skiers deserve to ski in a way that produces exhilaration and satisfaction from gliding over the snow. New shaped skis can help make this happen, but most skiers won't achieve their full potential without using the PMTS Direct Parallel methods. Obviously, because short skis are easier to turn than long ones, they will seem easier to use regardless of technique, but you will find that you can have a greater experience by using them correctly. Advanced skiing, such as bump skiing at the black level, requires quick reactions and short turns. And quick reactions require the use of small muscles and low resistance. Efficient skiing requires less effort and fewer muscles. Making it easier to turn, control and direct the skis with small movements is the biomechanical advantage offered by the new ski technology. If skiers have always skied correctly, they will require only fine-tuning and a little experience to be completely at home with shaped skis. My father is 80 years old and has skied since he was seven. He is a certified Austrian ski instructor who started on shaped skis four years ago and loved them immediately in all conditions. He has always skied by focusing on his feet, and in the last four years he has gone further by incorporating the ski tipping actions of PMTS Direct Parallel. Yes, he made minor adjustments to his skiing, but he also noticed that the skis were more forgiving, required less effort and reduced the strain on his knees.

However, skiers using traditional skiing techniques may gain no benefits from shaped ski technology. These are skiers who have developed skiing movements that use big muscles and large body parts as a result of receiving incorrect instruction or learning by surviving. In skiing, overworking occurs when fighting terrain or resisting gravity. Moving big objects or resisting large forces requires large muscle use.

Traditional Skiing Methods

The instructions from traditional teaching systems that engage the large muscles include

- Rotary movements: steering, turning, or rotating the feet or legs to turn the skis
- Timed and coordinated up movements or extensions of the body during turn transition
- Emphasis on turning the outside or downhill ski

All the traditional systems currently in use around the world are based on the snowplow, or wedge, and are biomechanically similar, whether French, Austrian or American. Even systems that are marketed to make skiers believe they are immediately on their way to parallel skiing, for example, the "Fast Track Parallel," are still snowplow-based. The snowplow movement progression imposes clear and long lasting biomechanical disadvantages on a skier's technique.

These methods teach skiers to apply muscular force to redirect the ski they are standing on. This means twisting, steering and skidding the outside or downhill ski. Successfully turning the ski by twisting causes it to rotate, torque the knee and start to skid out from under the body. The twisting and steering causes the ski to become unstable. Survival instincts tell a skier to stand on a consistent, secure platform, so the skier fights to stay over a ski that is moving away and to the side, displaced and skidding. As it continues to skid, the skier fights harder to stay over it, caught in an eternal trap. The easiest way to get out, to escape, is to **stop steering and twisting** and **start tipping, tilting or inclining** your skis.

PMTS Method

PMTS breaks with this tradition, using different mechanics, and setting new standards. Balance acquisition and free foot movements are the basic components of PMTS.

PMTS teaches skiers to balance on one ski and move the other. There are distinct and separate roles for the stance foot and ski and the other (free) foot and ski. The stance foot is the stable, balancing side, allowing the skier to develop confidence. The free foot and ski create the movements to make turns. Applying the combination of **tipping, tilting or inclining** to the inside ski is called the **Phantom Move**. When properly performed, it is smooth, progressive, and barely detectable, hence its name. Balancing over the stance foot and using the free foot to engage the stance ski will cause the skis to arc across the snow. Shaped skis turn virtually by themselves using the Phantom Move. The stance leg remains stable. I started this section of the book by stating that skiing has become easy; what could be simpler or easier than the Phantom Move?

The techniques that skiers learn from the basic PMTS Direct Parallel system give them access to the full advantages of the ski's design by using a series of easy movements that are more efficient, giving the skier a "biomechanical advantage." This is the reason for the amazing success of the PMTS Direct Parallel system.

I am not saying that skiers have never had access to ski design before PMTS was developed. Isolated components of PMTS have been around for some time, but only as fragmented, unrelated snippets, not as a streamlined, complete system. The very best skiers use PMTS movements when they ski. Since PMTS espouses efficient movements and the best instructors teach efficient movements, it makes sense that the most expert and effective instructors have used parts of PMTS.

Some skiers I work with tell me that their instructors use certain aspects of PMTS. Although it may be a well-intentioned effort to jump-start traditional teaching, using some parts of the PMTS system is only a partial solution. Since the basic movements developed by traditional teaching systems cause problems in long-term skiing development, it isn't sufficient simply to "spruce them up" with PMTS components. For many skiers, adding a PMTS movement may yield an initial benefit, yet inefficiencies will still plague their technique. It is my job to reverse these encumbrances by introducing the complete use of PMTS Direct Parallel.

The PMTS method was developed in an effort to make skiing simpler and more effective. When viewed in its entirety, the fundamentals of PMTS are unrelated to other teaching systems. PMTS is based on a simple sequence of moves related to each part of a turn (beginning, middle and end), which provides marked, immediate improvement. In addition, it is easier to understand and to learn because PMTS omits most of the complicated, widely held tenets of traditional ski teaching. (Those who are interested in the theory and logic of PMTS should read the *PMTS Instruction Manual*.)

It has been said that simple solutions are best. That is certainly true for PMTS! Now that PMTS has been used in over 100,000 lessons, skiers and instructors who use it agree that it works faster to produce successful skiers. They ski more easily, experience less fatigue and have more fun.

> *"When I started teaching PMTS, I immediately noticed more rapid improvement and instant breakthroughs for my students, and huge advances for the instructors in my program."*
> *John Clendenin*
> *Two-time World Freestyle Champion, director of the Aspen Ski & Board Doctors*

Expert Learning Theory

Most skiers have a history of traditional instruction, so I have applied innovative learning theories to make acquisition of PMTS movements rapid for all skiers. Our skiing clients arrive with a vast assortment of movement concepts that are based on traditional instruction. These tips are a virtual hodgepodge they have accumulated from ski instruction — a little from every "bag of tricks" instructors carry with them. It is obvious students don't dream up this string of often contradictory movements by themselves.

It isn't necessary to travel far to determine the source of these lessons. The instructions can be heard when riding a lift over practice slopes in some of the best ski resorts in the USA. A phrase like "up and around" is a common instructional cue repeated in traditional ski schools. It seems to be the accepted practice: instructors shout these commands to students, reinforcing debilitating movement patterns.

By contrast, as you are introduced to PMTS, you will discover functional information.

Analysis

When I watch skiers, I do a quick inventory check of their movements. Using PMTS, it requires only two turns for the trained eye to see what I call "limiting movements." I mentioned most of them earlier in the section on traditional skiing methods. Once you have learned the basic PMTS movements and know the order in which they are performed, you quickly will be able to see what other skiers are doing on the slopes. In fact, one of the most surprising things about my students is their ability to analyze skiers. I don't train them to notice the limiting movements of skiers. But limiting movements are glaringly obvious; they stand out. I even have had students tell me they see the deficiencies in the skiing of their previous instructors. Once these limiting movements are identified and replaced with PMTS techniques, you will experience a ride you never expected.

Learning New Techniques: RAM and the Hard Drive

There are two levels of consciousness that exercise control over movement: the conscious and the subconscious. Let's explore briefly how these two levels of consciousness interact as you learn new patterns of movement.

The conscious state is the one in which you can introduce new movements and direct control over your actions. When you begin to ski, your conscious mind loads what you want to work on – a new movement, perhaps. Your old technique, ingrained in your subconscious, resides immediately below your conscious mind. In situations in which you stop concentrating on new movements, or when you become apprehensive or unsure, the conscious mind stops controlling movements, and the old information in your subconscious immediately takes over control of your movements.

The conscious mind is like RAM (computer shorthand for random access memory or, as I like to call it, on-screen memory) in a computer. I refer to working in the conscious as working in RAM because it is fleeting and stores little information. If your new movements reside only in RAM, or the conscious mind, they will go away when you cease concentrating on them. They are not yet written on the hard drive.

The subconscious mind is like the hard drive. Once material is written there, it can be reaccessed even if the RAM is wiped clean (perhaps by fear of a steep mogul run). The subconscious is a storage area for the movements and reactions you have learned over a lifetime and use without conscious thought. Your mind automatically applies movements from the hard drive in times of emergency, or when you are fearful or unsure. In these situations, the information loaded from the hard drive takes over; the new material in RAM is wiped away.

Learning new movements is a matter of writing material from the conscious mind onto the subconscious. Until you overwrite the old material on the hard drive, it will return any time you are unable to focus consciously on technique.

The first step when learning new techniques is focusing the conscious mind on concise, effective movements and practicing them. It is the successful repetition of these new movements that causes the body to start recording them in the subconscious, or hard drive. By writing over the old information, new movements are substituted for the old. Once acquired, these movements can be accessed from the conscious mind by beginning the movement. The speed of acquisition depends on the complexity of the moves. Simple, logical, effective moves are learned faster than complicated, confusing, or extensive ones. In other words, the material you are working with in RAM must be in small bits, repeatable and simple.

Fooling the System

Even when we understand how new movements are acquired, it can be difficult to write new dependable information to the hard drive. Anyone who has ever taken lessons probably has experienced this situation. You are doing very well; you seem to be learning new movements. Then the instructor takes you to a slope where you have always had trouble, and you immediately freeze up and revert to what you were doing before the lesson. This reaction is normal. The information from the hard drive is used. The new techniques you have been learning have not replaced them yet, because the body doesn't trust them yet. New movements have to be repeated successfully until the body believes in them and records or writes them to the subconscious or hard drive.

There is a way to open the pathway to your hard drive and allow it to accept new information more readily. The method is called "movement reinforcement" and it is supported by the use of "external cues." Changing deeply rooted movements lodged in the subconscious requires practice with trustworthy information. Learning with the concise, easily replicated patterns used by PMTS creates that trust. PMTS is designed to accelerate the acquisition of new movements using external cues.

External Cues

An external cue is a physical attribute that can be recognized, identified and even measured. To help skiers acquire efficient movements, PMTS relies on actions that focus on outside or external cues, such as the position of the skis or the boots. These cues will help you become more aware of your actions and will allow you to change or remove any ingrained movements easily. The cue can be visual or physical, but it should always be verifiable by observation. An example would be "lift the whole ski from the snow." The external cue is the ski completely away from the snow. You can look at the ski, or you can sense that the ski is no longer dragging on the snow. An added, or subsequent cue, could be "touch the tip of the ski in the snow" or even more specifically, "tilt the ski until the outside part of the ski tip is in contact with the snow." External teaching cues include references to parts of the ski, such as the tail, edge, inside edge, or outside edge. Action verbs presented with verifiable, external outcomes are also effective external cues. The examples used above are good: lift the ski, touch the tip and tip the ski.

Conversely, internal cues are related to body position, movement of the body, or location of parts of the body. Some examples are such classic statements as "hands forward," "bend the knees and ankles," or "move or point the knee out." Success in these instances is subjective and not easily verified or replicated. It's difficult to know how far to move the body part in these examples, and whether the attempt at moving created a desirable outcome. It is even more difficult to repeat the move exactly so that the result can eventually be written to the subconscious.

PMTS was developed as a predominantly external cue movement system. On snow, presentations of primary movements are described by actions and outcomes that can be verified visually, such as "stand on one ski, lift the other ski and tilt it to the little toe edge." Students are encouraged to glance down at their skis to see what they're doing, but not to pay much attention to the position of the body or certain parts of the body. This maintains the external focus or attention on the resulting action itself.

Mastering Movement

It is fair to ask whether there really is such a big difference in the rate at which people learn with external cues, as opposed to internal cues. I've found there are virtually no internal cues that are better than action words or cues to external objects. Even small differences, such as "pull the inside foot back," rather than "pull the inside ski back," are important to note. Although many may find that the foot is synonymous with the ski, others seem to do better if the focus is on the ski rather than the foot.

I don't honestly know whether such a subtle difference will have an actual impact on the learning or success rate. I am familiar with several studies that seem to show significant improvement in learning rates using external cues. Researchers who have performed multiple studies on external cue learning believe quite strongly in eliminating any internal reference if an external one can be used. It's exactly that approach that produced striking variations in performance on a ski simulator studied by Wulf et al (1997, 1998). They focused on the feet (internal) as compared to the wheels of the apparatus, just below the feet (external), and found large differences in learning. There is also a study done by Dr. David Bacharach et al (2000) from St. Cloud University that revealed similar results in performance.

To knowledgeable people, it may sound like splitting hairs to say that movement instructions with well defined outcomes, such as "invert the foot" or "articulate the ankle" should not be used because they are internal cues. However, in dealing with students, I've found that such cues can cause the focus of attention to shift in the wrong direction — away from the resulting action. Using the example of inverting the foot, a preferable instruction would be "show the base of the ski to the other boot" or "dip the tip into the snow," although the difference seems trivial. We should be aware that when discussing technique or theory with someone it is important to understand the internal workings of the body. In this case you don't always have to have an external focus, but when teaching, the material and content should be focused externally.

Now think back to your traditional lessons. Were they focused on internal or external cues? Here are examples of teaching that I've heard or read from traditional systems: "move your hips forward," "use more leg rotation," and the best one yet, "change edges by simultaneously turning your legs."

These are strong examples of internal cues, which typify traditional teaching systems. Compare these with the external cues of the PMTS method.

Learning is Fun

Since repetition is a natural and necessary part of movement learning, learning new movements always should be fun. When new movements quickly improve your skiing, your fun is increased and so is your motivation.

Intricacies of Understanding

Most of us learn new movements successfully if the presentation is
1. something we want to learn.
2. easy to understand.
3. realistically achievable.

Although you may be highly motivated to learn skiing, you easily can become more or less motivated during the learning process. Few of us will go blindly where we have never gone without some insight into the process. Even if you are totally confident that the instructor is "all knowing" and you are ready to do anything he or she wants, there is still an opportunity to increase motivation.

How to Increase Your Motivation:

1. Be given an opportunity to discuss your expectations.
2. Establish agreeable, realistic goals.
3. Receive lessons tailored to your expectations.

If you come to a lesson with expectations that are too high for your immediate capabilities and the instructor isn't aware of these expectations, the lesson will seem a failure to you. You may leave frustrated, even if the instructor has given you what he knows to be the correct lesson for your level of skiing.

PMTS Direct Parallel initiated an instructor training and accreditation program in April 1998. Instructors who are accredited in PMTS Direct Parallel are trained and tested to use methods that evaluate the student's goals and expectations on an ongoing basis during a lesson. This method is called "Student Directed Ski Instruction" and was first introduced by Kim Peterson. Since then, with Kim's guidance, PMTS has developed an accreditation program that focuses primarily on the teaching abilities of instructors. PMTS instructors are unique in the field of ski instruction, because they are the first to be trained and accredited in "Student Directed Ski Instruction."

Fulfillment of Expressed Expectation

In order to set reasonable expectations for yourself, you have to be able to evaluate your own skiing. You should recognize when you are doing something beneficial and know you are doing it successfully. If you have been depending on your instructor to tell you that you are on track or doing something right, then your skiing is not in your control and is dependent on outside confirmation. If you find yourself thinking, "I can't remember whether the instructor told me to turn my uphill ski or my downhill ski," then you aren't evaluating your own skiing. An instructor is useful if he can teach you how to reproduce efficient movement. With PMTS movements it is easy to observe your results and track your progress. When you know what movements to select, and how to generate them with conscious movement cues, you will be able to learn more quickly. With PMTS movements it is easy to observe your results and track your progress. You will also be able to discuss your expectations with your instructor and decide how to work together to achieve them. PMTS instructors are trained to help you become your own best coach.

Become Consistent

As a young ski racer there were days when I was very hot and others when I was not. Some days everything worked beautifully; other days I was lost. This is normal for skiers who don't have a concrete, solid repertoire of skiing movements. This hasn't happened to me since I started to use movements with an external focus that developed balance. I can now produce the same consistent skiing and put myself into my skiing comfort zone on the very first run of the day. I believe every skier can achieve this consistency with the PMTS system of movements and technique.

Let Your Subconscious Take Over

Now that you are accustomed to the idea of controlling your movements by using your conscious mind to give movement cues, I must prepare you to ski without them. When will the right occasion present itself for you to let go? When you race! One of the worst things a racer can do is to think about instruction cues and technique while racing. The conscious focus has to change and turn to selecting terrain, locating turning points and just reacting. Technique is secondary in these situations. An expert skier skis with his eyes and lets the body react to deal with challenges. The mind becomes clear of instructional input and is exclusively fixed on reading terrain and sending that information back to the brain. It is obvious that the brain has to know what to do with the information once it arrives. This is part of what we will discuss in the application of various approaches to all the mountain disciplines.

A great way to learn to rely on movements imprinted in your subconscious is to take racing lessons. Skiing through gates requires that you react rather than think about how to turn. When you are concerned about where to go, you suddenly forget technique. You respond with movements you have trained and learned. This is the ultimate test of your technique and your learning process. If you have learned valid, effective movements, they will stand the test of the racecourse. If the movements are inadequate, you will have problems negotiating the course. The same can be said for skiing in the bumps, powder and steeps. If you are confident with the movements you have learned, these conditions will require only small adjustments and a little experience to master.

In this introduction we have launched many new ideas about ski teaching and learning. The concepts will be reinforced throughout the book. Since this is a self-guide to PMTS Direct Parallel you may want to review this section at a later time. It will be helpful to understand whether you are skiing from your old "hard drive" or using your new programs. Determine when you are ready to rely on movements you have written to your "hard drive". Have you programmed it properly with new efficient movements? The rest of the instructional portions of the book will refer to the most effective external cues. Try to become familiar with them, and possibly invent your own, as you become aware of what works best for your skiing. Now that we have introduced some learning and self-coaching theory, let's begin the PMTS Direct Parallel Undergraduate Course.

Chapter 2:

Balance

Defining the Role of Balance in Sports

As time management becomes increasingly important in everyone's life, accurate, effective training and instruction methods become essential. After performance goals have been defined, it's important to research the best methods for achieving them. For the sport of skiing, a delicate balance — no pun intended — must be struck between physical preparation and technique. Anyone who aspires to become an expert skier on all black terrain must dedicate some training time to physical conditioning. Precise balancing movements and ability do greatly reduce the need for strength. But skiing repeated runs for half a day or longer on black terrain will be beyond the ability of any skier who has no prior basic endurance training. Still, most of the time that a professional or recreational skier has to devote will be spent on technique, not on physical training. Every sport has its own requirements, and training management becomes critical for the participant. Therefore, it is important to determine what the most pivotal component is for progress and then to pursue it.

Although I have trained athletes for competition in other sports including tennis and bike racing, most of my time and energy has been dedicated to skiing. Are you surprised that I recommend a training program radically different from the traditional approaches? The reason I do is because it achieves results. I have been skiing for almost 49 years and coaching for 27 years, and I have observed a fair number of skiers develop over that time. Some of them are skiers whom I followed and emulated in my youth. Many are now in their 60s and 70s and are skiing very well. In fact, many are skiing better than when they were younger.

Let me explain. Skiers who ski well on black terrain don't have to lift weights, run 20 miles a week or take their bikes on century rides. In the off-season, they may go hiking, fly-fish, play golf or tennis, or work in the garden. There is one thing these people have in common: they all learned to ski using balancing movements, and therefore they ski with minimal muscular and physical effort. If this makes sense, why isn't everyone teaching skiing this way? I can only guess that most instructors haven't been trained to understand the process of creating a "biomechanical advantage," which is achieved only when we are in balance.

Let's look at some current trends. When I read about some of the touted shaped ski carving techniques, I have to shake my head in disbelief. They advocate extreme body positions and a very wide foot position. These are fads and aberrations, and some possibly may be dangerous to joint stability and health. In many cases, these techniques advocate static positions with a locked, unbalanced body. Any position in skiing that adds lateral and rotational loads to the knee and accentuates the knock-kneed position makes the knee vulnerable. In these positions, shifting weight results in an unbalanced two-footed stance. It takes great strength to recover from these positions because they don't use efficient balanced body alignment. The terms "gorilla position" and "hunched" are appropriate names to describe these techniques. They lack finesse and balance refinement and should be avoided by skiers who want to minimize muscle fatigue and joint trauma. These techniques are very limiting, producing one kind of turn not transferable to any other types of skiing.

Ski instruction that produces the results you want has to integrate balance into its program. Balance enables the skier to ski with better control and stability and with less fatigue: in other words, with more fun. This is what most skiers hope to achieve by taking lessons. Some of you may be wondering if traditional teaching systems use balance in their teaching. The answer, unfortunately, is that most don't use it to the extent necessary to move skiers to higher levels rapidly.

So what training should you be getting? I suggest it should be an approach that combines balance and technique. My method is designed to develop balancing skills and offers an appropriate mix of activities that quickly improve skiing ability. In fact, in PMTS, the instructors spend more time teaching balance than technique because the skiing techniques are designed to guide the skier through the balancing activities that are needed in skiing.

The Question of Skiing Balance

What is the particular relationship between skiing and something as fundamental as balance? Balance is basic to efficient movement. When you take skiing lessons, you probably hear the word "balance" used by the instructor at least once a session. You may be told about a "balanced stance" or position. And you probably also are told how to find it by standing near the center of your ski. What does the overused yet rarely defined cliché, "standing near the center of the ski", really mean? Don't the bindings already control where you stand?

Standing in balance means we are able to move freely and in a range to recover. Standing in the middle means we are not predisposed to leaning on the front or back of the ski boot. We are standing between the front and back. When we lean on the back of the boot to stay upright, we are not standing in balance; we are leaning back. To be balanced, we must stand in the middle of the boot confines.

When you take lessons do you work on finding your balancing ability, and are you aware of how to stand? Do you perform exercises that test or refine your balance? Do you learn how to determine whether you are in balance during a turn? If you don't, then you are not skiing in a system that uses balance, and therefore the system isn't efficient. If you can't analyze your ability to balance while moving on skis, how do you know whether lack of balance isn't the biggest factor limiting your progress? You may be skiing with a great deal of apprehension and not understanding why. Without a foundation of balance in your skiing movements, your body may be leaning into the slope without your knowing it. Leaning into the slope reduces control and causes the skis to feel uncontrollable; it's logical, then, to feel apprehensive.

Balance versus Stability

We must clear up one point: balance and stability are not the same thing. Standard ski instruction has neglected balance and accepted a low performance standard — stability — which is achieved by using a wide, evenly weighted, two-footed stance. A wide stance may feel stable at first, and it may prevent you from tipping over, but it doesn't develop the balancing ability required to progress to the expert level. If you've been taught this way, you really never have experienced balance. The irony is that once you start skiing faster and on more difficult terrain using these techniques, you'll find that skiing becomes increasingly difficult and unstable. This adds another reason to be apprehensive.

In fact, skiers never become experts by trying to achieve stability. If you watch experts ski, you see them moving continuously with their skis, always in balance. Their bodies are often far to one side of their skis, which is definitely not a stable position, but they don't tip over. Their stability results from their balancing ability. Unfortunately, balance doesn't develop when a skier strives for stability.

A lack of balancing ability will hold you back. Often when skiers try a new PMTS balance movement they say that they feel as though they're out of balance. I try to reassure them that finding balance can be unnerving at first, particularly if they have experienced standing only in a wide, two-footed stance. If you feel as though you're out of balance as you try these new movements, it means only that you haven't learned the balance needed to perform them yet. Finding and maintaining balance complements the advantages of the shaped ski's design. As you acquire the balancing movements that enable you to access the ski's design, you will be pleased to see your skiing improve and to discover that your potential is unlimited.

Technique, Balance, and the Expert Skier

It's time to take a different look at learning to ski. Developing into a good skier is not well understood. What constitutes good ski technique may, therefore, be even less well understood. In an effort to explain how my approach prepares skiers on-snow and in the off season, I will describe some characteristics of expert skiing.

Skiing at expert levels comes easily with a high degree of innate balancing ability. Balance is the ability to stay in equilibrium, but it's more than that: it's comfort in an unstable world. If you are comfortable, you feel confident and safe. Strength, endurance, and power are secondary requirements for expert skiing. Technique should guide the body through the specific balancing movements needed to learn to ski at a desired level. Traditional techniques limit the development of consistent balance, while PMTS develops balance and allows the body to be comfortable when descending in all mountain environments. Skiing in equilibrium is efficient: it requires less focus on technique and less physical effort.

Learning to Balance

I said that expert skiing requires high levels of innate balancing ability. This is certainly true for skiers competing at the world-class level. Ski racing is a competition of balance. Video clearly demonstrates that the best skiers in the world — World Cup racers — are actually in a balancing competition. The ones who win races are the best ski balancers on the planet in that given race. The racer with the best balance needs to make fewer adjustments and compensations on the way down the racecourse.

Adjustments and compensations reduce speed. Fortunately, those of us who weren't born with a high degree of natural ability can improve balance. In my coaching and skiing career I have concentrated on balance development for both competitive and recreational skiers. The results have convinced me that with proper ski technique and exercises, everyone in reasonable health can raise his or her balancing ability. Wherever you begin with PMTS movements, they will improve your balance and therefore your skiing.

When you learn to ride the stance ski and move the free foot, you are developing your system of moving in balance over the stance ski. When we insist that the free ski be moved to line up with the stance ski, we are creating balancing parameters in your skiing. These are parameters that develop basic elements of efficient ski use with a balanced body. We need to be thorough and accurate about the movements that create balance and those that don't. In PMTS we clearly outline what creates balance and reject the movements that don't. If you deviate slightly from the PMTS prescribed movements, balance is compromised. A movement like steering is a disrupter of balance. Steering, defined and introduced as in traditional methods, causes the learning skier to impart skidding and rotational motion to the body and skis. These both disrupt balance. Anytime there is rotational movement of the upper body, it can cause steering, which overpowers engagement of the ski. An upper leg steering movement that changes ski direction or edging eliminates the platform for balance. As soon as the inside ski is planted and used as the second stance ski during a turn, your body shifts toward that ski and to that side. This shift is a loss of balance. When you are no longer standing balanced on the stance ski, it begins to react undesirably. The first thing you notice is that it wants to go straight. The ski will continue to go straight until you can twist it back to the line you intended. Now you are caught in the "twist it to turn it" techniques. You are no longer using ski design to ski. You are using strength and inefficient movements. Accurate description and demonstration of movements is a strong point of the PMTS system. When inaccurate movements are allowed to creep into the system, the results are diminished. As you develop the PMTS basics like a Phantom Move or drawing the free foot toward the stance ski, you will find balance developing. When you don't use these movements, your standards will lower and the quality of your turns will drop.

The unfortunate state of ski instruction is that traditional systems don't intentionally set balance loss and inefficient movements as their goal, but the basic movement progressions are so disruptive of balance that they leave the skier no choice but to use gross, inefficient movements to survive.

Balance Training

I've been impressed by the large gains in skiing performance that can be achieved by balance training in the off season. Skiers now can save time by focusing on simple exercises, and therefore be ready to take advantage of additional ski lessons. No amount of instruction can improve your skiing if your balancing ability is not equal to the requirements of the new movements your instructor is trying to teach you.

As part of the PMTS program, I recommend many different balance training devices, including the use of a tightrope. I have skiers who have taken this advice seriously and built tightrope installations in their back yards. Chris, one of our clients, is devoted to expert skiing and has seen significant improvement in his technique, which he credits largely to his newfound balancing ability. In addition to using the tightrope cable, he supplements his summer balance training with in-line skating and other exercises.

Another tool that I have found to be very effective for PMTS movements is the Skiers Edge trainer. The machine with its newly designed stance plate allows independent tipping of both feet.

Finally, we use a number of one-footed exercises both to diagnose balance problems and to improve balance. My book *Ski Flex*, co-authored with Paul Frediani, includes numerous dryland warm-up exercises that incorporate balance for skiers. Some of them are described here.

Basic Dryland Tests and Exercises

Block of Wood Test

Fig. 2-1. Block of wood exercises

Fig. a. Stand on a block of wood, a 2″ x 4″ or, if you are very confident, a 4″x4″. Keep the free foot off the floor.

Fig. b. Tap the toe of your free foot behind you as far as you can reach without flexing the stance leg.

Fig. c. Now flex your stance leg and see whether you can reach farther.

Fig. d. Tap the toe as far to the side as you can reach.

Fig. e. Tap as far forward as you can reach.

Have a partner mark the spots you are tapping. Repeat the exercise on the other leg. Do five repetitions on each leg.

Block of Wood Exercises with Rope

Place a rope in a circle connecting your tap points from the previous exercise. Stand on the block and follow the rope outline with your free foot. Do this exercise non-stop, very slowly. Start at the back, move the free foot to the front and retrace the circle following the rope on the way back. Repeat the activity five times.

Fig. 2-2. Block of wood exercises with rope

Fig. a. Stand on the block and reach back with the free foot as far as you can.
Fig. b. Reach back and behind your stance leg.
Fig. c. Reach out to the side.
Fig. d. Reach and follow the rope to the front.
Fig. e. Reach across the front to the side.

Bench Step

With a mini step bench or wooden box, place one foot on the lower step. Without using the leg on the floor, step up to a full extension on the bench.

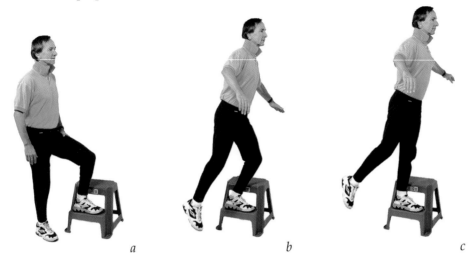

a   *b*   *c*

Fig. 2-3. Bench step-up and touches

Fig. a. Place on foot on the first step.
Fig. b. Stand up on the step.
Fig. c. Stand up to a full extension.

Front and Back Foot Touches

For an increase in balance and strength training while standing on the first step, tap the toe of the free foot on the floor to the back, side and front of the bench for a circuit as in the previous exercises. Repeat five times.

Increased Difficulty

Place your foot on the top step for increased training difficulty and perform the same routine.

Basic Lunges

Fig. a. Place one foot ahead of the other by a distance of approximately 2 feet.

Fig. b. Flex the front leg until the knee of the back leg touches the floor. Come back up to standing and repeat the exercise 10 times. Change legs and perform the exercise again.

a   b

Fig. 2-4. Basic lunges

Advanced Lunges

a   b   c

Fig. 2-5. Advanced lunges with bench

Fig. a. Stand with your back toe on the bench. The front foot should be about 2 feet from the bench.

Fig. b. Slowly flex the front leg to 90 degrees.

Fig. c. Athletic and well-conditioned skiers may continue flexing until the back knee touches the floor. Do not attempt the full lunge if you have knee problems.

One-Legged Squats

a *b*

Fig. 2-6. One-legged squats with chair

Using a chair for additional support, squat down on one leg while you keep the other leg a few inches off the ground. Begin with a quarter squat and move up to a 90-degree squat, as shown, after you have developed enough strength. For advanced training do the 90-degree squat without assistance from a chair. Ten repetitions on each leg is an indication of very good leg strength.

Rubber Cord

Fig. 2-7. Rubber cord rear extension

Fig. 2-8. Rubber cord front extension

Attach one end of a sport or surgical cord (found at most health clubs or exercise stores) to a fixed object. Attach the other end to your ankle. Facing the fixed end, move back until the cord is straight on the floor and the ankle with the cord is off the floor. Standing on the stance foot, pull the free foot back until the leg is stretched out behind your body, then return to the starting position. Reverse your position and face away from the fixed end. Move away from the fixed point until the cord is straight. Extend your leg forward until it is straight out in front of your body. Repeat the leg extensions 10 times in each direction for each leg. This exercise provides a triple benefit. It strengthens the leg on which the cord is attached, it utilizes co-contraction of leg muscles like in skiing and it develops balance on the stance leg.

This exercise also can be done to the side. Stand to the side of the fixed point and pull the cord with the free leg away from the fixed point. The resistance for all of these exercises can be regulated by the tension of the cord before you begin the extension.

Tipping Board

The tipping board is a balance awareness and refinement tool. It produces activity in the muscles that balance the ankle joint. Skiers who are not aware of the ankle's influence on balance while skiing may want to build or order a tipping board for balance training. You can find instructions for building a tipping board in the dryland portion of Harb Ski Systems' Web site at **www.harbskisystems.com**.

a

b

Fig. 2-9. Tipping board

Fig. a. Tipping board.

Fig. b. Using ski poles for added support, stand on the tipping board on one foot and lift the other foot off the ground. Lift the poles off the ground and see how long you can balance.

Fig. c. Center your balance foot on the tipping board.

c

On-Snow Balance Test: Self Check

How can we be assured we are maximizing our skiing ability? Here are some simple on-snow exercises to test your balance. If you can perform them without difficulty, you are well on your way to becoming an expert skier. If not, there are several ways we can help. A program of the above dryland exercises should definitely help your on-snow performance. If you still have problems, you also may need help with alignment and proper equipment selection. First, try these three tests based on the balanced traverse.

Balanced Traverse

The balanced traverse is nothing more than the basic ability to cross a slope with skis parallel. In the first decades of skiing in the Alps, a traverse was very important because it was sometimes the only way to avoid a steep or difficult slope. Today, at most ski areas, the traverse is rarely used or needed. Turns are connected, and skis are designed so we can easily form round arcs. However, the traverse is still a good way to introduce new movements to skiers as well as a great test of balance. It is incorporated into all Harb Ski Systems' PMTS Direct Parallel lessons. Follow these steps to test your abilities.

Safety Check

Before attempting any of the exercises in this section, you must look in both directions and up the slope. Pick a spot where you can see any skier traffic, and make sure that the slope is clear before moving forward onto the slope.

Criteria

When doing the traverse exercises, try to leave a single thin line with the edge in the snow. The line should be straight. Balance should be maintained the whole way across the slope with the lifted foot off the snow. If you are not able to do it perfectly, do not give up. Practice picking up the lifted ski while standing across the slope; this helps to develop one-foot balance experience. How many skiers have never tried to balance on one foot?

1. Downhill Ski Traverse

Find a spot on an intermediate slope that is clear of traffic. Stand on one side of the slope aimed so you can traverse to the other side. Drop your tips slightly and push off, aiming for a spot on the other side. Make a straight line standing on the big-toe edge of your downhill ski while lifting the uphill ski off of the snow. If you cannot make a straight line across the slope with one ski lifted, you may have an alignment problem. Now turn around and perform the exercise in the other direction on the other foot.

2. Uphill Ski Traverse

This is the same exercise as the downhill ski traverse, except this time you stand on your uphill ski and lift the downhill ski off the snow. Traverse the slope on the uphill ski's little-toe edge. The goal is to scribe a thin, straight line in the snow. Again, turn around and perform the exercise in the opposite direction. The same criteria from above apply here. When you can accomplish this traverse in both directions, you are ready to become an expert skier.

3. Straight Run

On a flat slope with a run out, point your skis straight down the slope. Push off and pick up one ski; hold it off the snow until you have traveled at least 20 feet. Make the skis go straight. Once you have traveled 20 feet, alternate your feet and ski on the other foot for another 20 feet, continuing to keep the line straight.

If you are having trouble balancing on one ski, you may have an alignment problem. No amount of instruction can make a difference in your alignment. First you must align your feet, ankles, boots and skis to the rest of your body before true skiing success can be achieved.

Why Can't You Balance?

When we can balance on one foot, it shows we are able to balance with co-contraction of the lower leg and foot muscles that support the ankle. Co-contraction simply means that opposing muscles are working in cooperation to stabilize the joints.

Co-contraction enables stabilizing movements around a joint to provide fine-tuning and balance. In a ski boot, the range of motion available to the foot and ankle is restricted by stiff plastic. In addition, the shape of the boot determines the angle at which the lower leg exits the boot. If your leg is angled laterally too far to either side, you may not be able to keep your body centered enough to balance on a ski. Proper alignment and a custom-made foot bed can alleviate this situation to a large degree.

Are You Aligned?

Are you suspicious that your skiing isn't right and it's not your fault? Do your friends ski better than you, though you are the better athlete? Have you been struggling at the same level in spite of lessons? Do you feel a difference between one side and the other in your turns? These are the most common situations that have brought the majority of skiers to my alignment sessions.

Evaluate Your Alignment

Proper alignment can change your skiing in one day. It immediately lets you access your balancing ability. I have been developing the process for the last 20 years, and I see the results every day at our alignment center. There are many alignment gurus around — self-professed experts on alignment and boot fitting. If they don't give you a complete on-snow evaluation, they may be missing the most important part of the alignment process. My first book, *Anyone can be an Expert Skier*, has a detailed discussion of alignment, describing what to expect from an alignment clinic, how alignment is improved by the choice of appropriate equipment and the different performance characteristics of various designs of skis and boots.

Equipment and Posture

Skiing is a dynamic and fluid sport. Expert skiing is not the result of assuming certain positions on your skis. It's the product of maintaining balance and using the right movements. However, just as you have a certain posture when you stand in bare feet or in street shoes, your body will have a "skiing posture" as a result of your equipment.

The way you stand on your skis – the posture you display – is to a great extent determined by the geometry of your boots. For each individual, certain brands or models of boots will produce a functional posture. Others will produce a non-functional posture. Ideally, you'd like boots that enable you to

- stand centered on your skis without having to push against the front or back of the boots
- adjust fore/aft pressure on the skis subtly, with small movements of the feet and legs
- recover from losing your balance in either direction.

Ski Boots

In an alignment evaluation we begin with the ski boots because skiers are more likely to receive inappropriate information and advice about boots than about any other piece of equipment. Knowing how your boots will affect your progress is important, because they can have a major positive or negative effect on your balancing ability.

Ski boots are the most influential part of your equipment, the place where the most can go right or wrong. The ski industry — including ski shops, instructors and manufacturers — has demonstrated to me a serious lack of training and understanding in boot selection and fitting through the failure to match boots to skiers. I have numerous skiers who come to my ski camps and alignment centers with the impression that they have had custom boot fitting and alignment done correctly by experts who came highly recommended. During the on-snow skiing assessment, I identify and clients begin to recognize that often they are handicapped by a combination of improper boots, poor foot bed design and misalignment. If you are interested in learning more, the details of how alignment and foot beds need to be measured and made appear in my first book, *Anyone can be an Expert Skier*. Here, I'll describe the influence and limitations of unsuitable boots and how these limitations often lead to incorrect instruction and skiing advice.

You maybe be surprised to know that some of the most popular boots could be the most detrimental to your skiing progress. So then why are they popular, and why do they keep selling? The manufacturers may advertise a lot. The boots might be very comfortable in the ski shop. They may "look good." The ski shop employees recommend them. Professionals who ski on the boots recommend them. Some ski shop employees may have motivations beyond your skiing needs to sell certain boots. It is very easy to end up with the wrong boot for your body type and skiing needs. The shop salesperson doesn't know how you ski, and most traditional instructors receive minimal training about the influence of boots on posture and movement. I said it in my first book: "No ski boot should be sold without an alignment and stance evaluation."

Since the appearance of my first book, in which the characteristics of lateral and rotary boots were discussed in detail, I have received many queries from readers and clients who are anxious to know what kind of boots they should have. Let me briefly summarize the differences in the two types of boots. Lateral and rotary are performance designations that refer to the manner in which a boot transmits edging or tipping efforts from the leg to the ski.

Lateral boots are designed to transfer tipping energy directly to the ski without introducing any pivoting motion. They have stiff sides and a cuff that flexes forward or to the outside. The forward lean angle of the cuff shaft is fairly upright (close to vertical) and the forward flex is controlled to prevent excessive knee drive that causes pivoting on the ball of the foot.

Rotary boots are designed to allow the lower leg to rotate internally before the boot applies lateral tipping forces to the ski. The cuff hinges and rivet positions generally allow the cuff to flex to the inside, letting it move with the legs as they turn and track. Some boots also have significant forward lean, or forward inclination of the shell and cuff. This lean contributes to the transfer of pressure forward to the ball of the foot and therefore produces excess rotation (twisting) of the ski. It causes the ski tail to skid because it becomes light or less engaged. The skier's knee is flexed and the shin rests against the boot tongue. Trying to tip the ski in this position generates strong twisting forces.

One other feature needs to be checked: the boot's ramp angle. This is the angle formed by the heel's being higher than the ball of the foot on the standing surface inside the boot. Ramp angle, when combined with forward lean, can have a profound effect on your fore/aft balance. It also affects your ability to tip the ski on edge, even if the boot has lateral attributes, such as stiff, high sides and a hinge point that allows the cuff to flex straight forward.

Rotary boots may feel great in the ski shop, but once on the slopes they severely hamper your balance and edging ability. Several models from well-known manufacturers cause the most severe skiing performance problems. Don't automatically disregard this explanation because you thought the ski shop salesperson sold you the best product. You may have been told to buy the most popular boots only to find they don't do anything for your skiing. For most skiers, rotary boots are the enemy of high performance expert skiing.

What specifically makes a ski boot rotary? Check all the following factors. Any one may cause your boot to make you lose your edging in skiing.

- If the rivet (that attaches the boot cuff to the lower boot) on the inner or medial side is lower than the one on the outer or lateral side, the cuff can flex to the inside and move with the legs.
- If the forward lean angle of the boot's upper cuff is extreme, uncontrollable, constant loading on the front of the boot may occur.
- If the boot's sole ramp angle is higher than 7 degrees, it may put excess pressure on the front of the foot, leaving the ski tail light and likely to twist out.
- If the boot board is either flat from side to side or has a valgus angle, this will cause excessive pronation. (Forefoot varus and valgus are the amount of twist or torsion of the forefoot, or ball of the foot, relative to the hindfoot, or heel. If the big-toe side of the foot is higher than the little-toe side when the ankle joint is neutral, there is a twist in the foot known as forefoot varus. If the big-

toe side is lower than the little-toe side, the twist is called forefoot valgus.) When the boot board has valgus it means the big-toe side is lower than the little-toe side. Valgus in the boot board causes internal rotation up the kinetic chain. A good foot bed can mitigate this condition.

While any single feature from these examples may not have immediately recognizable effects on certain individuals because of leg length and leg proportions, these are the most common characteristics, either individually or in combination, of boots that are detrimental to skiing performance.

Boot Geometry and Body Posture

Boots come in many different shapes, styles, flexes and geometries. People come in many lengths, shapes and proportions. Different boot geometries will produce different skiing postures for a person of a given build. Some of these postures may be functional, while others are not. It's very important to match the boot's geometry to the individual's in order to produce functional posture. A model of boot that might be perfect for someone 6'2" with long legs may not work at all for someone 5'6" with short legs.

A boot with a high ramp and forward lean angles can force you to stand and ski in an overflexed position, with the ankles, knees and hips flexed. This position may put your hips behind center, forcing your thigh muscles to be contracted constantly. This situation is rarely discovered during the excitement of trying on boots. It's only when you go on the hill that you discover your thighs burning and your tails sliding. Tall skiers with long legs are less likely to be adversely affected by boots that have high ramp and forward lean angles, while short skiers rarely ski well with that boot configuration.

Are You Pushing Plastic? *(And I don't mean credit cards!)*

My philosophy about ski boots is simple. You should be able to stand in a boot and not have to flex the plastic when you ski. There is a huge misunderstanding in the ski industry about this subject. Most skiers, instructors and boot shops will tell you that you need to be able to really flex your boot. I disagree.

If you are out of balance in a boot when you stand in it, you have to flex the boot to reach the point where you are balanced, and then it had better be a soft boot because you'll be pushing it constantly while you ski. If you are forced to stand in a less-than-optimal position because of the boot's ramp or forward lean, you will have to flex the boot every time you want to turn. You will have to push forward and flex into the plastic to achieve tip pressure. This effort requires a tremendous amount of work and is not very satisfying. If this is your situation, you will likely not venture too far away from the groomed slopes, as it's a difficult and daunting task to ski in moguls, powder or steeps with this imbalanced posture. Of course, if you are out of balance as you stand in your boots, a stiff boot will make it very difficult for you to ski, as you won't be able to flex the plastic to get to the point where you are centered.

A better solution is to use a boot that puts you in balance in your nominal posture in the boot. In this case, you won't need to push against the boot all the time to find balance. I prefer to select and adjust my boots so that I am in balance between the front or back of the boot. I ski in very stiff boots.

The range of balance in my boots is between the front at the tongue and the back where the back spoiler touches my calf. When I ski, I rarely load the back or the front of my boots unless I get out of balance. If I do get out of balance, I use the stiff front or back to rebound back into a balanced middle between those two spots.

The beauty of a balanced posture in your boots is that small movements are all that you require to make turns. If you are constantly finding yourself in the back seat and working to re-center, it's most likely not your fault, nor is your boot too stiff. I am not advocating stiff boots for every skier. I am advocating a boot that allows you to stand centered and balanced, so that small movements are all you'll need to perform turns. Boot flex shouldn't be softened to make up for an imbalanced stance.

World Cup racers ski in very stiff boots. I find it hilarious when shop sales people talk about Hermann Maier being so strong that he needs a really stiff boot. Hermann Maier has stiff boots because he wants the boot to hold him in fore/aft balance within the extremities of his boot. If he loses balance, the stiff boot can hold him and immediately help return him to a balanced position. The reason he can ski in stiff boots is that he doesn't need to flex the plastic to get balanced; he needs a supportive, stiff boot to regain balance.

The Right Ski Boot

The simplest solution is to buy boots that have ramp angle adjustment and forward lean adjustment. Make sure that the medial rivet on the boot is higher than the lateral rivet.

Foot Beds

Most ski shops try to sell you a foot bed or "comfort insole" with a boot. "Comfort insole" is a euphemism for a $150 piece of plastic to stuff under your foot. A foot bed that will actually make a difference requires a complete process of foot and ankle measurements. (For a detailed explanation, see *Anyone can be an Expert Skier*.) Even foot beds derived from exacting measurements will not produce the correct results unless the technician understands the dynamics of co-contraction. Therefore, a hunk of rigid plastic under your foot won't help your balance. In fact, it may immobilize your foot and ankle to the point where you are required to use large muscles higher up on the leg to balance and make turns — a definite no-no. Old thinking is to lock the lateral movements of the ankle in the ski boot. Our approach at the Harb Alignment Centers is to stabilize the ankle and reduce pronation, but not to lock out the co-contracting ability of any joint.

Co-contraction is not a complicated fancy word used only by biomechanics students. It is one all skiers should know about, because it plays a large role in their skiing success. And it also may help prevent injury. When muscles around joints are acting to stabilize the joint, the joint is protected from exceeding its natural range of motion. The forces of movement are distributed up through the skeleton, forming an "ideal skeletal force line," rather than exceeding the lateral load capabilities of the ligaments. Once you have felt co-contraction and skied using it, you will experience a new sensation: balancing through your skeleton.

PMTS teaches movements that keep your joints stabilized through co-contraction and therefore in balance. External forces are directed through the joint centers and are supported by the skeleton, rather than off-center forces that must be counteracted by ligaments and muscles. Proper alignment and the right boots bring the forces of skiing through and closer to the functionally stacked skeleton for a large majority of skiers.

Skiing Results

Shaped skis, I have repeatedly stated, should make skiing easier and more fun. The reason that skiing on shaped skis is easier is directly attributable to their wider tip and tail. The design allows the ski's tip and tail to cut into the snow when tipped on edge, bending the ski into an arc that creates a turn. The skier benefits because there is less fore/aft balancing adjustment required to make the turn. Shaped skis have eliminated the need to make the big fore/aft body adjustments and tip pressure that were required on traditional skis to engage the ski tip and start a turn.

The coaching in this book rarely mentions leaning forward or pressing forward. Our demonstrators for the book are well-balanced skiers who stand centered over their skis. They ski by standing normally in their boots, and thus balancing on the center of the ski. A proper stance, or balanced posture, distributes pressure as needed to the front and back of the shaped ski. When you are properly positioned and balanced in your boots and you need more tip pressure, you can achieve it with a simple, subtle, easily controlled movement that doesn't disturb your overall balance. PMTS advocates pulling the free ski back to increase tip pressure on the stance ski. The pull-back move is described in two places in the book: Chapter 6, "Free Foot Management"; and Chapter 13, "Bumps."

Instruction

Unfortunately, many skiers don't experience the benefits of shaped skis when they try them. I read and hear that many skiers are still told to press forward or move forward to engage the tips of shaped skis. I find that this motion disrupts balance and is excessive for turn transition. This movement is necessary only when the boot is compromising your position. If you are out of balance to the rear, then you'll need to battle forward to begin each turn. The advice to apply tip or forward pressure is usually circulated by instructors who have a compromised situation in their own skiing, or who find most of their students in a locked, rearward position. Typical instruction to cure this malady focuses on driving your knees and projecting your hips forward. These instructions are ineffective and cause many other problems not related to the fore/aft situation.

Imbalanced posture should be remedied with boot modifications, not by technique. No amount of ski instruction will change your stance. In fact, altering the ramp and forward lean angles of the boots can change your stance quickly. Again, more information on this topic can be found in my first book.

Much ski instruction is a band-aid for a poor equipment set-up. Even a good instructor at times will have to teach you adaptive movements based on your stance and alignment. Adaptive movements don't facilitate your skiing progress; they do allow you to get down the hill better for that lesson. This situation is less-than-acceptable as the next time the snow or the slope changes, the adaptive movements you were taught won't apply. There is real skier stagnation built into this predicament. You are always working on overcoming inappropriate movements and poor balance due to your equipment, alignment or a position that results from that combination.

Performance Check: The Phantom Javelin

Balancing ability should be the defining mark of every expert skier's competence. The path to your skiing success is outlined and presented in a step-by-step program throughout the chapters of the Undergraduate Course. One of the standards is the Phantom Javelin turn. The exercise of practicing and learning the Phantom Javelin is worth the effort as it is not exclusively a test of balancing ability. It also produces functional angles for resisting forces and maintaining balance through natural reaction to the lifted and positioned free ski. If you can perform this exercise as described in the photos, you are ready to move on to the Undergraduate Course. If you cannot perform it at this time in your development, spend extra time working on stance foot balance as you venture into the Undergraduate Course. The Undergraduate Course is a valuable guide to becoming a versatile all-mountain skier, and solid stance foot balance is a prerequisite for success.

Fig. 2-10. The Phantom Javelin turn

Fig. a. As early as possible, lift the inside ski and hold its tip slightly crossed over the tip of the stance ski. Notice here that the ski is lifted into position well before the skis aim down into the fall line.

Fig. b. Hold the lifted ski over the tip of the stance ski while you tip the free foot to the outside, increasing the ski's edge angle.

Fig. c. Keep the inside hand level with the outside hand.

Fig. d. Keep the lifted boot close to the stance boot.

Fig. e. Use no steering or turning. Your outside leg should stay long or straight while the stance ski does all the work. As no leg steering is used and the upper body remains quiet and stable, it's easy to maintain balance on the stance ski.

Fig. f. Ready the pole plant by swinging the tip of the pole forward.

Fig. g. Prepare to set the lifted ski on the snow and to transfer balance to that ski. After the transfer, the previous stance ski becomes the new lifted Phantom Javelin ski. Make sure the ski is lifted and in place during the upper third of the turn.

Undergraduate Course

The Undergraduate Course teaches you the "bulletproof" turn for all-mountain skiing.

If we were to compile a list of the requirements for success in various sports, the composition of this list would be surprisingly consistent. Whether it is skiing, tennis, golf, biking or fly fishing, each has a fundamental set of basic movements that must be mastered before you can enjoy the activity. Acquiring strong fundamentals is a process that requires dedication to details as well as practice. But if there is strong enough motivation to reach the level at which you enjoy the activity, then the time spent developing the basic skills properly will be well worthwhile.

If your only interest in skiing is in being outdoors, then dedication to acquiring precise fundamentals is less critical. However, even if you aren't determined to become technically proficient, there are certain essential skills needed to function in a mountain environment. Establishing control is one of the necessities that requires a certain mastery of technique. So why not learn techniques that not only give you complete control but also lay the foundation for becoming a proficient skier? PMTS Direct Parallel offers both in one package.

If the goal is to experience the thrill that sliding combined with g-force excitement brings, then going well beyond fundamentals is critical. It is no coincidence that the best extreme skiers in the world have years of formal training behind them. Magazines and videos may give the wrong impression of extreme skiing. These skiers are highly trained professionals. This training can come from a number of different skiing backgrounds, such as freestyle, bump competition or racing. Acquiring the fundamentals or basics is a necessary foundation for assuring ongoing growth in any discipline. It can't be done without real dedication.

Consider Tiger Woods. What makes him the greatest golfer of all time? Besides his innate talent, it's in large part his dedication to improving his game. He is already a great and consistent golfer, yet the day before the US Open, he still felt it was important to practice putting for two hours. He did this because he thought his ball wasn't rolling properly. And the night before the last round of the PGA Championship, the manager of the practice range had to ask Tiger to leave, because he was closing the facility for the night. Anyone who applies a fraction of that dedication toward developing proper skiing movements can master the basics for all-mountain skiing. Remember, Tiger didn't wait until he had a chance to win to start applying himself; instead, he is favored to win major titles because he has dedicated himself to his game from day one.

Our culture, in an attempt to make learning more fun, seems to leave out some important words that are integral to success, such as "dedication" and "effort." Because "work" doesn't sound like fun, it is the one word we really avoid mentioning. My point is obvious: if you are willing to dedicate yourself to learning functional, effective techniques, then becoming an expert skier in all-mountain conditions is possible. The information in this book will provide the techniques; from there, the amount of dedication required depends on how expert you want to become.

My frequent discussions with ski instructors have yielded some interesting observations about the need for fundamentals, particularly in relation to those who believe they are ready to learn different forms of off-piste (ungroomed) skiing, as well as to skiers already accustomed to skiing on black, or expert, terrain. The reality is that many of these skiers haven't been introduced to the fundamental requirements needed to handle these situations, even though their dedication is at the right level! What most skiers don't realize is that their training has been based on techniques that get them onto the slopes with an emphasis on control. The use of traditional techniques described in the first chapter creates skiers who use too much power and strength to ski. These are skiers who overuse their joints and muscles to stay in control and who rarely venture into powder and bumps. Such skiers have yet to develop a complete game or to complete the Undergraduate Course. Valid fundamentals needed for all-mountain skiing are rarely incorporated in these traditional progressions, which means that even those who are already skiing on black terrain will acquire new skills and increase their skiing pleasure with PMTS Direct Parallel.

Tennis provides a great analogy. To play tennis, you must first learn to get the ball over the net. Much of your beginner time is spent hitting the ball back and forth, forehand and backhand, but those moves don't make the game. The fundamentals of the real game are rarely learned. Components that make you a tennis player — not just a hitter — such as the serve, volley, half volley, approach shot, movement at the net and overheads, are rarely learned. Tennis novices can be compared to skiers in this sense. They haven't learned the different elements to develop a complete game. To ski bumps, powder and crud, and even to carve, requires a complete game; that is, a command of all the fundamental elements. These fundamentals rarely made an appearance in the lessons you received when you learned to ski. It therefore stands to reason that most skiers are unsuccessful and have great difficulty skiing in off-piste conditions.

Common scenarios for skiers who want an advanced off-piste lesson often unfold in a typical manner. Usually the instructor recognizes a skier's lack of fundamentals at the beginning of a lesson and suggests they spend some time on a groomed slope to smooth out the rough edges. Unless this refresher includes a package of strong "all-mountain tools," it won't further the skier's ability to ski off-piste. A specific course of movements for all-mountain skiing needs to be demonstrated and practiced. Without some clear, basic abilities, all-mountain skiing will not become a reality. The instructor has to know these fundamentals or you will be rehearsing the same movements that you have already learned and which proved inadequate in the first place.

Developing effective, all-mountain techniques can take a very long time if you are coached with traditional methods. No one wants to become an ongoing experiment, learning through trial and error with a coach as the cheerleader. The actual proven skiing skills you need are introduced in this section of the book and can take as little as a few weeks to learn if you follow the program with determination. If you are motivated, you can become an expert in the all-mountain realm. Below is a list of what constitutes the complete game of skiing. It provides you with a self-check to confirm that you have achieved the necessary basics. Evaluate your progress using the book. "To thine own self be true" — and you won't fear or have reason to be concerned in all-mountain conditions.

The Basic Short Turn

This series of photos of advanced, carved short turns demonstrate the complete game. When a skier can ski with these movements, I know we can move on to expert terrain and all-mountain conditions.

Some readers will identify Harrison, my son, from his appearance in my first book at the age of seven. He was 10 when these photos were taken. Many will say he is a natural skier, so of course skiing comes easily to him. I can say this isn't the case. Harrison skis several weekends a season and a week or two with me, but he is not in an organized ski program. He is involved in many sports, including soccer and hockey. He has worked very hard to achieve this level of skiing using PMTS and will tell you that his balancing and free-foot tipping took concentrated effort before they became second nature in all-mountain conditions. If Harrison hadn't learned using these movements, he easily could have fallen into the skidding and rotating methods that hold back skier development.

The Complete Game of Skiing

Fig. a. Harrison establishes complete balance on the stance ski.

Fig. b. In almost exactly the same position as the previous photo, he tips the free foot further on edge. He has the capability to hold the free foot under his body, as indicated by the ski tail, which is held higher then the tip.

Fig. c. He moves his balance slightly aft by raising the ski tip, but otherwise, the stance ski is making the turn.

Fig. d. He raises the pole tip to prepare for the pole plant.

Fig. e. He relaxes the muscles of his legs to flatten the skis.

Fig. f. Harrison raises the free foot of the next turn so he can begin tilting it toward the outside edge.

Fig. g. Tilting the free ski further to establish firm balance on the stance foot starts the ski carving.

Fig. h. Holding the free foot back under his hips brings more pressure forward to shorten the turn radius.

Harrison demonstrates all of the important abilities that let me know he is ready for all-mountain, double-black diamond slopes. These abilities are

- a clear command of his balance from one turn to the next
- a functional, flowing pole plant with no upper body rotation
- the ability to maintain his skis at the same edge angles
- turns that result from balancing and tipping with no sign of leg steering or twisting
- the ability to control fore/aft balance with his free foot
- hands and arms held in a natural, supportive position to allow freedom of pole swing
- upper- and lower-body coordination.

One additional ability is missing from the list of fundamentals for all-mountain terrain. Can you name it? If you said "leg steering," you will have opportunities to learn a great deal about skiing later in this book. The answer is flexion or leg retraction. Although Harrison didn't need to use it here, he didn't demonstrate any up-unweighting either, so I am confident he will be able to use absorbing or flexing movements to release the ski on steeper bumpy terrain.

The above list of fundamentals in Harrison's "Complete All-Mountain Game" for expert powder, bumps and carving can be divided into three categories:
• Balance Management Protocols
• Upper and Lower Body Coordination
• Foot Use and Ski Edge Angle Awareness

To ski the whole mountain, you'll need a solid short turn. The first chapters of the Undergraduate Course will teach you the basic elements of the short turn — the fundamentals. The later chapters will refine the short turn, and you'll learn how to apply it specifically to ungroomed snow. There is an extensive chapter on coordinating the upper and lower body and using the poles properly, which are essential for skiing off-piste.

It all begins with two fundamentals to help you balance: the "Quick and Easy Changes" of Chapter 3.

Chapter 4, "Releasing," makes sure you start each turn on the right track. It breaks down the exact movements you'll need to start every turn. The release has several variations — all are important to the all-mountain skier. Learning an effective release may make the most difference in your skiing.

Begin by trying the releasing movements in your short turns. Test your balance in short turns by doing a series of connected turns with a very slow release as I demonstrate in the photos. You may find you can't perform the slow release perfectly at first. When you do these exercises slowly, it emphasizes balance and correct movements.

Use the external cues described in each of the exercises. Gradual, progressive flattening of the skis, starting with either the two-footed release or the release from the uphill edge, will determine your success. You are training yourself to control ski-tipping. If you lose control and flatten the ski too quickly, it will grip or lock on an edge and restrict turning. The ski that will redirect to the fall line should remain almost flat through the release until it's in the fall line (pointed straight downhill). At that point it is important to stay balanced on that ski. Balanced in this case means that the other ski is light and tipping to create actions of turning. No turning should be initiated on the stance ski. After the skis complete the turn back across the hill in the other direction (almost to a stop), make sure you are balanced fore/aft, ready to release for the next turn. You may stop after each release at first as you learn to coordinate the movements. Refine the movements of the free foot introduced in these chapters to build on your balance and ski control abilities. After practicing, you'll have better dexterity in using your skis.

After learning an effective release, you'll want to make sure that your movements to complete each turn complement the efficiency of the release. You won't want any "limiting factors" to creep into your technique, make you work harder and hinder your progress. Chapter 5, "The Free Foot

Turns the Stance Ski," will help you learn the low-energy way to ski, getting the most performance from your skis. This technique works in all conditions, from carving deep trenches to zipping through the bumps to floating through powder.

In Chapter 6 you'll refine the actions of the free foot. The free foot controls all aspects of the turn after the release. You'll be able to control the size, shape, and radius of your turn using subtle movements of the free foot.

Most of the chapters in the book include a performance check so you can gauge your progress. If you have trouble achieving the performance standards, you may wonder whether you are doing something wrong. Often, it's not a matter of the wrong movement; it's just a need for a little more practice, or perhaps a refinement of the movements. Use the cues for success to guide your practice. If you are making the movements as prescribed in the chapters you are doing everything in your power.

An example of this very situation occurred last spring at a PMTS Instructor Accreditation course. One of the instructors trying for the Blue Level Accreditation was having difficulty with the bumps. His skis would split apart after a few turns and the downhill ski would jam against the bottom of a bump, tossing him out of rhythm. The condition clearly was being caused by a lack of balancing ability at the point at which the skis headed straight down the slope. The instructor was splitting the skis and using the inside ski as a balance crutch. I took him aside at the top of the next run and asked him whether he was pressing the releasing downhill ski against the new outside ski as soon as the turn began. It was obvious to me that he wasn't pressing enough. He said that he was trying to press the free foot against the stance foot throughout the turn and that by about the middle of the turn, he would lose his balance. I had him stand across the slope on the uphill ski and lift his lower ski. I stood above him. I used my pole to push his downhill ski away from the uphill boot. I asked him to press it back up and keep it in contact with the uphill boot. He pressed and he pressed and finally he was able to bring the boots back together. His comment was, "Is that how hard I have to press to keep my boots together?" I said, " Yes, at least until you feel how it works." The very next series of turns were his best in the bumps. He was astounded that a little thing like pressing harder made all the difference. His trainer who observed him skiing a run later couldn't believe the change in his instructor's skiing. The instructor was successful and achieved his Blue Level.

This example demonstrates how important the small things are in skiing. This breakthrough was not highly technical. It was simply a matter of refining a component in an otherwise effective skier. Take each new chapter or refinement in the Undergraduate Course seriously. The instructor I mentioned is just one person who will swear to the validity of this advice.

The following "troubleshooting guide" will help you to determine what to refine or focus on in order to improve your short turns.

Goal	Exercise or Focus	Benefits
Improve balance	Narrower stance (Chapter 3)	Easier balance transfer
More ski performance	Lighten or lift the releasing ski (Chapter 3)	Immediate transfer, early balance, early engagement of the ski
Connected short turns in balance	Shift balance to stance ski by lightening previous outside ski (Chapter 5)	Balance transfer
Shorter turn	Free-foot refinement, pull the free foot back toward the stance boot and hold it there (Chapter 6)	Increased tip pressure, centers upper body
Maintain corresponding ski edge angles	Flatten lower ski before upper ski (Chapter 4)	Clears lower ski (moves it out of the way) for stance ski to redirect into the turn
	Ball control exercise (Chapter 6)	Proper order of movement; tension between legs keeps legs acting in unison
Ski with less effort	Before turning, pull the free foot in toward the stance boot and tilt it to the outside edge (Chapter 5)	Creates movement of mid-body into the next turn, engaging the skis
Quicker transitions	Relax and flex the stance leg to start the release (Chapter 7)	Let momentum pull your body into the next turn; the quicker the flexion, the quicker the transition
Controlled release	Release from the uphill edge (Chapter 4)	Immediate and balanced direction change, develops edge change versatility
Upper body coordination	Stabilizing pole plant (Chapter 10)	Keeps mid- and upper body stable while you actively tip the skis

Chapter 3:

Toward a Solid Short Turn

A solid short turn is the prerequisite for all-mountain skiing. I notice that most skiers don't have this short turn in their repertoire. Of course, they can make a pushed, skidded short turn, but that's not good enough. You must have at your command a short turn that will stand up to the demands of all-mountain skiing. The short turns used by most advanced intermediates and even some advanced skiers commonly have the following deficiencies:

- pole swing and plant not synchronized with the turn, or a lack of upper and lower body coordination
- turn transitions without a transfer of balance
- skis held at different edge angles to the snow, at turn entry and exit
- outside ski twisted, skidded, and pushed to an edge set
- inside ski constantly trying but failing to catch up with the outside ski to achieve a parallel position.

A short turn is the universal tool for the all-mountain skier. Without it you basically are going into gravitational warfare without weapons. Skiers with an inadequate short turn usually describe it like this: "It's fine on the blue terrain, but when I get on something steep or bumpy, I can't control my speed."

If this description seems at all familiar, take heart, you are on the verge of a breakthrough. The good news is that if treated early and properly, the patient has a long, strong, healthy skiing career ahead. As of now, PMTS has not failed anyone who showed up with these symptoms. Unfortunately, about 90 percent of skiers have these symptoms.

Two Quick and Easy Changes

Through the Undergraduate Course we are going to build a short turn you can rely on and use to advance to the Graduate Course. The Graduate Course introduces you to all-mountain, condition-specific tactics. However, you don't have to wait until graduation to notice improvement in your skiing. If we override a few old habits with one or two simple new movements, an immediate change is at hand.

The first two changes to your skiing will seem almost too simple and easy to be believed. The results are immediate improvements. The changes may contradict what you have been learning and conflict with your present movements and skiing. However, there's no need to be concerned, as the explanations for the changes are given below, and the results speak for themselves. Your satisfaction will be the determining factor; I have no doubt that you will enjoy seeing your skiing efficiency increase. Let's jump right in and start with the wide stance.

First Change: Narrow Your Stance

Here I make a short turn in a relaxed, easy-to-hold stance. The free ski is completely free to tilt or to pull back under my hips. I can switch balance from one foot to the other easily in this stance. If I encounter powder, bumps or crud, I don't need a different technique. This one is completely versatile.

Fig. 3-1. A functional, narrow stance

Fig. a. Lighten the free inside ski and tip it toward its outside, little-toe edge.

Fig. b. Flex the legs to prepare to release.

Fig. c. Maintain both skis at same edge angles.

Cues for Success

• Keep the inside ski light or off the snow to confirm balance on the outside ski.

• Touch the inside boot to the stance boot to learn a narrow stance.

Biomechanical Advantage

• With a narrow stance, your body can move quickly as a result of small adjustments at the feet.

A wide stance is one of the most enfeebling positions in skiing, yet it is taught every day. A wide stance forces you to distribute your weight between both feet. The wide position makes it difficult to shift balance quickly and precisely as needed in bumps and steep powder runs. In bumps, a wide stance will put your skis on completely different levels and pitches, and it may not fit in narrow troughs. In powder, a wide stance generally puts the skis at different edge angles. In the softer snow, this makes the skis converge or diverge quickly and unexpectedly. The results are frequent face plants. A wide stance also forces you to ski mechanically with gross movements of the legs. Now someone will surely ask, "By gross, did he mean 'large' or 'ungainly'?" I mean both. Skiing with your skis and feet apart is ugly and inefficient, requiring large, tiring movements. Almost all skiers who come through our system are comforted to learn that they are permitted and encouraged to ski with their feet in a narrower stance. Say what you like about skiing, most people want to look elegant and ski with style. A wide stance doesn't do anything for your skiing image or the new outfit.

Narrow is Not Glued Together

The kind of narrow stance we are talking about developing is not the locked feet of the wedel technique from the 50s and 60s. The feet should have the flexibility to move independently, but your legs should stay in contact. Separation of the feet (the distance between the boots) is important to achieve, not in width but in the vertical plane. The inside ski boot can be separated from the outside boot but still lined up close to the outside leg. Space between the ankles in a lateral plane should remain narrow (a couple of inches), as in *Figure 3-1*. Note that the amount of vertical distance (one boot is higher then the other) employed in this aggressive turn can be large. My free foot is close to the stance leg but separated vertically from the stance boot. This distance is not only acceptable, it is critical to achieving acute body angles to the snow.

Fig. 3-2. Lateral proximity vs. vertical separation of feet

Second Change: Transfer Balance, Stand on One Foot

Diana demonstrates a clear, clean balance transfer to the new stance foot. She does it by raising only the back of the ski and tilting the whole new free ski and foot to the outside edge. No steering or turning actions are initiated on the stance leg or ski. All the actions at the stance ski are passive, reactions to the initiating actions of the free foot.

Fig. 3-3. A clean transfer of balance

Fig. a. Balance on the outside ski through the previous turn.
Fig. b. Get ready to release by swinging the pole and increase flexion/relaxation of stance leg.
Fig. c. Previous stance leg has released and lifted. Notice how free ski and boot are pulled back and held under body.
Fig. d. Free foot is tipped and held close to establish balance on and engage new stance ski.
Fig. e. Turn is established, balance is solid on the outside ski.

Cues for Success

• Lift the free ski tail just a few inches from the snow.

• In transition, keep the free foot against the stance boot.

Working on lifting one ski and balancing on the other is a simple and quick enhancement to your short turns. Stop standing on two feet! I still can remember during my racing career running in the fog at Whistler Mountain in the National GS Championships. My downhill ski was bouncing like a water ski crossing the boat wake. I was losing precious distance every time the ski bounced. I only realized later that I was never in balance over my ski. Each edge change resulted in too much of my weight being on or over the inside ski, on the uphill side. The outside, lower ski had weight on it, but my balance was never in line with the supposed gripping edge of the lower ski. Once I realized I was making these errors, I made it a priority to build a decisive balance transfer into my skiing. Concentrating on deliberately transferring and establishing balance allowed me to develop a powerful GS turn, even on the toughest, bumpiest runs.

Incorporating these hard-earned lessons, the PMTS system has helped countless students learn more quickly and enjoyably. Teaching one-footed balance right from the beginning instantly makes you a better skier. Understanding and recognizing the feeling of your body balancing over the ski as it cuts the snow is a world apart from the jarring vibration of a bouncing ski, yet few skiers are aware of the difference.

Developing the ability to lift the ski for a particular exercise or in a series of turns is a basic requirement for learning balance in skiing. After you have learned to sense and perform the lift, you will notice how your turns are more stable and balanced. The difference between your new turns and your previous turns is so great that the two no longer will be comparable. Skiing on all surfaces with a newfound ability to transfer and balance, will increase your confidence dramatically. Once you have completely assimilated the balance and transfer technique, the necessity for a strongly lifted ski is reduced. You can and will leave the ski on the snow or lift it when necessary. Lifting the ski is done initially to help you recognize and confirm the transfer of balance and to judge how well you maintain balance through a turn. Quick, connected short turns are learned more easily with a lift to transfer balance. After you are able to identify how much unweighting is needed to balance on the stance ski without completely lifting the free foot, just lightening will be sufficient.

How High Should You Lift?

This exercise doesn't require lifting the ski 12 inches off the snow. One inch is just as effective as one foot, as long as the movement to raise the ski causes a complete transfer of balance to the other ski. As you become familiar with balance and are able to transfer with precise timing, lightening the ski will be sufficient.

Fig. 3-4. Sufficient lifting of free foot

Fig. a. Transfer is complete; slightly lift the back of the free ski.
Fig. b. Pull the heel of the free foot back to hold it under your hips.
Fig. c. Keep the free boot lined up with the stance boot; the tail is still slightly lifted.
Fig. d. The free ski can be placed on the snow but only with light contact.
Fig. e. The tip of the free ski can be lighter than the tail to finish the turn.

d

e

Cues for Success

• Lift the free ski tail to transfer balance completely to the stance foot.

• Keep boot toes even fore/aft.

Fig. 3-5. Free foot lifted too high

Too High

In *Figure 3-5*, the free ski is lifted too high, which causes too much pressure on the front of the boot and ski, potentially causing the tail of the stance ski to skid. The leg muscles are overworked by lifting and holding the ski so high. This position is tenuous in rough terrain.

The Wide Stance Myth

Remain assured that there are instructors and coaches who will insist that lifting the ski is out of vogue and passé. These are the teachers who have their young racers and students struggling with balance transfer and stability on rough terrain. You may notice that at times the best World Cup skiers ski with both skis on the snow and at other times lift one ski. The reason for this is that they know how to balance and when to lift. They have spent hours training and learning balance transfer. They are able to lift a ski when needed, or leave it on the snow at any given point in the turn. If you can balance on one ski, you'll certainly be able to balance on two; if you know how to stand only on two feet, you won't be able to balance on one. For skiers who have not learned balance on one ski yet, a locked, wide, two-footed stance is their only possible method. The irony here is that when World Cup skiers are on perfectly groomed snow, they can ski in perfect balance and transfer balance perfectly with both skis on the snow. Coaches are so eager to have their racers emulate this that they teach only that position. They believe immediate success is just a matter of widening the stance and keeping both skis weighted or pressured. What they fail to realize is that the World Cup racers have done their homework. They can balance efficiently while skiing in a wider stance. They have learned it through the formal steps that you have begun to use to develop balancing ability. Many developing racers miss the important development stages. Most recreational skiers are stuck in the two-footed, wide stance like many of our young racers.

Chapter 4:

Releasing

The release is the important first action that begins a turn. When we ski in powder or in crud we cannot afford mistakes in technique which is why I have devoted so much effort to developing the release. A correct release sets you up for success through the rest of the turn, while you'll struggle to make up for a poor release. It is important to understand the basic mechanics of the release. I have broken it down in a number of different ways to present examples of how releasing movements can influence your skiing as well as to demonstrate that releasing has applications in all forms of skiing.

The releasing mechanics described here are not a review of *Anyone can be an Expert Skier*. The short turns in this book are more advanced. In the first volume, several chapters are dedicated to the development of the basic release. If you are not familiar with those releases, it would be helpful to review them first. The advanced release described here is developed from those fundamental techniques.

All-mountain skiers must have a solid two-footed release, and preferably a strong ability to perform both an uphill ski and a downhill ski, or weighted, release. Precise control of ski edge angles, often absent when inefficient mechanics are used, is much more critical on variable snow, powder, or bumps than in groomed conditions. The advanced release explanations and exercises will help you learn to keep the skis at the same edge angle from the start to the finish of a turn.

Because one of the goals is to achieve a functional two-footed release, we must learn how to have both skis change edges and maintain the same edge angles to the snow. The beginning Phantom Move, which you encountered in the previous chapter, instructed you to lighten or lift the releasing ski, which can evolve into a two-footed release. The basic movements are the same with only a refinement of the lifting and tipping, making this easy to accomplish with relatively little practice. These types of releases are covered in this section.

Later, in Chapter 8, you'll learn the Weighted Release. After you complete the releases and understand the movements thoroughly, you will learn the "float." At that time you will see how two-footed releasing helps to develop the float, which is so important in powder and crud skiing.

The Two-Footed Release

Prepare Your Boots and Skis Before You Release

From a starting point standing across the slope, focus your concentration on your skis and the rest of the body will take care of itself. The lower ski, or stance ski, will be weighted and gripping the snow. The uphill ski starts out tilted to its uphill, little-toe edge, at the same angle to the snow as the lower ski. You should notice that in this starting position it always requires more effort to move the uphill ski to the same angle as the lower ski to achieve equal angles because external rotator muscles don't have as much tipping, pulling or turning leverage as internal rotators.

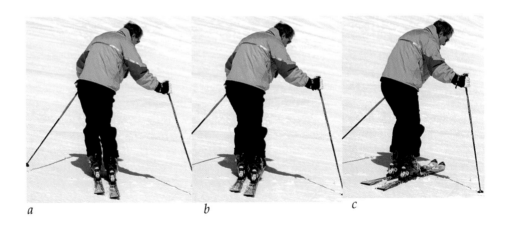

a   *b*   *c*

Fig. 4-1. The two-footed release: the basic release for short turns

Biomechanical Advantage
• Holding the free foot back, so your boots are even fore/aft, creates a strong turning force on your stance ski.

Fig. a. Start on a blue slope standing across the slope and put the lower pole into the snow for support.
Fig. b. Begin to flatten the lower ski, and let the skis move together.
Fig. c. The tips will begin to fall to the slope. Press the lower ski toward and hold it against the upper ski.

Cues for Success

• Squeeze your feet together as you flatten the downhill ski.

• Pull your free foot back to keep the boot toes even.

• Tip your free ski so its outside edge drags on the snow.

Refinements

There is one common glitch that happens during this exercise: moving the uphill ski to an edge. This is evidenced by the uphill ski flattening before the downhill ski, or by the uphill tail flaring open. If you continually push the uphill ski to an edge before the downhill ski is released to the fall line, begin with the next exercise: "release from the uphill edge". Pushing the uphill ski to an edge indicates that you are not releasing the lower ski.

When the skis reach the fall line, pull the free, inside foot back and tip it strongly to the outside edge. This movement usually requires more tipping action than you have used previously. If the ski is on the snow, slide the foot back and tilt the ski until its outside edge is dragging on the snow.

d

e

f

Fig. d. Use the pole for support and stand on the outside stance ski. The skis will move forward and down slightly.

Fig. e. Notice that I have not moved down the slope, as indicated by the pole, which is still planted in the same spot. Begin to tip the free ski as you hold it to the stance boot.

Fig. f. Keep the free ski back, holding the boot back and lined up with the stance boot. Be prepared to begin a release in the other direction. Use the same set-up as at the beginning of this release by planting the ski pole downhill below the feet.

Debunking the Myth of Simultaneous Edge Change

Traditional teaching systems use the term "simultaneous leg turning," to explain how to move when switching edges and steering the skis from turn to turn. I have to warn skiers that this term is misleading, and implementing it may hinder their progress. The reason so many skiers have difficulty making a strong parallel turn is because they try to steer their legs rather than tip or tilt their skis. Using leg steering movements to make turns results in converging tips and skidded turns. I know this phenomenon well. The focus on simultaneous leg steering in particular causes many skiers to suffer from wedge turn entries, while they actually believe they are making a parallel turn. A true parallel turn always will require sequential movements — but the correct sequential movements, done properly. The confusion and misunderstanding of this issue arises because the movements were described after analyzing photos of expert skiers, rather than from studying biomechanics. I admit that if I focused on describing what the legs were doing in some parts of an expert turn solely from photos, I would have to say the legs turned or rotated. However, what we cannot learn from a photo is whether the leg action is actively creating the turn or passively following from an earlier movement lower in the kinetic chain.

In PMTS, the ski tipping or tilting movements that start at the base of the body — at the feet or skis — do have an effect on parts of the body higher up the chain. When you focus on these movements, you can easily and precisely control the skis' angle and direction. You also are able to put yourself in balance immediately and maintain it. We will see the results of effective movements from the base of the chain in the following example: stand across a slope and move your skis to increase the angle of both skis to the snow. Use the tipping and tilting movements of your feet and ankles to increase and then decrease ski edge angle. If you continue to move the skis to and from a sharp angle, you will notice that your legs rotate toward the slope as the skis increase edge angle and away from the slope when the skis' angle decreases. Your legs follow the angle changes of the skis. We call this *passive, secondary,* or *resultant leg rotation.* Leg rotation may result from tipping the skis, but it should not be a focal point of expert skiing.

Active leg rotation occurs when you intentionally steer or rotate your legs to turn your skis. The large or gross motor muscles of the upper leg must initiate this action. These muscles have little fine-tuning ability to control the skis' direction or edge angle. Therefore, initiating turns with steering and changing ski direction by gross movements such as leg steering, diminish your skiing control and limit your progress.

You will notice that in PMTS Direct Parallel the description of releasing focuses on the outside or downhill ski of the previous turn. To release from a turn, this ski is activated first to initiate a sequence of movements, some separated by only a fraction of a second, which make the transition to a new turn. It is absolutely essential to master them. As the turn progresses, especially if it is a short, aggressive turn, the old outside ski, which becomes the new inside ski, must continue to tilt more actively to its outside edge after the release. This movement is emphasized because it is more difficult to tip a ski to its outside edge than to its inside edge. The muscles on the inside of the leg which control internal rotation have greater mechanical advantage than the external rotators. Because of the way the muscles are connected, in a turn transition, the uphill foot, ankle, leg and ski have an easier time moving to the big-toe edge than the downhill ski has moving to the little-toe edge. The downhill, or new inside, leg must flex and rotate externally under the body. Accomplishing this movement often requires some training. If this release is new to you, focusing on it exclusively at first will provide long-term results.

Release from the Uphill Edge

The release from the little-toe edge of the uphill ski is a skill that all expert skiers must develop if they are to continue improving. Slowly reduce the edge angle of the uphill ski until it begins to slide downhill. The tip drops and the rest of the ski will follow. Hold the free foot and boot close to the stance ski. Press the inside ankle rivets of both boots together to hold tension throughout the turn. If the free foot drops or touches the snow before completion, you have lost balance; start over. Tip the lifted ski strongly toward the outside edge as soon as the your stance ski points downhill. Try to complete the turn within a vertical distance of two ski lengths.

a   *b*   *c*

Fig. 4-2. Release from the uphill edge

Fig. a. Pick up the lower boot and hold it against the upper boot. Do not allow them to separate during any part of this exercise. You may look down to see whether the boots separate.

Fig. b. Start to tip the lifted foot toward its little-toe edge. Use the pole to help you balance as the stance ski rolls from upper, little-toe edge to lower, big-toe edge, as a result of free foot tipping.

Fig. c. Control the rate at which the stance ski rolls to flat – keep it slow.

Fig. d. Continue to press the free boot against the stance boot while you tip it toward the outside edge. Pull back slightly on it to keep the boots even fore/aft.

Fig. e. Notice again how little forward travel is accomplished, yet the skis have changed direction, now pointing downhill. This is achieved not by twisting the ski but by releasing the edge, tipping the free foot and balancing on the stance ski.

Fig. f. The stance boot is blocked from view because the free boot is lined up exactly fore/aft with the stance boot. Holding the boots like this creates turning power. You are accessing your biomechanical advantage.

Biomechanical Advantage

• Lifting the free foot brings a level of balance awareness needed in short, snappy, energetic short turns.

d

e

f

> ## Cues for Success
>
> • Balance on one foot, and keep the free foot lifted throughout.
>
> • Hold your boots together.

Action and Timing for Each Leg

In the transition of the turn, the action of each leg is different. The legs move or rotate in different directions from each other, which is why it is important to begin moving or releasing the lower ski first. If you try to move your legs at the same time, the dominant uphill leg, rotating internally as it rolls from its outside edge to its inside edge, will react more easily and quickly. The "internal rotation response" is already very strong in most skiers. The downhill, or stance, ski must release from a gripping big-toe edge, flatten, and then tilt to its little-toe edge. Because the lateral movements toward the big-toe, or inside, edge require less concentration and happen more readily, they need to be slowed, delayed or controlled. If you try to grip too soon on the new big-toe edge for the next turn, you will force the tail of that ski to flare out and cause a wedge entry to the turn. This is active leg rotation. When we understand this process, we can see that the lower ski needs to tip first, before the upper ski, in order for both skis to maintain the same edge angles during releasing and engaging.

It is difficult for many skiers to learn this new sequence because traditional systems reinforce the opposite movements. If you learned to ski with conventional movements, as most of us did, you learned the snowplow and stem Christie early. As a result, your dominant movement pattern is to move to the big-toe edge by adducting and internally rotating the upper leg, which produces the steering used to turn the ski in the wedge progression. Traditional teaching systems depend on these movements for control and turning.

In the PMTS system, releasing the downhill ski, using the opposing set of muscles, produces turns and creates an external rotation of the stance leg to the little-toe edge, which releases the stance ski and starts the turn.

To become an expert skier, you have to unlearn leg steering and rotating movements, which is why I referred to traditional teaching progressions in my first book and video as techniques that teach skiers dead-end skills. It is frustrating to try to advance to the expert level with these outside-ski steering movements dominating your technique. Few ever achieve expert skiing this way — and those who do usually have improvised and learned on their own.

By using PMTS Direct Parallel, you can reverse these ingrained movement patterns involving leg rotation and learn correct movements. The focus in PMTS is on the external cues of tilting or tipping the skis, which make the legs react in a controllable and predictable manner. Other benefits are improved balance and ski hold, both achieved with less physical effort. When you learn to release using the PMTS way, your center of mass or mid-body moves toward the new turn in a completely different way: deliberately, and under your control.

Two-footed Release from Traverse

Just as you hold your feet and ankles at an angle to maintain your grip while walking on a steep side hill of a golf fairway or a hiking trail, you must grip a snow slope with the edges of your skis and boots. The feet and ankles control gripping actions. Before you start, make sure you are able to hold your skis at the same edge angle while stationary on the slope. Releasing is done with both skis. Stand well centered over your skis and keep your feet directly under your body. Begin by flattening the lower ski first, letting the upper ski follow. Keep the lower or bottom ski weighted as you flatten. Again, this technique is different from the basic release in which the ski was lightened as it was tipped. Avoid the tendency to tip the uphill ski flat faster or sooner than the downhill ski. This caution is the key to avoiding the common problem of digging the big-toe edge of the uphill ski into the snow when releasing.

Fig. 4-3. Two-footed release from traverse

A Different Look at Releasing

Another way to begin this two-footed release is by lessening the edge grip of the lower ski. Press the ski down toward its outside edge. Press or let the outside edge of the ski drop toward the snow. Let the upper ski follow, and then continue moving both feet and ankles together. Be aware that the upper ski will have an easier time releasing, as it is moving toward its big-toe, or inside, edge. As the skis flatten and grip less, they will skid slightly. Make them slide together as one unit, as if the skis were made in one piece like a mono ski. Presenting the skis to the surface at the same angle will make them easier to control and more predictable. It will be easier to stay balanced.

Flattening movements should be progressive – they shouldn't suddenly flatten or roll all at once. See that both skis flatten the same amount. The tips will start moving downhill together. This moment is when skiers have a tendency to lean or sit back on their skis. Instead, keep your feet under your hips and move with the skis as they begin to slide forward and down the mountain. No muscular effort is needed to direct the skis; simply let the tips aim down the mountain. When the skis are pointed directly downhill into the fall line, the release is complete. Both skis should be flat on the snow. Let the skis run; there should be no hurry to twist them into a turn at this point. If it is difficult to feel when the skis are flat on the snow, go to a place on the mountain where you can experiment with a straight run. Take the time to learn what your skis feel like when they are truly flat on the snow.

Skis Flat at the Same Time

In the process of releasing from one set of edges and rolling toward the other, you have no choice but to go through a point where each ski is flat on the snow. Either both skis become flat simultaneously or one is flat before the other. It is very important to be aware of this transition point in a turn. You must be able to determine how your skis are lined up at the transition. In uneven snow or deep, soft snow conditions, both skis should become flat at the same time. Try to keep them flat as long as you can; avoid tipping the outside ski for the turn to its big-toe, or inside, edge. You will achieve parallel skiing with control and balance throughout the turn by managing the new inside ski and allowing the outside ski to come to an edge passively.

Straight Run

Become familiar and comfortable with your skis when they are flat on the snow by skiing this way as often as you can. There are multiple opportunities on a ski run to have your skis flat. Whenever you reach a point on the mountain where you can run straight, do so — especially on cat tracks or on flat sections. Bring your feet together as you try to keep the skis flat on the snow. Find the spot where your skis are completely flat to the snow and hold them there, keeping them flat and parallel. Take a peek down at your skis to make sure they are flat. I can't tell you how many students come to me who are desperate to learn to ski parallel. As soon as we come to a flat area, I have them allow their skis to run straight. Most are amazed when I point out to them that their skis are in a wedge position while they are in the straight run. If you are not aware that your skis are wedging, you will never ski parallel. You may be surprised at how closely together you must hold the skis for them to ride flat on the snow. Many skiers have never become parallel skiers because they have been trained to ski with their feet apart. A wide stance keeps the skis on both inside edges, which means they are not flat, parallel or at the same edge angles. In a straight run, make sure your skis are flat and parallel.

Performance Check

If you can bring your skis flat at the same time for each edge change in transition, you are on your way to skiing success. On flat terrain with no obstacles or skiers around, look down at your skis during edge changes to make sure you are controlling your skis and edges properly. Slow down and watch your skis between turns to see that your skis remain parallel throughout the transition and that they reach flat together as you roll or tip them from the previous edges to their new edges.

Chapter 5:

Tip the Free Foot to Turn the Stance Ski

The first conventional skiing concept we must reverse is the idea that we turn the skis. Skiing by trying to turn your skis is counter-productive. To bring back the pleasure of skiing,
don't turn your skis.

You will learn the key components in PMTS that allow you to make better turns without turning your skis. In this chapter we review the Phantom Move introduced in *Anyone can be an Expert Skier*. In subsequent chapters you'll learn how to relax between turns and give yourself time to achieve balance by using the "float." This new concept will quickly undo the old habits related to turning your skis. The other unfortunate technique, stemming from the lack of PMTS fundamentals that must be reversed is nicknamed the "unibody turn." This requires specific efforts to overcome. I have developed several new approaches that will unlock the body and develop "upper and lower body coordination."

By incorporating the simple changes I proposed in Chapter 3 — narrowing your stance and standing on one foot — you can quickly eliminate two of the most progress-hindering problems in skiing: skidded turns and loss of balance. You may have noticed that it isn't difficult to reverse some of the techniques you were taught and get on your way to becoming a much improved skier. In fact, when we review the Phantom Move, you will be able to eliminate almost all the wrong movements and be on the road to acquiring the right ones.

Analysis of Limiting Factors

Before you can change your skiing, it is important to become aware of the factors that are limiting your progress. The real skill is the ability to differentiate between the actual cause and the visual manifestations of limiting factors. Here is an example: most instructors easily can see when skiers rotate the upper body too much when turning. A logical diagnosis here is that you are compensating for lack of leg steering by employing extreme upper body rotation. Most traditional instructors will tell you to increase leg rotation, or steering, to turn your skis, which in turn should reduce the need for upper body rotation. In addition, they may suggest countering movements of the upper body for you to work on while you increase leg steering.

This solution may seem logical. Perhaps your rotary skills are insufficient. The problem with this approach in actual application is that no increase in leg steering will make you an expert skier. First, it is very difficult to control or sense the degree of leg rotation because this is an internal cue. As discussed earlier, internal cues are ineffective for producing functional movements and results. Second, it is almost impossible to become more active and forceful with leg steering without incurring mid- and upper body rotation — exactly what you are trying to reduce because gross motor muscles are required to move the thighs and trunk. And, finally, steering your skis and rotating your legs to create turns eliminates access to and use of the ski's design — your biomechanical advantage disappears.

The actual limiting factor is the turning of the skis. Here is how I overcome upper body rotation with PMTS Direct Parallel: in the case of the skier described above, there is little or no activity at the base of the body, or base of the kinetic chain, as I call it. The needed movement is tipping the free ski toward its outside edge to engage the side cut of the stance ski, thus using the biomechanical advantage. I begin by introducing new activities that make the student aware of the skis and the angles of the skis to the snow. These cues are external, enabling the skier to judge his or her own performance of the tasks. The object is to substitute new and efficient ski tilting movements for the old forceful leg rotation and steering actions.

There is an important consideration when changing someone's skiing. Even if the technique is incorrect, it is the only way the person is able to ski at the moment. If you are going to take away a movement the skier has relied upon, you must replace it with one that creates a better result. In this example, the skier is rotating the upper body. Only after the student has learned how tipping the skis helps produce a turn will he or she be able to diminish the need for turning the skis by rotating the upper body.

If you are planning to use this book to teach yourself, which I encourage, you are becoming your own instructor. When you are ready to learn a new movement, you must know how to introduce it in a way that makes it easy to learn. To help you succeed, break the movements down into sufficiently small components so that you can build on the exercise.

Let's apply this approach to the case above. The process begins on a flat slope, learning the exercises that create recognition of free foot tipping and stance foot balance. I would start with an introduction to free foot tipping or tilting by describing how to take the downhill ski and roll or tilt it toward the outside edge, flattening it to the snow. This releases the ski from the turn, so a new turn can develop automatically without a deliberate steering force. The focus for the rest of the turn remains on this ski. Next, continue tipping it toward its outside edge until the other ski starts to turn.

This example demonstrates the key ingredients of a successful beginning for a student: easy steps and external cues. The next step is to learn the building blocks that create a balance transfer, which are the basis of the Phantom Move. The Phantom Move, introduced in my first book, has grown in reputation and become legendary thanks to its effectiveness. Lito Tejada-Flores has adopted it in his teachings, and refers to it as "phantom edging."

Fig. 5-1. The Phantom Move

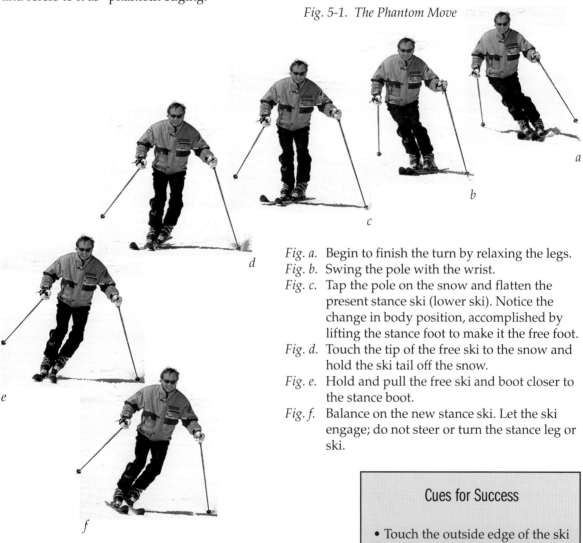

Fig. a. Begin to finish the turn by relaxing the legs.

Fig. b. Swing the pole with the wrist.

Fig. c. Tap the pole on the snow and flatten the present stance ski (lower ski). Notice the change in body position, accomplished by lifting the stance foot to make it the free foot.

Fig. d. Touch the tip of the free ski to the snow and hold the ski tail off the snow.

Fig. e. Hold and pull the free ski and boot closer to the stance boot.

Fig. f. Balance on the new stance ski. Let the ski engage; do not steer or turn the stance leg or ski.

Cues for Success

• Touch the outside edge of the ski tip to the snow, and hold the tail a few inches above the snow.

• Touch the free boot to the inside ankle of the stance boot.

The Phantom Move

The mechanics of the Phantom Move were well known to me before the name evolved. I have used it in my skiing since I was 14, and I have coached Olympic athletes and National Ski Team members using this technique. The name came about by chance. I was coaching a group of instructors at Aspen. I told them I was going to make a turn, and I asked them to tell me how I made my skis turn. They were unable to come up with the answer, so I explained it to them, saying, "I gradually tipped my inside ski for the next turn to its outside, or little-toe, edge." I didn't lift the ski because I didn't want to give away the answer. I lightened and removed most of my weight from the ski and slowly tilted the ski toward its outside edge and the other ski started to turn as a result of the tilting action. When you do the Phantom Move in this way, it looks as though both skis turn together. One of the instructors piped up and said, "That's a phantom turn." I thought it described brilliantly the subtle, almost unnoticeable, mechanics. The untrained eye has difficulty seeing the actual movements when they are done smoothly with both skis on the snow. I later changed the name to the Phantom Move.

Release, Transfer, and Engagement

In a series of turns, the Phantom Move is a continuum of three movements of the free foot: tipping it toward its little-toe edge, keeping it light, and keeping its heel pulled in toward the stance foot. It creates the three components of linked turns: the release, transfer, and engagement. Tipping the stance ski toward its outside edge, flattening it to the snow, starts a new turn; these moves comprise the **release**. Lightening that foot until the ski lifts slightly off the snow causes balance to **transfer** to the new ski. Continued tipping toward the outside edge, combined with the balance transfer, pulls the stance ski on edge – the **engagement**. Pulling the free heel inward makes it easier to balance on the stance ski and increases the effectiveness of the tipping movement. I call the sequence of tipping, lightening and keeping the heel pulled in a "continuum," because those movements or efforts must be performed throughout the arc of a turn until the turn is complete and it's time to release again. They are not just one-time occurrences to start a turn.

Basics for All Skiers

Many of the undergraduate exercises may seem too simple at first. The black slope skier especially may decide to overlook them. However, I encourage all skiers to perfect them, for they will pay dividends later. These techniques are more challenging and eye opening than they may seem at first. It is my experience that few skiers are proficient at these exercises. Of those who are, many are already experts in most skiing situations.

Pulling Movements

Movements to pull the feet back and in are rarely introduced in ski lessons. There is little use or understanding of them in traditional skiing. Skiers may at first find these movements of PMTS Direct Parallel challenging. They are not difficult, just new. Pulling the free foot toward the stance foot at the release or beginning of a turn becomes second nature after practice. Pulling the free foot back under the hips is another pulling movement that will gain importance as you venture from groomed terrain. Start using and learning it as soon as you get onto snow.

Don't Turn the Skis

Let's get back to the issue of turning the skis. Remember, we take the phrase "don't turn your skis" seriously. In the description of the Phantom Move, I never said to turn your skis, feet or legs. Turning the skis requires steering or turning efforts with the large muscles of the legs, which diminishes balance by moving the skis out from under you and shifts the body's normally strong skeletal alignment to a weaker position. In fact, trying to turn your skis prevents you from progressing in your skiing. Look at *Figure 5-1* of the Phantom Move description and at the sequence below, *Figure 5-2*. Notice how the stance ski tail stays in line with the direction of the tip. The tail is never displaced or pushed out. This turn is carved or mildly brushed. These turns result from the use of PMTS. You will see them demonstrated in various ways throughout the book. The techniques that produce quick, efficient turns with balance use precise timing of releasing movements.

Fig. 5-2. Don't turn the stance ski

Biomechanical Advantage

• Balancing on the stance foot and tipping the free ski engages the ski's sidecut to make the turn.

Downhill Ski Edging

Throughout this book there is little reference to edging the downhill ski or pressuring the downhill ski. The movements of PMTS create balance on and grip by the downhill ski. I intentionally avoid too much discussion about downhill ski edging or pressuring because correct movements result in proper balance and edging. Emphasizing downhill ski edging and pressuring in the first third of a turn, the old-school approach embodied in the command "get an early edge," often produces exactly the opposite result: an early skid. As a PMTS turn progresses to the point where the skis are headed back in the new direction, pressuring the downhill ski can increase. Extending the downhill leg and tipping the free foot achieve pressuring and edging. Edging the downhill ski can increase after your skis have crossed the fall line and have started back across the slope. When your outside leg is extended, slight ankle movements to adjust edging can be effective. Press the ankle gently toward the medial wall of the ski boot to tip the ski further onto its big-toe edge. Avoid driving the knee to the inside whenever possible.

Performance Check

The performance test for this chapter is the Phantom Move with complete balance control. Complete balance control means that you can

- transfer balance before a turn begins
- balance momentarily on the little-toe edge of the new stance ski before it starts to turn
- hold the free foot off the snow throughout the arc of the turn until it is time to transfer for the upcoming turn
- turn as a result of the free foot's tipping toward its outside edge.

Break the Phantom Move into these small steps and manage your turns with the tipping actions of the inside ski rather than steering or turning the stance ski, and you will become successful as an all-mountain skier.

Chapter 6:

Free Foot Management

Refining the Release

The subtle actions of the free foot that truly make for expert skiing are rarely taught or discussed. Although the release that we covered in Chapter 4 is the basic PMTS method of finishing a turn and connecting to a new one, there is more to the transition then meets the eye.

I have seen students and instructors alike have problems with this part of the turn, even though many have read my first book. I also have been pleasantly surprised at how quickly the transition improves when the actions of the free foot are refined. Having read, and hopefully rehearsed, the movements described in Chapter 4, you know that the original downhill or outside ski becomes the free ski for the next turn. A successful release depends on that ski flattening. What you may not have practiced yet are the additional actions of the new free foot, beyond tipping to the outside edge and lightening. The free foot plays an important role in creating and modulating balance for the coming turn. By keeping the free foot close to the stance foot in transition, both side-to-side and fore/aft, balance on the stance foot is improved.

I teach our system almost daily to skiers and instructors, and I am continually amazed at how few skiers have that skill. They are even more amazed at how quickly they improve once they acquire the proper technique. The following photos show the concerted effort that must be applied to the movement of drawing the free foot toward the stance boot for the next turn.

Pulling the Free Foot into Alignment

a   b

Fig. 6-1. Pulling the free foot into correct alignment with the stance foot

Hold the Free Foot Back

The skis and boots should remain parallel throughout the release, and they should stay even fore/aft. The ski tips and boot toes should remain side by side from the beginning to the end of the release. The tendency I see is for skiers to let the old downhill ski – the new free foot – slide ahead. Instead, maintain tension to keep the free foot pulled back under the hips. Flex that ankle and pull the free heel back under the hips. This prevents the inside foot from sliding forward. It is important to keep the free foot held back for the upper part of the turn. Developing this tension will make the turn transition easier. It should become part of your expert skiing repertoire.

De-emphasize Stance Ski Edging

Another important refinement during release and transition that is rarely developed by skiers is in the role of the new stance ski. Again, I must refer to the difference between traditional and PMTS instruction. Right from the beginning of instruction, this area is another in which the biomechanics of PMTS and traditional systems are opposite.

c

Fig. a. Stand across the hill on the uphill ski.
Fig. b. Lift the downhill ski and pull it toward the stance ski and boot.
Fig. c. After making contact, tilt the free ski toward the outside edge. Although the downhill ski tail crosses over the uphill ski, this is not an intentional move. There is no effort to cross the tails. Rather, it results from tipping the free foot and holding it against the stance foot.

Traditional instruction is focused on early engagement of the inside or big-toe edge of the new downhill ski which is emphasized through the wedge progression. Wedge and wedge Christie turns require you to slide the tail of the new downhill ski away from the tail of the other ski before beginning a turn.

PMTS de-emphasizes the effort to roll the new stance ski to its inside edge. On gentle terrain, practicing the release with PMTS movements and the Phantom Move, delay engaging the new stance ski. Actually make an effort to keep the stance ski flat on the snow, rather than tipped onto its big-toe edge. The stance ski will change direction more easily as a result of free foot tipping, tilting, or rolling if it is kept flat to the snow. It will require no active steering, twisting, or displacing of the tail to make the stance ski turn. The actions and refinements of the free foot create "resultant turning" of the stance ski.

De-emphasize edging the stance ski at the beginning of turns and use correct free foot actions, and you'll be able to turn your skis completely within a ski's length of vertical distance. Speed control is achieved largely by reducing vertical distance in linked turns. Use the free foot actions and refinements of this chapter along with a less-edged stance ski to create tight short turns. Many skiers will need to "rewire" their movements and reactions in order to incorporate the delay in edging the stance ski. Focus on it, for once you have learned it, you'll have functional speed control for off-piste conditions.

What to Do When the Tips Aim Downhill

After the release, when the skis start to slide downhill, many skiers panic. To become comfortable and secure with the feeling of releasing, practice on a wide-open, gentle slope with few skiers. Make sure you are able to stop on this terrain, and that you are not afraid to let your skis run straight downhill on this slope. After you have released and let the skis drop to the fall line, use the Phantom Move of the inside ski to complete the full turn. To start the Phantom Move, lift the back of the inside ski. Focus on the back of the ski, while keeping the ski tip on the snow. The inside ski boot should be held close to the outside boot. Many skiers separate their skis at this point. Balance and stand on the outside ski.

Fig. 6-2. From a release, when your skis aim downhill, perform a Phantom Move

Explanation of Tipping Mechanics

Tipping can be defined as tilting or rolling the ski in a side-to-side direction. People often like to describe the activities that occur inside the ski boots to explain what happens outside. Here are the internal actions that create tipping of the ski: rolling a ski from its big-toe edge to its little-toe edge can be achieved by changing pressure from the inside edge to the outside edge of the foot. Articulating the ankle inside the boot, applying a lateral force on the sidewall, creates this action. The lateral force tips the boot and ski to or from an edge. Since this movement begins at the base of the kinetic chain, muscles higher up are recruited as needed to assist in the tipping actions. While this explanation may help you understand the mechanics of ski tipping, it is not the best way to teach this movement.

A continuing search for effective ways to describe and teach PMTS movements has led me to use external cues. I am convinced that this approach makes success more easily attainable for my students. However, I don't want to limit explanations to only external cues, when biomechanical or other information can provide additional motivation or understanding. I think it is important for skiers to have as complete an understanding of the mechanics as possible, for understanding can help some learn faster. I realize, though, that others are not motivated by that kind of information, preferring to access as little extra information as possible, while learning by experimenting with the movements. I have tried to accommodate both learning preferences in this book.

Additional Free Foot Exercises

The "Pole Press" and "Release with Ball Hold" exercises are designed to help you successfully release with the skis at the same edge angle. Both exercises will help you learn just how much effort or muscular tension is required to keep the skis parallel at release. This knowledge will be especially helpful when you venture off the groomed slopes.

Starting position for the Release with Ball Hold

Pole Press

The actions of the releasing ski are important for the success of the turn. After the release has begun, when the downhill ski from the previous turn is flattening and releasing and becoming the new free ski, you must continue to focus on that ski until you are well into the turn; this is the continuum of movement mentioned earlier. Retaining control over the releasing ski and boot in order to keep it in line with the stance ski after the release seems to be difficult to learn. The movements required to draw the free foot in toward the stance foot and keep it there do not seem to develop naturally, and they are rarely taught. Traditional teaching systems haven't incorporated pulling movements or actions of the inside foot. Though it may be new to your skiing, active pulling is extremely effective. This exercise enables the skier to develop the tension required to move the new free foot toward the stance foot and line it up for the turn.

For this exercise, you need a partner who will attach a ski pole to your downhill ski by placing the tip of the pole under the boot, between the boot and ski. Have your partner push the boot down the slope away from the other boot with the pole to create resistance. You must try to bring the boots back together by overcoming this resistance. Once you can duplicate that pressure to bring your free foot toward the stance boot in an actual ski turn, you will be ready to slice the snow.

This movement of drawing the old stance ski toward the new stance ski is critical if skiers are to become expert in bumps, crud and carving. It also has the same positive effect on skiers who ski on ice. Have you been unsuccessful on ice? You probably didn't have the free foot aligning forcefully enough with the stance ski.

Practice this pole press exercise until you are comfortable and think you can do the same thing with your boot after you release the ski from an actual turn.

a   *b*

Fig. 6-3. Press against your partner's pole to bring in the free foot

> ### Cues for Success
>
> • With the free boot touching the stance boot, have your partner push harder while you press inward to maintain contact between the boots.

Fig. a. Have a partner place his pole tip under your boot between the boot and ski.

Fig. b. Lift this boot and press it toward the stance boot.

Fig. c. Have your partner push the boot away.

Fig. d. Try to overcome your partner's push and press your lifted boot toward your other boot until you can make the boots touch.

c

d

Release With Ball Hold

Earlier, I said I would provide exercises to validate your progress and make sure you are performing the new movements correctly. The next series of photos demonstrates a foolproof way to test your abilities. You must practice making a turn while holding an object between your boots. Don't be discouraged if you aren't able to perform it perfectly at first. Holding a ball, glove or large car-washing sponge between your feet while you turn is not easy, but it ensures that your feet and skis are correctly positioned throughout the turn, with sufficient tension to keep them there in ungroomed snow. The sponge is the easiest of the three props to use; the ball is the most difficult.

Drop the Ball and You're Out of the Game

What are the factors that enable you to hold the ball in a turn?
- You must press the free boot against the stance boot.
- You must keep the boot toes lined up fore/aft.
- You must release the downhill ski first.

_a_

_b_

_c_

_d_

Fig. 6-4. Release holding ball between feet

Cues for Success

• Keep constant pressure with the free boot against the ball.

• Keep the new stance ski flat on the snow until the fall line.

- You must prevent the uphill ski from rolling on edge prior to the downhill ski, or your boots will separate and you will drop the ball.
- You must make a precise balance transfer from one ski to the other and maintain balance throughout the turn.
- The boot and ski angles of both feet must be the same at all times.

If you can do all of these things in a turn then you are an expert skier and you pass this test! I have demonstrated this exercise to skiing champions as well as expert skier candidates. They found it very instructive. The exercise reveals any weaknesses in your technique and provides instant feedback about your skiing mechanics. A well-trained instructor can point out these weaknesses and help you change them.

I am demonstrating the exercise with a Nerf football. This exercise is difficult with a football because it has very little contact area. I found the large car-washing sponge most user-friendly.

Fig. a. Begin by standing across the slope. Place the ball between your boots and press the uphill boot against the lower boot just enough to keep the ball in place.

Fig. b. Begin to flatten and lighten the lower ski, shifting your balance to the upper ski. Press the lower boot against the upper boot to keep the ball in place.

Fig. c. Lift the free foot slightly off the snow. Pull the free ski back to prevent that boot from scissoring forward. Keep the new outside ski flat on the snow, not on edge.

Fig. d. Be patient with the turn; let the skis turn themselves. Continue to keep the outside ski flat on the snow.

Fig. e. Notice that there is no lead change or scissoring; the boots and ski tips are lined up perfectly.

Fig. f. The hard part is over. Press the free foot toward the stance boot as you tip it to the outside edge.

Fig. g. Both skis are tipped to the same edge angle as you stop.

e

f

g

Linked Turns with Ball Hold

This exercise is really useful. If you can make two consecutive turns holding the ball you are truly skiing with expert movements. If you use a traditional movement when you are in the position of *Fig. b*, you immediately will disqualify yourself from the exercise. No referee is necessary; the ball will roll down the mountain. A traditional movement here is flattening and putting the upper ski on edge first. You will notice in *Fig. d* that you must tip the lower ski onto its outside edge or it will catch in the snow. This exercise forces you to make the correct movements. The skis always must remain at the same edge angle. You may lift the free foot slightly to clear the snow, but you will have more chance for error this way.

Fig. a. Plant pole to establish balance for the release.

Fig. b. Lighten and flatten downhill ski of previous turn. Maintain constant pressure with new free foot toward new stance boot. This role change of the feet is critical. During the previous turn, the uphill boot was the free foot side that was pressing against the lower stance boot to keep the ball in place. Now the lower foot presses its boot uphill toward the new stance boot. Notice how the free ski boot and leg are tipped further on edge than the uphill stance ski and boot.

Fig. c. Stand balanced on the outside ski. Press the free foot toward the stance boot to hold the ball.

Fig. d. Continue tipping the free ski to establish the ski edge angles for the turn.

Fig. e. Hold the free boot back, even with the stance boot, or the ball will drop.

Performance Check

Using the large car sponge, you should be able to perform at least a release with ball hold in each direction to ensure that you manage your free foot adequately for off-piste skiing.

Cues for Success

• Squeeze the ball with the free boot against the stance boot.

• Deliberately flatten your stance ski to release.

Fig. 6-5. Linked turns holding ball between feet

Chapter 7:

Use the Force

Use Your Momentum to Reduce Your Effort

Lateral movements of the feet and ankles control ski edge angles, the rate of ski tipping, as well as turning. When we observe expert skiers, it looks as though their legs are turning in the same direction that the ski edge angle is tipping throughout a turn. The legs move toward the slope when the ski tips to a higher edge angle. The legs move away from the slope when the skis flatten to the snow. From the middle to the end of a turn, the body moves closer to the slope, inside the arc of the turn.

To begin a new turn, however, the body must move down the hill, away from the slope, out of the turn which can occur efficiently only if we begin releasing movements with the downhill ski. Tension in the downhill leg and the edge angle of the downhill ski resist the turning forces and keep the body inside the turn. If you release by flattening the downhill ski and relaxing the downhill leg, the turning forces will pull you in the desired direction, down the hill. Correct timing of the release makes it possible to use your momentum from one turn to move your center across your skis into the next turn.

Trouble arises when incorrect skiing mechanics are used instead of the release. Traditionally, the incorrect mechanics take the form of pushing off from the stance ski or extending from the uphill ski to move the body down the hill. After these movemetns are used, from that point on in the turn, inefficient compensating movements must be made. Skiers who use incorrect movements don't take advantage of the turning forces; therefore, they must incorporate compensations in order to extract themselves physically from the turn and launch themselves into the new turn.

When the turn is initiated properly through the release described above and detailed in Chapter 4, the skis tip to the new set of edges and the body moves into the new turn very quickly, with minimal effort. The idea is to minimize physical effort (relax the stance leg) by taking advantage of momentum and gravity. In effect, you are giving in to the turning forces that are pulling you down the hill. This causes your center to move across your skis and down into the next turn. Use the force; save your muscles.

> ### Cues for Success
>
> • Deliberately flex and shorten your stance leg as you flatten that ski to release.

Fig. 7-1. Use your momentum to start the new turn

Fig. a. Tip the inside ski to increase edge angles and turning.

Fig. b. Flex the inside knee as you tip to build the angles that resist gravitational and turning forces.

Fig. c. Begin to relax the legs and flex to reduce angles developed earlier in the turn.

Fig. d. Flex and pull up the knees toward the body. Flatten the skis with the pull of gravity and your momentum. Use the pole for stability.

Fig. e. Let the skis float to the surface and prepare to tilt the stance ski to its outside edge.

Tipping, Not Steering

Most instructors are trained to tell you that to achieve the turn of *Figure 7-1* you must steer your legs toward the hill. They will instruct you to rotate your legs away from the hill to start the new turn. Those movements do not create the turn I am demonstrating here. You may see how someone can be misled and made to believe that leg steering creates expert turns. The quest for this turn will be lifelong and unfulfilled if you use active leg steering. If you use the forces provided by the mountain and the tipping actions you can produce with your ankles and feet, you will create turns like the one I demonstrate.

The actions we just discussed are associated with letting go of the last turn. You will achieve an important breakthrough in your skiing when you realize that you should be expending more energy to keep yourself in a turn than to redirect your skis for the next turn. When you are able to do this, you will appreciate why I say that skiing should be effortless. You will no longer be concerned with turning your skis, just with how quickly you can relax, balance, and tip to make the transition.

The expert skier releases by relaxing the muscles in the stance leg. It can be difficult to tell a skier how to relax a muscle. Let's look at other, more obvious signs that a skier is relaxing the muscles of the leg to begin a release so we can develop an external cue that helps you learn to relax the stance leg. When you look at the photographs in this series, you will notice pronounced flexion of the legs at or near the end of a turn to begin a release. The flexing is initiated by the relaxing of the leg muscles. Skiers who want the release to happen very quickly will actually try to lift their knees and bring them into their chest. This is an important addition to your skiing for powder or in bumps to absorb pressure and change direction.

Practice Relaxing with Leg Flexion on Groomed Terrain

The next exercise is to link short turns on groomed terrain with a distinct relaxation and flexion (shortening) of the legs as you release. Perform the flattening and lightening of the old stance ski as you flex both legs. Keeping the legs in contact along their length will help the skis to work in unison. As you develop confidence in the timing and the movements, try this exercise on steeped terrain, where you'll be more aware of the flexion pulling your body downhill over your skis.

The photos on the next page may appear to be spread out because the release seems to take a long time to perform. Looks are deceiving — the release actually happens very quickly. The photos are spread out so that you can see the individual frames. If the individual frames were located correctly according to the turn, they would almost be stacked in a pile.

Fig. 7-2. Short turns with flexion at release

Fig. a. Begin to relax the leg muscles.

Fig. b. Prepare for the pole plant.

Fig. c. As soon as you feel the legs flex and the skis flatten, pull your knees aggressively to your chest.

Fig. d. Here I timed my pull with a slight bump to get an "air transition." This same move can be done in the bumps for spectacular air turns.

Fig. e. To land correctly for the new turn, tip the new free foot to the outside edge and pull that foot back.

Fig. f. Tip the free foot and keep it pulled in and back against the stance foot.

Fig. g. Managing the actions of your free foot will set you up perfectly for every turn.

Cues for Success

• Pull your knees up toward your chest to achieve leg flexion.

• Pull your free foot in and back to maintain contact with the stance foot.

Biomechanical Advantage

• Relaxing the stance leg and flattening that ski uses reduced energy and effort to begin a turn.

Chapter 8:

Weighted Release

The "Weighted Release," developed in PMTS Direct Parallel, is a sequence of movements designed to improve your turn transition technique. Keeping weight on the stance ski as it tilts to its outside edge reduces your dependence on big-toe, or inside, edge engagement, and internal femur rotation. The Weighted Release moves the body into the turn with assistance of "the force". We teach it to skiers who are ready to advance to expert status.

Watching skiers every day on the slopes gives me new ideas. I see their attempts to create proficient, fluid movements hindered by interruptive ski braking and gross, body-swinging actions. In an effort to solve these problems and provide immediate solutions, I develop exercises and movements that can be done quickly and easily. The Weighted Release is such an exercise. If you learn to perform the movements of this exercise as prescribed, you will become less dependent on big-toe, inside edge engagement, and you will have ultimate control over how much time you spend in transition between turns. There is an added advantage for knock-kneed skiers: the Weighted Release can reduce the tendency to ski knock-kneed. The Weighted Release also eliminates the step-off or push-off from the downhill ski that many skiers use at the end of a turn to project their bodies uphill into the next turn.

The problem knock-kneed skiers have is that they can't grip, or achieve enough edging, until their outside leg has rotated so far inward that their knee points at their inside leg. This extra internal rotation that they require to get an edge puts them in an "A- frame" position. The same is true for skiers who use leg steering and rotation to direct their skis. Often these skiers look knock-kneed but aren't. They actually have twisted the ski out from under the hips until they no longer have edge grip.

Normally the only way out of the situation is by stepping or pushing the uphill ski up and out onto its big-toe edge. These energy-intensive movements are limiting in all-mountain conditions and are hard to overcome. The Weighted Release can help to change these old movements. It enables skiers to keep the skis at the same edge angle during the release and engagement for the next turn. Many skiers, once they achieve edge grip, have great difficulty letting go of it. Holding onto that edge, not releasing it, keeps the body up the hill. Fluid skiing in powder, bumps, or steeps requires learning how to let go of the mountain. The Weighted Release will help you discover how easy it is to enter the next turn when you let go of the mountain. When properly executed, the turn happens almost effortlessly; that's why this exercise is so powerful. The Weighted Release leaves the skier no alternative but to move the body into the new turn. As you develop your Weighted Release, you'll be accessing the force as described in Chapter 7.

The first movement initiating a new turn should always be made by the stance ski of the previous turn. The ski closer to the bottom of the mountain is the downhill, or stance, ski. The other ski is the uphill, free, or unweighted ski. The stance ski is on its big-toe edge near the end of a turn. Watch and use that ski!

Make the initiating movement for the new turn by flattening the stance ski. First, relax the muscles of the stance leg — that will flex the leg slightly and allow the ski to come away from or off of its edge. Help the ski flatten by tipping the foot flat. Stand on the downhill ski; don't lighten it or shift your balance from it, as you would do in a regular release. This stance is what makes this a *weighted* release. As you flatten the stance ski, the uphill ski flattens along with it. Control the flattening of the uphill ski to maintain it at the same edge angle as the downhill, weighted ski. You can keep the uphill ski light or slightly weighted but both skis should be tipping at the same rate.

Fig. a. Through the end of the turn, balance on the downhill ski. The pole tip is already swinging for the pole plant.

Fig. b. Prepare the pole to tap and begin to relax the stance leg.

Fig. c. Flex and flatten the lower ski first; let the upper ski follow.

Fig. d. Keep the same amount of pressure on the lower ski as you had through the turn.

Fig. e. Bring both skis flat at the same time.

Fig. f. Begin to lighten the inside ski to make it the free foot.

Biomechanical Advantage

• The Weighted Release keeps your body moving into the next turn.

Fig. 8-1. Actions of a Weighted Release

Cues for Success

• Stand on the downhill ski as you flatten it.

• Relax and flex the stance leg as you flatten it.

Weighted Release with Lifted Uphill Ski

As mentioned earlier, knock-kneed skiers have difficulty letting go or rolling the downhill ski to the little-toe edge. It is more than just a knock-kneed skier problem; it is almost a universal problem. Even well trained, experienced skiers can be seen in a knock-kneed position at the end of turns. The combination of proper boots, alignment and movement can reduce even the most severely knock-kneed skier's A-frame position.

This exaggerated version of the Weighted Release, with the uphill ski lifted, is another step toward learning to let go of a turn so you can transition quickly into the next turn. Both approaches to the Weighted Release result in extraordinary benefits. Skiers who have difficulty moving their bodies into the next turn should practice both versions of the Weighted Release to appreciate and develop the feeling of letting go and transitioning into the next turn.

The lifted Weighted Release is like the previous Weighted Release, but with more emphasis on keeping all the pressure on the stance ski as it transitions to becoming the inside ski. To practice this exercise, lift the outside ski as you enter the turn, making the beginning of the turn on your inside ski. There is no balance transfer to the other ski during transition. Remain balanced on the stance ski during the edge change. If you're having trouble starting the turn, pull your lifted ski back so that the boots are even fore/aft. This will pressure the ski tip sufficiently to help the turn begin.

d

e

f

g

Cues for Success

• Balance only on the downhill ski throughout the release.

• Keep the lifted boot even fore/aft with the stance boot.

Fig. 8-2. Weighted Release with lifted uphill ski

Fig. a. Finish the previous turn by relaxing and flexing the stance leg.
Fig. b. Continue to stand on the downhill ski as it is flattened.
Fig. c. Tip the downhill ski to the outside edge while standing and balancing on it.
Fig. d. Use the inside pole to help maintain balance by dragging it on the snow.
Fig. e. The outside ski is still completely light.
Fig. f. Turn and balance on the little-toe edge of the inside ski.
Fig. g. Lighten and lift the outside ski. Keep it lifted until the end of the arc. At the end of the arc place the outside ski on the snow and transfer pressure and balance to that ski. Begin the next lifted Weighted Release by balancing and staying on that ski.

Biomechanical Advantage

• Balancing on the downhill ski throughout the release automatically brings your body downhill over your skis to start a turn.

Performance Check

The Weighted Release can occur only if there is no balance transfer during the transition. Weight and balance remain on the old outside ski while you tip it to the outside edge. The outside leg must relax and flex to begin the roll of that ski to the new edge. The transition happens on the edges of the downhill ski. The edge change is from the inside edge to the outside edge of the same ski. The other ski, not weighted, follows. Once the stance ski of the previous turn comes to its outside edge it becomes the inside ski of the new turn. Standing on the previous downhill ski as you roll it to its outside edge may sound opposite to everything you have been told — and it is — but the exercise is invaluable, as it forces the body to commit downhill into the next turn. This transition that makes your body cross downhill over your skis is essential for all-mountain skiing. When you are able to begin turns with the lifted upper ski Weighted Release, you will have achieved the next required step in the Undergraduate Course.

Midterm Performance Check

You are sure to have tested your short turns before you come to this "midterm performance check", which is an important step in learning. There are many ways to test or gauge your success with your turns throughout the Undergraduate Course. Before you continue with the Undergraduate Course and learn the refinements needed for true all-mountain conditions, you should be able to ace the following short-turn test.

Short-Turn Test

On the steepest blue terrain you should be able to make 15 short turns in a space no wider than a cat track without picking up speed. The path left by a groomer is an ideal width corridor. Connect the turns without a traverse before the release. The vertical distance you cover in a single turn should be no more than two ski lengths. Keep the same speed for the whole run. If you can perform this exercise, you have a functional short turn, ready for the enhancements that will take you off-piste. Typically, skiers who have learned PMTS require two to three full days of concentrated effort to perform short turns with a controlled release. This may seem like a long time, but it's worth the effort. This short turn is the basis for all-mountain skiing.

Chapter 9:

The Float

Pause Between Release and Engagement

Learn to float and your life will change. I'm tempted to begin every new component or movement series in PMTS with the claim "It will change your life or give you a skiing breakthrough" because these techniques do exactly that. I watch the transformation of skiers daily. The float is an addition to your ski technique and understanding that will fit right in with the Weighted Release. The float is not so much a technique as a place between ski turns where time stands still. Have you ever wondered, "How can expert skiers look so controlled, no matter how steep or how uneven the surface? They never seem rushed." Now the secret is yours: they have a place of tranquility between turns, a point in time to look around and evaluate without rushing the next move. The float is accomplished simply by pausing tipping movements so you feel as though you are suspended in mid-air.

Even if you aren't a tennis player, you may appreciate the similarities between these aspects of the sports. Recreational tennis players are always rushing around trying to get to the ball and making it at the last minute with an off-balance swing. If you watch the best players, they never seem rushed when they hit the ball. They are always in balance as they swing the racket. The reason they are able to stay in balance comes from what I call the "moment of stop." Just as they swing the racket, their feet stop and the body stabilizes. As a result, the racket can take its prescribed path to make perfect contact with the ball. Players need this moment to adjust their eyes and establish balance in preparation for the fast-moving on-coming ball. Intermediate players don't have this moment in their game. Expert players can repeat it time and time again — that's one reason they rarely miss.

Let's find out more about this moment of stop for skiers. From the time your skis enter the bottom of an arc until the end of the turn, your body is up the slope or above your skis. The beginning of the next turn will change that. Your body will move across the skis toward the downhill side. During this process, the skis go through an edge change, or transition, initiated by the releasing action of the lower foot and leg. The skis are flat on the snow at some point in the transition, which is where the float occurs. The idea is to exaggerate and maintain the floating time. Release to bring the skis away from their edges, then pause the tipping of your inside foot and hold your legs and body at an angle of ninety degrees to the skis as they approach the flat. Stay over the skis and move with them as they continue forward, keeping them flat to the snow surface as long as you can. Delay the engagement for the briefest moment.

Fig. 9-1. Actions of the Float

a

b

c

d

e

At the moment of float, when your skis are flat to the surface, you are actually beyond vertical. Your body has moved downhill slightly over your skis so that you are perpendicular to the slope. There is no reason to panic. You aren't going to fall over. The pause in your releasing movements will make you feel suspended in mid-air, and you will experience the "moment of stop." Your body eventually will continue to move on its path to the inside of the next turn. As your skis roll onto their new set of edges, you will feel secure. Your skis will arc around the turn until once again your body will be above them.

Fig. a. Tip the inside ski and flex the inside leg to increase edge angle to the snow.

Fig. b. Balance on the outside ski and continue to pull the free foot back. The tipping and flexing actions have paid off to complete an aggressive short turn.

Fig. c. Begin to relax the leg muscles and flatten the ski.

Fig. d. The momentum from the previous turn will propel you over your skis.

Fig. e. Pull the knees up, start to flatten the downhill ski, and then pause the tipping action to let the skis float.

Fig. f. Keep both skis flat as long as you can — this is the float. Prepare to pull the new free foot in and hold it back under your hips.

Fig. g. To leave the float and continue moving your body into the turn, resume tipping by aggressively tilting the inside ski to its outside edge.

> ## Cues for Success
>
> • Relax, then actively flex the legs to release.
>
> • Pause in tipping the free foot while the skis are flat on the snow surface.

f

g

If you have a tendency to push or roll the upper ski onto its big-toe edge before the lower ski is on its little-toe edge, you won't feel the float. Experts can perform the float and therefore can ski powder, bumps and steeps without difficulty. The float gives you time to adjust your balance before entering the next turn. If you are out of balance at the end of the turn, as many skiers are, you have little chance to recover unless you use the float to regroup. Without the float, you are caught going from one out-of-balance turn to the next.

Do you see how this whole program fits together? We first focused on keeping both skis at the same angle to the snow during the release, which we accomplished by flattening the lower ski first. Then, the Weighted Release helps to connect more directly the flattening action of the downhill ski to the movement of your body across your skis in the transition. If you can do that, you are on your way to learning the float. It's just a matter of pausing briefly between release and engagement while your skis are flat on the snow. Practicing the Weighted Release gives you more control over the rate of your release and your ability to float between turns. With the float, you can adjust your balance and be prepared for any situation the mountain can throw at you. You're on your way to skiing bumps and powder successfully.

a

b

c

d

Fig. 9-2. See the float from the side view

Cues for Success

• Look for both skis to be flat
at the same time in transition.

e   *f*   *g*   *h*

Fig. a. Finishing the previous turn, begin to relax the leg muscles.

Fig. b. Flex fully to absorb the bottom of the turn.

Fig. c. Relax the legs so the skis unbow.

Fig. d. Flatten the downhill ski to bring both skis flat to the snow, timing the pause to adjust the length of flat time.

Fig. e. Float with the skis flat. Prepare to become more active with inside boot pulling toward and holding to the stance boot.

Fig. f. Continue moving into the turn by resuming tipping of the inside ski to its outside edge.

Fig. g. Pull the free foot back to move the body forward over the skis.

Fig. h. Now you are balanced to begin flexing and tilting the inside leg and ski aggressively.

Performance Check

You can tell whether you are performing the float properly by looking at your ski tracks. The float occurs in the transition and is defined by the skis running flat on the snow between the release and engagement. When you examine your ski tracks between turns, there should be a section where you can see flat tracks from both ski bases, with neither ski tipped on edge. You should try to have the skis flat for at least a full ski length. If you have two flat tracks between turns with no edge impression, then you are performing the float correctly.

Chapter 10:

Upper and Lower Body Coordination

In ski books, there are countless mentions of the relationship between the upper and lower body under a variety of names. You may have heard it called a countered position, dynamic anticipation, upper- and lower-body separation, or blocked hips, to list just a few.

Upper- and Lower-Body Coordination, or "ULBC" as I call it, is the ability to coordinate counteracting movements of the upper body with turning actions of the skis, boots and legs. While good upper- and lower-body coordination makes it easy to ski with power, control, quickness and balance, many skiers have difficulty implementing this coordination in skiing. For that reason, I have put together a series of movement exercises that will increase your coordination. These are approaches I have tried that have proven to be effective for skiers. In conjunction with the movements of the feet and ankles, you will feel how ULBC exercises incorporate complementary movements of the upper body that will energize your skiing.

In PMTS we introduce upper- and lower-body coordination with an innovative approach. There is no single position that represents ULBC. Instead, it's a dynamic coordination of the upper and lower body throughout the turn. We teach ULBC while skiing, with movements and cues that produce this dynamic coordination rather than a static, ineffective position. You can use these movements immediately in all skiing situations. Simply put, the PMTS approach creates the movements that produce results and lets the body react to those counteracting movements.

Because the feet, ankles and shins are held securely by ski boots anchored to the skis, the movement of the lower body, from the thighs down, is influenced largely by equipment. You must learn to move your pelvis and upper body separately in response to lower-body movements. The feet are tipped to release and engage the skis. Increased tipping actions of the feet require that the thighs (femurs) rotate to keep up with the increasingly angulated skis. If the pelvis is held stable, both femurs can rotate under it without having the upper body follow. Remember in the descriptions of releasing how we referred to the rotation of the legs following the tipping skis, but described the upper body as remaining stable? Unfortunately, many skiers have difficulty creating this freedom of movement between the femurs and the pelvis.

Let's look back at some of the terms in skiing that have been used to describe ULBC. One is "countered position" and another is "upper- and lower-body separation." When the pelvis and upper body move with, or follow the rotation of, the femurs, few so-called counteracting movements are being used. Counteracting movements are being used correctly when the skier's upper body remains stable and quiet. It doesn't move, swing or rotate with the skis; thus the term upper and lower body separation. If the pelvis is held stable while ski edge angles increase through tipping the free foot, the thighs need not turn or steer in the direction of the turn. Counteracting movements that turn the pelvis away from the turn allow the body to increase mid- and upper-body lateral movements and therefore edge angles. When the body moves laterally into the turn and the pelvis is actively held or moved opposite to the turn direction, it minimizes or eliminates the need for femur rotation until the legs are flexed at the release. The introduction of shaped skis has changed technique in this profound way. Steering isn't a necessary part of skiing any longer, even at the intermediate level. Flexing at the bottom of the arc is an effective leg activity that complements modern ski technology. If you absorb the bottom of a turn by relaxing your muscles, the legs will flex. This is a progressive way to prepare for a release. As the pressure on the skis is reduced by flexing, the skis can be flattened easily. The ability to use the legs this way to release is dependent on how well you used counteracting movements at the beginning of the turn. If leg rotation or steering is used rather than counteracting movements early in the turn, the shaped ski design has less influence on the turn, and the ski is engaged less, reducing the possibility of the body moving inside the turn to help create edge angles.

We can start to feel and understand what stabilizing or counteracting movements mean by using indoor exercises. In my new book, *Ski Flex*, I introduce warm-up and stretching exercises that develop upper and lower body coordination while indoors. The indoor wall sit is one of these exercises.

Indoor Wall Sit

Fig. 10-1. Indoor wall sit

When sitting against the wall with flexed legs, you can begin to experience upper- and lower-body coordination. Turning your feet to one side, take note of how your legs move under a stable pelvis. Keep your pelvis and shoulders in contact with the wall. Place your arms against the wall to stabilize the upper body. Try to make counteracting movements with the hips by holding the pelvis against the wall before you turn your feet in a new direction. This movement sequence is the similar to what you will feel when the skis turn and your legs want to follow the turning skis. By counteracting the turning skis with the movement that keeps the pelvis flat on the wall, you will set up to develop body angles rather than knee angulation. Counteracting movements allow for a quicker, more powerful direction and edge change at the release. Because counteracting movements coil the body like a spring ready to let go of its energy, as soon as the release begins, the legs follow the flattening skis. Counteracting movements at the pelvis should be initiated immediately as, or just before, the skis begin turning.

The Poles and Upper and Lower Body Coordination

I have read most of the books on ski technique published over the past 20 years. Few, if any, accord pole use its true, deserved significance, which is an oversight, as skiers need expert pole use for expert skiing.

a   *b*

Fig. 10-2. Expert pole use for expert skiing

Fig. a. Prepare well ahead of the release with the pole swing.
Fig. b. Plant the pole and use it as a third point of contact for support and balance through the float.

Pole use has a major influence on upper and lower body coordination. However, integrating them can be tricky. Should pole use be developed before learning upper and lower body coordination? Is either more important and should one be learned first, or can they both be learned together? I hate to complicate the teaching, or leave open a point that might be misconstrued, but here is a dilemma: because coordinating the upper and lower body in skiing is largely supported by proper pole use, I feel that a correct pole plant should be developed first.

> ### Cues for Success
>
> • Hold the hands still while swinging just the basket of the pole.

I have seldom, if ever, encountered a skier who effectively coordinates the upper and lower body without a well-developed pole plant. On the other hand, I have never witnessed a skier with incorrect or mistimed arm and pole action achieve coordinated upper- and lower-body movement. So a correct pole plant can make upper and lower body coordination easier to learn.

Every sport has its key instruction cliché. In tennis, it's "keep your eye on the ball"; in golf, it's "keep your head down as you hit through the ball." Skiing has it own set of teaching clichés. One that applies to pole use is "don't drop your inside hand." With this negative instruction, it is no wonder the suggestion is rarely heeded. Most people respond better to "keep your hand up", a modified version of this cliché.

This suggestion is valid and provides several sought-after benefits: better edge grip, carving control and upper-body stability. Before you work on keeping the hand up, you might want to know where your hands are during your turns and poling action. Find out immediately using a skiing partner.

Pole Use Test

Have a friend or family member ski behind you as you make short turns. Instruct your partner to give you immediate feedback on your hand position using a loud voice. Here is how it works: if both of your hands stay in the proper position, to the side of the body as you pole plant, your hands should stay visible to the skier behind you. The skier following shouts out "yes," to provide positive, immediate feedback. If the hand planting the pole disappears in front of your body, your partner immediately responds by yelling "no." As you make turns, the word "no" will indicate to you that your hand has moved from the side of the body to the front, obscuring it from the view of your skiing partner (who continues to ski behind you). You will have immediate feedback about your hand position and poling method. Over-rotation and reaching with the hand both cause the hand to disappear. The pole plant should be a swing of the pole tip, not the all-too-common forward driving action of the hand. See photos of this test in action on the following page.

Fig. 10-3. Test of pole use

Fig. a. Here's the correct pole hand and arm position – both hands are visible from the rear as the pole plants.

Fig. b. Elbows are bent, and hands are out to the sides.

Fig. c. Both arms are visible. Their position changes little from frame to frame.

Fig. d. Pole swing begins. The basket swings forward while the hand remains in place.

Fig. e. Inside hand and pole (here, the right) are up and forward.

Fig. f. Pole tip points downhill before plant.

Fig. g. Pole is planted – both hands are visible.

Fig. 10-4. Expert skiers have a relaxed arm position, and use counteracting movements of the hips early in the turn. Steering or turning the skis does not produce this result.

Effective Hand and Arm Position

One of the most misleading instructional cues I hear on the slopes is "keep your hands forward." Although this is well intended, it still causes many problems. Pushing or holding the hands forward is unnatural and actually makes the skier's shoulders and arms stiff. Expert skiers have a very relaxed arm position. Keep the elbows bent, hands to the side and shoulders relaxed.

Holding and Swinging the Poles

What is the secret to achieving a relaxed arm position? Try these tips. Bend the elbows so the forearm is angled slightly toward the upper arm, and keep the hands to the side of the body rather than forward. Now with just a slight lift of the elbows, you have a relaxed, consistent useful arm and hand position.

From this position, use your wrist to swing the tip of the pole forward and downhill for the pole plant. Review the photos and notice how the arms stay in the same place, but the pole tip moves a long distance. Using this method will quietly and properly position your pole, hands and arms.

With your hands and arms in this position, try the test again. After several series of turns, you should be able to adjust your pole swing. If you still are not able to make turns in which your observer becomes a "yes man," your hand is still disappearing to the front of your body. You may need a pole swing makeover. The test gives you an instant status report about your pole plant mechanics. Although we will review pole use here, additional information and other approaches can be found in two of my other books, *Anyone can be an Expert Skier* and the *PMTS Instructor Manual*.

Before attempting to develop upper and lower body coordination, try to establish a proper pole plant rhythm. As soon as one pole touches the snow, the other pole basket should start to swing forward, and so on. If this becomes too difficult, you can work on the upper and lower body coordination exercises without using any pole plant. If you prefer to learn upper and lower body coordination first, that's fine; take up the pole plant afterwards. The order of presentation in this chapter is pole use first, then upper and lower body coordination. If you feel you want to learn pole use first, read on; if you want upper and lower body coordination first, skip this section for now and come back to it after reading the next section.

Once you have integrated upper and lower body coordination with a pole tap, you are on your way. There are few experiences that can equal the thrill of controlled floating of your skis over powder. Without command of upper and lower body coordination and pole plant, achieving that level of expertise will be difficult, if not impossible. The upper body must be well balanced and solid to achieve the "float" in powder. A well-developed pole plant and upper and lower body coordination provide this solidity. Skiing powder without the solid pole plant and coordinated upper and lower body is like racing the Indy 500 with street tires. You can get around the track, but you are bound to skid into the wall at some time. The natural reaction is terror; driving a car in these conditions is not a pleasurable experience. I have skiers who tighten up from fear when they get in powder due to previous, unsuccessful experiences. Face plants and fear are reduced when a skier combines the float, a pole plant, and upper and lower body coordination.

Review

If the timing of your pole swing is off, or if the swing creates rotation of the upper body, then it must be changed. If you are pushing your pole-planting arm forward and at the same time trying to control hip rotation, for example, you will find it very difficult to perform these movements in tandem. An incorrect arm action rotates the shoulders, which helps rotate the hips; therefore, you are fighting your own movements. Now you can see why the pole use test is so effective: it gives you immediate feedback about your pole habits. To stabilize your upper body in powder and bump skiing, the pole plant needs to have purpose and must be done in a strong, deliberate fashion.

Fig. 10-5. Holding and swinging the poles properly make it easier to ski the ungroomed

Fig. a. Prepare early for a stabilizing pole plant – the pole is in position, pointed downhill, prior to planting.

Fig. b. Straighten the elbow after the pole tip has pointed downhill.

Fig. c. Plant the pole and release the skis (the legs have relaxed and flexed, and the skis are flattening to the snow). The body should move as a unit toward the pole as it sinks into the snow.

Fig. d. Use the pole to stabilize the body during the float, where the skis come to the surface. Hold the pole firmly so it can provide support.

a

Cues for Success

• Swing the basket forward early so it points downhill momentarily prior to planting.

• Hold your pole firmly so it can support and stabilize your body.

b

c

If it looks as though I'm vaulting my body off the planted pole shaft in Figures c *and* d, *you're right. I am using it here to support my body.*

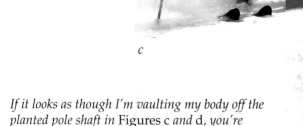

d

Exercises for Pole Use

Home Base

Where you normally carry or hold your poles and arms is called "Home Base." Home Base should be a wide position, with hands at least 12 inches away and out to the sides of the body. If you keep a relaxed, bent elbow position with the hands away from the body, you'll be fine in most cases.

g   *f*   *e*

Fig. a. Hold the hands to the side, not stretched forward.

Fig. b. Use the wrist to swing the pole basket forward in preparation.

Fig. c. Plant the pole and immediately move the planted pole hand forward and over the pole tip so that it stays in "Home Base."

Fig. d. Start to swing the other pole basket forward.

Fig. e. The pole points downhill well ahead of the pole plant.

Fig. f. With hands in home base, hold the pole at the ready.

Fig. g. Tap the pole to begin the release. It signals flexing the legs and flattening the stance ski.

Biomechanical Advantage

• Home Base aligns the upper body for easier balance on the stance ski.

• Home Base diminishes rotation of the upper body and makes it easier to release into a new turn.

Fig. 10-6. Keep your hands in "Home Base"

a

b

c

d

Cues for Success

• Move the arms very little from Home Base.

• Prepare the pole early so you have time to point it downhill prior to planting.

• Always look downhill at the location where your next turn will finish.

Two Types of Pole Plant

The pole swing is thought of primarily as a timing device for starting turns, but it is much more. A pole plant can help solidify counteracting movements, it can stabilize the upper body, and it can reorient the body for the next turn. It definitely is an aid that complements the basic upper and lower body coordination exercises. Two basic types of pole plants can be used for different purposes. In the first type of swing, the flowing pole plant, the movement comes from the wrist and elbow. The shoulder is not part of the pole movement. Flowing plants are used on groomed terrain and in medium to large radius turns. The actual plant is more of a tap, and the tip of the pole is not held on the snow for very long. A stabilizing pole plant is used in steeps, short turns, bumps, powder or crud, where speed control and upper body balance and stability are necessary but are often jeopardized. In many cases, the stabilizing pole plant is held in the snow until the body has passed and turned around the point where the pole was planted.

The Flowing Pole Swing

The basic swing is good for everyday use on groomed or open terrain. The first thing to understand is that "pole swing" doesn't mean moving the pole grip or hand forward. On the contrary, to begin a swing, the hand and wrist are moved slightly up and toward the shoulder. Remember, we are trying to swing the tip of the pole, not the handle. The wrist and hand should move up only enough for the tip of the pole to be released in a forward swinging arc. When the tip of the pole is clear of the snow, you can swing the whole shaft using a small wrist movement. Swing the tip until it points down the slope, and hold it for a fraction of a second. When you have the tip pointing down the slope, aim it directly at the bottom of the mountain and extend the elbow until the pole tip touches the snow. Once the pole touches the snow, push the hand forward. Now your hand and the pole handle make an arc over the point in the snow where the pole tip is planted. Moving the hand forward in this way returns the hand to its original home base position. As the hand arcs over the planted pole, the other hand and wrist begin the swing movements to maintain uninterrupted rhythm.

Fig. a. From the home base position, bend the elbow and wrist to bring the hand toward the shoulder.

Fig. b. Swing the pole with the wrist to point it downhill.

Fig. c. Tap the pole tip in the snow.

Fig. d. Immediately move the hand forward over the pole tip to return to home base.

Cues for Success
• Bring the elbow in and the hand up.
• Use only the wrist to swing the basket forward.

Fig. 10-7. The flowing pole swing

The Stabilizing Pole Plant

The second, more advanced type of pole swing is really the same but with a pronounced and more deliberate pole set in the snow. This swing is used on terrain where speed control is desirable, where you'll be completing your turns with the skis headed almost 90 degrees across the fall line. The stabilizing pole plant gives your upper body control and balancing assistance. The timing of this plant requires a longer pause in preparation for the turn, where you hold the pole tip pointed down the slope. The planting action is deliberate and delayed until your skis cross the fall line. Because the pole plant is held longer and more weight is applied, it helps move the upper body and shoulders down the slope, towards the planted pole and the center of the next turn, which helps line up your upper body for the next turn as you begin the tipping, releasing actions of the ski.

a

b   *Fig. 10-8. The stabilizing pole plant*

Fig. a. Line up the upper body solidly to the fall line, plant pole firmly to stop upper body movement.
Fig. b. Release skis and use pole for balance during float. Keep the pole planted as skis continue by it.

There is another important demonstration here. In Chapter 5, I discussed the need to *not* turn the stance ski when starting a turn. Notice here how from *Figure a* to *b* my skis have flattened and released, but they have not changed direction.

Cues for Success

• Keep the hands in home base before and after the plant.

• Plant and grip the pole firmly so that it stabilizes the upper body.

Preparing for the Stabilizing Pole Plant

c

d

Fig. a. Develop the pole swing as the turn begins by bringing the hand toward the shoulder.

Fig. b. Use the wrist to bring the pole tip forward. Notice how there is little change in any other part of the body.

Fig. c. Flex the wrist to bring the pole tip higher, aiming it downhill. This action prepares for a stable transition.

Fig. d. Extend the elbow to help reach the pole into the snow. Hold it firmly.

a

b

Fig. 10-9. Preparing for the stabilizing pole plant

The slight delay and holding the pole in the snow longer maintains the upper-body position and keeps it from rotating in the direction of the turn, constituting an upper-body counteracting movement. In effect, counteracting movements of the upper body conserve energy and store it for use in the release. Keep the pole in the snow as long as you can while moving the other hand and pole forward into position for the next turn.

Cues for Success

- Keep arm and shoulder stable.
- Use wrist and elbow to swing the pole.

Pole Basket Push

The pole basket push is a great exercise for orienting the upper body level to the snow. It also reduces the amount of pole and arm movements of the upper body, which is called "cleaning up extraneous movements." Read the explanation carefully. The pole basket push is so contrary to many skiers' pole habits that they find the concept difficult to grasp.

The first part of the explanation is very simple. This exercise requires that you keep your pole tips forward of the boot toes at all times during the turns. You can feel yourself accomplishing this by pushing the pole tips along the snow. Do a straight run while holding your poles vertically and drag the tips along the snow. Use your wrists to create pressure on the pole handles to keep the baskets forward of your boots; don't let the baskets drag back along the snow, so that you can feel the resistance created by the pole drag that you'll have to counteract with your basket push. In the pole basket push exercise, continue to create the same forward wrist pressure with the inside pole, preventing the baskets from dragging backward. Your hands will be high and the pole tips will be to the side of the binding toe pieces.

Right after you make a regular pole plant, before you move past the spot in the snow where the pole is planted, lift the pole tip and push it forward (remember the wrist action from above) along the snow. Lifting the hand and flexing the wrist toward your shoulder is how this movement is accomplished. It requires that you keep pushing the bottom of the pole forward as you move through the end of the turn. Keep pushing the pole basket while you prepare the other hand for the next pole swing. It's as though both pole baskets are swinging forward, one to prepare for the plant, the other pushing forward along the snow to stay ahead of the boot toes. After you plant the pole on the other side, push its basket forward in the same way you did for the last pole plant. Using the pole basket push on both sides with both poles will keep the poles well forward of the boot toes and keep the hands and poles positioned higher by your hips. This technique results in very beneficial upper body discipline.

Fig. a. Set up the pole plant with a wrist swing.
Fig. b. Plant the pole and be ready to drag the tip forward on the snow before it gets behind your binding toe pieces.
Fig. c. Use the wrist to push the pole tip along the snow.
Fig. d. Press the basket forward and well uphill of the feet so it doesn't snag. Prepare the other pole for planting.
Fig. e. Swing the outside pole basket ahead for its pole plant, aiming the pole downhill prior to planting.
Fig. f. Plant the downhill pole and repeat the drag on that side.

Fig. 10-10. The pole basket push, shown with the right pole

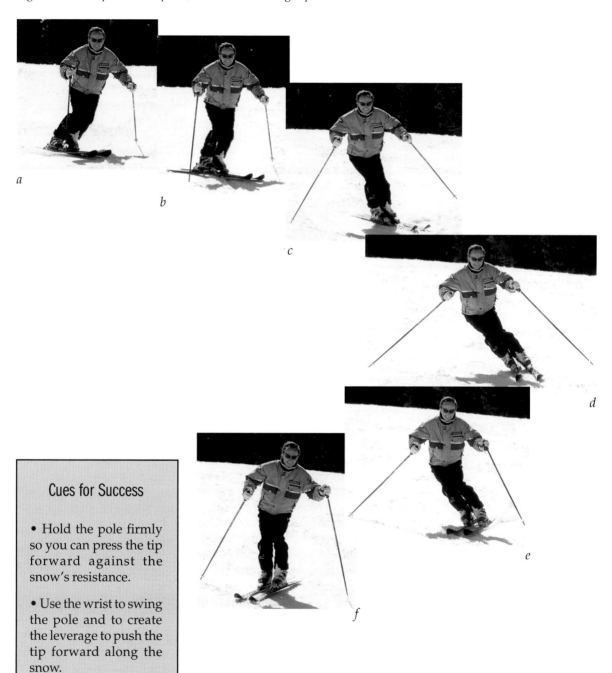

Cues for Success

• Hold the pole firmly so you can press the tip forward against the snow's resistance.

• Use the wrist to swing the pole and to create the leverage to push the tip forward along the snow.

Effective Pole Use Develops Upper and Lower Body Coordination

In short turns, to manage speed control and turn frequency, the pole movements must never stop. As one side is moving the pole into position for a pole plant, the other arm and hand prepare for the turn. After you plant the pole and you begin to move past the spot where the tip was planted, the hand and arm move forward, resuming their home base position. The inside arm is in the "strong-arm position" that maintains upper body position and stability. "Strong-arm" is a phrase I developed in the PMTS Instructor Manual. I point out what it is in the photos describing pole use. More terrain-specific pole use situations and descriptions will be illustrated as we move into the off-piste topics. I must reiterate that pole use has been largely ignored in skiing instruction. It is the one area in which you immediately can make big changes in your performance. Skiing more difficult terrain will not be fulfilling or enjoyable without well-developed pole skills.

Exercises for Upper and Lower Body Coordination

Building ULBC will take a two-pronged approach. The first set of exercises builds body balance and awareness. The second set of exercises builds the actual movements for dynamic turn-to-turn applications.

Counteracting movements, rarely used or understood by skiers, are part of the upper and lower body coordination program. Some form of a countering movement is part of every turn and is described by a turning action of the pelvis and upper body in the opposite direction of the turn. This movement counteracts and offsets the possible rotational movements created by the lower body as the ski's side cut engages to generate arcs. The counteracting movements can be active as in a steep energetic bump run where the upper body actually turns in the direction opposite to the skis, or the pelvis can be held stable to allow the femurs to follow the arc of the skis and turn under the pelvis.

The exercises introduced at the beginning of this section will also benefit your pure carving performance. Pure carving is a function of tipping the skis without slipping. The first set of exercises develops the body balance and awareness for riding on your edges rather than on the bases. Skidded turns have significant contact between base and snow. Carved turns have very little base-to-snow contact, unless the snow is soft. The carved turn on very hard snow is predominantly pure edge contact.

Let the Legs and Torso Become Independent

The beginning exercise is simple, safe and straightforward. It may remind you of the old Austrian starting position or traverse exercises that their ski schools used during the 1960s. Don't worry — this situation is temporary to loosen you up and make you aware of your mid-body range of motion. Make sure you look up the mountain to avoid traffic before beginning any exercise that takes you from the side of the slope into the slope.

Before you start moving, the upper body is turned in a pronounced manner, to face downhill. The skis are tipped onto their uphill edges. Hold yourself with your poles to prevent sliding before you begin to position the skis and upper body. Balance so you can stay upright; turn your uphill hip forward so that your backside is to the slope. When you are in balance, let the skis go. Let the skis run on their edges without turning or slipping. If you don't travel forward far enough across the slope, do the exercise again, but this time, begin by pointing your skis more steeply downhill. If you are on carving skis, you will notice they will immediately take you back up the slope, describing a round arc, leaving two thin edge lines in the snow. Because of their design, the skis want to scribe a semi-circle or half-moon on the slope and don't require any assistance from the pilot. This action is what we are trying to achieve when we say,

"let the skis do the work."

Edge Lock Traverse

Fig. 10-11. Starting position, edge lock traverse

Fig. 10-12. Skis scribing arcs in edge lock traverse

Start with the skis aimed slightly downhill, rolled on edge. Balance with the skis on edge and your back facing up the slope. Let the skis run. Tip the skis to a higher angle, turn your back to the slope, and lean out over the downhill ski.

*Fig. 10-13. Edge lock traverse -
emphasize free foot tipping*

Fig. a. Traverse on your skis' edges with the skis pointed slightly downhill.

Fig. b. Balance while you ride the arc scribed by the ski edges.

Fig. c. Tip both skis evenly and sufficiently to prevent skidding.

Cues for Success

• Tip both skis evenly before sliding.

• Aim your back uphill.

• Look for clean sliced tracks in the snow to confirm your performance.

The secret is timing. PMTS instruction will tell you

"don't turn your skis, they should turn by themselves,"

without physical assistance. Lito Tejada-Flores, my good friend, refers to this effect of the skis turning themselves as the result and benefit of his emphasis on "dynamic anticipation". Although we may not call these actions or techniques by the same name, they are the same thing. We are referring to the same coordination of upper and lower body that we know is a component of expert skiing.

In the exercise, the idea is to keep the skis cutting the snow so they leave two clean, distinct edge cut lines on the snow. The only way you can achieve this amount of edge-hold is by balancing properly over the skis. If the upper body or pelvis rotates you will lose balance and the skis will skid. Most skiers require two or three tries in both directions before they feel the skis locking into the snow and carving an arc.

Garland Release with Reengagement

The garland release with reengagement is a refinement, test and more advanced version of the traverse edge lock. You have to be able to flatten and then reengage the skis while sliding forward.

Set up the same as for the previous exercise. Let the skis go. As you begin to slow down near the bottom or belly of the arc, when your skis are pointed across or slightly up the hill, release or flatten the skis to the snow. You will have to relinquish your edged or angulated body position to flatten or release the ski. "Angulated" means tipping the ski to a high edge angle. The "angulated body" results from balancing on that edge angle. Let the skis flatten completely until they redirect and start to point down the slope. When the skis become flat to the slope and your tips have aimed downhill as steeply as your starting position, reengage the edges and hold the skis on edge to finish a new arc. This

Fig. 10-14. Garland release with reengagement

Fig. a. Traverse with the edges locked on angle and cutting a clean line.
Fig. b. Flatten both skis, initiating with the downhill foot, and let the ski tips start to drop downhill.
Fig. c. Tip the downhill foot to the outside until both skis become flat to the snow.
Fig. d. Quickly tip the skis back on edge, initiating by tipping the uphill ski uphill and keeping the flat of your lower back facing uphill.
Fig. e. Hold the skis on edge and maintain balance.
Fig. f. Keeping your back aimed uphill and the skis on edge, let the skis run until you stop.

exercise is basically an edge release garland, with extreme body angulation. The reason for introducing extreme angulation is to make you familiar with a range of body motion that you may never have achieved before. Skiers rarely discover on their own how far they can or need to move to create aggressive body angles relative to the snow. Expert skiing on all terrain may require moving in these ranges. Expert skiers may reach the extremes of this range in split seconds when they ski quickly in bumps and while carving.

Cues for Success

• Tip the uphill ski and move your hip uphill to engage the skis without skidding.

• Keep the uphill ski pulled back so the ski tips are even fore/aft.

Straight Run ULBC Exercises

Now do the edge lock exercise from a straight run. With this exercise, you begin moving to the edges of the skis and riding on them. Try to put the skis on edge without skidding and then balance over the edges. As you increase the edge angle, move your body in the opposite direction from the turn. Just as you did in the traverse edge lock exercise, turn your backside slowly to aim to the inside of the turn. You will know when the skis engage as they may feel like they are on tracks or rails taking you for a ride. Don't panic: enjoy the sensation. Establish balance by increasing the amount of body turn in the opposite direction to the ski turn. Make sure you have less pressure on the inside ski — there should be just enough to leave a groove. Quick or aggressive movements will put you off balance, so take your time developing these movements. Once the skis have changed direction enough to feel the arc, gently and gradually bring them flat and start tipping to the other set of edges. Notice that you are skiing on all four of your edges from one turn to the other. Skiers who have alignment problems will have difficulty keeping both skis at the same angle. Don't give up; remember, tipping the inside ski is very difficult for a knock-kneed skier. Staying balanced on the outside ski is difficult for the bowlegged skier.

Make sure you choose a low traffic area on a flat slope for this practice.

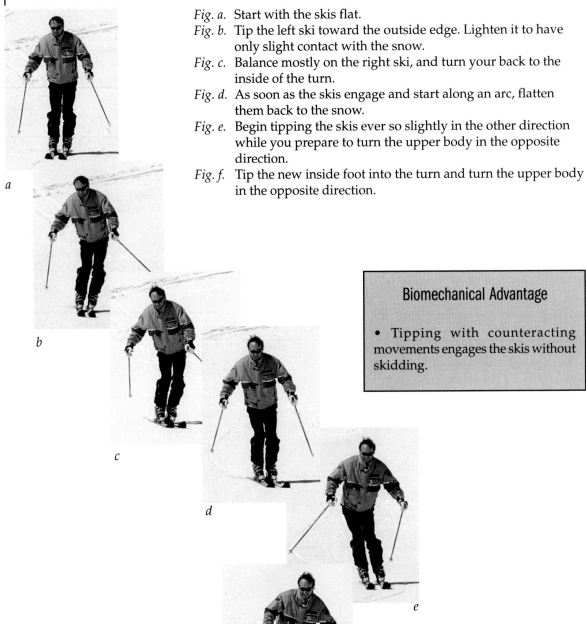

Fig. a. Start with the skis flat.

Fig. b. Tip the left ski toward the outside edge. Lighten it to have only slight contact with the snow.

Fig. c. Balance mostly on the right ski, and turn your back to the inside of the turn.

Fig. d. As soon as the skis engage and start along an arc, flatten them back to the snow.

Fig. e. Begin tipping the skis ever so slightly in the other direction while you prepare to turn the upper body in the opposite direction.

Fig. f. Tip the new inside foot into the turn and turn the upper body in the opposite direction.

Biomechanical Advantage

- Tipping with counteracting movements engages the skis without skidding.

Fig. 10-15. Straight run ULBC exercises

Fig. a to b. From a straight run with skis flat, turn your upper body to the right and tip the left ski slowly on to its outside edge.

Fig. c. Stay balanced over the edges and let the skis track until they change direction.

Fig. d. Bring the skis back to flat with your body facing forward, as you started.

Fig. e. Tip your right ski onto its outside edge while you turn your body to face the left, with your back aimed to the inside of the new turn. Engage the skis cleanly.

Cues for Success

• Look at your tracks to gauge your performance. You should leave two clean arcs, then a brief section with two flat base tracks, then two new arcs, with no skidding or brushing marks.

• Turn the body before the skis tip on edge.

• Ride on the edges and let the side cut dictate the path.

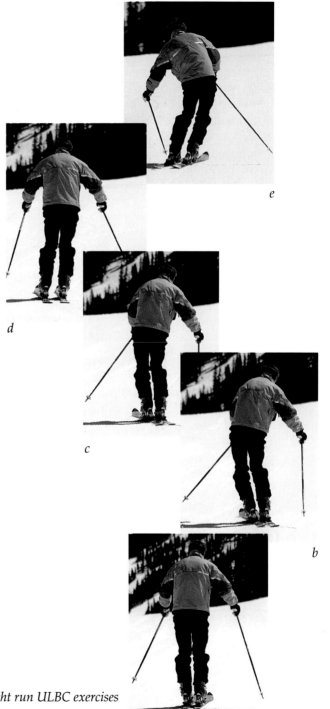

Fig. 10-16. Straight run ULBC exercises

I have taught the straight run ULBC exercise frequently to both advanced and high-level expert skiers. Even these skiers often require at least a run or two, sometimes an afternoon, to master the exercise. Start by gradually and progressively tipping the skis. To be very clear, I said tipping and I mean tipping only. Most skiers, whether they are aware of it or not, have rotation and skidding built into their every movement. Rotation is an unnecessary and debilitating habit that must be eradicated. Once you have completed the Undergraduate Course and can tip your skis and engage them without inadvertent skidding, I will demonstrate how you can increase the turning or redirecting of your skis using efficient and accurate movements. Skiing is traditionally taught with an overemphasis on rotary and steering movements, which results in body rotation and skidding skis, because skidding has been the only understood means to change ski direction, especially for beginning and intermediate skiers.

I recommend that you develop all the exercises in the series to a satisfactory skill level, as they will pay off when you encounter your first powder day. Learning the basics on a powder day is a frustrating waste of a potentially great day. Your friends are out shredding the snow and you are digging yourself out and cleaning your goggles. Try these exercises and learn to incorporate them into your skiing technique. The edge lock traverse deserves at least three tries in each direction before you start the straight run ULBC exercise. The straight run version deserves at least an afternoon. Check your tracks frequently to make sure you are practicing the right movements. If you have trouble leaving two clean arcs, practice the edge lock traverse.

Dynamically Coordinating Upper and Lower Body in Skiing

Now that you have practiced the exercises that help you isolate your upper and lower body and learn balance on cleanly engaged edges, you're ready to progress to the second prong of the ULBC. The next exercises help you coordinate your upper and lower body in linked turns in the manner that will take you off-piste with success. Use the range of upper and lower body movements you experienced in the previous exercises.

Arch/Hand Lift, Poles Horizontal

This exercise is one of the most effective from the upper and lower body coordination series I developed. I am unaware of any other instructors who use this approach. It can be included any time you are ready to begin coordinating your upper and lower body. The Arch/Hand Lift is a variation on the Phantom Move that adds a role for the upper body. Coordinating ski and foot action with upper-body counter tilting is the goal of this exercise.

If you have never practiced the Phantom Move in short turns, it might be a good idea to review and practice that first. Link short turns using the phantom lifting and tipping action with each turn. The first question I usually hear in response to this exercise is "Which foot do I lift?" First, think about lifting the arch rather then the foot, as this action will incorporate both the lightening and the tipping into one thought. Second, lift the arch of the foot in the direction in which you'd like to turn. If you want to turn right, lift the right arch. As an example of an external cue to help you gauge your performance, you might think, "show the base of your inside ski to the other boot." Balance and stand on the regular outside or stance ski. These should be short, shallow turns, with just enough direction change to head back across the slope. After a slight direction change, put the lifted arch or ski back on the snow and start lifting the other arch.

Once your short phantom turns are working well, you are ready to coordinate the lower body with the upper body. Hold your poles out in front of your shoulders as in the photos. Coordinate lifting the arch with lifting the same hand in the turn — i.e. right arch, right hand. As you begin lifting the free foot, lift the hand on the same side of the body. Keep enough tension in the arms so that lifting the hand also lifts the shoulder. You develop a functional relationship of the upper body to the lower body by coordinating these movements.

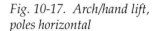

Fig. 10-17. Arch/hand lift, poles horizontal

Fig. a. Raise the inside arch and lift the inside hand at the same time.

Fig. b. Continue to tip the inside ski and keep the inside hand slightly higher.

Fig. c. Place the inside ski back on the snow, raise the other arch and lift the other hand.

Fig. d. Complete the turn by holding the inside hand high and keeping the inside arch lifted.

This combination of movements will swing all of your body weight over the outside ski; it will also create increased body articulation. You should start to feel a difference in the way your body reacts to turns. The first sensation many skiers report is a pinching at the lateral part of the ribs and hip on the side over the outside ski. This feeling makes complete sense as the exercise tips your upper body toward the downhill side, in turn, stretching the uphill side of the body. Notice in the carving section of the book (Chapter 12) how the upper body is still slightly angled toward the outside ski despite the extreme body angles attained. Keeping the body angles slightly toward the outside ski increases edge grip, especially on hard and icy snow. In the carving section of the book you will notice the emphasis on moving the hip and mid-body into the slope, but not the upper body, head or shoulders. This exercise will help you develop this ability. Leaning the upper body accomplishes very little except loss of balance. Your upper body will develop tremendous angles to the surface after you achieve lateral balance.

Fig. a. Lift the new inside ski.
Fig. b. Tip the inside ski to its outside edge and raise the inside hand.
Fig. c. Set the ski back onto the snow and bring the hands to level.
Fig. d. Begin to lift the right ski and right hand.
Fig. e. Increase the lift of the right hand and the right arch through the turn.
Fig. f. Increase the tipping of the lifted ski to increase the body angle to the slope.
Fig. g. A slightly lower outside hand and higher inside hand is a good indication of a stable body.

Biomechanical Advantage

• Coordinating your upper body with the lifting of the free foot establishes solid balance on the stance leg.

Cues for Success

• Hold the poles out in front of you.

• Lift the arch and hand together.

Fig. 10-18. Arch/hand lift, poles horizontal

c

b

a

Fig. 10-19. Arch/hand lift, proper pole position

Arch/Hand Lift, Proper Pole Position

Once you have coordinated the arch lift with the horizontal pole lift, you are ready to hold the poles in their normal position and try the exercise again. The idea here is to feel the extra edge hold and angulation that can be achieved by upper body coordination. Hold the poles away from the body, and as you lift the your arch/ski, lift the hand on the same side. The movements of this exercise feel extreme, but when I look at the photos we took after the photo shoot, I am always amazed at the excellent body position that the exercise provides. I don't think we should ski every day using this extreme upper body outward tilt, but the exercise conveys to skiers how much more tilt is available in their regular skiing.

Biomechanical Advantage

• The reaction of the body to the arch and arm lifting engages the ski's sidecut without skidding.

Fig. a. Keep the hands level in transition.
Fig. b. Lift the back of the inside ski and start tipping it.
Fig. c. Lift the inside arm.
Fig. d. Flex the legs to release.
Fig. e. Prepare to lift the back of the new inside ski. Here, in transition, the hands are level again.
Fig. f. Lift and tip the inside ski, and lift the inside arm.
Fig. g. The inside ski is tipped, and the inside arm is slightly higher. This position is truly balanced.

e

f

g

> ## Cues for Success
>
> • Lift inside hand, arm, and shoulder.
>
> • Lift the arch and arm together.

Performance Check

The performance check for this chapter has several components. Coordinating the upper and lower body is critical to success in any "graduate conditions" — ungroomed snow or high-angle carving.

Pole Use

Enlist a friend to help you judge your pole use. You should be able to pass the pole use test in linked short turns on groomed expert terrain: when viewed from behind, your hands will be visible at all times on each side of your body.

In linked short turns on groomed intermediate terrain, you should be able to perform flowing pole plants. Have your friend watch to be sure that your pole touches the snow just before your release, and to be sure that the rhythm of pole swing and turns remains constant for at least 10 turns.

To be prepared for the Graduate Course, you must link at least 10 turns on groomed expert terrain with stabilizing pole plants. Have your friend watch to be sure that your pole is firmly planted before your skis release, and to be sure that your speed remains controlled and constant over the 10 turns. At the end of each turn, your skis should be pointed across the hill while your upper body faces downhill.

Upper- and Lower-Body Coordination

The performance check for ULBC comprises two tasks. First, you should be able to perform a garland release with reengagement to a locked-edge traverse in both directions. Second, you should be able to perform the straight run ULBC exercises with a locked-edge engagement in both directions. For both of these tasks, you can judge your own performance by examining the tracks your skis leave on the snow. When you perform the exercises correctly, you'll see that the skis roll onto edge without any skidding or sideways travel of their tails. In the straight run ULBC exercise, you should see two clean edge arcs, then a momentary flat track from the ski bases, then two more clean arcs.

Poles and ULBC

Check that you can coordinate your body and the pole swing by performing the arch/hand lift with the poles in their regular positions. You should be able to link at least 10 turns on groomed intermediate terrain without gaining speed.

Final Performance Check

Congratulations! Achieving upper- and lower-body coordination is the final step before you proceed to the Graduate Course — carving, bumps, powder, or all three topics. If you have succeeded at the performance checks for each chapter in the Undergraduate Course, you're ready for the final check. All that remains is the Linked Release Test.

Linked Release Test

For the final test, you should be able to perform at least 10 linked releases, coming to a complete stop after each release. Any of the releases from the Undergraduate Course (two-footed, weighted, or from uphill ski) is fine as long as the skis remain parallel throughout the exercise. The requirements are:

- a stabilizing pole plant is in place as you come to a stop
- you stop within two ski lengths
- the arc of your turns is less than two ski-lengths wide.

Graduation!

Upon successfull performance of the Linked Release Test, you're ready to take the Graduate Course. The graduate chapters will apply the technique you've learned through the Undergraduate Course to specific conditions and performance. As you read through the graduate chapters, if you're not confident with the techniques presented, look back at the appropriate chapter in the Undergraduate Course and practice again on easier terrain if needed.

Chapter 11:

Carving

What can be said about carving that hasn't already been repeated, plagiarized or trivialized? According to comments posted on the German Amazon Web site by a reviewer of my first book, "Finally, a simple approach to carving that can be learned by all skiers." I think that just about sums up what we teach in PMTS. We regard carving to be the standard for basic turns, although carving seems to be considered an elusive goal by many skiers. Carving has many faces and can mean different things to different skiers. In some circles, carving has grown into an almost separate sport within skiing, just as bump and mogul competitions are not mainstream skiing, and driving contests are not really golf games for the average player. Bump skiing is still fun and a long drive off the tee is a thrill.

PMTS Direct Parallel defines its turns as consistent with carved turns. The principles of sound parallel skiing should be based on carving. Some say that PMTS puts too much emphasis on carving. I think that those who believe carving isn't the whole game see it as a one-application turn with specific technique. I see carving, through the application of the accurate biomechanics in PMTS, as the ultimate expression of using shaped skis as they are designed. When I ski bumps or powder, I use the basic PMTS movements with minor modifications. When I carve, I use the same PMTS movements, but with appropriate tuning for the snow surface and ski design. I don't use a completely different technique, as many would suggest is required.

This isn't a new controversy, but PMTS Direct Parallel has rekindled the flames and added a new wrinkle. Carving has been in dispute since the 1970s when Warren Witherell basically threw down the gauntlet and insinuated that racers carve and instructors skid and teach skidding. I know

Warren well and contributed to his book *The Athletic Skier*. I think most of his initial assertion is still valid. It isn't surprising that some ski technicians and theorists believe that learning to ski with carving movements limits skiing development. I think this point of view is prevalent because they believe that carving requires specialized technique and movements. I agree that, compared to traditional movements, carving is a new and different technique, but I disagree with the idea that carving limits a skier's potential. Unfortunately for skiers, this position has restricted development of skiing techniques for shaped skis on a global scale. PMTS is a different viewpoint: it demonstrates that biomechanically efficient movements can be versatile enough to include carving as well as mild brushing.

A Moderate Speed Carved Turn

PMTS technique and movements are the same at the basic level as at the uppermost expert levels. The distinction between the levels is the intensity and speed of movement. Quicker reactions are needed when skiing faster and on steeper terrain. The following photo sequence introduces carved turns on blue level (intermediate) terrain. The only difference between this moderate carved turn and a high-level, high-speed turn on steep slopes is the reduced dynamics that result from lower speed and slope angle.

Pure carving usually results in wider and larger turns at first, as you want the skis to produce the arc. With pure carving the turn radius is dependent on side cut, ski bend and ski angle. A carving novice will not know immediately how to bend the ski or increase the edge angle. It is necessary to learn both if you want to carve at high speed with large edge and body angles.

The radius of a carved turn can be reduced (the arc tightened) by increasing pressure on the ski. Think of a bow and arrow: as you pull the arrow back further, the bend of the bow increases. The arm supporting the bow can be compared to the outside leg in a carved turn. When you extend the leg in a carved turn, you bow the ski. The tighter bow of the ski creates a tighter turn as the ski edge bites into the snow and the ski slices along that edge. Tipping the ski to a greater edge angle also tightens the turn arc by pressing the wide ski tip and tail into the snow. The wider tip and tail bite into the snow more than the narrow waist, so again the ski bends into a tighter bow.

In the days of traditional skis, when the side cuts were almost nonexistent and the sides of a ski were virtually parallel, it took a great deal of pressure to the forward part of the ski to make the tip dig in. In those days technique was dictated by ski design. Expert skiers of that era had the capability to "get forward" far enough to bend the tip and begin carving the ski. Intermediates were taught to twist the skis because it was believed that they didn't have the strength or technique for the expert's forward move. Shaped skis don't require nearly that forward pressure to bring about a carved turn; therefore, more skiers can learn to ski like experts. As I have demonstrated a number of times, the old method not only won't be needed, it actually overpowers the shaped ski, making the tail wash out. Let's look at the photos on the next pages and learn the new way to carve.

Fig. 11-1. Carved turn at moderate speed

g

f

e

h

i

Cues for Success

• Tip the inside ski onto its outside edge.

• In transition, relax the legs so your body moves downhill across your skis as they flatten.

• Show your back to the inside of the turn.

a

b

c

d

Fig. a. You're still in the turn, prior to transition. Keep your outside leg almost straight, and your inside ski light and tipped. Your lateral balance should be solidly on your outside ski.

Fig. b. The turn is almost complete. Begin to swing the pole, slightly relax and flex the legs.

Fig. c. Flexing the legs flattens your ski angle, and starts your knees and body moving downhill over the skis.

Fig. d. As you relax and flatten further, your body's momentum directs your center downhill over your skis. Balance now on both skis – the float.

Fig. e. Tip your lower ski onto its outside edge to draw the uphill ski onto its big-toe edge. Your legs will follow the tipping actions. Only use tipping movements of the feet, as steering or turning the legs or rotating the upper body will eliminate your balance and therefore also the carving.

Fig. f. Here is where you start to use the movements of Chapter 10, "Upper and Lower Body Coordination." As the turn progresses, bring your inside arm forward and hold your uphill hip back. You may think of the movements as "showing your back" to the inside of the turn.

Fig. g. Here, the relationship between your upper and lower body should resemble that in the straight line ULBC exercise, *Figures 10-15* and *10-16*. Here, with speed, you will be much more angled to the snow, toward the center of the turn.

Fig. h. Continue tipping the inside ski, controlling the upper body. Not much is effort is required — just let the ski do its job.

Fig. i. Tip the free ski further onto its outside edge to increase your body angle. The inside ski can touch the snow, but you should keep it light. If you are able to lift it slightly from the snow, then you are skiing in balance. As you approach the bottom of the turn, let your shoulders and hips start to turn with the skis, as in *Figure a*. Bringing the upper body to square off or turn with the skis at the end of the turn is a natural progression of a completed, round turn and preparation for the next turn.

Carving and PMTS Movements

You may realize that the first skiing movements you were taught didn't include parallel carving ability. Traditionally, conventional teaching tries to minimize and trivialize the importance of carving. Some try to suggest that PMTS teaches an aggressive version of a carving turn too early in the learning process. I agree that beginning skiers with the ability only to rail their skis down the beginner slope using the side cut of the ski are dangerous to themselves and others, but this isn't what happens with skiers who learn PMTS. On the contrary, most skiers learning PMTS learn a brushed carve and brushed direction change. The great advantage of PMTS is that it is designed to quickly bring a skier who is ready up to the level of a carved turn.

If a skier has a natural tendency to rail the ski, which, incidentally, is not carving, de-tuning this to a brushed carve turn is a natural outcome of the PMTS process. We also differentiate between a skidded turn and a brushed carve. We do not teach skidding; we teach movements that create ski and speed control. A brushed carve is a turn with a slightly less aggressive edge angle in the snow that produces a wider track. You will probably acquire that turn through PMTS before you learn the complete locked carved turn. When learning a carved turn, the aggressive skier should be able to leave two clean, single, narrow tracks in the snow, while the less aggressive skier produces a mildly brushed turn. Neither of these turns conflicts with the ski's design. Skidding does! If you find yourself using different techniques to carve or skid your turns, or to make long or short turns, you haven't learned the right technique yet.

It is probably obvious by now that the fundamental movements of PMTS will enable you to ski using parallel carving. Those who want to achieve a higher level, such as skiing at high edge angles with pronounced body angle, will have to work with greater concentration on these skills. If you apply everything you learned in the Undergraduate Course, you will be able to carve just as Diana and I demonstrate in the photos. The technique doesn't change. The timing and movements are described in detail with the photos.

a

b

c   *Fig. 11-2. Roles of inside and outside leg in carved turn*

> ### Cues for Success
>
> • Flex the inside leg and tip that ski on its outside edge.
>
> • Keep the outside leg extended and the ski pressured while you balance on it.

Fig. a. Carved turns at a high edge angle and body angle result from the dynamic version of movements described in the previous photo series. Strongly flexing your inside leg and tipping your inside ski allow you to tip to this angle.

Fig. b. This position is almost the same, but it is further along in the turn. Continue to tip the inside ski onto its little-toe edge. Flexing your inside leg while you tip that ski enables your body to move closer to the snow, further inside the turn. As you flex the inside leg, keep the outside leg extended. Many skiers believe that the body is being pushed into the turn by the extension of the outside leg. This is not the case, and attempting to do so likely will make you lose your balance.

Fig. c. Keep strong muscle tension in the outside leg to resist the forces and to bend the outside ski. Doing so will store energy in the bent ski. When you flex to release, the stored energy will propel you into the new turn.

Equipment for Carving

A number of the Alpine nations of Europe host carving competitions based on skiing around cones, like water skiers in a slalom. They use techniques that are defined by a wide stance and very specialized equipment. In contrast, the photos you see in this book are taken using basic skis and normal equipment. Carving competitors use very short, narrow-waisted skis, with very high lifters under the binding and boots. They don't use poles and they reach their arms out to the snow to keep from falling over. Most of the skiers in such competitions use upper-body rotation to bring the skis around more quickly. As you can see, this form of skiing is very specialized — not a method for everyday use.

Ski racers also carve because it is the best way to maintain speed and control. They have more disciplined upper-body movements than those in the carving competitions, but they do use specialized equipment.

What can we aspire to in carving? We have to take equipment into consideration. I had a number of clients last year who had great difficulty learning to carve on wide-waisted all-mountain and "free riding" skis. When used for what they are designed to do, they're good skis, and skiers who can already carve may be able to do so on these skis. However, they aren't carving skis, and the salesperson should let you know that when you buy them.

As mentioned above, the photos in this section of the book are taken of skiers using normal equipment that anyone can buy. I don't like to provide too much information about specific equipment models within company lines, as after a year many of the models no longer exist, and after two years improved technology is usually available. In my case, the skis I am shown using are Elan Hyper Carves. The Hyper Carves can be skied in the bumps or in all-mountain conditions; however, they have an aggressive shape, a side cut that generates a turn radius of approximately 14 meters. Skis like this are made by all major companies and should be available for a number of years to come. Head has the Cyber Slalom Ti and the Cyber X-60, for example, and Atomic has the BetaCarve 9.14 and the even more aggressive 9.11. I recommend any of these skis for a carving fan, and especially for the skier who aspires to learn carving.

To the Realm of High-Angle Carving

What will take us beyond regular carved turns and let us achieve high-angled carved turns? Remember the section in the introduction about not turning your skis? If ever there was a situation in which trying to turn your skis will eliminate success, it is in carving. Only movements that change edge angles and tipping actions that move across the skis at 90 degrees to the direction of travel produce success. In the upper- and lower-body coordination ("ULBC") section of the Undergraduate Course, you will find the basics for lateral movements required for high-angled carved turns. The slope doesn't have to be steep! In fact, a moderate slope is better to learn on. The photos for this book were all taken on blue terrain. Intensive and aggressive movements are required to develop high angles in turns. Your allies in this endeavor are the skis' side cut and the greater momentum that develops as you pick up speed and engage the skis. Literally, you let the ski do the turning. This may sound too simplistic, but it couldn't be easier.

Fig. 11-3. Set up the angles, then refine your balance

Cues for Success

• A good release sets up early turn angles.

• Fine tune your balance with your inside "strong arm."

Fig. a. Diana demonstrates a powerful early angle in this turn. A perfect release from the previous turn helps you achieve this early and extreme body angle. It lets the energy from the previous turn launch you into this position in the new turn.

Fig. b. Tighten the arc further by flexing the inside leg and tipping the inside ski further

Fig. c. Now it's just a matter of maintaining balance. Often you can refine and improve your balance on the stance ski with subtle changes to the inside "strong arm" position; fine adjustments such as lifting or lowering. Use simple movements such as tipping and flexing to establish the turn, and then focus on maintaining balance with small adjustments.

Fig. d. The turn is almost over. Start to relax your leg muscles, giving in to the turning forces that will take your body over your skis into the next turn.

Fig. 11-4. Tighten the arc by tipping the inside foot

Fig. a. Diana demonstrates the dynamics of a carved turn with balance on the outside ski and strong flexion and tipping of the inside leg.

Fig. b. Increase the body angle and tighten the turn radius by tipping your inside ski further. This is evidenced by the external rotation of Diana's inside femur. Ski angles are identical. This extremely dynamic skiing cannot be accomplished with the "skis-apart-weight-on-both-feet" school of carving. Keep the inside boot touching the outside leg. As you flex the inside leg, draw it up along the outside leg. You'll increase the vertical distance between your feet — not the horizontal distance — making it easier to maintain balance on the outside ski. During the release, as your leg length evens out, your skis will once again be side-by-side.

Cues for Success

• Tip the inside ski onto its outside edge far enough that the inside thigh moves outward.

• Keep the inside foot along the outside leg.

Fig. 11-5. Tighten the arc by flexing the inside leg

Cues for Success

• Tip the inside ski and shorten that leg to pull your body into the turn.

• Keep the free, inside foot in contact with the outside leg.

Fig. a. Again, flex the inside leg and tip the inside ski to draw your body down into the center of the turn.

Fig. b. Increase tipping and flexing with the inside leg to tighten the radius and give you a tighter turn than what the side cut alone would yield. Again, keep your inside foot in contact with the outside leg throughout the tipping and flexing.

Relax the Stance Leg to "Use the Force"

As with everything simple, some background information may help. What I presented in the ULBC section of the book is still applicable. Balance is the key to carving, as it is to most other things in correct skiing. If you can change the direction of your skis by tipping the skis and leaving two thin lines in the snow, then you have the basic skills necessary for learning high-angle carving.

The next thing that you must add to your repertoire is leg retraction, or flexion. This is just what we covered in Chapter 7, "Use the Force." At the precise moment that the ski tips start to head back across the fall line at the bottom of the turn, you must flex your stance leg aggressively. Flexing is the opposite of pushing off the ski. It means shortening your leg under control so your body center moves closer to the ski. In almost every turn in this book, you will see that at the turn transition, the skier's body is moving closer to the ski at the release. We have discussed how this is accomplished numerous times. Relaxing the stance leg begins the release, but in carving you want to use the energy from one turn to take you into the next. The timing and speed of the transition become very important. If you are too late, you cannot take advantage of your body's optimal momentum in the direction of the new turn. Quickly flexing your leg will move your center closer to the ski and bring your skis flat to the snow. If, at the same time, you add the elements of the Weighted Release, the transition is even faster.

Review, if needed, the elements of the Weighted Release in the Undergraduate Course. Keeping your weight on the stance ski as you relax to release literally can propel you into the next turn.

Fig. 11-6. Control the relaxation of your stance leg

Fig. a. Coming out of the turn requires a relaxation of the leg muscles and fine control of the rate of flattening. Here I'm just beginning to relax.

Fig. b. Just a slight relaxation of your stance leg muscles will bring your body back over your skis. Maintain balance on your outside ski until it is completely flat on the snow, then lighten it and tip it on its outside edge so it becomes the inside ski for the new turn.

Cues for Success

• Control your rate of relaxing and flattening.

• Balance on your outside ski until it is completely flat on the snow.

Fig. 11-7. *Time your release for a quick transition*

Fig. a. Lead the tipping actions with the inside ski to draw the outside ski on edge at an equal edge angle. Keep your outside leg long so the inside ski tipping will pull your body far inside the turn.

Fig. b. Begin to relax the legs – they'll flex more (shorten), your body will start to move downhill over the skis, and the skis will start to flatten to the snow.

Fig. c. The turn is complete – let the turn forces pull your body into the new turn. Notice how quickly the skis and body change angles from one turn to the next.

Fig. d. Committing to the next turn is easy if you keep the inside ski light at the beginning so the body can be pulled into the center of the turn.

Fig. e. Early body angle in the turn is possible when the inside ski doesn't interfere with letting the body drop into the turn. If you place too much weight on the inside ski, it will stop your body from moving into the turn. The body and ski angles are blocked from increasing, and the speed and carving energy is lost.

Fig. f. Let your inside ski skim over the surface, ready to increase tipping angle.

Cues for Success

• Keep the outside leg long until the last 3/4 of the turn.

• Keep the inside ski light, just skimming the snow.

Chapter 12:

Bumps

Bumps or mogul competence is considered a milestone or rite of passage to expert skiing. A standard we often set for our skiers at the Loveland Ski Area in Colorado is to ski the whole Avalanche Bowl (rated double black diamond) without traversing or stopping. You are on your way to becoming an expert when you can meet this challenge. I have assembled many examples of skiing steep bumps at high speed in order to highlight the different skills needed and to help you achieve this level of skiing. If you have already developed the basics for short turns, you have the essentials to master bump skiing. It goes without saying that a solid short turn with a strong pole plant is a necessity. I'm not saying you can't ski in the bumps without those abilities, but you will not ski like an expert. You'll get down, but you'll struggle. It will take you a long time to feel confident without a command of the basics introduced in the Undergraduate Course, if you ever are able to achieve that confidence. The essential components for bumps or mogul competence are listed in order:

1. short turn
2. pole plant
3. upper- and lower-body coordination

If you learned to use the movements in the previous sections and are comfortable with the techniques presented, you're ready to start the graduate bump course that follows.

Strong young skiers may decide to skip the Undergraduate Course in the first section of the book because they believe they can learn by doing. Many readers of my first book confessed to me that they made that error in judgment. They told me that after looking through my book and selecting what they wanted to learn from the many photographs and montages, they turned right to their favorite sections. They immediately went out on the slopes and tried the movements. Fortunately, most of them were successful, in spite of incomplete background preparation. Only later did they read the whole book. They confessed that after going through the whole book, they gained a greater understanding of how to use my system and were rewarded with even greater improvements. It is human nature to reach for instant success and read the most intriguing part of the book first. Some of you may be reading this section before any other.

If you find that this chapter produces immediate results for you with a direct approach, I can't keep you from trying it. But if you find you are having some difficulties, go back and read the introduction and study the Undergraduate Course; it will make a difference.

Without the fundamental movements introduced earlier in the book you may develop a defensive bump-skiing technique. Another downside of improvised bump skiing is the physical grind and the beating your legs will take. When the new shaped skis came out, I realized that I had been avoiding bumps on my 204 cm slalom skis. The new skis opened the door for me. Traditional skis, with their lack of side cut and enormous length, required considerable effort to wiggle through a steep bump field. All that leg torquing and ski bending takes power and strength. If you have a weak link like I do — a bad knee — it can be very painful. Bump skiing can be experienced with less pounding and impact by using efficient movements. Extraneous movements take time and energy; expert bump skiing doesn't have room for these inefficiencies. I use the primary movements exactly as explained in the beginning photos and montages of this Graduate Course.

Control and graceful movement with flair and energy are my goals for bump skiing. Scary, uncontrolled airtime and physical beatings are not my idea of sophisticated bump skiing. Timing your turn to take advantage of the bump's shape and contour is an important part of tactical bump skiing. Before you can use a well-synchronized release that matches a bump's contours, your movements must be ingrained and rehearsed. One of the benefits of learning PMTS is that you can make the movements as quickly or as slowly as you wish to control speed.

Line or Timing of Movements in Bumps

Achieving a line in the bumps is similar to trying to stay on line in a racecourse. If you haven't developed the movement capabilities to stay with a line yet, all coaching and descriptions won't get you there. I frequently see a lot of fuss being made about line. It's putting the cart before the horse. You can't control where you are going unless you have the technique to get there. Just as steering and skidding your skis won't keep you on the ideal line through a racecourse, these techniques won't keep you fluid and in control through the bumps. Learn the proper technique, and you will be successful in the racecourse and with picking your turns in the bumps.

The fastest way to find the ideal line through the bumps is by using correct movements at the top, on the other side, going down and in the hollow between bumps. If you use the series of movements developed in PMTS you will be able to

- engage by tilting the inside ski at the top of the bump.
- let the outside ski come to an edge on the front face of the bump.
- increase edge angle by tipping the inside ski through the turn and extending the outside leg to stay in contact with the snow.

Use these prescribed movements, and the outside leg will be extended, and the ski will be change directions. By the time you approach the hollow between bumps, you will be in balance and in the perfect position to flex the extended outside leg which will absorb the hollow and bump lip while releasing the skis for the next turn.

Rarely do we have much choice about what we are facing next in fast, steep bumps. Choosing the ideal line in bumps is more a reaction to the bump directly in front rather than an established line you have chosen. Bump skiing is a game of reactions. Looking ahead to the next bump, after you have figured what to do for the one you are in, is the answer. Just because racers study the course doesn't mean they are always picking the line they will ski. In fact, the truly great racers study the general contours and direction of the course, but they make adjustments on the course to gain more speed. If you are planning for an ideal line, you may be restricting your freedom and be late with your movements. A racer — and I have known a few who prepare in this manner — who is overly concerned about exactly where to be on every gate usually will have a slow run. Looking ahead to the next gate and using accurate movements that bring the skis to the best arc is a successful tactic.

Rarely is a bump run as uniform as a racecourse. If you deviate slightly on a racecourse you can get back on line within a gate or two. If you deviate on a bump run from an intended line you will run into a completely new configuration of bumps. A true bump skier is versatile and adaptable, ready for any change in terrain.

If you are new to bumps, start your preparation on intermediate bump runs. Try connecting two or three bumps at a time. In this case, you can see far enough down the slope to plan a line. Develop your turning by tipping just as in all levels of PMTS. When you can bring the short turn movements practiced earlier into the bump, you will find the success you are looking for. The description of bump skiing at this expert level completely applies to bump skiing at the introductory level; only the terrain changes.

Foot Speed

One of the essential capabilities for bump skiing is foot speed. You may ask, "what is foot speed? It sounds important, and I think I'd like it, but what does it mean?" I asked that question when I first heard about foot speed in skiing. Does it mean I must move my feet more quickly? I thought runners or tennis players needed that ability, not skiers. In fact, many of the great skiers I coached had slow feet and ran poorly. Again, I think this term stems from the visual impression of skiers who are changing direction very quickly. It does make sense because all the movements associated with changing direction involve the feet and skis. To the untrained eye, it looks as though great skiers move their feet very quickly. Not just any quick foot movements will do; being quick with a selected set of movements is the key to bumping without thumping.

Fig. 12-1. The basics in bumps

Figures 12-1 and *12-2* are the same turn. *Figure 12-1* has been expanded so you can see the actions in the individual frames. *Figure 12-2* shows you the actual placement of the turn in the moguls. These bumps are big and tight on a steep hill, and the turns are very short and quick.

Fig. a. Plant the pole and begin the release.

Fig. b. Hold onto the pole for stability. Let the skis float, avoiding any urge to twist them. Begin tipping and rolling the inside ski strongly to its new edge.

Fig. c. Keep the inside hand moving forward after you have passed the pole to keep your upper body lined across the fall line. After the float phase, the body is back in balance over the skis.

Fig. d. Swing the pole tip for the next pole plant.

Fig. e. Plant the pole and allow the skis to float.

Fig. f. Push the inside hand forward while preparing the other hand for the new swing. Always keep the pole plant movements going. One pole or the other should be swinging to a plant at all times.

Fig. 12-2. Use the release to generate foot speed

Fig. a. As the skis float (run straight and flat for the briefest moment), pull the lower ski back under your body while tilting it toward the outside edge.

Fig. b. Tilt the new inside ski until its outside edge touches the snow. Continue tilting and flexing to bring the skis around the bump.

Fig. c. The next release has redirected the skis to point downhill. Finish the turn by tilting the free foot strongly and pressing it against the stance ski.

The movements you must learn in order to improve your direction change in the bumps are the release and balance shift, or transfer. If you start a new turn without re-establishing your balance, you are in for an uncomfortable thumping. Shifting your balance from one side, or foot, to the other is the key movement for successful bump skiing. So you always need to prepare to shift your balance for the next turn. Balance results from having a solid platform. Releasing shifts your body, establishing a new stance foot, but tipping engages the stance ski, creating a solid platform with the new stance foot.

Weighting the Skis

To purists, weighting or unweighting technically may be the wrong words to describe functional skiing actions. But when I ski, I can feel pressure building under my foot as I increase the push against the ski by extending my leg. I also can feel more pressure as my ski tips to a greater angle to the snow. The feeling of increased pressure or weight under my ski or foot indicates to me that my body is changing position or shifting in response to the forces of the terrain. Pressure can be sensed and described by skiers in many ways; weight shift is one of these ways. When we use efficient movements, the body naturally will move to balance over the new stance ski or foot. The body responds to the changing forces by aligning itself over the ski to stay in balance. As I release from the downhill edge of the previous turn, my stance ski becomes my free foot. My balance shifts to the new stance ski and I create contact with that ski by extending the leg. This is the switch in pressure to the new weighted, downhill side of my body. The former downhill side of the body is now the less weighted, or free, side. The free side should continue tipping to engage the ski, and is able to make movements that improve and maintain balance. Most of these explanations are descriptions of how the body should behave and react. These examples are different from external cues. However, sometimes an explanation of this kind creates additional insight for skiers and offers another way to understand the techniques in addition to those developed solely through the use of effective external cues.

Earlier in the book I wrote that the primary purpose of technique should be to create balance. I prefer to limit the use of technical explanations and references such as "weight shifting" or "pressure shift" because they become too technical. Using the idea of transferring balance makes more sense. If you transfer balance you have no choice but to shift pressure and weight, and as they shift, balance is re-established. The big advantage of thinking about transferring balance is that you produce the appropriate amount of edge angle, body alignment and pressuring in the right place, every time. Think about balance first and you will do only what you have to do to achieve balance. This method is an economical way to move and a first-class way to develop consistency. I like to use simple movements and get results by focusing on cues that combine many actions. This approach gives the skier less to think about and produces superb results.

Fig. 12-3. Chris Anthony demonstrates the actions of the free foot

Fig. a. Flex the legs to absorb the bottom of the turn. Let the skis float, and hold firmly to the planted pole.

Fig. b. Still holding the pole, flex the inside leg and tip it to the outside edge.

Fig. c. Tipping the inside ski redirects the skis, as in a release.

Fig. d. Extend the outside leg to reach for the surface and prepare the pole plant.

Fig. e. Flex the legs and absorb the transition.

Fig. f. Let the skis float, but focus on pulling the inside ski back.

Fig. g. Pulling the skis back causes the skis to match the angle of the slope for the next turn.

Revisit the Phantom Move

We come back to the Phantom Move to demonstrate how one simple action begins a chain reaction of movements for the whole body. The Phantom Move sounds almost too simple to work, but it is effective beyond expectations. I love to hear comments about the Phantom Move from the traditional ski-teaching community, which criticizes PMTS as a system that has only one move, not believing that something so simple can work so well.

PMTS is a complete system, not a "single move." The criticism shows a lack of understanding about PMTS, but I take those comments as compliments. If you can ski like an expert by thinking about only one movement, what a great achievement! When you break the Phantom Move into smaller parts, it can become very complex. As with many simple concepts, there is complex reasoning behind it. In this case, skiing does become rocket science, but you don't have to know the science to ski it — that's the beauty of PMTS. The Phantom Move is much more than one move; it sets into action a chain or series of efficient movements.

When skiers analyze the Phantom Move, they find they are actually performing the following movements:
- releasing the skis by flattening the angle of the outside or stance ski;
- transferring to the new outside ski by lightening or lifting the previous outside ski, making it the free ski or the new inside ski;
- engaging by tilting or tipping the inside ski to the little-toe or outside edge and continuing to tip that ski through the finish of the turn.

This description is a complete breakdown of the actions of a Phantom Move. The Phantom Move makes it possible to get out of a turn, move the body directly into balance over the new outside ski, engage the skis on their new set of edges and continue completing the turn. A simple description of performing the Phantom Move is to lighten the old downhill ski and tip or tilt it toward its outside edge. Once you learn this sequence of movements, your lower-body focus can be the Phantom Move.

In *Figure 12-4*, Chris Anthony, Alaska Extreme Champion and veteran World Extreme Championship competitor, demonstrates a direct line in a steep bump run. He is very quick from one transition to the other, performing linked Phantom Moves. The critical time in these turns is after the release. The transfer and engagement must be performed early in the turn so balance is maintained. Notice how early Chris uses his free foot to set up the ski and body angles. The beauty of the Phantom Move is that one move can influence the whole turn set-up, which is the biomechanical advantage of using PMTS in the bumps.

Biomechanical Advantage

• When the stance ski turns as a result of free-foot tipping, you are able to extend the stance leg rather than twisting it. You maintain snow contact, and get the full range of flexion to absorb the crest of the upcoming bump.

Fig. a. Here at the end of the turn is the last moment your edges are gripping. Swing the pole basket forward to prepare for the pole plant.

Fig. b. Relax the legs and let the skis flatten and float.

Fig. c. Gather in your releasing foot — now the free foot — by lifting and pulling it in toward the stance foot.

Fig. d. As the free foot comes in to match the stance foot, tip it toward the outside edge. Notice how much direction change is accomplished.

Fig. e. The next pole plant stabilizes the upper body and coordinates with the release.

Fig. f. Chris releases the edges and lets the skis float. He prepares the downhill ski to be pulled back and tipped for the next turn.

Fig. g. His free foot's tipping and pulling-in actions have set him up perfectly for the next turn.

Cues for Success

• Pull the previous downhill ski and boot in to touch and hold against the new stance ski.

• Pull the free foot in prior to the next hollow.

Fig. 12-4. Linked Phantom Moves directly in the fall line

Connected Phantom Moves allow very quick edge changes and therefore quick direction changes or turns. Quick feet are important to bump skiing, but how do we achieve them? Quick feet result from a quick relaxation to create a release and a quick pick-up of the ski; actions that are specific to bump skiing. These movements begin the chain reaction I talked about earlier, enabling the body to align with the forces of the next turn. But if we try to think about all the movements that need to happen in a turn transition, we'd never get to the next turn. If we focus on the bare essentials of the Phantom Move, the lift and tip, the deed is done. Technically speaking, it isn't just the feet that must be moved to make quick direction changes. The muscles of the upper and medial side of the leg, hip and lower back all contribute and are recruited. All the mechanisms are put into place and activated without conscious thought. Keep your mind as clear as possible; simplify. Develop your ability to move in the bumps by learning to link Phantom Moves.

Wrist Management

Diana demonstrates superb timing and wrist management in this steep bump run. Early pole preparation is a mainstay of expert bump skiing. You need to feel that your pole plant is part of your support system in the bumps.

Going into gravitational games without a stabilizing pole plant is like showing up at a gunfight without a gun. You're just not going to be in the game. Study the upper and lower body coordination section of this book before you ski bumps. The photos and captions here explain and demonstrate the importance of the stabilizing pole plant.

Cues for Success

• Keep the pole in contact with the snow long enough to use it.

• After the pole is released, bring your hands and arms back to Home Base.

• Swing the outside pole early to prepare for the upcoming turn.

Fig. 12-5. Using a stabilizing pole plant in bumps

Fig. a. Diana prepares to absorb and change direction for the next bump.

Fig. b. The pole is planted and the legs are relaxed and flexed to absorb the bump.

Fig. c. Diana lets the skis float out from under her body in an aggressive manner but keeps them in control with a strong free foot pull-back and tipping movement. The pulling back of the free foot results in the tip-down position of the free ski.

Fig. d. The results are perfect. As soon as her skis redirect from the release and tipping, her body has caught up and she is in perfect balance. Her outside leg is extended, maintaining contact and preparing for flexion.

Fig. e. She extends the legs to be able to absorb the next bump.

Fig. f. She keeps the movements going with another early preparation of the pole swing for the upcoming bump.

The Pole is Another Point of Contact

A strong pole plant is paramount for successful expert bump skiing. As you learned in Chapter 10, "Upper and Lower Body Coordination," the pole swing and timing must be in synch with the turn and release. Here is the plant and release example.

Skiing with a correct pole plant is like manually shifting gears in a car while turning the steering wheel to match the curve. Millions of drivers have learned to drive a manual transmission and sports car buyers still demand a stick shift. If all these drivers can accomplish this feat, skiers can learn how to use a stabilizing pole plant for the bumps.

a

b

Fig. 12-6. Plant the pole for an additional point of contact

Fig. a. Complete your turn with a strong, stabilizing pole plant.
Fig. b. Flatten both skis and allow them to float out from under your body. The pole still is strongly planted for added support.

Biomechanical Advantage

• Flattening the skis uncoils the strong upper-to-lower-body counteraction of the previous turn.

Float with Foot Retraction

Sometimes you must absorb sharp bumps that you know will launch you airborne otherwise. The best thing to do is stop tipping, relax the legs and flex the knees quickly. You will be in a seated position coming over the other side of the bump as in *Figure 12-7b* (following page). The benefit of this unweighted or lightly weighted situation is that it makes the skis easy to manage. While the skis are still light, organize the free foot for the next turn. While extending the outside leg to make contact with the hollow of the next bump, pull the free foot in toward the stance boot and back under the body. These movements will bring you over your skis and in balance for the turn finish.

Recovering balance in bump skiing requires that the free foot be pulled back strongly in the transition between turns. I first started pulling the free foot back 20 years ago because, like all racers, I was often getting caught "in the back seat" — racer terminology for being too far behind your skis. Racers normally don't park, or camp out, in the back seat; they usually find themselves stranded there as their feet and skis accelerate forward without warning. You may have experienced this sensation. Out of nowhere in an aggressive turn, your skis lock onto an edge and they jet forward, leaving you sitting back with your legs levered against the back of your boots, out of control and hanging on for dear life. Skiers whose normal stance tends to be on the verge of leaning back find themselves in this situation more often. Losing your feet like that is a frightening experience and can have long-term effects on your confidence. If you are skiing in fear of another occurrence, it could severely hamper your progress and dampen your enthusiasm for all-mountain skiing.

The only solution for this problem was to instruct skiers to lean forward or place their shins on the front of the boots. Other frequently heard recommendations were to stand up more, flex your boots more, lift your rear, project your hips forward, or hold your hands in front of you. Unfortunately, none of these recommendations is adequate. The fastest and most effective way to get yourself recentered fore/aft over your skis is to move your base of support back. Moving your foot back has the effect of moving your hips forward. How should you get the skis back? Generally in skiing, your weight or pressure is on the downhill, or outside ski, making this ski very hard to move once it is set on edge. Skis that are floating, or unweighted, in the transition between turns are easy to control and move. In the short turn section of the Undergraduate Course, I introduced pulling the free foot back as one of the basic necessities for all-mountain skiing. Now you can apply it to bumps.

Fig. a. When there is a sharp kicker, as on this bump, be ready to flex by bringing your knees up to your chest and letting the skis float.

Fig. b. Balance on the pole while you organize the tilting movements of the free foot.

Fig. c. Tilting the inside foot, bringing it against the stance foot and extending the outside leg have brought my body back over my feet.

Fig. d. Increase the flex of the inside leg and tilting of that ski to make a sharper turn.

Fig. e-f. Relax and flex both legs to suck up the bump.

Cues for Success

• Organize the free foot while the skis are light or floating.

Fig. 12-7. Retract the free foot to stay centered in bumps

Extend the Legs After the Release

a   *b*   *c*   *d*

e

Fig. 12-8. Extend the legs after release to have a full range of flexion

Fig. a. Reach out with the legs to make contact after the bump.

Fig. b. Flex the legs to absorb the bump.

Fig. c. Plant the pole for balance and to time the release. Let the skis float between turns.

Fig. d. While floating, tip the inside ski (the previous stance ski) to prepare for the direction change. Pull and hold that ski back to produce a balanced stance for the turn.

Fig. e. Notice how Chris is organized with both skis at the same angle, feet close together both fore/ aft and laterally, and legs extended to absorb the hollow of the next bump.

At the point in the turn at which you are ready to release your edges, focus on the lower or downhill ski. Your pole should be firmly planted in the snow, as in *Figure c.* Your skis should be flat at or just before the crown of the bump. As your ski tips become free of the snow and stick out over the bump, tip the new inside ski or free foot to the outside edge and pull that boot back under your hips, as in *Figure d.* These two movements can be accomplished simultaneously. Pull the heel of the free foot back. This is the move that will keep you in balance and turning, make your bump skiing successful. The contour of the bumps makes this move extremely important. After you drop off the top of the bump to its front side, the face of the bump becomes much steeper. If you are skiing fast, the lip of the bump tends to launch you. Stay calm, use your pole and free foot, and you will land in balance, headed in the right direction.

Cues for Success

• Flex the inside leg more than the outside.

• Press the free foot against the outside boot.

Pull the Free Ski Back to Drop the Tips

Diana comes into an abrupt transition with speed. She has her work cut out for her to avoid getting launched off the bump. She sucks her knees up quickly and tips her previous downhill ski to the outside edge. Holding the inside ski back as she crests the bump allows her to change the fore/aft relationship of her upper body to her lower body. Her upper body moves forward and her boots stay under her hips. This is the technique skiers have been searching for to stay balanced over their skis in the bumps. No amount of hip thrusting or knee driving will achieve this re-centering. Use the biomechanical advantage that Diana demonstrates here – pull your free foot back to stay centered.

A well-prepared bump skier will simply pull the free foot back and therefore be able to drop the tips to match the steep contour on the front side of the bump. All the components of the Undergraduate Course are applied at this moment. If you omit any one of them, your likelihood of success drops dramatically. The pole plant must be solid as demonstrated by the accompanying photos. The free foot must be held back and tipped to match the stance ski angle. Although it seems like the skis are too far ahead of the body after the release, this situation is quickly rectified when the skis react to the tipping actions initiated in the release. Your skis will float if you release at the right time: that is, at the very transition or crown of the bump. This is the time to initiate a strong backward pulling action by the free foot, while at the same time tipping the ski. Study the photos that accompany this section and practice this movement in easy terrain before you try it in the bumps.

a

b

Biomechanical Advantage
• Pull your free foot back so your body can keep up with your skis.

Fig. a. Come into the hollow fully extended.

Fig. b. Flex the legs to absorb the transition.

Fig. c. Tip the inside ski and pull it back at the top of the bump to change direction.

Fig. 12-9. Pull the free foot back to drop the ski tips

c

Keep the Upper Body Facing the Fall Line

e Fig. 12-10. Keep the upper body facing downhill

In *Figure 12-10* on the previous page, Craig McNeil, a former pro freestyle competitor, shows an athletic, aggressive bump approach.

Fig. a. Craig comes into the hollow fully extended and in balance.

Fig. b. He plants the pole and flexes to absorb the bump.

Fig. c. He goes for good air but his skis are turned, his tips are aimed down to match the steep face of the bump, and his body is already lined up for the next turn.

Fig. d. He is in perfect balance again thanks to his release and the tilting of the inside free ski.

Fig. e. Craig reacts to the release of the last bump by letting his skis float and is ready to tip for the next turn.

Notice that for an instant after the release, the skiers let their skis float ahead of their bodies. As soon as the skis are tipped and the free foot is pulled back and close to the stance boot, matching the ski edge angles, the body catches up and is in balance over the skis once more. The photos were taken on very aggressive, steep bump runs. You might want to start learning this advanced set of movements on more forgiving intermediate bumps. Remember, this is a progression starting with effective short turns. If you first become proficient with these very same movements, described in the Undergraduate Course of the book, your ability to use them in bumps will come much more quickly.

Carving in the Bumps

Most skiers are taught to ski bumps by rotating their legs and twisting their skis at the top of the bumps and sliding down the other side to control speed. This method is limiting and keeps the skier at a very low level. Anyone can learn the methods described and taught here. With these methods you make up your mind. Do you want to be blue level proficient at bumps or an aggressive black level skier as demonstrated here? You won't have any limitations of technique if you use these methods. How expert or aggressive do you want to be? These methods will allow you to make the decision rather then have limitations imposed through improper movements.

Fig. a. The most important moves are right at the top of the bump: plant the pole and then lift the downhill ski to make it your free foot.

Fig. b. Tip the lifted foot to the outside edge. As you lift the foot, the stance support disappears. Your body naturally "falls" to the side of the lifted ski.

Fig. c. Keep the inside ski tucked back and hold it close to the stance ski. Notice how the outside ski is tipped well on edge as a result of the inside foot actions. This is as close as you can get to carving in the bumps. I like to ski bumps with a carving technique as it provides better control and uses the ski – the biomechanical advantage.

Fig. d. Tip the inside ski and stand on the outside ski to move your body inside the turn. Extend the outside leg so you'll have a full range of absorption at the bottom of the bump.

Fig. e. Keep the upper body facing downhill. Use counteracting movements of the hips and the strong inside arm position practiced in Chapter 10.

Fig. f. Relax and allow the bump to flex the knees up into the chest. Let the skis float, pull the downhill ski in and back and tip it over to the outside edge.

Fig. 12-11. Carving in Bumps

Carving in the Bumps — The Actual Line

Fig. 12-12. Montage of previous turn, carving in bumps

This is a montage of the frames from *Figure 12-11*. In this montage, the skier appears in his actual position on the slope, giving you a realistic perspective of how quickly and sharply the turn can be made using tipping and absorbing movements. This is a very aggressive line on a steep slope, but that doesn't mean you need to make huge recoveries. The actions of the free foot and ski are clearly demonstrated. The fastest way to transfer is to lift the inside ski, which is accomplished in the second frame. Hold the free boot close to and pressed against the stance boot as in the ball hold exercise. When you press the boots together, edging and body angles develop quickly and with balance. Notice how by the third frame the outside ski is already on a strong edge. My shaped skis for this run are not radical; these are all-mountain skis, yet I still let the side cut take me around the turn, demonstrating carving in the bumps.

Upper and Lower Body Coordination

The next montage, *Figure 12-13*, is part of the same run but further down the slope. I used strong counteracting movements at the beginning of this turn to help achieve this extreme edge angle. The counteracting movements presented in the Undergraduate Course are very important if you want tight, short arcs on steep bump runs. This turn is an example of the power that countering movements offer to redirect the skis for the next turn. Just as in the wall sit, keep your back up against the imaginary wall behind you up the slope. My upper body is facing down the slope, and my skis are turned fully across the slope. As I flatten my skis, I let them float out from under my hips. My pole is planted firmly in the snow for important added support and upper-body stability. My upper body is almost suspended from the pole as the skis are flattened. Once the skis are flat to the snow, press the inside boot against the stance boot and tip the inside ski toward its outside edge. Notice in the third frame, *Figure c*, the pole is no longer supporting my upper body, and my old downhill ski is no longer gripping; therefore, my body moves to the inside of the turn. It is not free falling as some would call this point in a turn. My outside ski is already edged and gripping the snow, and my outside leg is extended to maintain contact with the snow. My tipping actions earlier in the turn brought the outside ski to the correct edge angle. Some will interpret my turn by saying, "Look at how he rotated his legs to steer his skis." I can state unequivocally that I don't use rotation and leg steering to turn. The turning action is a result of balance on the stance ski and tipping of the free foot. I never think about rotating or steering my legs when I ski. I can't feel or sense my edges or the surface when I focus on steering my skis or legs. Instead, I focus on sensing the edge angles of my skis.

Notice in the photos of this chapter, the release occurs on the lip of the bump. Consequently, most turns are initiated at this point. Tipping the inside ski at the crest creates the direction change of the skis. Avoid trying to turn or steer your skis at the top of bumps. Turning or twisting the skis requires that you flex your legs, which keeps you in a low position. With this approach, you have no extension or absorbing ability for the next bump. The muscles required to steer or turn your skis are most effective when your legs are flexed; therefore, to achieve enough force to turn the skis, your legs must stay flexed. In contrast, tipping the inside ski edges and redirects the skis in an efficient manner, providing superior edge grip and control. If you tip the inside ski rather than steer it, the outside leg extends, allowing you to edge and grip with the body balanced on the gripping edge. High-energy, high-speed bump skiing as in the photos in this chapter, is a game of releasing the skis and letting them float. The PMTS approach to re-centering over your the skis is to use the retracting and tipping actions of the free foot. Trying to stay centered all the time, maintaining the same position over your skis while skiing bumps, is also possible by using the same movements, but only with much less speed and more rounded turns. The runs shown here are for expert bump skiers on steep black diamond bumps. The lines demonstrated here are very direct and close to the fall line. If you are developing your bump technique, use exactly the same movements described here in easy bumps on blue terrain. You will find you will be able to stay balanced over your skis and control your speed.

Fig. 12-13. Strong upper- and lower-body counteracting movements in bumps

Cues for Success

- Keep your back square to the fall line.
- Tip the new inside ski first.

Long Legs, Short Legs

Fig. a. John Clendenin, former World Freestyle Champion, demonstrates a rounder line with larger turns. He has time to completely extend the legs between turns.

Fig. b. John relaxes and flexes to absorb the bumps just as we do in the more direct line sequences.

Fig. c. John's early inside foot tipping allows him to be well positioned and already edged, coming down the front side of the bump.

Fig. d. Increased tipping brings the skis across the hill and in position to absorb the next bump.

a

c

b

d

Fig. 12-14. Full extension and flexion of the legs

Keys for Practice

Now you're ready to go out and ski some bumps. I've taught many recreational skiers and instructors how to improve their bump skiing using these techniques. Keep in mind the must-have and must-know moves of your mogul repertoire:

- Manage your free foot, bringing it close to the stance foot and drawing it back before you start your turn.
- Have a solid, stabilizing pole plant before the release.

Chapter 13:

Powder

Mysteries of Natural Snow

Ever since I was a child, I knew powder skiing was recognized as the ultimate skiing experience. Unfortunately, it was some time before I actually got my chance to try it. In the years leading up to my first experience, the topic of skiing powder always raised conflicting advice from both instructors and experts. I didn't really know what to expect. My feelings of inadequacy were more than just a passing glitch in confidence; they revolved around my complete lack of practical knowledge and experience on real western snow conditions. My first try in deep powder came in 1968 at Castle Mountain ski area near the Crowsnest Pass, in Alberta, Canada. The heavy wet stuff we used to plow through as kids in the Laurentian Mountains in Eastern Canada was no training ground for that.

Coming from the east coast, I found I was out of my element. The best advice I could garner from my racer buddies was to sit back and twist my skis, and if I got out of control, to lean back and sit down before I ran into a tree. Sound advice for an 18-year-old from an 18-year-old. Advice I received from instructors and other experienced skiers didn't provide much better information. Some said you sat back in powder, others said you hopped. None of the advice made any sense at all to me while I was screaming down through the trees in hip-deep snow. Eventually, I had to admit that my buddy's advice about sitting down to avoid hitting a tree was my most reliable tactic. By the end of the day a combination of guts, close calls and quick reflexes added up to a few connected turns that made me think that there might be something to this powder skiing after all. The rest of that winter I skied all over the west, but mostly in Banff and Lake Louise. I met Mike Wiegele, who was the ski school director in Lake Louise at the time. I skied with everyone I thought could help me and I stuck with Mike whenever I could get him out for some runs. I learned a lot from him, and that experience started my transition to an all-mountain skier.

Most of us don't have the time or the physical capacity to learn to ski powder the way I did, so I have developed a much shorter and safer route.

Looking Good

Powder technique has advanced since those days, although it is not always accompanied by succinct instructions. Ideally, instructions for specific, effective movements are most helpful. You may notice I rely on "how to" movement cues rather than observations or explanations of positions. My coaching experience has taught me that to look good on skis you must be making correct movements. Expert powder skiers look graceful and move effortlessly. Such skiing is attainable by using small movements that create big results, not big movements that require strong muscles.

The snow in this next photo sequence is new powder that has been blown by the wind. In some places it is a foot deep, in others it is only 3 inches over frozen crust. Delicate pressuring was required, especially at the top of the turn. Notice how I describe making the pressure even from ski to ski and flexing both legs to keep them moving laterally as one unit.

Handle the Pressure

Fig. a. Balance with more weight on the outside or downhill ski than on the inside ski to continue turning at the bottom of the arc.

Fig. b. With the pole plant, begin to flex and relax the stance leg. When the stance leg flexes to match the flex of the inside leg, balance on both skis to keep them pressured equally.

Fig. c. Flex your legs and let the skis float until they come to the surface. Keep them at the same edge angles. Use the stabilizing pole plant to balance as the skis surface.

Fig. d. As you flex, press the downhill boot toward the uphill boot and tilt the downhill ski first. Make sure the legs stay pressed together while tilting. Flexing the legs equally and keeping the skis at the same edge angles controls your float.

Fig. e. Do not rush the tipping action - make sure both skis tip together. Flattening the downhill ski and releasing will commit your body to the perfect position for the next turn. PMTS technique lets the body move as a unit into the arc of the new turn, organized and balanced despite the variable snow conditions.

Fig. f. As the skis tip, gradually extend the legs. The edge angle causes the skis to redirect. Then increase the tilt of the inside ski. Notice that the skis changed direction when they were above the snow as a result of tipping the free ski and holding the legs together to work in unison. No active leg rotation or steering is needed.

Fig. g. As the turn comes back far enough in the other direction, begin to flex and release.

Fig. 13-1. Handle the pressure

Biomechanical Advantage

• Both skis will turn together when you keep them at the same edge angles.

• Flexing and tipping to release will move the body into the new turn.

Cues for Success

• Press the entire length of your legs together.

• Stand evenly on both skis during the float.

• Use a stabilizing pole plant.

First Requirement – Mastering the Pressure

Skiing ungroomed snow is a piece of cake if you use the balancing movements you developed from the PMTS Undergraduate Course and trust your skis' side cut to turn. One of the basic skills you should acquire from PMTS is foot awareness and the ability to pressure the skis independently. You can increase or decrease the weight on a ski, or you can transfer balance from one foot to the other. We showed how to develop these abilities in the Undergraduate Course (refer to the float and Weighted Release). In powder, we play with equalizing the pressure on both skis, as well as increasing and decreasing pressure from one ski to the other. Pressuring by extending a leg will sink that ski into the snow; flexing and retracting the leg causes the ski to rise to the surface. When both skis are pressured evenly, you can sustain or increase your buoyancy via the process of quickly flexing or retracting your legs. When we pressure both skis evenly and tip them in the prescribed order, they can behave as one platform. Making the pressure even on the skis is used to develop a release. This technique is described in Chapter 8, "Weighted Release."

Although you try to develop even pressure on both skis coming into the release, in other parts of the turn you still may require different and varied pressure on each ski. You can adjust the pressure with the same movements we have used throughout the PMTS short turn progression, flexing and relaxing the leg to make that ski lighter and extending to create more pressure. In powder, the difference in pressure between the skis becomes more obvious, as the more pressured ski will sink into the snow and the lighter ski will rise to the surface. The emphasis of PMTS Direct Parallel, from the first lesson, has been on shifting balance from one foot to the other. Alternating balance from one ski to the other is stance mastery and is probably the most important prerequisite for skiing off-piste. Reducing the edge grip and the pressure build-up under the skis by the releasing movements starts a new turn in powder, as in all other skiing situations.

f

g

h

i

j

This simple warm-up is useful for powder, soft snow or crud snow. The hopping helps to develop and feel a range of motion in the legs. Landing with legs flexed and tipping the inside boot puts the skis on edge and develops a feel for balance as the skis start to engage and turn. Hopping again gives you the opportunity to pressure both skis evenly at take-off. This warm-up also lets you practice the non-stop pole plant needed for powder skiing. To maintain balance, your upper body will need to coordinate with the legs. Revisit the straight run ULBC exercises in Chapter 10 if needed.

Fig. 13-2. Hopping powder warm-up

Fig. a. Start with a straight run. Plant the pole for a direction change to the left.
Fig. b. Hop and tip your skis to the left.
Fig. c. Hold your legs together in the air. Start to swing the basket forward for the next pole plant already.
Fig. d. After you land, tip the inside ski (here, the left) more than the outside ski, but press your legs and boots together.
Fig. e. Flex the legs and settle down on the skis. Let the angle of the skis to the snow create the turn.
Fig. f. Pole plant again and hop. Push evenly off both feet to hop.
Fig. g. Start the next pole swing while you're in the air.
Fig. h. Prepare the new inside ski for tipping and make sure the legs and skis stay together.
Fig. i. Tip the inside ski as you land on the snow, and flex the inside leg further than the outside leg.
Fig. j. Keep minimal pressure on the tipped, inside ski to set the skis into a turn.

Release, Transfer, and Engagement in Powder

In powder, getting into a series of turns from a standing start can be the first and one of the most difficult hurdles. As illustrated in the hopping powder warm-up, *Figure 13-2*, from a straight run begin by extending your legs to push both skis into the snow. You will discover how much resistance the snow has to offer. Once the skis stop sinking you can react. Quickly pop your skis back to the surface by bouncing or flexing, and pulling your knees toward your chest. You can do this 2 or 3 times to pick up a little speed and determine the snow's density. After you have felt the skis reaching the bottom of your extension and know how dense the snow is, plant your pole the next time the skis surface and begin tipping your skis. Try to keep the first turn very short — just enough for a slight direction change. As soon as you tip the skis they will take a set in the snow. A set means the skis are now angled against the directional pull of gravity and pressure will build under the bottoms as they sink. Once the pressure builds sufficiently, the skis will begin deflecting more quickly, causing a turn.

Imagine you are beginning a turn to the left. Keep the inside, left ski pressed against the stance ski boot as they both tip to the inside of the turn. Always initiate tipping by tilting or rolling with the inside ski; let the outside ski and leg follow. Be aware at this point that the inside ski will try to separate from the outside ski. Keep the legs squeezed together in powder to help both skis do the same thing and stay at equal edge angles. As the skis take their set in the soft snow, extend the outside leg. When they stop sinking in the powder, immediately begin to flex the outside leg. Flexing will cause the body to move toward the skis and down the hill. Pull the downhill ski out of the snow as you flex to speed up the transition and transfer your balance to the other ski. Extend the new outside leg and keep tipping and flexing the releasing ski. Now your body is lined up with the new outside ski and you are in balance for the new turn.

The movements of releasing and transfer in powder are the same as in the rest of the book except you may need to be more deliberate with the downhill ski at the end of the turn. You may, in addition to flexing, need to pull the ski out of the snow. In effect this is like kicking one leg out from under a card table. As we all know, the table collapses quickly toward the side of the removed leg. Similarly, the body reacts by falling toward the collapsing, folding, or flexing leg as you remove the support of the old stance leg. The release has begun and is automatically followed by the transfer and engagement. Continue these movements with a stabilizing pole plant and you have the basics of powder and crud skiing.

The first photo sequence of this chapter, *Figure 13-1*, is continued here. Note that it's important not to overload the downhill ski at the bottom of turns in this snow. To come out of powder turns with your shiny side up, flex both legs to release, especially the outside leg, because it will always be longer, or more extended. By flexing it earlier, you have a chance to even out the pressure between the skis. Once the skis are evenly pressured, pull your knees toward your chest to put both skis flat quickly.

Biomechanical Advantage

• When the body moves across the skis to start a turn, keeping the skis at the same edge angle, the snow will deflect the skis together in the turn.

Fig. 13-3. Control the pressure with flexion and extension

Fig. a. Plant the pole and bring both knees up together to get out of the turn.

Fig. b. Hang onto the pole and let the skis float out from under the body. Tip the inside ski.

Fig. c. Lighten the inside ski and tilt it for the new turn.

Fig. d. The releasing and engaging movements of *Figure c* will draw your torso inside both skis. Extend the outside leg to maintain contact with the snow.

Fig. e. Keep the inside ski held close to the stance ski for easier tipping actions. Notice how the inside leg extends with the outside leg.

Fig. f. Strong counteracting movements help to keep you in balance with equally angled skis.

Fig. g. Increase the flex of the inside leg as you tilt that ski to keep pressure equal on the skis and edge angles the same just before the release.

Cues for Success

• To exit the turn, flex both legs, starting with the downhill leg.

• To maintain the turn, continue tipping the inside ski and extending the outside leg.

Make the Skis Behave in Unison

The idea in powder and uneven snow is to make both skis behave like one ski. I imagine a snowboard or a mono-ski. Even as it is tipping, a mono-ski has a more weighted side (the side in the snow) and a less weighted side. But this evens out and reaches a constant state as the wide ski compacts or traps snow under the base surface. As the snow packs under the ski, it begins to feel light and controllable. If you are on two skis, the ski that is completely weighted will sink more deeply, making it difficult to control or turn. Skiing on powder and crud is different from skiing on packed snow, for you are in a more fluid-like medium. Like water skiing, each ski must stay afloat. Quickly overloading or over pressuring one ski relative to the other can make it react unfavorably, probably diving deep and pulling apart from the light ski. Remember, as I said in my first book, "Don't surprise your skis." Independent pressuring of the skis is still necessary in powder, but it must be done in a subtle, more progressive way.

Let's try to create the same effect that gives the mono-ski or snowboard its flotation advantage in soft snow. With the new skis you have, in effect, the opportunity to have a mono-ski on each foot, especially the mid-fats or all-mountain skis. Any ski 70 mm wide under the foot is wide enough to provide great flotation and control in powder or crud, if used correctly. Regulating the pressure from one ski to the other by either flexing or lightening to create float is appropriate. Extending to increase and maintain contact of the outside or stance ski at the beginning of the turn provides momentary balance, but the skis must line up side-by-side at the same edge angle before the turn progresses very far. I will demonstrate how these movements work in different all-mountain conditions in the photo sequences throughout this section. When both skis are lined up before engaging in the new turn, you can maintain consistent turning throughout the arc. During the release, even pressure is beneficial for flotation and is necessary for smooth transitions. The ability to regulate pressure with flexion and extension will allow the skis to behave as one wide platform.

a *b* *c* *d*

Fig. 13-4. Make the skis behave in unison

There are situations in powder, as shown in this montage, in which the stance or downhill ski gets caught in the snow and does not release as desired. Take the time to organize the releasing ski, lining it up with the new outside ski, before the skis engage.

Fig. a. The turn is almost finished and it's time to get the ski tips out of the snow. Begin to relax the downhill leg.

Fig. b. Flexing the legs will reduce the ski edge angles and will bring your body or torso closer to and over the skis. Try to keep equal pressure on both skis and flex both legs so the skis are lighter on the snow. Let the skis move forward and flatten as you flex.

Fig. c. Synchronize leg flexing and ski flattening with the pole plant to bring the upper body into the next turn. You are controlling your body's entry to the new turn with the angle of the skis. Pull the now lifted and retracted leg and ski in toward the stance ski.

Fig. d. Begin tipping for the next turn. The tipping of the inside ski helps to commit the body into the new turn.

Second Requirement – Keep the Skis at the Same Edge Angle

The ability to keep your feet, skis and boots at exactly the same angles while moving laterally to and from an edge is the second requirement for skiing in soft snow. Here, mastery of the ball control exercise (Chapter 6, *Figure 6-5*) is a must. If you can make your skis and legs tip in unison well enough to ski gentle turns with the ball between your feet, controlling your skis in powder and crud is within your reach. The movement sequence for the release, discussed in the first section of the book, becomes critical when you reach this stage in your skiing. Now in powder and crud you will be able to determine whether you have practiced these techniques sufficiently. The movements of the Undergraduate Course really pay dividends at these upper levels of skiing.

Where Does it Break Down?

Skiers with an A-frame or knock-kneed stance have difficulty keeping the skis at the same edge angle. The A-frame stance is not necessarily a circumstance of poor alignment. It can result from a dominant urge to move the downhill ski to an edge first. Remember, unlike hard pack, powder and crud conditions provide minimal resistance to tipping because they are soft. You easily can tip the new downhill ski too far. I only remind you of this possibility because when you first try to ski in powder you are likely to revert to old habits. This typically stems from an attempt to get the ski turning, on edge, or across the slope. We discussed this in detail in Chapter 4, "Release." However, unless you have properly prepared and applied yourself to learning PMTS Direct Parallel movements, the wrong movement still can return when you are in stressful situations. You are not alone; for most skiers and even for some instructors the tendency is to turn the new downhill ski, especially in powder. This survival instinct is very strong — a default movement pattern that is deeply ingrained. If you still use this default movement, read on and you will learn to change it shortly.

History

In the first section of the book and the early undergraduate chapters, I explained why traditional instruction makes it difficult, if not impossible, to become an expert. Traditional systems rely heavily on commands such as "turn the outside ski," "steer the legs," and "stand on the downhill ski," and are making you work too hard in an incorrect manner. When you apply movements like these to powder or crud snow, you will be in for unpleasant surprises. These traditional movements train you to engage the downhill ski well before the inside ski, thereby putting the skis in a converging relationship, the A-frame. Unfortunately, by the time the inside ski can match the outside ski, the skis are crossed or the downhill ski is overloaded and digs in. Even if you are an inside ski "quick steering sensation," you will get caught crossing your tips from time to time on powder and crud slopes.

Foot Separation

Keep the skis and boots close together or they may act independently. Use the cue of touching the boots to ensure they stay close enough. When your feet are more than an inch apart in soft snow they are more difficult to control. If you don't press the legs together, the skis will pull apart. Once you are in the turn, your skis may separate vertically, but you must keep the inside boot close to the outside leg. If your skis should separate to shoulder width or more in the transition, you quickly will need to pull the free foot back in line, as in *Figure 13-4*. The closer the feet are together, the easier it is to adjust the pressure subtly on each ski. When the boots are together, one movement can control both skis. Remember, the goal is to have two skis behave as one. I like to keep my legs touching so they can react as one unit. In this position, the legs still are able to adjust for up and down, extending and flexing movements. The femurs can still turn under a stable pelvis when your boots are together. If this weren't the case, Jonny Mosely wouldn't be able to survive in the bumps with his locked foot style.

Skis are Rudders

The snow doesn't know whether you have two skis or one wide ski. It responds to what you give it. If you present your skis at two different angles to powder snow, the skis, especially shaped skis, will act as if they each had a mind of their own. Skis in powder are like rudders; they take off in different directions as soon as their angles to the snow differ. They force the boat, or in this case, each leg, to head in different directions. Tipping the wrong ski first pressures it and causes it to react quickly. If you have difficulty now in 4 inches of powder, those movements will only be worsened in 10 inches of snow. This tendency of the skis to separate when tipped at different angles reinforces the idea that shaped skis should not be turned, which is doubly true in powder. Proficient powder skiing can be achieved with simple tipping movements. It's important to remember that in powder, the edges don't have much influence on your turning or holding. The bases (flat, wide, bottom surface) of the skis do. Like the wing of an airplane, the bases are the flat surface area and its exposure to the snow controls direction. Powder skiing requires a different understanding of skiing, but the same PMTS movements can be used successfully.

Ski Action and Reaction

When the skis are tipped at an angle against the direction of travel, the snow gathers under the ski and deflects the skis in a new direction. The idea then is to pack as much snow under the outside ski as under the inside, in order to keep the pressure under both skis the same so that they will change direction together. If you start by tipping the inside ski to the little-toe edge, for example, that ski will deflect and move out of the way, making room for the outside ski to follow. This movement will lean or tilt the body slightly inside the turn, thereby tipping the outside ski appropriately. After that initiating movement of the inside foot, angle both skis equally and they will stay parallel. By tipping the inside ski first, you cause a reaction further up the body that moves your center into the turn. The tilting of your body causes the stance ski to tip on edge passively and thus turn. The outside leg should extend and the inside leg should shorten to keep both skis turning at the same radius through the lower half of the arc.

Fig. 13-5. Keep the skis at the same angle

Fig. a. After the skis have floated, tip the inside ski to the little-toe edge.
Fig. b. Point the pole tip down the hill.
Fig. c. Begin flexing and releasing as you plant the pole.
Fig. d. Flex your legs so that the skis rise to the surface.
Fig. e. Use the stabilizing pole plant for balance.

The ski angles must remain the same if the skis are to act in unison during the turn. After the last turn, the skis were allowed to float and the inside ski was tilted. Keeping both skis together helps keep them under control and facilitates balance adjustments. With the skis working together, very little effort is needed to turn the skis — just small tipping and flexing movements. These movements reduce physical effort and maintain balance. Since you have tipped the skis to make the turn, no body swinging is needed to horse the skis around. Use counteracting movements of the hips to stabilize the torso. Counteracting movements also set up the turn for a powerful release by coiling the upper body against the legs. From *Figures c* to *e* you will notice how the flattening of the skis uncoils the legs. You don't have to concentrate on the legs to achieve this releasing power. Releasing the skis and using the upper and lower body coordination movements we presented in Chapter 10 will produce this effective and efficient way to ski.

Focus on Your Feet to Control the Legs

On intermediate terrain, once you start a turn you have to be prepared to move quickly to turn back in the other direction. You must head back the other way before you go too far across the slope. If you stay in the turn too long, you may lean over and fall to the inside of the turn. Keeping your momentum going down the hill keeps you upright, so use a series of connected turns. Prepare to change direction as soon as you feel the pressure under the skis taking them in the new direction. Change direction by flexing the stance leg, which lightens the stance ski and reduces the pressure on it. Because the stance ski is pressed deeper in the snow throughout the turn, it must be prepared for the transition prior to the inside ski. You may have to flex aggressively to pull it up out of the snow. Flexing the leg will take the pressure off the ski and reduce the snow's influence on it. When the ski starts to flatten, flex both legs equally, and flatten both skis to the snow. When they are both flat on the snow, you will be in between turns and your legs should be bent the most. By flexing your legs, you allow your skis to float and come closer to the surface. When they are near the top, they are easy to tip and redirect into the next turn.

Turning the Skis is Tiring

Many skiers I talk to feel that they need tremendous power to turn the skis in powder. I've seen them grinding away and twisting their legs to change direction. If you feel your muscles starting to burn as you try to overcome the turning resistance, you are working too hard. Turning the skis in powder should be effortless. You shouldn't feel that the skis are hard to turn. We discussed using "the force" in Chapter 7. Releasing the downhill ski allows you to use your momentum and gravity to keep your body moving down the slope rather than trying to stop your momentum with a stiff stance leg and pushing off it to begin a new turn. That's too much work.

If you find yourself working too hard, what's causing this wasted effort? Earlier I described how to extend the stance leg and where to use it in the turn. In powder, most skiers rarely use extension. Instead, they stay in a flexed position. Not only can this be more tiring for the muscles, it doesn't allow any further relaxation of the stance leg to create an effective release. Those skiers hardly ever use "the force." Without a release, the only way to start turns is by jumping and twisting your skis using the larger, leg-turning muscles. These muscles only impart their full twisting power to the skis when they are bent or flexed. If you are trying to turn your skis in powder, you are using these muscles and you have to stay flexed throughout the turn. PMTS saves you from this exhausting and frustrating spiral, but first you must recognize your limiting movements and replace them with efficient PMTS movements.

Flexing and Extending the Legs

In PMTS we advocate flexing the legs but in a completely different way. Flexed legs have turning power, while straight legs have little turning power but are strong for edging. Now you will learn how to use the relationship between turning power and edging power. Imagine making a turn to the left. When your skis flatten after the release, continue tipping the left ski from flat toward its outside or little-toe edge. Allow the right ski to react naturally and keep some tension holding your legs together. The right ski will follow the direction of the left, tipping ski. At the same time, it will have to stretch out or extend to maintain contact with the snow as your body moves inside the turn. Remember, I said "stretch out," not push against the snow. The extension of the right leg on the outside of the turn will tip that ski to an angle in the snow causing the ski to turn toward the fall line. The inside ski leads the tipping activity and should always be angled slightly earlier than the outside ski. The turn has been set into motion. All that is required after this is fine-tuning by making tipping adjustments. As the snow packs under the right ski, it pushes back against the leg, especially as you cross the fall line; the same is true for the inside ski. Keep extending the right leg to pack the snow under the ski until you are ready to start the next turn. The inside leg is more flexed. The body has reacted to the primary movements of tipping the skis. The legs are extended, resulting in strong edging.

For the next turn you must again relax and flex to begin the flattening and tipping of the skis. Here is where flexed legs help to redirect the skis. During transition, the legs follow the flattening and re-engaging of the skis. During edge release, the legs move from uphill of the skis to downhill of the skis. This movement across the skis changes the edge angles and imparts passive steering to the skis. The more flexed the legs are during transition, the more they move across the skis. Thus, flexed legs have greater turning influence on the skis. Remember that you are focused on lateral tipping, not leg turning. Focus on flattening the skis and flexing the legs, and you will achieve the amount of ski redirection you need.

Figure 13-6 shows fresh tracks in wind-packed snow. It is denser than powder, so the skis will react more quickly in it.

Fig. a. The skis are floating, ready for inside ski tilting to increase the body and ski angles to the slope.

Fig. b. Increase inside ski tilting and your body will drop to the inside. Now both skis are angled to the snow. Offering resistance to the snow by extending the legs causes the skis to turn more quickly.

Fig. c. The body is angled to the slope and legs are extended, causing pressure to build under the skis. The skis deflect in the snow to the new direction.

Fig. d. Keep the legs extended until the turn is far enough around to begin releasing. Notice how the pole swing has developed with the wrist movement. Now plant the pole and begin flexing both legs to release and flatten the skis.

Fig. e. Flex both legs and shorten the downhill leg to match the length of uphill leg and pressure of the uphill ski.

Fig. f. Move the downhill leg out of the way by shortening and tipping. This movement will transfer balance and prepare the body to move into the next turn.

Fig. 13-6. Flexion and extension of the legs

a

b

c

d

e

f

g

h

Fig. g. Even with strong flexing, crud and wind-blown snow offer strong support and energy to the skis as they are released. I lift out of the snow without jumping or hopping, simply as a result of the skis' planing on the firmly compressed wind pack. Proceed with tipping the inside ski and you will land in perfect balance.

Fig. h. Keep tipping the inside ski to tilt the outside ski on edge. Do not move the outside ski to get it on edge. The edge angle will result from the body's tipping into the turn. Any attempt to put the outside ski on an edge will result in the tail pushing out as well as unequal ski edge angles.

Extending the Outside Leg

The outside leg should be extended to maintain contact and to compress the snow under the ski. You must be judicious with how you extend. Too soon and too much will cause you to push your body down the hill, resulting in loss of balance. The idea is to use the force. Let the tipping action of the inside free foot, momentum and gravity move your body into the next turn. Don't push your body down the hill with your extended outside leg. Tipping the inside ski and flexing the inside leg help to bring the body to the inside of the turn once the transition has begun. As the body moves inside, the outside leg naturally has to extend to stay in contact with the snow, providing an advantage later in the turn when it is time to change direction. An extended outside leg has a large range of flexion and can be used to absorb pressure at the bottom of the turn. When flexion is active and fast, the skis quickly come to the surface and flatten in the process. Keep the upper body facing the same direction during this process of flexing and releasing. Notice from the photos how important the role of the pole plant is to help hold the upper body in position until you are ready for the next turn.

Timing of Linked Turns

Determine when it is time for another turn by how much direction change or turn completion you want. If you are on a very steep powder slope, start flexing the outside leg earlier to slowly control the body's rate of descent into the fall line and the next turn. Don't wait too long or the skis will start into a traverse, carrying your momentum across the hill, no longer available to help with the release. If you have a traverse between turns you will be forced to use the muscle-taxing techniques discussed earlier to initiate the next turn. Timing the flexing and relaxing of the outside leg will dictate your turn size, rhythm and speed. Slow flexing will lengthen the turn; quick, aggressive flexing — almost pulling both legs out of the snow — will create short, quick powder turns.

Retracting the Legs

Retracting the legs or flexing the knees to shorten the legs is a powder power move that often is needed for skiing in very steep powder runs. Many skiers have difficulty practicing this move because they rarely want to learn by experimenting in challenging conditions. Practice the retraction and flexing movements demonstrated in Chapter 7 in your regular short turns and you will become familiar with the movements.

PMTS movements develop an extended outside leg near the middle of the turn. This extension of the leg offers a complete range of flexion. Near the end of the turn, it is important to use this range of flexion to get out of the turn. If you quickly retract and flex your leg, you are taking the pressure off your ski. The ski, therefore, floats to the top of the snow. Hold this float position for a moment until you are sure that both skis are at the same angle and you are in balance. Now, with both legs flexed, you can begin tipping the outside or lower ski toward the outside edge to begin the transition. In powder, relaxing and flexing the legs to end a turn has a greater impact than on groomed snow. As the flexing brings your skis flat and up to the snow surface, you are ready to begin tipping. Once your legs are flexed sufficiently and you have placed your pole, you are ready to let the skis float.

Fig. 13-7. *Retract the legs for a clean release in crud*

Fig. a. Strong flexion and retraction (pulling up on the legs) allow my skis to float over this crud.

Fig. b. Strong, quick inside ski tipping engages the skis.

Fig. c. Short turns in this crud again require strong flexing.

Fig. d. Flex the legs and pull the knees up when the snow is sticky.

Fig. e. When the skis are free from the snow, tip in the new direction.

Fig. f. When the legs are strongly flexed, as in this sequence, tipping has an instant turning effect. As at the top of a bump, a large direction change can be made by tipping the flexed legs.

Dryland Training for Leg Flexion and Extension

Quickly flexing and retracting the leg is not a natural movement. One of the best ways to practice strong flexing and retracting actions without powder, or even lift lines, is the dryland skiing machine called the Skier's Edge. If you are having trouble performing the leg retraction and flexing movements described here, try the Skier's Edge. It duplicates the extension and absorption movements in your own living room, and, if you set up a mirror, you can watch yourself to ensure your legs flex and extend. The machine also allows your feet to tip and reproduce the controlling movements that keep the skis at the same edge angles. If used correctly, it duplicates the movements of PMTS.

Pole Plant and Arm Rhythm

There is no substitute for good hand and pole use in powder skiing. All the principles demonstrated in Chapter 10, or in the *PMTS Instructor Manual,* will help you develop strong pole use in powder. The arms and poles shouldn't be conducting an orchestra in any kind of skiing, unless you are in trouble and need a gross reaction to recover. The arms and poles can't create a release, but they can time movements and stabilize the upper body. No amount of arm reaching or swinging will start a turn unless you release the skis. Early preparation for the turn by pointing the pole tip down the fall line is a great way to keep the body in line and prepared for the eventuality of the ski's release. Proper arm and pole use will keep the upper body in position and efficiently balanced. After the pole is planted in the snow, punch the inside hand forward to keep from over-rotating the upper body. Often, in the excitement of a steep powder run, this movement is forgotten. The hand and arm are dragged back by the pole plant, the body swings around to face the side of the trail, and you overturn. I recommend you practice continuous arm movements in your warm-up runs to establish the proper poling activity. Prepare your pole early for the turn. Pull your hand toward your shoulder so you can swing the tip of the pole and point it down the slope before planting it into the snow. This movement will assure proper shoulder and arm positioning prior to the turn, just as I explained in the sections on pole use (Chapter 10).

Steep Powder

After riding powerful motorcycles, jumping out of an airplane, and racing on a World Cup downhill course, I still believe steep powder runs are the most exhilarating feeling in sports. They're not only exciting, but you'll find that steep powder runs can be very safe if you are in the right place at the right time. The ideal powder for this experience is dry. Wet powder slows you down too much and requires very steep slopes where cliffs and rocks often become hazards. My best experiences with steep powder were at Snowbird, Alta, Berthoud Pass and the Canadian Bugaboos and Monashees. I am sure other powder experiences exist, but for easy access, Loveland and Berthoud Pass in Colorado, and Snowbird in Utah, are the most readily accessible. You must be crafty to take advantage of the powder at Snowbird these days, because the local population knows how to use up the untracked snow in short order. One option is to take a guess on the weather or a storm pattern. Stay overnight up in the canyon before they close the road and have the mountain to yourself the next day, for no one can get up the canyon when it is snowed in. For me the best is Berthoud Pass, about a half-hour from my house; I get a big jump on the Denver traffic even on a weekend day. Once you have found that steep section you want with no tracks and no one around, don't hesitate. The next skier may not stop to look around and check the view. He will most likely just ski right past your perch and poach your run. You may have heard the saying, "No friends on a powder day." Remember though, before you take on something new, it is best to know the area you are about to ski. You never know what is beyond the next tree or steep drop.

Free Falling

You are ready, you push off, but the first turn seems heavy and the skis don't respond. Powder skiing requires momentum just like carving high-angle turns. Let your skis go at first and make less direction change. Definitely keep your poles moving, and make strong continuous pole plants. In powder, never stop moving your hands and wrists. You must prepare constantly for the next turn with an early pole plant. At this point, many skiers try to slow themselves down by making sharper turns before they reach cruising velocity. You may be holding yourself back from experiencing the most thrilling ride of your life by bailing out too early. Even on very steep slopes, the powder should be enough to slow you down; try not to use sharp turns to control speed. If you do, your skis will dig in and you won't be floating over the surface; you'll be on the ground. The real experience of flying in powder means that you shouldn't touch the packed snow beneath the new. The flying sensation comes from staying above the hard surface and well up in the new snow. Speed control isn't the issue; you eventually will reach maximum velocity and stay at that speed for the rest of the run. Snow density and deepness determine maximum speed. Turns can help to reduce speed, but not to control it. Most important, as I said earlier, know the slope and the run-out area. Free falling on skis is not for everyone, but if you are ready to experience this thrill, make sure you have more than 6 inches of new snow. In fact, you really need at least a foot and a half to two feet to experience this type of skiing.

Trees

Skiing powder in the trees is simple if you have mastered the basic technique. Figure it out on open terrain first. In the trees is where you should use the fat powder skis. In open snowfields, regular-waisted shaped skis are fine because you can use speed to keep them floating. In the trees, you may not want to have as much speed as you need to keep such skis above the snow. In fact, this happened to me on a cat powder skiing tour at Steamboat. I could ski the steep powder on my longish skis when I was in the open. But when the aspen trees were close together, I often missed great skiing lines because my skis would bog down in the tight turns dictated by the trees. I immediately switched to wide, shaped powder skis and the world changed. All of a sudden I could keep a rhythm going, make the turns around the trees, and still stay on top of the snow.

Trees can be intimidating and they should command your respect. Using them as slalom poles is not a good idea. Kim Reichhelm, the former world extreme champion, once used a large pine for a GS pole while filming for a Warren Miller movie and found it wasn't forgiving. She tore her shoulder and went bouncing down the slope. Tactics for tree skiing are similar to those you use in mountain biking. Never look at the trees! Always look for the light between the trees. Give yourself more than 3 feet from the edge of the tree well (the hole around the tree trunk) because your body has to be angled toward the tree to make the turn. If you have to sneak by trees that are close together, move your upper body outward over the stance ski. Some of the best snow ever found is in the trees, but there are also obstacles such as fallen logs and thinly covered rocks. I suggest you wait until they have all been covered by a number of big snowstorms before you get started.

References

Bacharach, D., Seifert, J., Dean, K., Shultz, D., and Rice, L., (2000). Coaching Cues via Radio Enhance Practice Performance of Junior Alpine Skiers. *Abstracts*, 2nd International Congress on Skiing and Science.

Harb, Harald (1997). *Anyone can be an Expert Skier*. New York: Hatherleigh Press.

Harb, H., Rogers, D., Hintermeister, R., and Peterson, K., (1998). *Primary Movements Teaching System Instructor Manual*. Colorado: Harb Ski Systems.

Harb, H. and Frediani, P., (2001). *Ski Flex*. New York: Hatherleigh Press.

Tejada-Flores, Lito (1986). *Breakthrough on Skis*. New York: Vintage Books.

Wulf, G. and Wiegelt, C., (1997). Instructions about physical principles in learning a complex motor skill: To tell or not to tell… *Res. Qtrly. For Exer. & Sport, 68*, 362-367.

Wulf, G., Hoss, M., and Prinz, W., (1998). Instructions for motor learning: Differential effects of internal versus external focus of attention. *J. Mot. Behav., 30*, 169-179.

Announcing
a breakthrough in
the science of
Expert Skiing...

BOOK & VIDEO SERIES

Release the expert skier within you!

Join skiing pioneer Harald Harb as he teaches you with his revolutionary PMTS Direct Parallel method of ski instruction. The **Anyone Can Be An Expert Skier** book and video series is the most innovative and effective teaching system ever created! You'll learn to ski expert terrain with more ease and less effort than you thought possible.

Harald Harb has spent a lifetime perfecting the PMTS Direct Parallel method. It has been used in over 100,000 lessons worldwide. Skiers and instructors alike agree that it works faster and better than any other system available. The **Anyone Can Be An Expert Skier** series will show you how to master the mountain in record time!

The **Anyone Can Be An Expert Skier** series teaches you techniques of expert skiing that anyone can learn and shows you how to choose the proper boots and skis to maximize your skiing power. The door to enjoyable, exhilarating skiing is finally open for you!

Anyone Can Be An Expert Skier
books contain over 200 photos and unique photomontages. Plus, bonus tear-out "Pocket Instructor" cards allow you to learn on the slopes.

"I have learned a lot from Harald Harb. His insights into the multiple makeup of expert skiing—equipment, biomechanics, and functional primary movements—are vital, accurate, and above all, immediately useful."

— Lito Tejada-Flores

ORDER TOLL FREE 1-800-906-1234

Anyone Can Be An Expert Skier 1
The New Way to Ski

Harald Harb enthusiastically offers a step-by-step, easy-to-follow process that will improve your skiing no matter what your ability level. With Harb's revolutionary PMTS Direct Parallel method, you will be on the fast track to all-mountain expert skiing! What's more, you'll learn to recognize, correct and avoid the dead-end movements that keep you from achieving your skiing potential.

Easy-to-understand and impressively complete, this book is a "must have" for skiers everywhere. Quite simply, it is regarded as the foremost authoritative guide to the art of carving with shaped skis.

Anyone Can Be An Expert Skier 1–
The New Way to Ski
Book (ISBN 1-57826-073-6) .$19.95
Video (ISBN 1-57826-082-5) .$24.95

Anyone Can Be An Expert Skier 2
Powder, Bumps, and Carving

Revealed here for the first time: the secrets of the Biomechanical Advantage–a proven technique used by hundreds of pro skiers to achieve winning performance!

In this book and video, you'll learn how to handle challenging terrains and conditions with ease. Moguls, powder and crud, steeps––there will be no limit to your skiing horizons! The special section on advanced carving techniques will perfect your skiing style–giving you precision and control like never before.

Anyone Can Be An Expert Skier 2 is your ideal solution for all mountain conditions. You will discover the techniques that have helped thousands of skiers reach the pinnacle of expert status. Guaranteed!

Anyone Can Be An Expert Skier 2–
Powder, Bumps, and Carving
Book (ISBN 1-57826-074-4) .$19.95
Video (ISBN 1-57826-083-3) .$24.95

Harald Harb, skiing innovator, pioneer of ski instruction, and president of Harb Ski Systems, has made a life-long study of skiing techniques. Born in Austria, he raced the World Cup circuit with the Canadian National Ski Team and later was named Overall Champion on the Eastern US Regional Pro Circuit. As a coach, Harald directed ski racing programs that produced some of the United States' most successful National Team members and Olympic medalists. After working with recreational skiers, he became convinced that current teaching systems needed improvement, so he created the Primary Movement Teaching System (PMTS). Harb also reaches thousands of ski enthusiasts through his position as technical editor at *Skiing* magazine.

1. Manage your Free Foot

- Touch the inside boot to the stance boot.

- Keep the boots even fore/aft.

3. The Phantom Move

- Touch the outside edge of the inside ski tip to the snow, and hold the tail a few inches above the snow.

- Touch the free boot to the inside ankle of the stance boot.

5. "Ball Control"

- Squeeze the ball with the free boot against the stance boot.

- Deliberately flatten your stance ski to release.

7. Weighted Release

- Stand on the downhill ski as you flatten it.

- Relax and flex the stance leg as you flatten it.

9. Pole/Arch Lift

- Lift inside hand, arm, and shoulder.

- Lift the arch and arm together.

11. Carving in the Bumps

- At the top of the bump, lift the downhill ski, pull it in and back, and tip it over to the outside edge.

- Use a stabilizing pole plant, and the strong inside arm position.

4. Release from the Uphill Edge

- Balance on the little-toe edge of the uphill ski.

- Press the lifted boot against the stance boot throughout the complete turn.

- Flatten the stance ski slowly.

2. Pole Press with Partner

- With the free boot touching the stance boot, have your partner push your foot away while you press inward to maintain contact between the boots.

8. Float in Transition

- Relax, then actively flex the legs to release.

- Pause in tipping the free foot while the skis are flat on the snow surface.

6. Flex to Release

- Pull your knees up toward your chest to achieve leg flexion.

- Pull your free foot in and back to maintain contact with the stance foot.

12. Retract for a Clean Release in Crud

- Flex the legs and pull the knees up toward the chest.

- When the skis are free from the snow, tip the inside ski quickly.

10. Tighten the Carved Arc

- Slide the inside foot up along the outside leg to pull your body into the turn.

- Tip the inside ski onto its outside edge far enough that the inside thigh moves outward.

PHOTOGRAPHING WILD BIRDS

PHOTOGRAPHING
WILD BIRDS

CHRIS GOMERSALL

AMPHOTO BOOKS
An imprint of Watson-Guptill Publications
New York

Dedicated to the memory of my
mother, Jane (1930–1996)

I sing but as the bird does sing
That in the silence dwelleth
Goethe

First published in the US in 2001 by
Amphoto Books
an imprint of Watson-Guptill Publications,
a division of BPI Communications, Inc.,
770 Broadway, New York, NY 10003
www.watsonguptill.com

First published in the UK in 2001 by
David & Charles

Library of Congress Cataloging-in-
Publication Data
Gomersall, Chris.
Photographing wild birds / Chris Gomersall.
p. cm.
Includes index.
ISBN 0-8174-6416-6
1. Photography of birds. I. Title.
TR729.B5 G65 2001
746.43'20432--dc21

                              2001016061

Printed in Italy
1 2 3 4 5 6 / 06 05 04 03 02 01

Contents

INTRODUCTION 6

Appendices

(half-title page) **Atlantic puffin in breeding plumage**

(title page) **A female osprey at her Scottish eyrie**

(opposite) **Brent geese wintering on the Thames estuary**

INTRODUCTION

The most frequently asked question of all wildlife photographers must be, "How long did it take you to get that photograph?" When it comes my way in casual conversation, I often dismiss it with a peremptory "one thousandth of a second" – not because I mean to be rude or evasive, but because it would take too long to answer comprehensively.

Take the example of the backlit shot of a white-tailed eagle in flight that appears on page 135. If I were to consider only the day of photography, the reply might be "a few hours," but that would still be misleading, as that particular field trip had already taken more than a week, waiting for a suitable weather window and getting into position to take the photograph. Then there were several previous visits to the same area over three or four years, and the many less successful attempts at other locations dating back some 15 years. What about my years of learning photography and ornithology, and acquiring the field skills and practical experience to be able to capitalize on the opportunity when it eventually occurred? Should I go back to when I first began to look at and take an interest in birds, or when I took my first holiday snap? The only conclusion is that the most honest and accurate answer must be "all of my life."

Similarly, when people remark that you must have been very lucky, it's tempting to nod in agreement. Nobody really wants to hear about your enormous time commitment, but it's undoubtedly true that the harder you work, the luckier you get. The one thing that is sure is if you never go out with your camera, you'll have no luck of any kind.

Another comment that I hear with surprising frequency is, "You must have some really good equipment." And I tend to agree that yes, I have equipment that is good enough to do the job I need it to do. But cameras alone don't create great photographic images. Why is it that photography is generally held in such low esteem by so many people, even though I am quite sure they don't mean to insult its practitioners? Would the same people suggest that Gabriel Garcia Marquez must have a fantastic word processor with the

Hoopoe with crest raised
You have to be alert to capture the brief moment the hoopoe's crest is displayed, just after it lands.

very latest spellchecker to be able to write such wonderful books? Or that a good carpenter must have a brilliant set of chisels? It is plainly ludicrous to suggest that good equipment is the only explanation for their accomplishments, and yet it seems to be an all-too-common attitude with regard to photography. Perhaps it is because we see so many examples of good photography in our daily lives, and assimilate their messages so readily without the need to think too hard about how they were made. With particular reference to bird photography, the commentator has probably recognized the fact that you can't just walk up to a wild bird and expect it to pose for the camera. And I do acknowledge that technological developments are very much influencing the way all of us work, allowing us to shoot from a greater distance, and enabling more candid representations of natural behavioral activities

– this has got to be a good thing, for us and the birds. Still, the specialist hardware is only a small part of the whole deal.

So, when it comes to writing a "how to do it" book on photographing wild birds, I wouldn't wish to deceive you that there are any set menus of convenient short cuts, quick fixes, and tricks of the trade. It just isn't possible to provide a recipe book detailing precisely where to go and when, with foolproof formulas for obtaining perfect photographs every time. I'd be doing you a disservice if I were to pretend otherwise. What I can do is to pass on some of the benefits of my experience, relate a few techniques that have worked for my colleagues and me, and generally give encouragement. This will, I hope, make your understanding greater and your photography easier, but in the end it is your own experience, and learning from your mistakes that will count for most.

Short-billed dowitcher
Many migrant shorebirds such as this feeding dowitcher can be photographed on Florida's coast by careful stalking, in this instance using a 300mm lens with a 2x teleconverter.

The main ingredient for success must surely be a passion for birds and nature – without that you're unlikely to have the necessary patience and commitment to get very far. For this reason, I believe that an enthusiastic birdwatcher is more likely to become a successful bird photographer than an already competent photographer who just wishes to diversify. Imagine if I tried to switch to sports photography, for example. Even though many of the camera techniques are similar, it would be a hopeless quest if I didn't understand the rules of the particular game I was trying to cover. It might take some years of sitting on the touch line of a football pitch before I could hope to anticipate where the ball would be at a given time well enough to capture it on film with any degree of reliability. I would go so far as to say that you should go birdwatching for a while and hone your observational powers before taking up a camera in earnest.

Having learned my craft and done most of my work in the British Isles, I have grown up with the idea that wild birds are rather shy creatures and not at all easy to approach. It is also a given fact that British light and weather are very variable, if not to say downright unhelpful in the way they seem to conspire against all outdoor photography. I would like to think that this background has provided me with a sound foundation of the necessary field and camera skills, and shaped a responsible, well-rounded approach to photographing wild birds. It is certainly the main reason I have concentrated so much on the fieldwork aspects of bird photography, which sometimes seem to be taken for granted in other books on the subject. At the same time, I have also tried to reflect the more international nature of modern bird photography, and to allow for the fact that people are increasingly likely to travel outside their country of residence in order to pursue their interest. I hope there is sufficient cosmopolitan flavor here to interest readers on any continent.

It is my great privilege and your good fortune that we have been able to include the work of a number of guest photographers, all of whom are acknowledged leaders in their respective fields and styles. In fact, when my publishers suggested the idea to me, I confess to an initial reluctance. After all, it was asking for unfavorable comparisons to be made. The guests would be able to show one favorite image from their lifetime portfolio, while I could use examples of my own work to illustrate such unfortunate phenomena as red eye! But I was soon won over to the idea, especially as it meant that I wouldn't have to bluff that I had been everywhere, and done everything. I mean, why try to pretend that I'm an expert in high-speed flash photography when everybody knows that title rightly belongs to Stephen Dalton? To my amazement and immense gratification, everybody I invited to contribute said yes. Of course, I could have included many more beautiful photographs to illustrate the same points, and let me apologize straight away to the many excellent bird photographers I have excluded – honestly, no slight intended! It's a matter of regret, though, that there weren't more female role models from whom to choose.

There are a few ethical matters that need to be raised, relating to the way nature photographers conduct themselves. First and foremost, it has always been my belief that the welfare of the bird is more important than the

Great bustard male in spring plumage

It took many weeks of hide work to obtain a few satisfactory photographs of this shy and difficult subject.

Brent geese flock

*These birds were photographed
from the promenade at Southend
on the Thames estuary with an
80–200mm zoom lens.*

photograph, and that is an underlying premise of this book. As in all matters of conduct, the actions of an irresponsible few can seriously undermine the public perception of all wildlife photographers. To behave with due consideration to wild birds and other people should be the natural way of things, but unfortunately it is not always so – sometimes through malice, more often ignorance. Of course, you should behave impeccably at all times because it is the ethical thing to do, but even to take a purely cynical view, it makes sense to guard your reputation from the very outset of your photographic career. Mud sticks, and it is exceptionally difficult to shake off suspicions of bad practice. You might spend your whole life building the trust and confidence of others, whether landowners, licensing agencies, or fellow photographers, but you can blow it all with one stupid act. And then you find out just how much you depend on the cooperation of all these people and institutions. So for selfish as well as

altruistic reasons, it makes sense to behave responsibly and sensitively.

Bird conservation and biodiversity has always been the primary motivation for my photography, so the realization that not all bird photographers think the same sometimes comes as a surprise. Few things depress me more than hearing nature photographers complain about conservation organizations and their representatives, usually over some trivial matter of access or facility. This seems to me extraordinarily selfish and short-sighted. To those who believe their civil liberty has been in some way curtailed because a nature reserve has been established where they once roamed without restriction: wake up and consider for a moment what might be there now, or in ten years' time, if not for this or that environmental group. A shaky boardwalk, or restricted hide window view is really quite insignificant compared to the need for habitat conservation and management, isn't it? If the water level at a wetland reserve seems to be

inconveniently high for your photography on a particular day, it might well be because flooding is an important management tool in vegetation control, to create the best possible nesting conditions for certain species. Remember that, in the eyes of the warden or estate manager, you are part of just another special interest group, no more deserving than dog-walkers, rock-climbers or horse-riders, for example. It's up to you to convince them otherwise. Yes, of course photography can be a potent communication tool, and they will probably appreciate that too if you take the trouble to understand what they are trying to achieve – what we should all be trying to achieve. And do you know what? If successful, there might just be more birds for you to photograph at the end of the day. Again, only through our continued good conduct can we expect to be allowed any right of access at all.

The truth of the final image is an important consideration for all photographers, not just those working with wildlife. In our case, controversy and debate has long centered around whether the subject is genuinely wild, or "controlled" in some way by the photographer. The accepted code of good practice is that the photographer should declare prominently in the caption if the subject is captive. This generally satisfies everybody, even though the captive status is rarely referred to when the same image appears in print. That would be an editorial decision, and we might sometimes take issue with it, but on the whole it's a workable solution. But woe betide the photographer who tries to pass off a captive subject as wild and free – it might not seem like a crime of the highest order, but the perpetrator is usually viciously denounced if the transgression is discovered. Really, it's easiest to own up from the outset. There may be very good reasons for using a captive subject anyway. Perhaps it's a globally endangered bird that would be almost impossible to photograph in the wild, and to try to do so would further jeopardize its chances of survival. Perhaps you need a close-up of the hooked bill of a bird of prey to illustrate its feeding adaptation, and it's just not practical to attempt this with a wild

bird. Either way, it's a simple matter to declare the subject's captive status in the caption, even though you might think it would be obvious to most viewers anyway. For my part, I am happy to confirm that all of the images in this book are of wild birds, as the title implies. The single exception is the photograph of a pinioned duck on page 76, included specifically to show how to spot a fraud!

More recently these ethical concerns have

White stork in bell tower
Since the stork is traditionally associated with habitation, it seemed appropriate to show a little of its preferred nesting site.

(opposite) Black-tailed godwit juvenile in late summer
A 500mm telephoto lens and a hide were necessary for this close-up.

Stone-curlew incubating

Photography of this British rarity at the nest required a Schedule 1 license from English Nature.

(opposite) Distant gulls over intertidal mudflats

Not all bird photographs have to be frame-fillers to be effective; by exploiting unusual light conditions and paying attention to composition, you can create evocative images of nature. This was taken at the Wash estuary in eastern England.

extended to the potential for deception through the use of digital enhancement and manipulation. Indeed, it is possible to make totally convincing but wholly fabricated images of "nature" through the computer. This concerns me much less than it used to, as the technology and its application comes of age. The important thing is that there should be no intention to deceive. Quite honestly, I can't feel offended or deceived if an advertiser uses a digital composite to impart some witty message. We all understand the terms of engagement here. So context is everything. In editorial, we expect to be told the truth, and quite rightly so. On the few occasions where news and magazine editors have overstepped the mark in publishing misleading, digitally altered photographic images they have quickly been exposed, and often by the very photographers concerned. The usual response is a hastily amended editorial policy with regard to altered images; after all, the worst thing for them would be to lose credibility with their readers. All in all, I'd rather make my images in camera than in computer, and expect the editors to police their own houses.

I will undertake to declare any digital manipulation on my part, whether in the name of art or otherwise. As far as this book is

concerned, none of the images have been in any way modified or enhanced, other than the normal requirements of colour management and print production. Indeed, the great majority are shown full frame without any subsequent cropping, except where this would have seriously compromised the design of the page. But of course, you have no idea what I left out of my composition at the moment the exposure was made – this is potentially the greatest misrepresentation of all! However, most people would see that as an important part of the creative process. Ethics aside, the techniques of manipulating images in computer are not dealt with here. It would take a book on its own, and others are better qualified than I am to write it, so we'll stick to generating bird images from first principles.

Presumably you don't need any persuading as to the beauty and attractiveness of wild birds, or else you wouldn't have got this far. Like me, you would probably rather be outside communing with birds and nature. So now if you don't mind, after several months of being confined to my office writing this book, I need to get out into the field again. You will too, I hope, shortly after you have finished reading. Enjoy. I would wish you 'good luck', but as you know, luck doesn't come into it.

Chapter 1
EQUIPMENT

The image-making process must begin with the acquisition and understanding of our basic tools. Here we explore the various types of cameras, lenses, films and photographic accessories, their functions, and their specific relevance to bird photography.

WHERE TO START

Brown pelican and angler

Do you suppose it needed a special rod to catch this fish? The pelican, photographed at Sanibel Island in Florida, doesn't agree.
Camera: *Nikon F5*
Lens: *50mm f1.4*
Film: *Fujichrome Velvia*

(previous pages) **Dawn flight of pink-footed geese**

Photographed from a hide with a 50mm f1.4 lens, these birds were just leaving their night-time roost.

(opposite) **Avocet and recently hatched chick**

Avocet chicks move away from the nest within a couple of hours of hatching, so I had to plan for this event by estimating the hatch date and carefully maneuvering my floating hide into position over several days. My final camera position was only about 3.5m (11ft) from the birds, but the adult is clearly relaxed about it. Note the egg-tooth still visible on the chick's bill.
Camera: *Nikon F3*
Lens: *300mm f2.8 plus 2x teleconverter*
Film: *Kodachrome 64*
Exposure: *¹/₁₂₅ sec. at f8–11*

Obviously there is a minimum level of equipment required for serious bird photography, and we must all cross that threshold to pursue our interest practically. As a child wanting to take close-up photographs of wild birds and animals, I quickly became aware of the limitations of my Kodak Instamatic 126 camera. I remember being bitterly disappointed on being advised that it couldn't accept a telephoto or zoom lens, and all the more so when I discovered how much it would cost to replace with the recommended 35mm SLR camera system. Happily, what would have cost a lifetime of pocket money in the 1960s is now much more affordable, though it is still a significant investment to most people.

So where should you start? Firstly, how serious is your interest in photography? If you are basically a birdwatcher who wants to keep a pictorial record of birds you have seen, most likely as prints, then possibly a camera adapter for your telescope will best suit your needs. The advantage is that you save on weight, bulk, expense, and many hours of frustration. The disadvantage is that the quality of the photographs is nowhere near as good as with a purpose-built camera lens. You are restricted to a single, small aperture (typically about f13), which will mean using faster, grainier film stock and you won't have any control over depth of field. A telescope camera adapter is therefore not an advisable option for those wishing to strive for high-quality bird photography.

The next question is, which camera format to choose? Don't professionals usually use medium-format (120) and large-format (4 x 5in or 8 x 10in) cameras? Well, if their interest is mainly in landscape, studio, or portrait photography, then this is certainly true. But film emulsions are so good now, and the portability of equipment so fundamentally important, that 35mm is really the only sensible choice for bird photography. The

single-lens reflex (SLR) camera is the basic unit of a modular camera system that allows for interchangeable lenses, including powerful telephotos, and a whole range of other accessories. An SLR is relatively light, versatile and inexpensive, and most importantly for wild bird subjects, quick to use. The 35mm format shall be assumed from here on.

The main manufacturers of 35mm SLR camera systems are Canon, Nikon, Minolta, Pentax, Contax, Leica and Olympus, with the first two being the market leaders for wildlife photographers. Certainly there are great photographers creating beautiful photographs with all of these makes, but it is Nikon and Canon that you see most often in the field. I happen to use Nikon, and wouldn't easily be tempted to switch brands, because it does the job well and I am familiar with the layout and handling. However, I am pretty sure that if I'd got used to the Canon system I'd probably feel the same about that. Most objective critics reckon that Nikon have the superior camera bodies and light metering, while Canon have the more advanced lenses. But don't get too hung up about owning the "right" gear, just make sure you know how to get the best out of whatever you have.

If you can rent or borrow equipment for a proper trial before you buy, so much the better. You will want to be assured that the camera feels right, that the key controls are accessible and intuitive to use, and that it is well-built and reliable. Lenses need to be similarly well-constructed, easy to focus, and in balance with the camera. More than anything, you will want to see some results and check out how the equipment performs for you.

Contemporary cameras can be pretty intimidating at first, but as with a computer there is nearly always more than one method of achieving what you want – you just need to get familiar with the layout and functions, choose which suit you best, and gain confidence in using them. Using your camera system must become a more or less automatic response, and this can only be achieved through practice.

As well as camera and lenses, your basic kit will need a tripod, accessories like flash and cable release, and a backpack or carryall

to transport it all. If all this is beginning to sound like a bulky and heavy load, well, you are right – and it's a burden you'd better prepare for, or else reconsider your interests. Round shoulders and an aching back seem to go with the territory. Just as new weight-saving innovations come along and cameras and lenses should become lighter and more compact, there always seems to be some new, vital facility that
adds to the overall mass again.

CAMERAS

Before you get into all of the gadgets, and electronic and technical considerations of a camera, first try to weigh it up in terms of its general design and ergonomics. Does it feel comfortable in your hands, both horizontally and vertically? Can you reach and operate all the key controls without taking your eye from the viewfinder? Does your nose get in the way when you try to look through it? Such basic things as whether you are a right- or left-eye viewer, or whether you wear eyeglasses suddenly become highly significant. What about the lens mount – which bayonet system is employed, and is it back-compatible with any lenses you may already have? How heavy is the camera, and is there a central tripod mount? And crucially, can your fingers negotiate the buttons and dials? Remember that you will sometimes need to be able to work all of this with cold hands, through gloves.

Construction

Generally speaking, the more you pay, the more likely it is that a camera body will be strong and durable, resistant to dust and moisture, and fundamentally suited to the rigors of outdoor work. You will want to be confident that it can withstand the occasional knock, and you can't afford to worry about the odd shower of rain, although hazards like salt spray, blowing sand and prolonged periods of high humidity will always demand extra precautions. The point is, you mustn't be so concerned about protecting your equipment that you never take it out and use it.

Noise is an important consideration. Motordrive, mirror and shutter noise can be disturbing to bird subjects up close, but most birds habituate to moderate sound pretty quickly. Nevertheless, you may as well try to get something as smooth and quiet as possible: a soft, purring camera is so much more reassuring.

Examining the camera a little more closely, look for the essential details such as a depth-of-field preview button. Amazingly, there are still cameras being made that don't offer this basic facility, but it is an essential requirement. There should be a flash hot-shoe, and maybe even a PC (power cord) socket for using independent or older types of flash gun. What about a film cassette window? This simple provision is so useful, letting you check at a glance whether you have film loaded, what type it is and its nominal speed.

Buy the best you can afford, with a good guarantee. I wouldn't advise buying a second-hand camera body other than through an authorized dealer, as they are much too complex to assess at a glance. And remember that manufacturers' guarantees will be invalid if you purchase equipment through unauthorized "gray" importers.

Power supply

Just about every function on a modern SLR camera is electrically powered, with film advance, autofocus and image stabilization being particularly power hungry. All of these energy demands become greater at low temperatures; batteries need to be changed more frequently, and some camera functions may cease altogether in particularly severe cold.

The main choice to be made is between disposable and rechargeable batteries. Disposables are the most convenient. You don't have to have access to a power supply for recharging, and if you can utilize standard sizes, such as AA, you should be able to find these for sale pretty well anywhere in the world. Alkaline AA batteries are the cheapest and most widely available, while lithium cells are 30 percent lighter and last about three times as long, as well as being more reliable in cold weather.

Rechargeable batteries are clearly the greener option. Nickel-cadmium (Ni-Cd) have

David Tipling
Emperor penguins, Weddell Sea, Antarctica

The Antarctic is becoming increasingly accessible to photographers, with a wealth of organized tours to choose from. But to catch the end of the emperor penguin breeding season, David Tipling had to join a special expedition a month or so earlier than usual, before the sea ice broke up. David gives us some tips based on his experience there:

" *During a month-long camping expedition to the Antarctic, I worked in temperatures that varied from just above freezing down to an incredible –55˚C (–67˚F); combined with a strong wind, this made for a formidable wind-chill effect. I was relieved that my Nikon F5 performed admirably throughout, particularly when used with the Ni-MH rechargeable power packs, which I found lasted much longer than lithium batteries. Spare power packs were stored inside my jacket to keep them warm. Other necessary precautions included refraining from breathing over lenses or viewfinders, and not bringing camera equipment into warm tents and vehicles, to prevent condensation becoming a problem. And of course, it was important not to use liquid solutions for cleaning lenses as they would have frozen immediately.*

I also had a Fuji 6 x 17cm panoramic camera with me – a format that seemed to suit the wide-open spaces of this pristine wilderness – and I used this for the photograph you see here. As I was walking across the ice to keep up with the line of penguins, a tripod wouldn't have been practical, so I hand-held the camera with its 90mm lens at $^1/_{60}$ sec. With only four frames per roll of 120 film (I used Fujichrome Velvia exclusively), I had to compose and shoot discerningly as frostbite was a real danger when reloading; you could take your gloves off for a maximum of only 30 seconds at a time, and the brittle film had to be wound on very slowly and carefully. There were no electrical problems with the panoramic camera either, though it has no built-in lightmeter or motordrive and requires only a small alkaline battery to operate the electro-magnetic shutter, and this has a manual back-up facility. This photograph was taken at about 11 o'clock at "night." During the day at the penguin rookery I spot-metered off the gray chicks with my Nikon F5, but for this shot the exposure would have been estimated, based on readings from previous evenings. "

been the commonest type until recently, but the AAs hold less than half the charge of their alkaline equivalent. They should be discharged fully before recharging, otherwise they will not "top up" properly and you'll notice fewer and fewer films going through the camera between battery changes. Nickel metal hydride (Ni-MH) rechargeables are much the better option, as they can pack up to 100 percent more charge than Ni-Cds, perform better in the cold, and can be fully recharged every time without discharging first.

Battery failure is the most common cause of camera malfunction. If you are experiencing a problem with your camera, always try replacing batteries before looking elsewhere. You may need to do this more than once to be sure, as your new set could have one or more duds. The moral is: always carry plenty of spare batteries in your field kit.

Film transport

The long-serving manual lever wind has now pretty well disappeared and been replaced with the power winder or motordrive. So every time you press the shutter, an exposure is made and the film is automatically advanced to the next frame, with the mirror reset and shutter cocked ready for your next exposure. You will probably have a choice of single-frame or continuous-frame film advance, and maybe some variation in speed. In continuous mode, the maximum speed could be as fast as eight or ten frames per second on a standard camera body. Keep the shutter depressed, and a whole 36-exposure film can be gobbled up inside 4 seconds. This might be more useful than you would first imagine. You can wait all day for some interesting bird behavior to occur, only for it to be all over in a couple of seconds. At other times, you can shoot roll after roll of action on the continuous high-speed setting, to discover afterwards that only one or two frames have the bird in just the position you want. Even with static subjects, the continuous high-speed drive is very useful for making "in-camera duplicates," which will be of higher quality and cheaper than second-generation copies derived at a later date. So

take advantage of the faster drives, and regard yor film consumption as an investment.

Automatic film-loading is quite a bonus – you just need to lay the film leader over the take-up spool, close the back, and the film advances to the first frame. Motorized film rewind will also rewind film into its cassette, sometimes automatically after you expose the last frame, and this can gain precious time when reloading. How fast is it, and how quiet? Can you still rewind manually if you want to, to save on battery power or keep noise to a minimum with a sensitive subject? Can you rewind from any point in the film? There may

difference with moving birds.

Viewfinder information displays tell you about your camera settings via a series of LEDs or LCDs. Are you able to read these easily, and is there any information you would like to have that isn't there? For instance, you don't always get a check of the frame number in the viewfinder, or you might not be able to see the exposure compensation selected, both of which I would say are essential requirements. There should also be some method of viewfinder illumination, and you need only to try to use your camera in a dark hide to appreciate the importance of this. Is the light

do I have these?

be a custom function that lets you leave the film leader out of the cassette (useful for partially exposed film you may want to finish another time), but be careful as there is a danger here that you could confuse exposed and unexposed films.

Viewfinder and pentaprism

The pentaprism is the optical array inside the viewfinder, which makes it work, in combination with the reflex mirror, and lets you see just what the lens sees. Or a good proportion of it. Some viewfinders give close to a 100 percent representation of the final exposed frame, some a little less, and both types have their advantages. You will need to know what coverage you have for critical framing of your portraits, though you will rarely have time to think about such a subtle

easily switched on when you need it?

Image brightness is crucial for fast and accurate framing and focusing. For this reason, it used to be important to be able to change the ground-glass focusing screen to give a crisper image when working with long-focus lenses, but most modern cameras now come equipped with clear, bright screens. If you're using an older model that has a split-image or microprism-type focusing screen, it will black out with longer focal length lenses, so do try to exchange it for a plain matte version, ensuring that the replacement will preserve correct metering displays.

Some cameras have an eyepiece shutter (or blind). This is used for eliminating stray light that would otherwise affect exposure when your eye is away from the viewfinder, for example when using a cable release or remote-control

Continuous shooting
Use your motordrive in continuous high-speed mode not only for action sequences (great egret, above) but also to make in-camera duplicates of static but cooperative subjects while you can (eastern meadowlark, below). I was shooting at eight frames per second in both cases.
Camera: Nikon F5

Male capercaillie at lek

Exposure time for this early-morning shot in the forest was $1/8$ sec., even with my 500mm lens wide open at f4, and uprating Fujichrome Sensia 100 film by 1 stop. To overcome camera shake, which would otherwise have resulted at this slow speed, it was necessary to use a cable release and lock up the reflex mirror.

Camera: Nikon F5

apparatus, but it is easy enough to shield it in other ways. Eyeglass wearers will appreciate a viewfinder with built-in diopter correction, and an accessory soft rubber eyepiece.

Reflex mirror

The mirror reflects light from the lens up through the pentaprism, and is flipped out of the way immediately prior to exposure to allow light through the shutter to the film. It has to be reset at the end of the exposure to let you resume viewing. So you can imagine that this has to work pretty fast with motordrives working at up to eight or ten frames per second. Impressive as this is, there is an important down side to mirror vibration (also called "mirror slap"), as it is a major cause of camera shake and consequent nonsharp pictures, particularly at shutter speeds around $1/8$ sec. and $1/15$ sec. Mirror vibration can be overcome through the provision of a mirror lock-up facility, although as a result you lose the ability to see through the viewfinder, so it is only really viable with stationary subjects. You also lose autometering and autofocus functions with the mirror out of commission, so it is a slow and cumbersome operation – but effective. Not many cameras have mirror lock-up. Those that do are sometimes complicated to set, and may not allow multiple exposures with the mirror locked up. Mirror damping is improving all the time, but image-stabilization technology

may well be the long-term answer to this age-old problem, precluding the need for mirror lock-up altogether.

Shutter

The shutter opens to allow light from the lens to expose the film, so that the longer the shutter is open, the more light enters the camera. Doubling or halving the shutter speed is said to increase or decrease the exposure by 1 "stop." Faster shutter speeds "freeze" motion, while slower shutter speeds tend to blur it. These are absolutely fundamental concepts to be grasped, regardless of whether you choose to use automatic or manual exposure modes.

To overcome blur caused by camera shake, most people will need to use a shutter speed of $1/60$ sec. or faster when hand-holding a camera fitted with a standard (50mm) lens. Longer focal length lenses will magnify camera shake as well as image size, so your shutter speed needs to be faster. The rule of thumb for hand-holding is that your shutter speed should not fall below the reciprocal of the lens focal length in millimeters ($1/200$ sec. with a 200mm lens, $1/500$ sec. with a 500mm lens and so on). You can get better at hand-holding with practice. If you are using a tripod, you can afford to shoot slower with the same lens, and slower still with a cable release – $1/125$ sec. for a 500mm lens ought to be sufficient, but again you can improve this with care and practice. Much depends on the sturdiness of your tripod.

Overcoming blur caused by subject movement depends on how fast the subject is moving. A preening bird might well be arrested on film at $1/125$ sec., but to render the wing tips sharp and all the feathers well defined on a fast-flying songbird might easily need $1/2,000$ sec. Usually I would try for a shutter speed of at least $1/250$ sec. to feel confident if there is the slightest subject movement, and for larger birds in flight I would hope for about $1/1,000$ sec. Of course, blurs in the right places can be a good thing, adding to the impression of movement in a photograph. In practice, there often isn't sufficient light to allow shutter speeds faster than $1/2,000$ sec. and flash is

employed instead, and in this circumstance the flash duration is the determining factor rather than the shutter speed.

The most useful range of shutter speeds to a bird photographer is something like $1/8$ sec. to $1/2,000$ sec. Most cameras now offer at least this range, with a B setting as well (when the shutter stays open for as long as the button remains depressed). *Do I have?*

Potentially more important is the fine control you are able to exercise over shutter speeds within the range. Until quite recently, the shutter speed series used to go up in whole stops: $1/60$ sec., $1/125$ sec., $1/250$ sec. and so on. Now many cameras allow $1/2$ or $1/3$ of a stop increments. This is of great significance when you are shooting "wide open" (with the aperture as open as possible) and trying to get the fastest possible shutter speed; changing from $1/1,000$ sec. at f4 to $1/800$ sec. at f4 is so much more useful than having to suddenly switch to $1/500$ sec. Find out whether you have the option of selecting shutter speeds by a $1/2$ or $1/3$ of a stop. It is easier to think in $1/3$-stop

steps, since film speeds are also described in a $1/3$-stop series (25, 32, 40, 50, 64, 80, 100, 125, 160, 200, 250, 320, 400, 500, 640, 800, 1000 and so on).

The shutter-release button itself is usually thoughtfully located right where your index finger wants to go (if you are right-handed). Sometimes you get an extra button on the side to facilitate shooting in the upright position – this should have a lock to prevent accidental firing. In addition to the shutter-release buttons, it is vital that you are able to trigger the camera shutter via a cable release to reduce camera shake. Almost certainly the cable release will be an electrical device, but some cameras also have a socket for the older mechanical type. Frankly, although they're more expensive, the electrical ones are more reliable as well as being more versatile in that they lend themselves better to remote triggering devices.

Advances in shutter design have also allowed the normal flash synchronization speed to increase from $1/60$ sec. to $1/250$ sec.

Roseate spoonbill preening
The most usual cause of blurred photographs is camera shake. With a telephoto fitted, you should be looking for shutter speeds of at least $1/250$ sec. to avoid this hazard and allow for moderate subject movement (such as a bird preening or walking slowly). As light was not a limiting factor here, I opted for $1/500$ sec. to be sure. Naturally the lens was mounted on a tripod.
Camera: *Nikon F5*
Lens: *300mm f2.8 plus 2x teleconverter*
Film: *Fujichrome Sensia 100*
Exposure: *$1/500$ sec. at f8*

This is welcome because it gives more flexibility when photographing with daylight-balanced fill flash, and minimizes ghosting effects (where two images are recorded on the film from the respective, simultaneous daylight and flash exposures).

bird
I think

Moorhen among reedmace

Multi-segment "matrix" metering has successfully calculated this exposure, because there is an even balance of light and dark tones throughout the scene. Selecting a center-weighted pattern might well have resulted in overexposure because it would have been biased to the central, dark subject.

ch.

Camera: *Nikon F5*
Lens: *500mm f4*
Film: *Fujichrome Sensia 100*

metering by center of shot

Metering system

The range of through-the-lens (TTL) light-metering modes on a modern camera is perhaps the most bewildering aspect to a novice. First, there is usually a choice of metering pattern: where on the film format you want the meter actually to measure the light. Then you will have a choice of various automatic and program modes to set exposure, with a given metering pattern, in any permutation. Somewhere among all this there needs to be a good, old-fashioned manual setting – you may not think so at first, but this will be vital to your success in accurately and consistently determining exposure.

To deal with metering pattern first: the time-honored method of measuring light in the camera is the **center-weighted pattern**, which as the name implies gives most emphasis to the area in the center of your view, predicting that this is where your subject is likely to be. Typically, about 75 percent of the meter's sensitivity is assigned to a 12mm (^{1}/2in) diameter center circle, with about 25 percent outside the circle. Some center-

weighted systems are further biased to the lower part of the frame, in an effort to exclude the influence of bright sky. This is a useful and reliable workaday system, but will be fooled by "nonstandard" lighting situations such as strong backlight, for example.

A more sophisticated version of this is the **multi-segmented metering pattern** (Canon's "evaluative" metering, Nikon's "matrix" metering), where a large number of light sensors simultaneously measure light across the whole scene and interpret the results through a set of preprogrammed algorithms, to deliver a "smart" exposure value prediction. Multi-segmented metering will try to take account of more complex lighting situations, and what it is you're trying to do, with varying success. These multi-segmented patterns are probably accurate more often than the center-weighted system, but they are certainly not infallible. And they will work only with the designated lenses, which possess a built-in electronic chip to process the information and set the correct lens aperture.

Often, you will see the same light reading with both center-weighted and multi-segment metering, but there can be significant variations – try metering a scene with a bright sky filling exactly half of the picture to see an immediate difference between the two. Good advice would be to get used to using one or other of the center-weighted or matrix metering patterns, and keep it as your default; constantly switching between the two is bound to confuse matters.

Spot metering is a very precise method of light measurement, particularly when used in conjunction with telephoto lenses. The sensitive cone is especially narrow, so the active spot might be as little as 1.5 percent to 2.5 percent of the frame area. You can see the light reading fluctuate dramatically as you track the lens across a scene in this setting. Spot metering can be very useful in bird photography, but meter readings must be interpreted and applied intelligently. It is therefore a bit slower to use in practice, requiring more thought as well as cooperative subjects. The better spot-metering systems sensibly allow the metering spot to coincide with the active autofocus area.

Partial metering is a system exclusive to Canon, and is an expanded version of spot metering with a sensitive central spot of about 8.5 percent of the frame area.

Program-metering modes (usually designated P, sometimes mysteriously "green rectangle") are superficially attractive, inviting you to abdicate all responsibility for metering decisions. Both shutter speed and lens aperture are selected on your behalf. Variations within the program mode can tip the emphasis in favor of a faster shutter speed or a smaller aperture; but none of these program settings give you anywhere near enough control. Spurn them – not that you'll be able to buy a new camera without them fitted.

Automatic metering is commonly separated into aperture priority and shutter-speed priority modes. The former allows you to select your preferred lens aperture and automatically sets the shutter speed according to the current meter reading. The latter lets you choose your preferred shutter speed and automatically sets the appropriate aperture. Aperture priority automatic is the most useful in bird photography, as you so often want to select the widest aperture to obtain the fastest available shutter speed. An automatic exposure lock (AE lock) is normally provided so that you can maintain an exposure setting when recomposing. For instance, you can lock in a light reading off the ground to then photograph a bird in flight overhead, in order to prevent the meter being fooled by a bright sky background.

Finally, the **manual-metering** mode, while being the simplest and most straightforward, is absolutely indispensable. Make sure you have it. In manual, you set both lens aperture and shutter speed by reference to the lightmeter reading. It is best to have a clear analog scale to read from, so you can instantly see both the lightmeter reading and your selected setting, and how they relate to one another. The lightmetering scale is deficient, in my opinion, if you can't see at least 2 full stops either side of the median. As with shutter-speed settings, it is distinctly advantageous to be able to read and set $1/2$ a stop, or better still $1/3$ of a stop,

aperture values.

An **exposure-compensation dial** is a vital facility; it is used in conjunction with the automatic metering mode to make subtle but important adjustments to the automatically selected exposure. You should be able to add or subtract light relative to the automatic

exposure setting, using your experience and judgment, up to about 2 stops either side of the median. Again, this should be broken down in $1/2$-stop or $1/3$-stop increments.

Film speed setting has an important bearing on metering methods. The DX facility automatically selects the film speed on the camera by reading a pattern on the film cassette. It is best if you have a full manual override to the DX setting, so that you have more flexibility when "pushing" films, for example; setting the film speed manually leaves your exposure compensation dial free for its more usual purpose. In any case, I have known the DX facility to be unreliable and occasionally register spurious film speeds with consequent bad exposures.

Automatic daylight-balanced fill flash is one of the great brain-saving features of modern metering systems, in combination with intelligent, electronic flash. Camera, lens and flash communicate with each other, and the camera's CPU (central processing unit, or computer chip) balances measured ambient

Skylark in evening light
No automatic metering system would be able to interpret this scene and expose correctly as shown, without some intervention by the photographer. The dark background would be too strong an influence. For this reason, you need to have an exposure-compensation dial to override the automatic exposure or, better still, a manual-metering mode with spot-metering capability.
Camera: Nikon F5
Lens: 500mm f4 plus 1.4x teleconverter
Film: Fujichrome Sensia 100 uprated to EI200

Adult red kite

*Autofocus is of great benefit in
action and flight photography,
and the better modern cameras
allow for off-center subject
placement. The Nikon F5 used
here has five active AF brackets
arranged in a diagonal cross,
while the Canon EOS3 and
EOS1V have up to 45 selectable
AF points.*

Lens: AF-S Nikkor 500mm f4

*Film: Fujichrome Sensia 100
uprated to EI200*

Exposure: $^1/_{1,250}$ sec. at f4

light with an automatically selected flash
setting to deliver perfect fill flash exposures.
Photographs have a natural light appearance
with the flash barely noticeable, but all the
shadow detail is now miraculously illuminated
while preserving its tonal value.

Another modern refinement is
autoexposure bracketing, whereby
"bracketed" exposure values above and below
the average meter reading are automatically
selected, allowing you to hedge your bets.
Custom functions normally let you select the
number, order and size of bracketed
exposures. This is probably of limited value in
bird photography, but if you think you might
take advantage of it, investigate whether AEB
is available with all film advance settings.

Autofocus systems

To take advantage of autofocus (AF) lenses,
you must have an autofocus-capable camera.
That will include almost all cameras on the
market today, although autofocus systems vary

in speed and sophistication. Look for a system
that offers predictive AF or focus tracking,
designed to keep pace with a moving subject
and predict precisely where it will be when the
exposure is made. This is a tremendous asset
for photographing birds in flight, especially in
combination with a fast motordrive, although
it has to be said that such systems are fallible,
and all will struggle with a fast-flying bird
moving directly towards the camera. So far.

Canon have certainly been the pace-
setters in autofocus technology, having
developed the first really fast and reliable
system, although the other makes now seem
to have caught up. Before the Nikon AF-S (or
"silent wave") lenses were available, I had
never been persuaded of the advantages of
AF. It simply wasn't good enough to be worth
the extra expense. But I was appreciative of
the AF functions of the Nikon F4, and
subsequent models, which gave me a focus
confirmation light in the viewfinder even with
my manual focus lenses. This is very useful

when your eyes are tired during a long hide session, or when using extremely long focal lengths with the depth of field so narrow and critical. So it's still very useful when using newer AF lenses in manual mode. It even tells you in which direction to focus – good news for all the over-40s.

There are generally single servo (one-shot) and continuous servo (AI servo) AF modes, so you can elect for the shutter to fire only when there is a positive focus check (single servo), or to allow continuous firing even if the AF is still hunting (continuous servo). Both of these will be valuable at different times and with different kinds of subject.

Earlier autofocus cameras had only a single, central, active area for autofocusing. This hardly lent itself to creative composition. Then came selectable AF areas, permitting off-center subject placement. The Canon EOS3 and EOS1V now offer a staggering 45 AF areas grouped in an ellipse, although you can opt for fewer to improve selection speed. With systems that offer multiple AF areas, you may have the option of dynamic AF, and this is well worth having. Dynamic AF detects a moving subject and automatically selects the appropriate AF bracket or cross-hair, so this does expand your possibilities considerably. Use dynamic AF in combination with focus tracking in continuous servo mode, and you really do have a powerful system. Sometimes, selecting a slightly slower motordrive speed (say, six frames per second instead of eight frames per second) helps to keep it keen and effective.

The Canon EOS3 and EOS5 cameras even incorporate advanced eye-controlled autofocus where the camera can detect what you are looking at and focus on it automatically; an awesome prospect, but not always fully effective in field situations. It does give us some indication of where things are going, however, and how further exciting advances can be expected within the realm of autofocus; see also p. 32.

LENSES

Having selected a camera body, you will need to think about a lens or two to go with it. Ultimately, you will probably want a range of lenses to do different jobs, but don't be disheartened if you can't afford a full set of glassware in the beginning. It is the lens more than anything that will determine the final quality of the photograph, so have fewer better quality lenses rather than many cheap ones, and plan to build your system over time.

How lenses work

Lenses focus reflected light from an object on to the film plane in the camera. In simple terms, the distance between the lens and the focused image (on the film) is called the focal length of the lens. In practice, camera lenses are made up of several lens elements so they don't have to be physically as long as their nominal focal length. Lenses of longer focal lengths (telephoto) magnify the image, while lenses of shorter focal lengths (wide-angle) make things appear further away. It follows that the angle of view of a lens decreases as focal length increases, and this has an impact on perspective. So with telephotos you have a foreshortening effect and a flatter, more two-dimensional looking subject, while wide-angle lenses tend to extend perspective and distort the shape of objects close to. These characteristics influence our choice of lens, and how we use them.

Approximate picture-taking angle of different lenses:

Lens focal length	Angle
20mm	94 degrees
28mm	74 degrees
50mm	45 degrees
135mm	18 degrees
300mm	8 degrees
500mm	5 degrees

The iris diaphragm in a camera lens controls its aperture or opening, and thereby the amount of light reaching the film (in combination with the camera shutter). These apertures are described by a number called an f-stop or f-value, with the larger apertures having a smaller f-value. The f-stop progression on lenses follows a conventional sequence: 1.4, 2, 2.8, 4, 5.6, 8, 11, 16, 22, 32. Moving up or down between adjacent f-stops in this series either halves or doubles the amount of light entering the camera. Hence we refer to a decrease or increase of 1 stop, 2 stops, and so forth. You will remember that the shutter-speed scale on the camera also follows this doubling and halving formula, so that an exposure of $1/125$ sec. at f8 allows exactly the same amount of light to the film as an exposure of $1/250$ sec. at f5.6, $1/500$ sec. at f4, $1/60$ sec. at f11, or $1/30$ sec. at f16.

Changing aperture also has an effect on the depth of field (the amount of the final image that is in focus). Photographs taken at smaller apertures (higher f-values) exhibit a greater depth of field, and vice versa. This means that with the same lens and subject distance, more of the scene will be in focus from front to back with an aperture of f16 than at f11 or f8. This effect can be viewed by pressing the depth-of-field preview button on the camera (or lens), which operates the diaphragm, at various apertures, but of course the image will also be dimmer at smaller apertures so the effect can be hard to see. Many lenses have f-values inscribed on the barrel next to the focusing scale, and reference to these lets you work out depth of field more accurately. Note that depth of field extends further beyond the point of focus than in front of it, and this has relevance for critical focusing, not least when using long telephotos at wider apertures. A 50mm lens focused to 3m (10ft) shows that at f11 the depth of field extends from just over 2m (7ft) to 5m (16ft), not 2m (7ft) to 4m (13ft) as you might have expected. Actually, it is the reproduction ratio of the image that determines depth of field rather than lens focal length, so a bird imaged at 1:10 on the film ($1/10$ life size) at an aperture of f8, say, will have the same depth of field whether photographed with a distant 500mm or a closer 50mm lens. It is the angle of view and the distance between lens and subject that change. But in practice we think of longer focal length lenses as having a smaller depth of field because of the way we use them.

Lenses are normally defined by their focal length followed by their maximum aperture, thus 50mm f1.8, 400mm f5.6, and so on.

Types of lenses

With a 35mm format camera, the "standard" lens is considered to be a lens of approximately 50mm focal length. This is roughly similar to the diagonal measurement of the 24 x 36mm film frame, and gives a more or less normal angle of view and perspective, most similar to our everyday perception of the world. However, you would have to be standing very close to a bird to obtain a reasonable image size on the film. Standard lenses are not terribly useful in bird photography therefore, but they are relatively easy to manufacture and produce in bulk, so they are cheap and you may as well have one. They have the highest maximum aperture of all lenses, typically f1.8 or f1.4.

Wide-angle lenses are of shorter focal length than standard lenses (anything less than about 35mm is usually termed wide-angle), have a wider field of view, and record smaller image sizes than a standard lens with the same camera-to-subject distance. They can be used to exaggerate perspective and maximize depth of field in a scene, making them particularly effective for landscape and habitat photography. So although they may not often be suitable for taking bird portraits, they do have particular characteristics that can be exploited from time to time, for example with remote-control bird photography. Since they are quite small and compact, and not too expensive, you would be well advised to have one in your kit. Probably a 24mm or 28mm would be the optimum if you were to buy only one wide-angle.

Now to the main tool. Telephoto lenses have a much longer effective focal length than standard lenses and record a larger image size on the film at the same camera-to-subject distance. In other words, they appear to magnify the scene by a factor equal to the multiple in focal length of the standard 50mm; so that a 300mm lens magnifies about six times, a 400mm about eight times, and so forth. This is beginning to sound more useful, isn't it?

You will certainly need a lens in the telephoto range to be able to undertake any kind of serious bird photography. However, there seems to be a common misconception that all you need is a long telephoto lens, and suddenly you will be able to photograph a wren at the bottom of the garden or a golden eagle on a distant mountain perch. Unfortunately, the reality is somewhat different. You will probably be surprised at just how much work you still have to put in to get close enough to your subject. As the focal length increases, the weight and cost of lenses go up exponentially, and all sorts of other technical difficulties come into play. More light is required to work with the smaller maximum apertures, camera shake becomes a bigger problem than ever, and the depth of field is restrictively narrow. Telephotos of 600mm or longer really do take a bit of experience to be able to use successfully. My own favorite lens is a 500mm f4, which is still quite a weight (3.8kg/8lb) but it fits comfortably in my backpack and is

nothing like so monstrous as the 600mm f4 (5.9kg/13lb), so I'm not too discouraged from lugging it around and using it. Sacrificing 1 stop on the maximum aperture would save you a few thousand pounds and a couple of kilos! I would recommend starting with a telephoto of 400mm f5.6 or perhaps a 500mm as a practical compromise. If you can afford it, by all means go for one of the super telephotos of the type you see at sports events the world over, and you won't be disappointed.

Size, weight and cost are obviously key concerns when purchasing a telephoto. Other considerations will be: closest focusing distance, maximum aperture (or "speed"), and not least, the type of glass used in construction. This may sound unnecessarily technical, but there are great advantages to be gained in picture definition by going for better quality glass. This is because different wavelengths of light refract by different amounts as they pass each glass/air interface in the lens, so they come to focus at slightly

Atlantic puffin at breeding island

Not too many bird subjects allow such a close approach, but the use of a wide-angle lens in these situations can have quite an impact, allowing you to show both the bird and its habitat in focus.
Camera: *Nikon F5*
Lens: *20mm f2.8*
Film: *Fujichrome Sensia 100*
Exposure: *1/60 sec. at f16*

29

different positions at the film plane with a resulting loss of sharpness. Such refraction is more pronounced with lenses of greater focal length, but the effect can be minimized by using low-dispersion glass. Such lenses are said to be apochromatic and are variously described as APO, LD, L, ED, fluorite – all meaning basically the same thing. They are of course more expensive than lenses with "ordinary" glass, but well worth buying if your budget allows.

Telephotos are optimized in their design to work well at wider apertures. This is just as well, because you probably won't often use one at anything other than its widest setting, or perhaps 1 or 2 stops down. The virtue of this is in enabling you to work at the fastest possible shutter speed, minimizing camera shake and subject motion blur. So there is a lot to be gained from having a "faster" lens with a wider maximum aperture. You will also get a brighter, clearer image in the viewfinder, and faster, more positive focus acquisition (whether manual or autofocus). Another feature of working with wide apertures at long focal lengths is the narrow depth of field, and this can be used to your advantage to make clean, unfussy, out-of-focus backgrounds complement sharply focused subjects. There's no special trick to this, other than being alert to the distance between subject and background, and being prepared to move your camera position a little. But remember, to obtain an extra stop on the maximum aperture of a telephoto means a lot of extra glass and consequently a proportionally heavier, more expensive lens.

Minimum focusing distance varies quite a lot between different makes of lens. Typically, a 300mm lens will focus down to about 2.5m (8ft), and a 500mm down to about 5m (16ft), but you can find better and worse. You're probably thinking that you'd never need to be closer than that to any bird, and chance would be a fine thing. However, a tiny bird like a goldcrest (or kinglet) still only occupies about a quarter of the frame width viewed side on with a 500mm lens at 5m (16ft), so there are times you might wish to be closer. And you might be interested in photographing butterflies as well as birds. So pay close

attention to minimum focusing distance before purchasing, and I would say it should be no more than ten times the focal length of the lens (5m with a 500mm, 6m with a 600mm, and so on). Closer focusing can be achieved by other methods, however (see Teleconverters pp. 33–34, and Extension tubes, p. 34).

As well as the weight, also check the balance of a telephoto lens when mounted on your camera body, and whether you can easily hand-hold it for flight shots. Make sure that there is a tripod mount on the lens itself, which should be solid, substantial and attached to a rotating collar. How does the lens fit on your tripod head, and is there room for it in your backpack or holdall? Faster lenses should have a drop-in filter drawer to save you buying enormous, impractical and expensive screw-in filters for the front element, and it's even better if these are a standard size, allowing you to redeploy screw-in filters from your shorter lenses. Lens hoods are necessary for preventing flare on your photographs, especially when shooting into the light. Some seem to be unnecessarily long and cumbersome, but may be retractable or removable.

Zoom lenses are those that have a variable focal length, say from 28–80mm or 70–210mm. The change in focal length is achieved either with a push-pull operation of the lens barrel, or a twisting action. With push-pull types, ensure that the zoom mechanism is tight enough to prevent accidental zooming when pointing the lens up or down. With rotating zoom mechanisms, check whether you can cover the whole range of focal lengths without changing hand position.

There are clear attractions to having zoom lenses, not least the convenience of being able to use the zoom facility to quickly frame your subject without having to change camera position. You can also cut down on the number of lenses you need in your outfit and there are obvious benefits for traveling, reducing overall bulk and weight. A mid-range zoom, such as a 28–80mm or thereabouts is a popular alternative to a standard lens, though you'd expect to pay a bit more. Telephoto zooms are particularly advantageous to bird photographers, as you are more flexible when

Hannu Hautala
Whooper swans in flight, Kuusamo, Finland

Hannu Hautala is a master of the slow shutter speed action shot, which characterizes much of his work. He explains how he achieves this special mood in his flight study of two whooper swans:

❝*This photograph was taken from a hide situated on top of a birdwatching tower. The hide is built specially for photographing birds in flight, and the upper part of the hide,*

where the camera is fixed, turns around 360 degrees quite freely with the help of a ball bearing, so it is easier to follow flying birds with a long lens.

In the picture two whooper swans are fighting over nesting territory. The stronger bird drives away the other. I was using a Canon EOS 3 camera and a very long focal length of 1,200mm, by attaching a 2x teleconverter to my 600mm f4L IS-USM lens. The photograph was taken in evening light with the lens at its widest aperture (now f8), using a shutter speed between ^{1}/10 sec. and ^{1}/20 sec. on automatic exposure. Autofocus and the image stabilizer were very important in trying to get a good shot. **❞**

encountering different-sized subjects at different distances than with a prime (fixed-focal length) lens. They can really come into their own when working at close quarters from a hide, as to change a prime lens would almost certainly disturb the bird. Again, check for the presence of a tripod mount on the lens.

This convenience and versatility does carry penalties, however. The construction of zoom lenses calls for the use of more glass elements, and more elements mean that definition is compromised and there is a greater risk of lens flare. Zooms are also prone to optical

aberrations at their extreme focal lengths: "barrel distortion" at the short end (straight lines become convex), and "pincushion distortion" at the long end (straight lines become concave). But the quality of zoom lenses is improving all the time – a good zoom with low-dispersion glass can have better definition than a prime lens without it. Edge-to-edge sharpness can be a problem with cheaper zooms, and any deficiencies will be most noticeable at the widest apertures. Similarly, "vignetting" can occur at the wider apertures, giving darker corners to your pictures.

The main disadvantage to bird photographers is that the maximum aperture of a zoom will almost certainly be smaller than that of a prime lens in the range. In addition, it will probably vary according to focal length (known as "floating" aperture) so you might find it is described as f4.5–5.6 or similar, where the wider aperture will only be available at the shorter focal lengths. You pay more to get a fixed aperture across the whole zoom range, and this generally means sacrificing something on the zoom ratio too, for example with an 80–200mm f2.8.

Good signs in zoom lenses are a fixed maximum aperture and a low-dispersion glass designation. Pound for pound, the equivalent prime lens will still give you better quality pictures at a given focal length.

Macro lenses focus closer than other lenses, and are designed to work best at higher reproduction ratios – usually up to a ratio of 1:2 (subject imaged at $^1/_2$ life size on the film), sometimes 1:1 (life size) or greater, though this may require the addition of an extension tube. Typical focal lengths for macros are 50mm, 100mm and 200mm, where the longer the focal length the greater the working distance for a given image size. Macro lenses are by no means essential for bird photography, but are useful for close-ups.

Autofocus lenses

Autofocus is now pretty well universal. With shorter lenses, the autofocus function can be driven by a motor in the camera, but with telephotos it is better to have a coreless motor built into the lens, which will give much faster and quieter operation, with less of that tiresome hunting as the lens tries to find and lock on to a subject. Look for "ultrasonic motor" (USM), "hypersonic motor" (HSM) or "silent wave" (AFS) in the lens specification, to stand any real chance of being able to autofocus on a fast-moving bird.

Focus range limiters can assist the speed of autofocus, by setting near and far points for the lens to search. If you are working with a large subject like a heron or bird of prey, you can probably safely restrict the lens to a "10m

to infinity" AF range setting. If on the other hand you are focused on a drinking pond close to a hide, you would be better off selecting "5m to 12m" or similar.

AF works on image contrast. It is therefore still difficult to get snappy autofocus (or any autofocus at all) with low contrast scenes. A gull against a featureless, white cloudy sky, for instance, will cause any system to struggle. This is just one of several reasons why you might find it preferable to switch to manual focus. You might just want complete freedom to frame your subject without being confined to designated AF areas. So be sure that you have a complete manual override with easy switching between the two. Operate the lens in its manual mode and see how smoothly and positively it will focus – but don't ever do this while the lens is still in its autofocus setting as you could damage the AF motor. Some lenses have a dual M/A setting, which will allow for both, and the moment you press the shutter-release button, autofocus is reasserted.

With an AF telephoto it is useful if there are focus lock buttons towards the front of the lens – the natural left-hand position for many people when using long lenses – as well as on the camera. Usually there will be four positioned around the lens barrel so you don't have to search too hard for one.

It's worth pointing out that the clamor for these super new autofocus telephotos has led to some great second-hand bargains among the manual and older AF telephotos. Optically these are every bit as good as their modern counterparts, and are well worth considering, especially if you're just wanting to dip your toe in the water.

Image-stabilized lenses

Essentially, image stabilization detects and reduces pitching and yawing movements in a lens, enabling you to obtain sharp pictures at slower shutter speeds than normal, perhaps by as much as 2 or 3 stops. It might mean you can do without a tripod altogether for certain shots, or make do with a smaller maximum aperture lens, or use a slower film. The attractions are obvious, and not surprisingly such lenses have been greeted with much enthusiasm. The Canon 100–400mm f4.5–5.6 IS zoom is particularly popular, with a Nikon 80–400mm VR (vibration reduction) hot on its heels. For many people this might be the only big lens they ever need – great for trips overseas, great for hand-held flight shots.

IS technology is now being incorporated in a wider range of lenses, particularly the telephotos as you would expect, and looks like an exciting step forward for both bird and wildlife photography. But do remember that IS and VR lenses won't have any effect at all on blurring caused by subject movement!

Teleconverters

A teleconverter (or tele-extender) is a small, accessory lens that fits at the back of the main lens (usually a telephoto), increasing its effective focal length typically by a factor of 1.4x or 2x.

The relative effects of teleconverters
This curlew was photographed at long range from a car window, first with a 1.4x teleconverter (top), then a 2x teleconverter (bottom) fitted to my 500mm lens. The step from 700mm to 1,000mm effective focal length shows a significant improvement in bird image size. I used a beanbag to support the lens and the fastest shutter speed available.
Camera: Nikon F5
Lens: AF-S Nikkor 500mm f4 with TC14-E and TC20-E teleconverters
Film: Fujichrome Sensia 100 uprated to EI200.
Exposure: $^1/_{400}$ sec. at f8

There is a corresponding loss of light of 1 stop and 2 stops, respectively. So fitting a 1.4x teleconverter to a 300mm f2.8 lens would give you a 420mm f4 lens, in effect, while a 2x converter would make it a 600mm f5.6.

Teleconverters are a very neat and effective way of extending the capabilities of your main lens. They are certainly a cheaper solution than buying a whole suite of telephotos, and of course you save on weight and bulk. If you are working from a hide, teleconverters give you the ability to add to your focal length without removing your main lens from the tripod, although this is clearly a bit slower than using a zoom in the first place. There is some loss of definition, but this is barely noticeable with matched converters for a defined range of lenses. In this respect, a 1.4x would be a better bet than a 2x. Using a 2x teleconverter on a zoom would perhaps be asking for trouble, but even this is becoming more accepted practice.

It's worth remembering that a teleconverter does not affect the minimum focusing distance of the prime lens to which it is applied, so this brings an additional benefit. Your 300mm f2.8 can be a 600mm f5.6 which focuses down to 2.5m (8ft), with the addition of a 2x converter, instead of the usual 6m (26ft). Indeed, judicious use of teleconverters might influence your choice of telephotos, particularly if you aim to have more than one. A pairing of 300mm and 500mm telephotos for example, with the two teleconverters, can give you a range of 300, 420, 500, 600, 700 and 1,000mm focal lengths, and some useful close-focusing options. This is clearly more versatile than a 300mm and 600mm telephoto pairing.

Ideally, the corrected aperture reading should be displayed in your viewfinder when a teleconverter is fitted. A 300mm lens with a 2x teleconverter set at f4 on the lens will actually have an effective aperture of f8 so it is best to be reminded of this, but TTL metering will expose correctly in any case.

Ensure that your autofocus (and image-stabilization) functions are preserved when adding a teleconverter to a particular lens. Of course, you must use an appropriate AF converter, but even then AF functions can be lost at apertures smaller than f5.6 with some systems. And even if it works, autofocus will slow down as focal length increases and maximum aperture decreases. At focal lengths of 1,000mm or 1,200mm, you shouldn't expect too much of your AF.

Some adventurous photographers even stack their teleconverters on occasions to deliver monster focal lengths in excess of 1,200mm. It has to be said that this is hardly recommended as normal practice, but I have seen some astonishingly good results right up to 2,400mm, and they stand testimony to the tremendous advances in lens design. Nevertheless, expect to waste a few frames trying to get a sharp shot. When stacking converters, attach the 1.4x converter to the camera body first. Canon users must insert a 12mm extension tube between their teleconverters, while Nikon users have to have a slight alteration made to the teleconverter mounts, by filing off a small metal lug – not a service offered or officially approved by Nikon, but you can find reputable service centers who will do the job. This amendment also permits you to use AF teleconverters with your older Nikon lenses, albeit in manual focus.

Extension tubes

An extension tube (or extension ring) fits between camera and lens, but unlike a teleconverter does not have any lens elements of its own. Its effect is to reduce the minimum focusing distance of the lens, but you lose the ability to focus at infinity. Most camera systems have several sizes of extension tube, with a progressive effect on focusing range. As the tube gets longer you can focus closer, but you also lose more light. TTL metering will allow for this small amount of light loss, and an "automatic" extension tube lets the camera continue to operate the lens diaphragm through exposure. However, not all extension tubes preserve autofocus and full lens communication.

Ensure that extension tubes are compatible with the lenses you are using – some older models can damage the CPU contacts of newer AF lenses. Independent makes of tubes may be cheaper, but are more likely to cause vignetting.

FILTERS

There are not many filters that are practical for use in bird photography. Generally speaking you don't have time to fit one, or at least it's not top of your priorities. You would be well advised to fit a skylight or UV filter to the front of all your lenses, however, if only for protecting the front element; these cut out some of the blue end of the spectrum, with a skylight being ever so slightly "warmer" than a UV. Neither affects exposure. A "warming" or straw-colored filter, such as an 81A or stronger 81B, can be useful for photographing in shade or counteracting the blue light of dusk, and you lose only $1/3$ of a stop with these. This is the only extra filter I would normally carry. At a push, a polarizing filter might come in handy for cutting out glare, but the loss of up to 2 stops is usually too much of a disadvantage. Anyway, as object lenses and filter thread

The effect of a warming filter
This golden eagle eyrie was in shade for much of the day, so I decided to use an 81A warming filter to counteract some of the blueness that I knew would result on film, at the expense of $1/3$ of a stop. The top picture shows the scene with a standard skylight filter, while the bottom picture benefits from the 81A warming filter.
Camera: Nikon F5
Lens: 500mm plus 1.4x teleconverter
Film: Fujichrome Sensia 100

gauges get larger, polarizing filters become prohibitively expensive, especially if you're going to use them only very occasionally.

With the faster telephotos, a drop-in filter drawer in the narrower part of the lens allows you to use smaller, cheaper and more manageable filters. Your UV or skylight filter would normally be fitted at this position as standard, with a protective clear glass at the big end of the lens.

TRIPODS AND SUPPORTS

A sturdy tripod is an absolutely essential accessory (image stabilization notwithstanding), and generally speaking the heavier the better. You need the inertia of a solid mass to keep everything still and stable to combat camera shake. Most tripods are metal alloy, but carbon fiber is becoming increasingly popular. This does seem to afford strength and stability at relatively low weight, for a price, but there is a great temptation to go too light – I often see photographers with enormous heavy lenses on the flimsiest looking carbon-fiber tripods, which does seem a waste of time and money. If you can't afford the heavier, higher gauge carbon-fiber models, persist with a metal one.

The conventional tripod design is the equilateral triangle type, and this is quite sensible for everyday use and the least likely to blow or topple over. The Benbo or Unilock type is rather more versatile. A single locking bolt allows you to set up in some awkward spots, low down if you wish, in shallow sea

water if necessary, and can be arranged in a way that leaves room for your own legs when used in a hide. So there is much to commend this design, but the smaller sizes are really too light and flimsy for use with large telephotos, especially when the column is extended; its off-center positioning gives an unbalanced feel to the system.

Center columns are a bit of a liability altogether, usually preventing you from getting down low to the ground, and introducing unwelcome wobble when extended. You ideally want a tripod that will let you use your camera comfortably in the standing position, without the need for a center column. If your tripod does have a center column, adjusting camera position is a lot quicker and easier, but try to leave it down when working with your longer lenses.

Maximum working height and size when folded are important things to look at when selecting a tripod. With more leg sections, there is a greater risk of vibration creeping in, but it will be more compact when folded. Twist grips and locking screws on the legs are slower than latches, but more dependable.

Tripod heads

A tripod on its own is useless without a head. There are several basic designs of tripod head, and all come with their various advantages

Using a tripod
Ideally, you should be able to use a tripod comfortably in both the standing and prone positions. The Gitzo G1548 carbon-fiber tripod is shown in use at near maximum working height (right, and at minimum working height (below).

and disadvantages – you can't seem to get one type that suits every eventuality. Those that give great maneuverability don't support larger, heavier lenses so well, and those that have a generous platform and handle for your big telephoto just can't achieve all the positions you need with a shorter lens. It is very much a matter of personal preference.

Three-way pan-and-tilt heads are the most widely available kind of tripod head, and suitable for most types of work. Three locking screws or handles enable head movement in each of the three axes, and there is usually a larger panning handle at the back, which helps you to counterbalance the weight of a long lens. Actually, this handle might just as likely lock and unlock the tilt action, but it also helps to pan the lens from side to side – very useful and reliable for longer lenses. I have a trusted old Gitzo Rationelle #5 low-profile head of this type, and like it for its solidity and its large, secure base with the possibility of two lens fixing points. But the large base and handle are a curse as well as a blessing; they restrict the upwards elevation, and when using a shorter lens without a tripod mount (and the camera body attached to the tripod head), it is difficult to use in the upright shooting position. Gitzo and Manfrotto (Bogen) make a wide selection of pan-and-tilt heads.

Fluid heads are a refinement of the pan-and-tilt type, principally designed for use with film cameras and video camcorders. True fluid heads use a hydraulic oil to dampen movements, so they are especially suitable for the smooth pans required when filming, and you can "dial in" the amount of resistance you want. This is also appreciated by many stills photographers, not least because it prevents sudden and dangerous movements with valuable long telephotos. Fluid effect tripod heads mimic this kind of action through clever use of springs, making them lighter as well as cheaper. Both types will be "two-way" heads, meaning you have to level your horizon or change to vertical format by use of the tripod collar on the lens. For this reason, this type of head is appropriate only for longer focal length lenses. Miller and Sachtler are well-known manufacturers of fluid heads, while

Manfrotto (Bogen) and Gitzo offer good fluid-effect alternatives. Fluid heads tend to be heavy and expensive.

Ball-and-socket heads have become very popular in recent years. The large monoballs can cover more angles than any other type of head, offer more camera positions, and lock down with a single action, making them quick and positive to use. They are very versatile indeed. Arca Swiss and Foba are the most widely used among wildlife photographers. Arca B1 heads have adjustable tension settings on the ball, and lock with a knurled wheel. Foba opts for an angled lever. Both makes employ quick-release attachments, with various designs of quick-release plate to suit different lenses and camera bodies. You can also obtain a good range of quick-release plates from Kirk Enterprises and Really Right Stuff, for all the main combinations of camera, lens and ball head.

Personally, I find these quick-release plates on all my lenses and camera bodies a real nuisance, as they tend to snag on everything. And while I like to use ball-and-socket heads with shorter lenses, I have serious reservations about using them with long telephotos. When carrying the combined camera and tripod rig over the shoulder, the torque exerted by such a heavy lens tends to unscrew it from the head. Also, the locking wheel or lever easily rubs or catches and unlocks, letting everything swing loose. Most disconcerting! More seriously, the Arca quick-release locking screw only needs a glancing contact to dump your camera and

Different tripod heads
Popular tripod heads for supporting larger telephotos include the Arca Swiss B1 ball-and-socket head (top) and the Gitzo G1570 low-profile three-way pan-and-tilt head (bottom).

White-tailed eagle stooping

A monopod is useful where a tripod would be too much of an encumbrance, helping to support the weight of a heavy lens while allowing rapid reaction. It is the obvious choice when working from a boat, as on this occasion (see also pp.134–5).

Camera: *Nikon F5*
Lens: *AF-S Nikkor 500mm f4*
Film: *Fujichrome Sensia 100 uprated to EI200*
Exposure: *¹/₁,₀₀₀ sec. at f4*

lens on the ground – I've had this happen (but only once!), causing extensive and costly damage. Manfrotto and Gitzo make quick-release systems with a double-action failsafe locking device, which look more trustworthy. Another disadvantage with ball-and-socket heads is that dirt tends to build up inside the mechanism, causing them to become stiff and eventually seize up. They will probably need servicing more often than other types.

Gimbal heads like the Wimberley work very well with longer, heavier lenses such as a 600mm f4. Their unique design makes a big lens feel almost weightless, and enables you to follow a moving subject very easily, even at height. So they are becoming increasingly popular for action and flight photography with the bigger AF lenses. There are two locking positions, for pan-and-tilt actions, with any leveling or change to vertical format realized by rotating the lens in its collar. A "sidekick" variation in the basic design coupled with an Arca B1 head is a bit lighter and more compact, and quite suitable for lenses up to about 500mm f4 dimensions.

Monopods and other supports

As the name implies, a monopod is a single-leg support. Obviously, it gives less support than a tripod, and can't stand on its own, but a monopod can be very useful when stalking birds, being quicker to operate than a tripod

and giving you a bit more freedom to move about. I find a monopod particularly useful when photographing from boats, if only to take the weight off my arms and wrists. Monopods also double up as walking sticks, if you are treading some distance over rough ground.

Some monopods have an additional shoulder or chest brace to give extra stability. You can fix a small ball-and-socket head if you want more movements, but this can become pretty sloppy and unmanageable, and really you can do quite well by twisting and rocking with the monopod screwed straight on to the tripod mount of the lens.

If you are using a very long focal length lens on a tripod, you might seek additional support for your camera body to prevent too much flexing of the whole system, and a monopod is quite good for this job, too. Of course your subject needs to be fairly static, as it's slow to recompose with everything locked down. You can also get a support brace for this purpose, which attaches between camera body and tripod leg, and gives you a bit more mobility. Manfrotto (Bogen) makes one.

There are window clamps and other purpose-built camera supports on the market, and they seem to be the type of gadget that lots of photographers like to design and build for themselves. It always seems overelaborate to me, but the Groofwin pod from LL Rue is highly rated by others.

Beanbags

Beanbags are really quite the most practical, inexpensive and simple camera supports. No moving parts, nothing to go wrong! Sling them on to a rock, branch, hide window, car window, car roof, or anywhere solid and you get rock-steady performance, instantly. I like the double pocket type that flops nicely either side of a window ledge, with a tab for carrying it around. Choose a zippable one so you can empty it for traveling light. Fill it on arrival at your destination with the cheapest rice or dried beans available, and cook and eat them or give them away just before you leave. Some photographers I know fill them with bird seed, so they always have an emergency supply for baiting subjects. But whatever you use, it should be a reasonable mass – don't be tempted by lightweight polystyrene balls, which are quite useless. You need to fill the bag fairly full so it moulds well to the shape of the lens and doesn't slip around. Keep spare beanbags around the house and in the car – wherever you are likely to need one suddenly.

CAMERA ACCESSORIES

There are a few accessories that you are likely to need pretty well straight away. A cable release is the first, electronic flash second. Most other things can wait. I would add a pair of binoculars to that list, too – not really a camera accessory as such, but if you want to photograph birds you'd better be able to find them. A light, compact pair of 8 x 30 or thereabouts would be ideal.

Sometime later you might want to add more sophisticated gizmos like an infrared remote release, beam trigger, flash extender, external power pack, bulk film back, and so on. By all means check out the availability of such accessories when you first investigate a suitable system, but don't think that you have to get them all at once.

Carrying the load

One thing you will definitely need at the outset is a decent carrying case to protect and transport all your gear. It can be hard to find an ideal case or carryall to suit every situation. Sometimes you want the protection of a hard-sided case, or water-tight seals for an amphibious landing. At other times you just want to be able to dip in and grab a different lens. But on the whole, the best compromise for a wildlife photographer is a backpack. This is the most comfortable and healthiest means of carrying a heavy load of camera gear, and leaves you with both hands free. On the down side, you have to take it off to access your equipment, and this can mean laying it down in the wet and mud at times, worse still on sand. Whatever you choose, make sure it has a good built-in frame and a comfortable harness. Waist straps are also good for helping to spread the load. Allow for your main telephoto and a couple of camera bodies at least, with pockets for film, spare batteries, waterproof

and sandwiches. Try not to be tempted into buying something too large, because you'll always find more stuff to put in it. It might be optimistic to expect to attach a tripod as well, depending on your age and fitness. A good guide would be to limit yourself to what will fit in an aircraft overhead luggage locker. Tamrac, Camera Care Systems, Domke and Lowepro all make good camera backpacks, or you can adapt a walker's rucksack by inserting your own foam protection.

You might later want to add to this basic pack supplementary carrying systems like a belt pouch or a photographer's vest with loads of pockets. These can be particularly helpful when traveling, or when working light on a particular project.

FILMS AND PHOTOGRAPHIC MEDIA

It is more or less standard practice for nature photographers to use transparency (also known as "slide" or "reversal") film. Other professional photographers are very happy to use negative, which is easier to expose correctly and makes better prints – so why do we bother with transparency? Well, it's not just because we like to inflict our slide shows on reluctant audiences. Transparency film emulsions are inherently of higher contrast than negative film emulsions, and make colors look rich and vibrant, or "well saturated." They also tend to be finer grained, and appear sharper when reproduced in print. Since it is also easier for printers to see what they are aiming at and balance colors by reference to a positive image, transparency film has become the publishing standard. And many of us are aiming to get our work published, so we are happy to comply.

If your main aim is to produce prints, then there really is no reason why you shouldn't just go ahead and use color negative film. It is cheaper and easier to process, has wider exposure latitude, records a fuller tonal range, and makes beautiful photographic prints. It also scans very well.

Working with transparency film does call for careful and accurate exposure. Because of its reduced contrast range it is easy to burn

Transporting camera gear
Use a sturdy and dependable backpack for carrying your camera gear in the field, such as the Lowepro Photo Trekker AW seen here.

Mark Hamblin
Jay in falling snow, Yorkshire, England

A regularly supplied and intelligently placed feeding station can create good photographic opportunities for a steady flow of different bird subjects. Mark Hamblin relates how he enticed a normally shy jay within range of his camera:

❝ *Within walking distance of my home on the edge of Sheffield there is an old cemetery surrounded by mature oak woodland. In some years the bumper acorn crop attracts large numbers of jays, which often remain in the area throughout the winter, retrieving acorns that they have stashed in the autumn. However, with snow on the ground, feeding is difficult for the jays and so I set up a feeding station and began to put out peanuts. Jays and magpies, as well as the tits, soon found them*

and made regular visits to feed. For this particular picture I had previously drilled small holes into a dead branch and set it up in front of my portable canvas hide. Following a couple of days of snow I pushed peanuts into the holes of the branch out of sight of the camera, and settled into the hide. My hope was that I would be able to photograph jays and other birds, not only in the snow, but also with snowflakes falling around them. I worked with a Canon EOS 1-N camera and 500mm f4.5 lens. The light was poor and so I pushed the Fuji Sensia 100 film one stop to EI200 in order to achieve a reasonable shutter speed of $^1/_{125}$ sec. Bird activity was very slow during my session in the hide, but I was lucky enough to obtain a sequence of three or four shots of this individual. After landing, it quickly took several peanuts into its crop but then posed briefly looking back over its shoulder. This was my favourite image from a cold afternoon spent in the hide. ❞

out highlights and block in shadow detail. Take greatest care not to overexpose highlights, and let the shadow detail go if necessary (the opposite advice to working with negative). Slightly underexposed transparencies still record good tonal detail and can be salvaged in printing, scanning or duplicating. Slightly overexposed transparencies are invariably useless.

Film speed and sensitivity

Film sensitivity (also referred to as film "speed") is described by the internationally recognized ISO (International Standards Organization) rating. Daylight-balanced transparency films are commercially available at nominal speeds ranging from ISO25 to ISO1600. Doubling the ISO number represents an increase in sensitivity of 1 stop, so an ISO200 film is twice as sensitive as an ISO100 film. Therefore "faster" films are more sensitive and have higher ISO numbers, allowing you to shoot at faster shutter speeds or smaller apertures, while "slower" films are less sensitive and have lower ISO numbers. Slow films are finer grained and have better resolving power; fast films are coarser grained. The term "exposure index" (EI) describes a film speed different from the manufacturer's nominal speed, so an ISO100 film might be "pushed" or "uprated" 1 stop to EI200, calling for a corresponding increase in development time. You must therefore notify your processing lab of any change in exposure index. Pushing films tends to increase graininess and contrast and causes color shifts.

There is always much discussion among photographers about which films have the most lifelike color, and the conclusion is generally the same: it's all down to personal taste. When you think about the enormous range of colors throughout nature and all their nuances, the fact that chemical dye-coupling can come anywhere near to matching them has to be a source of some amazement and admiration. But most films have one or two subtle hues that they are unable to reproduce entirely faithfully, and you have to work out which you can most easily live with. Photographing with available light means that color temperature (the color of light, measured in degrees Kelvin) can fluctuate enormously, even minute by minute, and this has a much larger bearing on color rendition in final images, so take a pragmatic view.

Transparency films of low to medium speed (ISO64 to ISO100) are probably the most useful for bird photography, offering the best compromise between speed and grain. The best advice would be to find one film that you like and stick with it for a while. Settle on a professional lab for processing, and stick with that too. This way you will become familiar with a film's characteristics, how best to expose it in different conditions, and whether to make fine adjustments to the recommended speed. Report any gripes to the lab and work through any problems (as long as they're only occasional), and build up a good working relationship with them. Store unexposed films in a fridge, and have exposed films processed quickly.

THE DIGITAL ALTERNATIVE

Digital image capture is already making quite an impact across many photographic disciplines and looks likely to replace traditional photochemistry in due course. Digital systems are very much in favor with studio and news photographers, in particular. The former can make huge savings on film and processing costs, while the latter appreciate the speed with which they can deliver good enough images to their news desks. These benefits will also apply to bird and nature photographers of course; in addition, digital cameras work well in low light, you can use your existing lenses with an effective 1.5x increase in focal length, and you have unlimited, lossless copies of your "originals." On the down side, image quality isn't yet as good as the finest 35mm transparency, file transfer speed and data storage capacity are limiting, and you really need a laptop computer on hand to review your images properly. So at the moment there is a conflict between portability, speed and image quality, but probably not for long. Watch this space.

Whatever your equipment, and whatever medium you use to record your bird images, the essential techniques will remain the same. There will be many times when your equipment still seems inadequate, and even the most sophisticated camera cannot predict what you want to express in a photograph. That is part of the beauty, and the skill, of photographing wild birds, and where we must now turn our attention.

Brown pelican
Fujichrome Velvia is very fine-grained, high-resolution transparency film but, at ISO50, a little slow for much bird photography. With an obliging subject and Florida sunshine, it was the natural choice for me. Some photographers believe the colors to be too vivid, and swear by Kodachrome 64 for its more neutral color and proven archival stability. Velvia pushes well to EI100, but is prone to color shift.
Camera: *Nikon F5*
Lens: *80–200mm f2.8*
Film: *Fujichrome Velvia at ISO50*

Chapter 2
CONTROLLING
THE IMAGE

Having established what we need in the
hardware department, it is time to attend to
the more creative side of our photography.
This chapter looks at the theoretical aspects
of composition and light, and how we can
combine these ingredients effectively to
produce a synchronous whole. We also learn
about the quantifiable nature of light, how
to work with it, and how to create our own.

(right) **Fairy terns courtship**
feeding
Behavioral activity, and
interaction between birds, their
neighbours, and their
environment gives rise to
interesting compositions that
almost design themselves. But
keep the basics of framing in
mind at all times.
Camera: *Nikon F5*
Lens: *80–200mm f2.8*
Film: *Fujichrome Sensia 100*
Lighting: *SB-26 Speedlight on*
daylight-balanced fill flash

COMPOSITION

The subject of photographic composition is often spoken about in terms of rules and mathematical theory. This is not particularly helpful or appropriate when dealing with an uncooperative, wild creature. Most of your effort and concentration will have already gone into getting close to the subject, selecting the correct exposure and keeping focus. It is easy to neglect composition in the midst of all this. However, it is really worth pausing to consider the ultimate outcome and trying to visualize it in two dimensions. It is the difference between a haphazard palette of random colors and a work of art. In the end though, it won't be down to some academic exercise in aesthetics, but something quite personal, which you feel and express through the camera. Your awareness for composition will grow naturally as your technical skills become more proficient and intuitive, and will manifest itself in your own unique style.

Frame discipline

I use this term to describe the basic mechanics of framing a photograph. Frame discipline is the housekeeping side of composition, and is about avoiding sloppy oversights. Do you have the most appropriate lens fitted? Is the camera best in the horizontal or vertical orientation? Is the horizon parallel to the frame edge? Are there any awkward intrusions (such as out-of-focus twigs), distracting highlights (like surface reflections on water), or conflicting backgrounds (such as electricity pylons that appear to be growing out of birds' heads)? These questions should be going through your mind all the time as you look through the viewfinder. To rectify things might be a simple matter of moving a step to one side, turning the camera round, or zooming in or out. A continual state of alertness is required. Pay attention to the edges of the frame, and how your subject relates to them. Is there anything you can afford to leave out, that adds nothing to the picture? Reduce these unwanted elements as far as possible, and start thinking "less is more." On the other hand, perhaps you have been so preoccupied with trying to make a large image of the bird that

you have failed to see the better photograph? Consider your image size, and don't necessarily go for the biggest that you can get. And remember that with a 100 percent viewfinder the final image will be cropped slightly when the film edge is lost under the slide mount.

Designing bird photographs

Composition means going a step further than taking just a well-executed record shot. At its best, it should encapsulate a special moment, challenge the viewer's preconceptions, raise questions and impart meaning. This might

sound fanciful, but bird photography has a bit of a reputation for being rather staid and conventional, so let's aim high! At the very least, we can try to tell something about the life of the bird, its behavior, how it relates to its habitat, what might happen next. And we can also set about trying to design our photographs to best effect within the given circumstances. There should be no golden rules, but I can point to some devices that I think have worked for others and myself.

Arranging the elements of a photograph in a way that arrests the eye of the viewer is the simplest starting point. The result might be pleasing or it might be unsettling, but it must have the power to make people look. To do this effectively means being able to visualize how the scene will record in two dimensions, so try to assess your viewfinder image as though it were printed on paper. Look for strong lines, shapes, and patterns, real and implied, that will have an impact in the finished photograph, and think about how you can use them. Are there toning or contrasting colors and textures that could add to or detract from the subject? Are there any

Frame orientation and subject placement

All of these views of a common snipe are conventionally "good" compositions, complemented by the attractive perch and clean background. In the horizontal or "landscape" format (top), the bird is positioned more or less at the "intersection of thirds," and has space on the left to look into. This was a fortunate occasion where the bird posed long enough to allow further shots in the vertical or "portrait" format. With the bird low in the frame (bottom left), the rusty barbed-wire fence is excluded, but there is a lot of dead space above. With the bird higher in the frame, it appears better supported, and I quite like the way the rust color is echoed in the bird's plumage.

Camera: Nikon F3
Lens: 300mm f2.8 plus 1.4x teleconverter
Film: Kodachrome 64

interactions with other birds or the immediate environment? Make your mind up about what needs to be included and what might be excluded, and remember that the simpler compositions are often the most successful. Granted, you might only have this luxury with an obliging, perched bird, but often you can be thinking about it before the bird is even in the frame, and plan your approach accordingly.

Subject placement

One of the first decisions you must make is where to place your subject. The textbook formula is to locate your center of interest at one of the "intersections of thirds" – the four compositional strongpoints that fall within a rectangular frame. With a bird small in the frame, the center of the bird might be thought ideally placed at an intersection of thirds; with a bird large in the frame, make it the bird's eye.

The shape of the bird or group of birds will dictate the possibilities to a large extent, but anything off dead center generally looks good. In practice, look at the image in the viewfinder and try to achieve a sense of balance.

Usually it looks better if you leave space for the implied movement of the subject. So if the bird is looking or moving towards the left, you leave a bigger space on that side for it to move into – somehow it just seems the natural thing to do. However, you should always question whether it could be done better or differently. For instance, when a moving bird is leaving a trail or wake, it seems preferable to show where the bird has been rather than where it is going. Practicalities always intercede – the space you'd prefer to leave has a telegraph pole in it, or perhaps half of another out-of-focus bird, which would only result in a poorer photograph – so you need to adapt to the situation. With flocks of birds in flight, if there is a recognizable outline shape to the flock you will probably find yourself leaving room in front of the leading bird. It seems to matter much less if the tail-end birds are chopped in half. When the flock more than fills the frame, there's really no decision left to make.

In the upright format, compositions tend to work better with the subject placed in the upper third of the frame, so that it has some "support" space underneath. But beware too much out-of-focus foreground, particularly if it is cluttered and only just out of focus. With birds on or near water, pay particular attention to reflections and whether their inclusion might improve your shot.

Other considerations apply if you are shooting for stock libraries or aiming to supply your work to publishers. Then it is less important to have the perfectly composed photograph in camera, and much more important to leave options open to the graphic designer. So a smaller, centrally placed subject might be quite acceptable, allowing the picture to be cropped to fit the space available on the page. Think about leaving copy space (plain background that will take type) around your subject. Take lots of uprights – most books and magazines are printed this way up, and publishers are always on the lookout for good candidates for full-page

photographs. If you want a coveted front-cover shot you could improve your chances by leaving a space at the top for a title.

Camera viewpoint and perspective

Foreground and background will be affected by relative distances, focal length of lens and camera viewpoint. With telephoto lenses, because of the small angle of view, a very small shift in camera position can make a big difference to the foreground and background. Explore the possibilities of more pleasing, less fussy backgrounds by moving the camera up or down, and from side to side rather than just settling for the comfortable, eye-level view.

Foreground elements such as foliage or grasses might be seen as a nuisance, but look to see whether they can be used to make an interesting, natural frame and lend depth to the photograph, particularly if they are a contrasting color to the subject. Foreground framing generally needs to be either in the same plane of focus as the subject, or well blurred, not somewhere in between. This also helps the subject to appear more natural, at home in its habitat, undisturbed. Low camera viewpoints lend themselves to fuzzy foregrounds, and give a more intimate perspective for birds on the ground or water. Set the tripod at its lowest position, or rest your lens on a rock, camera bag or directly on

Goldeneye drake displaying
The silver wake of the goldeneye against the inky loch really begged to be included in my composition, and provided a good enough reason to break the "rules."
Camera: *Nikon F5*
Lens: *AF-S 500mm f4 plus 2x teleconverter*
Film: *Fujichrome Sensia 100 uprated to EI200*

The effect of changing camera position

Moving a couple of steps to one side can have a profound effect on background with long telephotos, because of their narrow field of view. These two shots of a red-shouldered hawk were taken moments apart, with only a meter or so difference in camera position.
Camera: Nikon F5
Lens: AF-S 300mm f2.8 plus 2x teleconverter
Film: Fujichrome Sensia 100

the ground to achieve that intimate feeling. It might mean getting yourself wet or muddy, but the end result justifies the pain. In contrast, looking down from high viewpoints with shorter lenses often looks awkward, suggesting tame or captive birds in a confined setting. Camera viewpoint is something you can change quite quickly and easily, so make it work for you. Get down, get dirty!

Remember that the focal length of your lens will also affect perspective. Assuming that you are using a telephoto, bird images will tend to appear flattened and two-dimensional. The longer the lens, the more pronounced the effect. It would be a shame always to portray birds as flat and shapeless, so don't use huge focal lengths indiscriminately. Other objects in view will also be foreshortened and compressed, making relative size and distance difficult to judge. This effect can be used to makes things appear closer together than they really are, stacking up a succession of tree trunks, waves, mountains, or whatever, in a way that enhances the overall composition.

Turnstone foraging on sea shore
I lay on the ground with my lens supported on a beanbag to achieve this low camera angle. This position presents less of a threat to the bird, and also seems to lend a certain intimacy to the photograph.
Camera: *Nikon F5*
Lens: *AF-S 500mm f4 plus 1.4x teleconverter*
Film: *Fujichrome Sensia 100 uprated to EI 200*

Shorter focal length lenses will incorporate more background, because of their angle of view, so don't forget the wide-angle option with larger, tamer birds (or with a remote-controlled camera). The use of a small aperture on a wide-angle lens can permit both bird and habitat to be shown in focus, but subject placement is critical so that the bird doesn't get lost against a cluttered background.

Depth of field

Depth of field plays a big part in composition, too. Use wide apertures to obtain soft, blurred backgrounds with telephotos. For a small to moderate-sized bird shown large in the frame you will need to stop down a bit to achieve sufficient depth of field, particularly if it is a front-on view. Employ your camera's depth-of-field preview to check. Focus on the bird's eye and let the tail go out of focus, if needs be. Where there is more than one bird in view, they seldom come together in exactly the same plane of focus, even though they often look as though they are in the viewfinder. Try a smaller aperture to show both (all) birds in focus, or perhaps switch to a shorter focal length. Alternatively, wait until one bird moves into quite a different plane of focus, use a wide aperture and deliberately make the bird(s)

behind well out of focus. With large flocks like grazing geese or waders at a roost, the best option is usually to focus on the front row.

Lines and edges

Diagonal lines and sweeping curves are usually more agreeable than strong horizontal or vertical lines, leading the eye gently into the picture, so exploit them where you can. For example, if you are photographing a bird on a tide line or stream edge, try to avoid the land/water boundary becoming a vertical or horizontal line in the photograph. Simply moving to one side or the other will transform the line into a more powerful diagonal, or exaggerate any curve. Where there is more than one straight line, look for convergences to make interesting triangles. These lines might be implied rather than real, a suggested link between the main subject elements.

Red grouse hen
Using a telephoto "wide open" results in a narrow depth of field. Distant backgrounds are rendered agreeably out of focus, while a small amount of out-of-focus foreground can help to frame the subject and give the photograph a feeling of depth.
Camera: *Nikon F5*
Lens: *500mm lens at f4*
Film: *Fujichrome Sensia 100*

Atlantic puffin with sand eels
Head shots are the easiest close-ups to compose, but remember that with this sort of reproduction ratio you'll need to be stopping down to smaller apertures to obtain sufficient depth of field. I stalked this bird by creeping up on my stomach with a 200mm macro lens hand-held, using my elbows for support.
Camera: *Nikon F4S*
Lens: *Micro-Nikkor 200mm f4*
Film: *Fujichrome Sensia 100*
Exposure: $^1/_{60}$ *sec. at f11*

Close-ups

Close-ups of parts of birds need careful thought. If you've just clipped the subject outline it looks pretty clumsy, as though you couldn't be bothered to frame properly. Half a bird looks a bit odd too, as if you weren't sure whether you wanted a close-up or not. Head portraits are pretty safe – you would expect to concentrate the composition around the bird's eye. Larger, tighter close-ups where you can't see any defining outlines may be very successful, such as of a wing panel or speculum, or the facial disc of an owl. It's often better if there is some mystery to the photograph and the identity of the subject isn't immediately obvious, so the viewer has to think a bit to work it out. Remember that with these larger reproduction ratios you will need to stop down to quite small apertures to achieve sufficient depth of field, and this in turn may require additional lighting.

Most often, this sort of photography will be possible only with birds in captivity rather than wild birds, but there are occasional obliging wild subjects. Photographs of bits of dead birds are depressing and usually all too obvious – a conveniently spread wing or tail, even if sprayed with water droplets, is unlikely to fool anybody. However, a recently moulted feather photographed in habitat might make a sensitive study, likely to require the use of a macro lens or extension tubes. What about a more abstract approach, such as a trail of footprints in the mud, or a powder down imprint on a window following a collision?

Photographing bird action

Not so long ago, bird photographers would not have considered attempting anything other than a static portrait of an incubating bird on the nest, hampered as they were with quarter-plate field cameras and having to estimate a $^1/_{50}$ sec. time exposure (at best) for their single plate. There simply wasn't that much choice. Fortunately, modern cameras and films allow us to be much more

adventurous in our approach, and we can capture bird movement and behavior in previously undreamed of ways. So rather than just illustrating a motionless subject on a fence post ('birds on sticks', as some editors rudely describe it!), try instead to photograph birds feeding, drinking, bathing, flying, singing, preening, or displaying. They do lots of interesting things, but you wouldn't always know it to look at the photographic record.

Action photography does of course call for some understanding of your subject, and an ability to anticipate its next move – skills you can only really gain through observation and experience. You will also need good reaction time and practice in the use of your equipment so that you are not fumbling around when the action does occur. The best advice is to be bold, and hit the motordrive whenever it looks as though something interesting is about to happen, and not be frightened about wasting film; you can toss the failures but you can't recover lost opportunities.

In practice, you will most likely be operating with a long focal length lens, though anything longer than 600mm takes some getting used to, just to keep your bird in frame. Start with the lens at its maximum aperture to obtain the fastest possible shutter speed in order to freeze subject movement. Use a predetermined manual exposure reading, or set to aperture priority automatic if shooting mainly mid-tones. You will probably need at least $1/500$ sec. to be confident of sharp results with moving subjects, and $1/1,000$ sec. or faster for birds in flight. Depending on the maximum aperture of your lens and the available light, you may need to opt for a faster film to be sure of a sufficiently fast exposure. With a 400mm f5.6 lens, a shutter speed of $1/800$ sec. or $1/1,000$ sec. ought to be achievable on ISO200 film in good light. Consider uprating ISO100 film to EI 200 for a sharper image and finer grain structure than a nominal ISO200 film, or use an even faster film if you can tolerate the grain. As you gain experience of action photography techniques, you will be able to judge when you can afford to use slower shutter speeds, and what is appropriate for particular activities.

Think ahead, and if you are within a couple of frames of the end of the roll, try to change films in advance of any action. Most probably, you will be photographing in the horizontal (or "landscape") format for ease, but do try to think about whether the camera would be better in the vertical orientation. It's a good idea to frame your subject in a way that allows space for it to move into; not only is this the more pleasing composition, but it's the most practical way of keeping up. And if you don't have the bird too large in the frame, you'll have a better chance of following the action and allowing room for taking off, wing-stretching, or sudden changes of direction. If the bird starts to run, swim or fly, keep your lens moving at the same speed to maintain its position in the frame, striving to hold that space ahead of the direction of movement, and taking short bursts of pictures with the motordrive set at its fastest rate. This can be difficult at first, and with the mirror flapping up and down you can easily lose confidence as the viewfinder image flickers, but try to pan smoothly with the subject motion and don't falter when you press the shutter button. It helps to have a good tripod head for this, with a smooth panning action. When you become accomplished at panning, it's possible to use much slower shutter speeds, perhaps even as slow as $1/60$ sec., and keep the main areas of interest sharp while blurring the wing beats and background to really give a feeling of movement. Don't expect every shot to work out, but if the eye and bill of the bird are sharp it is surprising what you can get away with. Streaky backgrounds are good for illustrating the speed of a flying bird, and become possible when panning at shutter speeds of $1/250$ sec. or slower. Water spray from birds bathing, fishing, or taking flight also adds dynamism to an action photograph – individual droplets will render well at $1/500$ sec. or faster, while arcs of spray result from slower shutter speeds of $1/125$ sec. or less.

With all of these things to think about, you could do without having to worry about focusing the lens as well. This is where autofocus can be of enormous benefit – in particular the advanced autofocus systems that

as birds flying directly towards the camera, or low contrast subjects against high contrast backgrounds (shore birds flying against a background of breaking waves, perhaps) – and you will soon become aware of your system's limitations. Try setting the continuous film advance to a slower speed – perhaps six frames per second rather than eight frames per second – to improve AF and focus tracking capabilities. When it works, autofocus really does expand your horizons and lets you concentrate more effectively on other important aspects of your bird photography. The rewards are there for the adventurous.

With a manual-focus lens, your best bet is to pre-focus the lens and let the bird move into the field of focus, pressing the shutter just as (or just before, if the bird is coming towards you) the viewfinder image looks sharp. Again, this is something that takes practice and you should expect waste. Use shorter focal length lenses by preference, say 300mm or shorter. At seabird colonies I have found a 200mm macro lens quite dependable for manual-focus flight photography, but have occasionally made sharp flight shots in manual at focal lengths right up to 700mm.

The use of slower shutter speeds for action photography in nature has become quite the vogue in recent years. While there is clearly some loss of detail in outline and plumage, the most successful examples of this kind of work portray birds in a beautifully impressionistic manner. Perhaps such images are a better approximation as to how we remember having seen a bird, in fleeting glimpse, than the more usual action-stopping interpretation. Some people, however, simply hate the style. If you want to give it a go, expect to take rolls and rolls of film perfecting the technique. Usually it works best at shutter speeds around $1/15$ sec. or $1/30$ sec., but much depends on the size of bird and its range and speed of movement, so be prepared to experiment. Although it might not be immediately obvious, image stabilization can assist greatly with this style of photography, as it reduces the camera shake element of the exposure so any resulting blur is solely attributable to subject movement.

Photographing flight
Same bird, same place, same time – but different treatment. This feeding black skimmer was photographed at both $1/800$ sec. (top) and $1/25$ sec. (bottom) to produce quite different interpretations.
Camera: *Nikon F5*
Lens: *AF-S 300mm f2.8 with 2x teleconverter*
Film: *Fujichrome Sensia 100*

have "focus tracking" capability. To some extent, these systems can predict the speed and direction of subject movement, but you still have to try to keep the selected AF bracket on the bird (although some claim to be clever enough to select the right bracket automatically, in "dynamic AF"). It may take a frame or two for the system to get up to speed, so again you need to grit your teeth and keep the shutter button depressed in the hope that the computer chip is doing its job. While autofocus technology has developed at great pace, there are still many situations where the best systems can't easily cope – such

Perches

An ugly perch can so often ruin an otherwise fine photograph. It might be out of proportion to the bird, introduce unwelcome parallel lines (especially if it is a wall or fence post or some other man-made object), lie at an awkward angle to the plane of focus, or just be a cluttered mess of twigs and foliage. Conversely, the right perch can transform a relatively dull portrait into a beautiful composition – a mossy bough, a lichen-encrusted rock or a spray of fresh blossom should complement a bird subject without competing for the viewer's attention.

There are occasions when you might be able to gently manipulate the perch a bird uses, perhaps by introducing one of your own choice or removing those you don't like. If you're erecting a fence post or branch for example, consider its angle and don't just plonk it down vertically. And avoid using the same one over and over again. Leaf buds and shoots should be pointing in the natural growing position, with pruning and gardening kept to a minimum and as inconspicuous as possible. If an introduced perch is too perfect with everything slap-bang in the plane of focus it can easily look faked (as it is). Decorating the perch with ivy is usually a dead give-away, but if you are working in your own garden or at a regularly visited site you could, with judicious pruning, train the growth of branches and climbing plants in a more natural way over a period of time to suit your composition.

More likely, in real-life field situations you'll have no choice in the matter of where a bird perches, but you should still take it into account, look whether a better angle might be achievable or just hang around a bit longer in case the bird moves to somewhere more agreeable. Just occasionally all the elements come together and combine to produce something exquisite.

Depicting birds in their habitat

Your bird doesn't always have to be a frame-filler to make a successful photograph. Sometimes it's good to show how a bird relates to its habitat, and a relatively small bird image can look spectacular in the right

Mike Lane
European bee-eater, Almeria, Spain

This beautifully composed portrait earned Mike Lane the *British Birds* magazine title of Bird Photograph of the Year in 1995, and illustrates his painstaking attention to detail. Mike tells us how he made the photograph:

" A single pair of bee-eaters were nesting in a bank, but I noticed that they were occasionally landing on a beautiful tobacco tree 200m (660ft) away from the nest. Droppings on the floor suggested that they sat here often, and I swept these away so that the following day I could judge if they had been back. They had, so I quickly erected my hide about 7m (23ft) away. The direction of the light meant I could only work between about three and six o'clock in the afternoon, and it took three afternoons before they landed in the right place. It was important to me that the bird was close to the yellow flowers, which so perfectly match the plumage, as do the green leaves. As a final touch, I smeared an ugly scar on the glossy black bark of the perch with a tiny drop of engine oil from the dip stick of my car, to disguise it.

The background is an out-of-focus sand dune. As ever in such hot conditions the wind was blowing strongly and the thin branch was moving back and forth as well as up and down. Consequently, not every picture was sharp.

I used a Canon EOS 5 camera body with a 600mm f4 lens. The film is Kodachrome 64, exposed at ^{1}/250 sec. at f8. "

Male whinchat

Small bird images can make marvelous photographs, if conditions are working in your favor. The vibrant greens and backlighting tempted me to try this ambitious composition, but it was the single bent stem straining under the weight of the bird that really clinched it.

Camera: *Nikon F4S*
Lens: *500mm*
Film: *Fujichrome Velvia*

composition. It takes some courage and confidence to pull back from a frame-filling opportunity, but it could be exactly the right thing to do. Most probably, before you look for the potential in the smaller image size, you will have already satisfied yourself as to your own fieldcraft abilities, and will feel safe in the knowledge that you could get closer if you really needed to.

Strong design, interesting light or texture, and a complementary background are required for this approach to work. A narrow shaft of sunlight spotlighting a bird and isolating it from a low-key background might be the ideal scenario. This is where the photographer's "vision" and creativity really have the chance to shine; when properly executed it will be obvious that the composition was intended, and not simply the result of the photographer being unable to get as close as he or she would have really liked. Such a shot can equally well be taken with a telephoto or wide-angle lens. Quite possibly, it could be regarded as an excellent landscape

photograph that just happens to have birds in it – they may be small in the frame, but they still play an important role in the integrity of the overall composition.

Some birds lend themselves to this treatment better than others, whether by their size, distinctive shape, gregarious behavior, or preferred habitat. A rail skulking in a reed bed might not give you much opportunity for any kind of photograph, let alone a considered composition. However, be alert to the rare occasion when it emerges from the reeds and its smooth curves contrast neatly with the regular pattern of vertical stems – there could be a masterpiece in the making.

LIGHT AND METERING

Judging by questions I am asked at lectures and workshops, metering seems to cause more problems and anxiety than any other aspect of photography. Transparency film in particular is pretty unforgiving of mistakes, so the anxiety is not without foundation. Let's take it from first principles.

Janos Jurka
Red-throated diver, Ludvika, Sweden

The photographs of Janos Jurka exhibit a great appreciation and understanding of space, often making use of small bird images but always in a way that makes a complete, synchronous composition. Nothing is wasted. He told me about his technique:

Respectful bird photography requires a good knowledge of the species one works with. It is important to understand birds' behavior patterns, as well as their individual traits, such as sensitivity to disturbance, aggression towards intruders, and so on. Individual birds of the same species can actually behave quite differently from each other.

I have photographed red-throated divers near my home in Sweden for more than 15 years, without using hides. In the beginning I used to visit their breeding lake once or twice a day, following the same route on foot and always wearing the same clothes. If the birds showed any sign of nervousness about my approach, I would turn back or stop and sit down for a while until they calmed down. Gradually they came to accept my presence, so that today I can sit at a distance of 10–15m (33–55ft) without disturbing them. Amazing, but true.

This method allows me to move around and select the best distance, camera position, and lighting effect when composing my photographs. Of course it wouldn't be suitable for all types of bird, and even when your presence has come to be accepted it is important not to abuse the birds' trust. Patience and respect will eventually be rewarded with special experiences, and photographs that capture the habitat and whole atmosphere – in my opinion, this is more important than being able to count the feathers on a close-up. Besides, once you have built up a trusting relationship with your subject there will be plenty of opportunities to shoot close-ups too.

This photograph was taken with a Canon F1-U camera and 85mm f1.2 lens, on Kodachrome 64 film.

How to use a gray card

When I photographed this outdoor scene including the Kodak gray card, a spotmeter reading indicated that the grass was actually 1 whole stop darker than the card itself. It is important to have the card angled correctly to minimize surface reflections and, significantly, Kodak recommends "for subjects of normal reflectance increase the indicated exposure by $^1/_2$ stop." This exercise also indicates that "grass green" should not be taken as an absolutely accurate representation of mid-gray.

Understanding your meter

The most important thing to know and remember is that all lightmeters are calibrated to mid-gray, or 18 percent reflectance (you can see how this looks by reference to a Kodak gray card). This is a long-established constant or standard of measurement, which is supposed to represent the average reflectance of the most commonly photographed scenes.

In a sense, it doesn't matter where the standard is set as long as you understand what it is and how to interpret it. Suppose, for example, your camera's lightmeter tells you that a given scene should be exposed at $^1/_{250}$ sec. at f8. Following this advice without any interpretation or amendment, most times you will get a fairly acceptable exposure. If you are photographing a family group, a landscape with some sky, or even a typical bird in its normal habitat, the average of the tonal range will most probably approximate to mid-gray, so you can pretty well trust your averaging meter. But were you to photograph a white swan in a snowfield or a raven in a shadowy cave on a straight meter reading, you would also get a mid-gray representation on film – not what you want at all. Of course, the meter doesn't know what you are looking at or how you wish to represent it in your photograph, and can only suggest the average setting. To keep your white bird white and your black bird looking black, you must overexpose or underexpose relative to the average meter reading. And, of course, there is a whole range of tonal variations in between that call for some amendment. More on this subject and how to expose correctly below.

The other point to bear in mind is that the human eye can perceive and allow for a much greater contrast range than any film. On a bright sunny day, the contrast range might be as high as 2,000:1, which might make you squint, but your eye and brain can adapt to and accommodate this brightness to make sense of the information. Color transparency film emulsions can only resolve a maximum contrast range of something like 32:1 (or about 5 stops) in comparison, and color negative about 128:1 (7 stops). Anything beyond this range will record on the film as

blocked-in shadow or burnt-out highlight, with no texture or detail. Sometimes, this high-contrast effect can be desirable and work to your advantage, but it's best if you know when those times are while they're happening, rather than arriving at that end point by chance. More often than not, the effect of a high contrast range on film (and especially on transparency) is erroneous exposure and consequently the loss of important detail in key areas of your photograph.

You can measure the contrast range of a scene by employing a spotmeter and taking a reading of different tones from highlights through to shadows, to see for yourself just how great the range can be. Even if you had time to calculate all your exposures beforehand in this way, unfortunately it's not good enough just to work out the median reading and opt for that as your camera setting. It will still be wrong a lot of the time (but it is in essence what an evaluative meter reading does for you). Really, you have to make a value judgment about what is the most important part of your picture and expose for that accordingly, often at the expense of other elements.

Another method of working is to find a mid-tone in your picture and take a spot reading off that. Fine in principle, but how do you recognize an accurate mid-tone with any degree of consistency? Is it green grass? Blue sky? You can carry a gray card and try to meter off that, but it's slow and not very practical for bird photography. Alternatively, you could use a hand-held incident lightmeter, and get an accurate reading that way. But what happens if your subject is more than 2 stops lighter or darker than mid-gray? It will still be incorrectly exposed!

Sunny f16?

There is a popular rule of thumb advanced by a number of North American authors, and first popularized by John Shaw, known as the "sunny f16" rule. This states that if the sun is shining, with your aperture set to f16, the shutter speed will be the reciprocal of your film speed or its nearest equivalent. Thus with ISO100 film you should set your shutter to

$^{1}/_{125}$ sec. (or $^{1}/_{250}$ sec. at f11, and so on). While this might be fine if you work only in Florida, in the middle hours of the day, with the sun over your shoulder, it's unfortunately not universally applicable. It seems to me to be no more scientific than glancing at the tip sheet in your film pack and going by that. Neither is it an incentive to work with more interesting light at the ends of the day, or in a snowstorm, or in any way that might produce exciting, evocative photographs. Now this is no way a criticism of the formidable work of John Shaw and others – it's a technique that seems to have worked well enough for them, after all. I can understand that it's useful to have a comprehension of what light reading you might expect in normal shooting conditions, if only to be able to judge when some bit of equipment is failing, but that understanding will generally come with

experience anyway. So, with respect to my American colleagues, I would urge you to give no credence to "sunny f16." In short, believe your meter and use your head.

Practical exposure control

I wish there were one definitive answer I could give to ensure perfect exposures at all times and in all conditions, but unfortunately it's not quite that straightforward. Even professionals don't get their exposures right all the time (and don't believe them if they say they do). However, there are some useful guidelines and tips to set you on your way.

Most of the time it is pretty safe to rely on your averaging meter in center-weighted or evaluative mode (remembering to get used to using one or the other). Try to judge the tonal value of your subject and background as seen through the camera viewfinder. If it is a pretty

Redshank in summer plumage
With a mid-toned bird against
a mid-toned background and
frontal lighting there's really
not a lot to go wrong, and an
automatic meter reading can
be relied upon.
Camera: Nikon F4S
Lens: 500mm f4
Film: Kodachrome 64

Mute swan on water

For consistently reliable exposure when photographing a white bird on transparency film, begin by taking a spotmeter reading of an area of bright white plumage where you want to retain some texture or detail – here I would have chosen the swan's forewing. In manual mode with your chosen aperture, set the shutter speed ensuring the meter indicator is 1^2/$_3$ stops above the center point of the analog scale. This should solve the problem, no matter what the background reflectance or relative bird image size.

Camera: *Nikon F5*
Lens: *AF-S 500mm f4*
Film: *Fujichrome Sensia 100*

uniform mixture of light and dark tones, or a mid-toned subject large in the frame, then it is safe to proceed in aperture priority automatic. As this will account for the majority of your subjects, I would recommend leaving the camera on this setting as a default, at least until you get confident. Common exceptions include particularly light or dark subjects, and light or dark backgrounds.

When dealing with lighter or darker subjects, their relative size in the frame determines how much they will influence the meter reading. Take the example of a white swan swimming towards you on a background of dark water. There is a point at which the automatic averaging meter will calculate the exposure just right, but it's decidedly risky to leave it to luck. If the swan's image size is smaller than that, the water will have a greater influence on the meter and the swan will be overexposed. When the swan's image size exceeds the critical point, it will reflect more light to the meter and cause the camera to progressively under-expose, if left on auto. You don't know where that critical point is, but

you can judge it with a bit of practice. The quick way to adjust exposure is to leave the camera on auto and use the exposure-compensation dial to make adjustments. Continuing with the example of the swan, assuming you are photographing this as your main subject so it is pretty large in the frame (about one quarter of the whole frame area), you would want to add about 1 stop to the autoexposure setting. Add more if the bird is very large in the frame. With the converse situation of a black bird against a lighter background in similar proportion, you need to subtract about 1 stop on the compensation dial. This gives you a better chance of an acceptable exposure on your subject, even if the background loses detail to blocked-in shadow or burnt-out highlight. Commonly used by many wildlife photographers, this is a fairly crude, pragmatic way of effecting a solution. You get better with experience, and can make finer adjustments with some degree of confidence.

A more accurate way of determining exposure, if you have time, would be to

spotmeter in manual mode. To take the white swan example again, select an area of bright white plumage where you would just like to retain something of the feather detail (ignore small areas of glare or totally burnt-out highlight). Spotmeter off this area and set it at $1^2/3$ stops higher than the mid-point on your analogue meter bar, so that you are effectively overexposing by this amount. It might work better for you at $1^1/2$ or 2 stops depending on your equipment, favorite film and so on, but this is a near foolproof way of keeping your whites white. And you can retain this setting for a short working session, using it for other swans in different positions, assuming the ambient light level remains constant. Periodically double-check the reading and reset your exposure as necessary. The most difficult part of the whole process is selecting an appropriate area of white plumage in the first place.

With a black bird such as a crow or raven, in manual metering mode, spotmeter an area of dark black plumage where you would like to keep some feather detail (not an inky black shadow where all is lost anyway), and set this to $1^2/3$ stops lower than the mid-point on the meter, or under-expose. Again, you may wish to adjust for your particular combination of camera and film. This will ensure you keep your blacks looking black, and not gray.

The number to remember is $1^2/3$. After that, the trick is to recall in which direction to compensate: overexpose light subjects, under-expose dark subjects. For light-toned birds that are not white, or dark-toned birds that are not black, estimate on a sliding scale between 0 and $1^2/3$ stops. With black-and-white plumaged birds you should aim to expose the white correctly and disregard the black.

A bright background such as a shiny water surface, snow, sand or cloudy sky, or a dark background such as woodland shade or deep blue ocean, can easily fool your automatic metering. Evaluative metering takes care of this to some extent, but is unlikely to give correct exposures in the more testing situations. Assuming the subject is reasonably well lit, ideally you should spotmeter in manual off a mid-tone – preferably some part of the bird's plumage – and keep that as your setting. It might be at the expense of burning

Black grouse male at lek

To expose correctly for black birds, place your manual spotmeter reading $1^2/3$ stops below the mid-point. It helps if you have low, angled sunlight to reduce contrast and show feather detail, and a catchlight in the eye always makes a big difference with black-headed birds.
Camera: *Nikon F5*
Lens: *AF-S 500mm f4*
Film: *Fujichrome Sensia 100 uprated to EI200*

out a background of snow, for example, but this shouldn't matter too much if the subject looks right. Failing this, look for another area of reliable mid-tone in the landscape, such as a branch, some rock, or foliage or grass. Assessing what is a good mid-tone is the crucial part. If in doubt, you might try spotmetering a few likely areas and averaging them, but of course this procedure uses valuable time. In practice, it's likely that you'll need to work more quickly, make a rapid

assessment of the scene and adjust with your exposure compensation dial. Again, overexpose against the averaged meter reading for light backgrounds, and under-expose for dark backgrounds.

With extremely bright backgrounds and a poorly lit subject, you probably ought to settle for a silhouette (or use fill flash). This can be pretty effective if the bird has a distinctive shape, or has assumed an interesting posture, and the background is something like

glistening water or mud. As a general rule, I would dial in an additional 2/3 to 1 stop over and above the meter reading to keep texture in the background. Silhouettes against a dawn or sunset sky also look great and are easy to meter. A straight meter reading is quite acceptable, but tends to make the sky a little too well saturated in color. I usually add 1/3 or 2/3 of a stop for a more realistic appearance.

For birds in flight against a white cloudy sky, you would need to allow at least 12/3

stops extra to keep detail in the underparts, and the results would still look pretty washed out and disappointing. Give it more exposure and the sky burns out to clear film. Sometimes you just have to tell yourself it's not worth taking the shot. Birds against a blue sky or leaden thunderclouds are a much better bet, especially if there is some light reflected underneath, say off snow, sand or water. Many photographers maintain that blue sky is a good approximation to mid-gray, but it varies considerably from the nadir to the zenith. At 45 degrees elevation, I would add 1/3 or 2/3 of a stop for a mid-toned bird. A meter reading that is taken off the ground (specifically green grass) tends to overexpose, in my experience. Best of all, spotmeter off a mid-tone area of the birds' underparts.

With dark backgrounds, again you would ideally want to spotmeter off your subject and let the shadows go. Alternatively find a mid-tone in the scene in order to achieve the same. If you're forced to stick to auto, under-expose by something like 1 stop (minus 1 on the exposure-compensation dial).

If you're still unsure, then bracket your exposures. There's no shame in this, especially if you're on an overseas, once-in-a-lifetime trip. A third of a stop either side may not have much effect, so go with 2/3 of a stop each way. Over the long term, you will probably move towards manual metering as your preferred method. You will find that it gets quicker and easier, and you are rewarded with a higher percentage of correctly exposed photographs.

A creative approach to light

When you're beginning bird photography you'll probably be pleased to find a subject within camera range and in good light, and all the more so if you are able to take a sharp, correctly exposed shot. Thinking about more creative aspects perhaps won't be high on your agenda. As your skill and confidence develop, you'll want to explore the possibilities of creating more "artistic" photographs. Learning to see and appreciate the nuances and subtleties of changing light conditions will figure more prominently in your photography.

Brent geese
With the sun against me and strong reflections bouncing off the mud, I knew that it would be difficult to show any detail in the plumage of individual birds. Instead, I chose to show them as silhouettes to emphasize their shape and gregarious habit, and to keep some texture in the mud. By simply overexposing 2/3 of a stop against the average meter reading I was taking a bit of a chance, but the birds were bound to come out black anyway.
Camera: Nikon F4S
Lens: 300mm f2.8
Film: Kodachrome 64

(previous pages) **Whooper swans**
on ice
A straight autoexposure of this
winter scene would have resulted
in gray swans and gray snow.
overexposing by 1²/3 stops
against a spotmeter reading of
white plumage ensured that it
was represented truthfully on film.

Photographing in full sun near the middle of the day in high summer will produce the worst possible results. The light is harsh, contrast high, and usually birds are quite inactive anyway – doubly so in the tropics. Take a siesta for a couple of hours either side of true midday, or find something else to do, but don't bother taking any pictures. The low light of northern winters, early mornings and evenings is so much more flattering, giving better modeling, surface texture, softer shadows and an overall warmer coloration. Basically anything is better than midday sun, so try to be adventurous. Although we might curse cloud and rain because it makes photography more difficult, requiring longer exposures, it can sometimes be a blessing in disguise. The softer, diffused light of a bright cloudy day often makes for the best possible photography conditions. Rain showers are frequently followed by crisp, clear intervals with interesting skies. And falling rain or snow can transform an otherwise ordinary photograph into something quite special, providing you have a reasonable amount of light to work with.

Cross-light is where the main light source is from the side of the subject, and backlight is where it is from behind. Rim-light is that moody, fringing glow resulting from very low backlight. All of these conditions make for more compelling photographs than straight frontal lighting, if used wisely. Suppose you have a whitish bird, such as a tern, in quite strong sunlight, so that you might expect the glare on the plumage to threaten to burn out on the transparency; either you can wait until evening when the contrast has reduced considerably, or hope for the sun to go behind a cloud, or you can photograph the bird against the light, so the whites and pale grays are now in shadow and rendered well on film. A bright halo defines the bird's shape and makes it stand out from the background – instant magic. So who cares if it will never be used in a photographic identification guide?

Catchlights

A bird in frame might be swimming or walking around, or just turning its head from time to time, but watch the changing light and try to capture the moment when it looks best. This might mean changing camera position. In particular, a "catchlight" in the bird's eye can make a huge difference to the success of a photograph, bringing life and sparkle to the subject. This is all the more important for black-headed birds, where the eye can so easily merge with the black plumage and be indistinguishable on a transparency. On the other hand, white-headed birds, large-eyed birds, and birds with a well-defined eye-ring tend to look good without a catchlight. In flat light conditions, a catchlight can be manufactured by punching in a small amount of flash. This looks fine if you don't overdo it, but out of place if the bird is obviously photographed against the light. A catchlight from a flash on camera can sometimes show in the lower part of the eye, and may therefore appear unnatural. Double catchlights look especially weird. These may result from the use of multiple flash guns, making the bird appear as though it has been photographed in a studio. They can also be entirely natural – for example, where the sun is reflected off water as well as directly in the eye.

MAKING YOUR OWN LIGHT

There are times when ambient light is simply inadequate to do the job, so you have to set about making your own. Tungsten lights are OK for studios but totally unsuitable for wild creatures, while we can pretty well discount mirrors and reflectors with mobile subjects like birds. What we're really talking about is electronic flash.

Electronic flash

A single flash on camera will provide you with a convenient bright light source for relatively close subjects. However, the light is "hard" and emanates from a point source, giving rise to dense, black shadows with no modeling on the subject. Built-in pop-up flash, such as found on some of the lower-spec SLR camera bodies, is not powerful enough to be of any real use to bird photographers. Moving the flash off camera, or using additional fill flash can restore a more natural appearance, but the chances

Wendy Shattil and Bob Rozinski

Snow Goose Night Roost, Bosque del Apache, New Mexico

This photograph was highly commended in the 1999 BG Wildlife Photographer of the Year competition. Wendy and Bob describe how they worked with the luscious evening light and translated their vision onto film:

66 *Preparation, perseverance and luck are required to capture special moments like this. Careful observation of the snow geese taught us where and when the flock returned to a night roost. The photo was taken about 30 minutes after sunset when some birds had arrived at the roost and others were still approaching. No hide was necessary. We selected Fujichrome Velvia film to hold the whites in the warm light and register the pastel pink and peach of twilight. Because of the $^1/_8$ sec. exposure, the camera was on a tripod and we selected a corresponding f16 aperture for enough depth of field to include foreground and background birds. Our lens of choice was a Canon 70–200mm on an EOS 1-N body. The zoom simplifies compositional adjustments, which is beneficial with moving subjects. We used a slow shutter speed to give the scene a sense of motion. In this image the geese in the water are still enough to be sharp, while the ones flying in are less defined but recognizable as more of the same birds. From half a roll of film taken to document the scene, there was considerable variability due to the incoming waves of geese, movement of foreground birds, and changes in the light. Only one frame was exactly what we wanted. The least expensive aspect of photography continues to be film, so it makes sense to be generous with it. We've worked this location off and on for more than 15 years without having all the elements work together this well, so we took advantage of a great opportunity and shot as much as possible. The cloudless sunset, lack of wind, and perfect location for the birds combined with our knowledge of working with light and equipment to produce a memorable image.*

No filters or other manipulations were used. Nature provided all of the elements we needed. 99

Song thrush singing

The twinkle in the thrush's eye, or "catchlight," is a straight reflection of the sun, but makes the subject really come alive – watch for its appearance as your bird turns its head, then hit the motordrive.

Camera: Nikon F4S

Lens: 500mm f4 plus 1.4x teleconverter

Film: Fujichrome Sensia 100

are that your photographs will still have a nocturnal look, the black background being caused by flash "fall-off." Remember the inverse square law of light? If your subject is 10m (33ft) away from the flash and the background 20m (66ft) away, the background will receive only a quarter of the illumination reaching the subject. Hence it records 2 stops darker on film – this is quite a difference, and enough to cause undesirable blocked-in shadows on transparency. Assuming that you can't bring the background and subject closer together, you are left with two choices. Either illuminate the background with more flash guns, or balance the flash output with the ambient light level, otherwise known as daylight-balanced fill flash (see pp. 70–71). The latter is usually the more feasible and produces the most natural-looking results. Of course, if you are photographing nocturnal subjects, such as owls, a black background looks perfectly natural and flash fall-off is not an issue, but it would still be better to use more than one flash for improved modeling on the bird.

Another difficulty about using flash in bird photography is that you need either very close subjects or a phenomenal amount of flash power. You can see already that there are a

number of ways of setting about using flash, and modern automated systems do make life an awful lot easier. I still try to avoid using flash in my bird photography wherever possible, preferring the subtler nuances of natural light, although daylight-balanced fill flash can complement it quite sensitively.

Flash features and accessories

Dedicated "smart" flash guns, such as those in the Nikon Speedlight and Canon Speedlite series, are powerful, sophisticated and easy to use. They offer various refinements, such as built-in fresnels for different focal length lenses, automatic daylight-balanced fill flash, infrared autofocusing, wireless through-the-lens (TTL) control with built-in slave cells, rear curtain (or second curtain) flash, strobe effect, modeling light, red-eye reduction, and so on. There is also a good range of independents on the market, including those made by Metz, Vivitar and Sunpak, and some of these models are compatible with proprietary TTL metering systems. For the beefiest flash output from a portable system, look at offerings from Norman and Lumedyne with their ability to run multiple heads from a high-power battery pack. You can also improve your flash recycle time by adding an external battery pack, either main brand or something like a Quantum Turbo battery.

There are a number of ways to diffuse or soften flash light. Studio photographers use umbrellas or softboxes to scatter light rays and produce a softer lighting effect, but these are too large and impractical for most bird photography (except perhaps for birds in enclosed settings like an owl in a barn or a swallow nesting in an outhouse). There are miniature softboxes, which attach to compact electronic flash guns, but you do sacrifice quite a lot in light intensity with these and they are still somewhat cumbersome. More practical is to use a soft white cotton, gauze or glass-fiber diffuser material – a rough and ready solution is to wrap a handkerchief around the flash gun and secure it with a rubber band. Then you have the translucent plastic boxes that clip on to the flash gun, such as the Stofen diffuser, and various homemade equivalents. With all of these diffuser devices, your in-camera TTL flash metering will take account of the modified

light output. Note that diffusers are more effective if they are placed further away from the flash gun. All of these are effective solutions for improving light quality, but at the expense of light intensity.

More likely you'll be looking for ways to increase your flash output, especially when working with longer telephotos. For this purpose you can deploy fresnel screen flash extenders, which attach in front of the flash gun, usually with two connecting arms. These act to focus light into a narrower beam, similar to the angle of view of your telephoto, and gain you an extra 2 stops or so. But they do need to be aligned quite carefully. The Better Beamer/Walt Anderson flash extender is a lightweight, collapsible flash projector that attaches straight on to the flash gun, and is quite simple to set up.

Flash synchronization speed is basically a function of the camera body and how quickly the focal plane shutter operates. Until recently $^1/_{60}$ sec. was the standard flash sync speed, but nowadays $^1/_{250}$ sec. is more usual. This

Lesser noddys at nest
These tropical seabirds were photographed with automatic daylight-balanced fill flash, to combat the shade of the foliage but still appear as close as possible to natural light.
Camera: *Nikon F5*
Lens: *80–200mm f2.8*
Film: *Fujichrome Sensia 100*
Lighting: *SB-26 Speedlight on camera*

allows more flexibility for daylight-balanced fill flash with a greater range of shutter speed options, and is also useful in high-speed flash photography by minimizing ghosting effects. If ambient light is lower than the flash output, then the flash duration will determine the effective exposure time rather than shutter speed. Flash duration might range from about $^1/_{1,000}$ sec. at full output to $^1/_{20,000}$ sec. or even faster at reduced power on a typical compact flash gun. Even the slowest flash duration is fast enough to stop most bird movement, while the faster speeds achievable make it possible to use these modern units for seriously high-speed flash photography.

Normally, flash is synchronized to fire at the start of the shutter opening, but some flash guns can be set to fire at the end of the shutter sequence. This "rear-curtain" flash lends itself well to creative action shots with slow camera shutter speeds, so that you can have a sharp image from the flash exposure with motion blur from the ambient light part of the exposure appearing to fall behind the moving subject (as opposed to in front of the subject with normal sync). Your flash gun might also have a rapid-fire strobe effect, allowing you to record several images of the same bird on a single frame, but to all practical purposes this is only an option with controlled or captive bird subjects. One of the more practical gadgets on modern flash guns is the infrared range finder, which can

autofocus your lens in total darkness as well as set the right flash exposure – I have used this feature to good effect when photographing shearwaters in dark nest burrows.

Determining flash exposure

The power or maximum light output of a flash gun is described by the manufacturer's guide number; the higher the guide number, the more powerful the flash. Before the advent of the smart flash, with its automatic TTL metering, all flash exposures had to be calculated by using the guide number, and it is still useful to know how to apply it (for example, in high-speed flash work). The guide number when divided by the flash-to-subject distance in meters tells you the aperture you need to set when using ISO100 film. A typical modern flash might have a published guide number of 45 (meters). If your flash-to-subject distance (read off the lens-focusing scale if the flash is mounted on the camera hot-shoe) is 5m (16ft), then you should set your aperture to f9 (45 ÷ 5) with ISO100 film. If you happen to be using ISO200 film, don't double the guide number, but work out in the normal way and then expose at 1 stop less – f13 in this case, or f11 $^1/_3$. Similarly, if you have ISO64 film loaded, simply add $^2/_3$ of a stop to the calculated exposure.

A note of caution: manufacturers' published guide numbers tend to be optimistic, probably in the assumption that you'll be photographing relatively reflective subjects such as people's faces. I recommend that you work out your own guide number for your flash gun by making a series of test shots on a mid-toned subject outdoors (no reflective surfaces for the flash to bounce off) and carefully recording distance and aperture. This will almost certainly show that your true guide number is somewhat less than that advertised and give you a better understanding of your actual flash output, even if you have no intention of working out your flash exposures manually as normal practice.

For a more accurate flash exposure calculation you can use a flashmeter. From the subject position, point the meter cone towards the camera lens and trigger the flash by means

Wedge-tailed shearwater in nest burrow

It's difficult to focus on a bird down a black hole in either manual or autofocus, if you don't have a flashlight on hand. However, an infrared rangefinder on a flash gun can automatically set the focus on a compatible lens and camera.
Camera: *Nikon F5*
Lens: *80–200mm f2.8*
Film: *Fujichrome Sensia 100*
Lighting: *SB-26 Speedlight on camera*

Blue tit and great tit on
peanut feeder
Multiple flash guns were used to
light this garden bird set, one
directed at the subject and two at
the background of shrubs. Flash
alone determined exposure
duration, and was fast enough to
freeze the wing movement of the
aggressive great tit –
approximately $^1/_{1,000}$ *sec.*
Camera: *Bronica SQ-Am*
Lens: *250mm f5.6*
Film: *Fujichrome RDP100*
Lighting: *Lumedyne flash system*

of an X-sync cable, or remote shutter release.
This can give you a digital exposure read-out
accurate to $^1/_{10}$ of a stop, and is very reliable,
but only in fairly controlled photography
"sets." Since you can't walk up to wild birds
with flash meter in hand, it's not often a
practical proposition out in the field.

In practice, it is more likely that you will
use the flash's own automatic exposure facility,
or better still the camera's integrated TTL flash
metering. A TTL sensor placed in the camera
measures light reflected off the film plane
and regulates the flash output accordingly.
Standard TTL flash is appropriate for dull light
conditions, and the automatic metering is
pretty reliable, provided the subject is within
flash range – there is normally a warning light
to alert you to under-exposure.

Multiple flash

Using more than one flash gun will expand
your creative options considerably. So if you
are working a regular site, such as a garden
pond, bird feeder or nest box, it is better to
light the "set" with two or more flash guns.
There should be one main light, which
provides most of the illumination, and this is
best set high and to one side of the camera to
give an obvious directional light source. Your
fill flash gun should be located nearer to the
lens axis (or possibly slightly to the other side

of the camera) and be set at about one
quarter of the power of the main flash (or
double the distance from the subject), so that
it softens the shadows but doesn't compete
with the main light. Be prepared to
experiment with the relative positions and try
moving the fill flash so that it doesn't produce
a second catchlight in the bird's eye. If you are
working with nocturnal subjects like owls, a
third flash firing behind the subject will
produce a halo of backlight and make the
subject stand out from the dark background,
emulating moonlight when executed skilfully.
Take care not to point the third flash directly at
the camera lens giving rise to flare, and again
you will need to experiment with relative flash
positions and lighting proportions.

The only reason I can think of for using
more than three flash guns is for illuminating
backgrounds. So for instance, at a bird-feeding
station photographed in daylight you want the
extra illumination to give better depth of field,
but you also need short flash duration at a
high sync speed to stop bird movement. Two
flash guns work fine on the subject, but you
still have the old problem of flash fall-off with
the background, and balancing to daylight
would force the camera shutter speed too
slow. The answer is to light the background
with a couple more flash guns, balancing their
output to that of the main flash. Test shots will

George McCarthy
Three barn owls, Sussex, England

These young barn owls were reared in a disused water tower, which they continued to visit after fledging. George McCarthy photographed them there, under license, while a new business park was being built around them. Although the birds were successful this particular season, the loss of habitat has meant that the barn owls have since found somewhere else to nest, despite the fact that the developers subsequently incorporated a new clock tower in the park with special provision for owl nesting, with the photographer's help. George explains how he made this charming image, and how he lit the scene:

66 *Photographs were taken from a 10m (33ft) scaffolding hide, which was built up over several days, carefully monitoring the birds' comings and goings each evening. At no time was there any problem with the adults accepting the hide, and in fact they and the young often used it as a staging post on which to land. Lighting was supplied by two Metz 60CT4 flash guns; the main light angled in from the left, with the fill flash positioned slightly to the other side and above the camera. I used a Canon EOS 5 camera with a 100–300mm f5.6L lens. The aperture would have been f11, which was calculated beforehand from a series of test shots using a white fluffy toy to ensure perfectly accurate exposures. My film was Kodachrome 64. I pre-focused the lens in daylight before each photography session, and was able to see well enough what was going on when the birds were present without the need for any artificial illumination.*

Although I was photographing over a period of several weeks, only on this one occasion did all three youngsters pose together, and then only for four frames as the recycle time for the guns was 13 seconds. I was delighted with the result, which continues to be one of my best-selling bird photographs. 99

be necessary to check the light balance and make sure that no telltale shadows are falling on the viewable background.

To calculate exposure for multiple flash using guide numbers, just use the distance of the main flash to subject and disregard the rest, so long as you have set their output lower as recommended above. Really it makes better sense to take advantage of built-in TTL flash metering if you have one of the proprietary systems. The practicalities of using multiple flash means using off-camera flash brackets or flash stands, and TTL cables with multi-connectors or the use of photo-electric slave cells to fire all the flash guns simultaneously. Fortunately the latest wireless TTL flash systems with built-in slaves eliminate the need for lots of expensive and unwieldy TTL cable, and take care of exposure calculation.

Fill flash

Daylight-balanced fill flash (or fill-in flash) is quite an asset in bird photography, and its automation is a godsend. Use it to fill in deep shadows with bright midday sun, or with subjects against the light, and especially when working in dappled light conditions such as under woodland canopy. It will also bring life into a bird's plumage on dreary, overcast days and produce a gleam or catchlight in the bird's eye.

Calculating daylight-balanced fill flash isn't such a mysterious art. Set the ambient light exposure in your normal way, say in aperture priority automatic with center-weighted metering, or in manual if you prefer, and then set the flash to deliver between 1 and 2 stops less light. In the past you had to think quite carefully about how to do this, and it meant cheating the autometering on the flash gun by setting a wider aperture or a higher film speed than that actually set on the lens and camera respectively. Now it's normally a simple matter of dialing in the appropriate adjustment on the flash compensation dial. Go for minus $1^2/_3$ stops as the standard for a mid-toned subject – this should be just enough to take the edge off the shadows without making your photograph appear too flashy or unnatural. With black birds, you will need to reduce this 1 further

The effect of daylight-balanced fill flash

For this series of photographs of a kingfisher the background was quite bright but the foreground in shade. An ambient light exposure with no flash (left) produced an acceptable result, but the bird still looked rather drab. The correct amount of fill flash (center) showed a marked improvement, with shadows subtly filled and colors well saturated, but not too obviously taken with flash. Too much fill flash (right) gave rise to a "washed out," unnatural light appearance.

Camera: Nikon F5

Lens: 500mm plus 1.4x teleconverter

Film: Fujichrome Sensia 100 uprated to EI200

Lighting: SB-26 Speedlight on camera

stop (minus 2^2/3) to account for the subject's low reflectance. For white birds, minus ^{2}/3 of a stop is nearer the mark. If you're doing it right, you still get a good exposure even if the flash hasn't fully recharged or you have a bad connection – you just don't get the flash element and will be stuck with the gloomy shadows. This can also occur if you simply don't have the flash power to reach the subject, so remember to watch for the flash under-exposure warning.

All of the above assumes that you are using the flash at its normal flash output or standard TTL setting, and not in the automatic daylight-balancing mode. The latter employs a pre-programmed fill flash level of about 1 stop below ambient light. It's perfectly OK to use this automatic mode, but you must take out about ^{2}/3 of a stop to achieve the same look as described above. This is the quick and easy method of fill flash, and it's reliable most of the time. Again you will need to use the flash compensation dial to adjust for light subjects (try plus ^{1}/3) and dark subjects (try minus 1^2/3), according to your own experience. For strong backlight, I tend to leave the compensation at zero. With the Nikon system, you can adjust the flash exposure (only) by making corrections on the flash gun, while adjusting the camera's exposure-compensation dial affects the whole exposure (both flash and ambient). With Canon, flash can be compensated on both flash gun and camera body but alterations made on the flash gun will override those made on the camera. Getting these two different flash modes (standard TTL and automatic daylight-balancing) straight in your own mind is imperative, and the key to mastering fill flash technique.

"Red-eye"

Some birds, particularly large-eyed nocturnal or forest-dwelling species, are prone to "red-eye," caused by flash reflected off the retina. To overcome red-eye, the flash gun needs to be relocated away from the lens axis using an off-camera bracket and lead. You might notice unnatural-looking catchlights with other birds at times, perhaps too low in the eye, and again this can be cured by moving the flash gun a touch higher relative to the camera. Unfortunately, you tend to notice these things only in the processed results, too late to do anything about it, but you can learn by experience to anticipate the problem with certain familiar subjects. Fill flash continues to work perfectly well with flash extenders and flash off-camera, if you use the right leads, because the camera's TTL metering measures light as it enters the lens and adjusts the flash output appropriately.

High-speed flash

The short duration of flash burst can be used to arrest the movement of fast-moving subjects and depict it in fine detail on film. It can be useful for photographing small birds in flight, for example. Purpose-built high-speed flash units deliver high illumination at fast speeds and still have a short recycle time, but they are neither cheap nor widely available. "High-speed" flash generally means flash speeds of $1/10,000$ sec. or less – faster than the shutter on any standard SLR camera. Such

speeds might be necessary for flying insects and a few fast-flying birds, but you can achieve a lot with two or three basic flash guns set at low output if you can get them close enough to your subject. Look for manual settings that deliver $1/2$ down to perhaps $1/64$ power output, and check in the handbook what flash speed this represents. On a Nikon SB-26 Speedlight, full flash output (1/1) would have a flash duration of $1/1,000$ sec. while $1/64$ would be $1/23,000$ sec. – easily fast enough for working with birds.

The more practical difficulties lie in persuading wild birds to use a predictable flight path within your flash range, and synchronizing the flash burst precisely to the bird's position. These problems should not be underestimated, and you may need to devote the rest of your life to perfecting the technique!

To fire the shutter it is common practice to use an infrared beam trigger device, where the moving bird passes through the infrared beam, completes a whole circuit and effectively photographs itself. There are a few commercially available beam triggers, of varying sensitivity and range, usually effective up to a couple of meters. The trouble is, by the time the mirror has flipped up, the shutter has opened and the flash has fired, the bird will be well out of frame. This time-lag can be reduced by about 30 percent by using camera mirror lock-up, but remember that this entails working in manual exposure and focus modes. Alternatively, you can use a Canon EOS-1N RS with the fixed pellicle (so no delay waiting for a reflex mirror to move out of the way) and retain your autometering functions. Whichever you use, there will still be a time-lag of some milliseconds to account for, and you will have to predict where the bird will be when the flash fires. This is a case of trial and error, and no small amount of luck, or getting into some very sophisticated electronics and specially designed shutters. Even when you are successful in getting the bird in frame, more often than not it will be in a poor position, with a wing across the head or something similarly unfortunate. Thus, high-speed flash photography undoubtedly requires a serious time commitment.

Barred owl, exhibiting "red-eye" syndrome

Flash located too close to the lens axis was responsible for this unpleasant phenomenon. I ought to have used an off-camera TTL flash cable to get around the problem, but that was one accessory left behind on this particular day.

Camera: *Nikon F5*

Lens: *AF-S 300mm f2.8 plus 1.4x teleconverter*

Film: *Fujichrome Sensia 100*

Lighting: *SB-26 Speedlight on camera*

Stephen Dalton
Wren in flight, Sussex, England

Stephen Dalton is a pioneer and recognized expert in high-speed flash nature photography. He insists that there are no trade secrets regarding his technique; in his own words:

" *Both my techniques and equipment are pretty basic. The high-speed flash and triggering system were designed in the 1970s and virtually none of my gear has changed since. Certainly far more advanced stuff is readily available these days.*

The wren was photographed around 1975 and completed within a day! It was nesting in the bank of a stream about a meter up from the water among ferns, mosses and liverworts. Wrens are among the easiest birds to tackle because in my experience they take little notice of the photographer. Often, as in this case, the hide can be dispensed with altogether. I just stood a couple of meters away and watched, making the odd adjustment every now and again.

Three high-speed flash guns, with a flash duration of around $1/25,000$ sec., were carefully positioned to emulate natural lighting. Triggering was achieved by a conventional light beam and photo-electric cell, which in turn fired the camera via an external solenoid attached to a mechanical Leicaflex SL. The lens was a bellows version f4 Macro Elmar. Film used was Kodachrome II, an emulsion, that was superseded by the inferior Kodachrome 25. The aperture was about f11.

It is very unusual for high-speed photography of this nature to take only a day or so to complete. Most projects carry on for several days or sometimes weeks. Positioning flash guns and making adjustments at ground level around a co-operative creature, particularly a bird that frequently returns to one spot, is a totally different ball game to working with an owl 10m (33ft) up a tree – as you can imagine! "

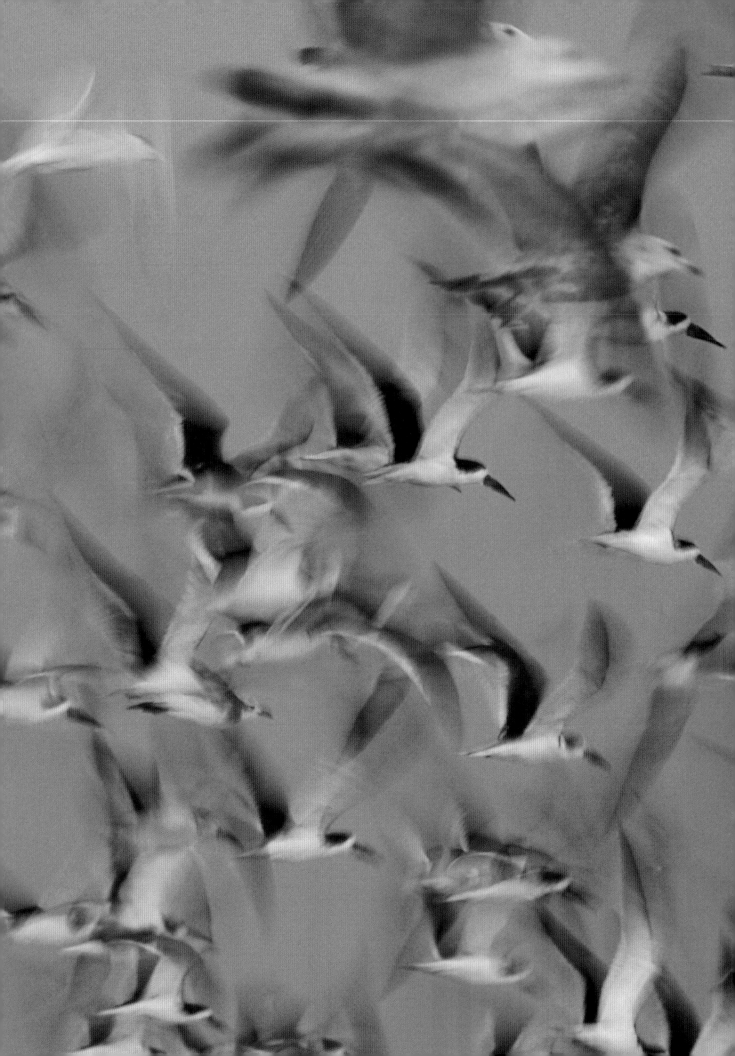

Chapter 3
IN THE FIELD

Learning to visualize photographs is half the battle, but you also need to know where to look for birds, how to approach them, and generally how to get about and work in the field. This is the practical part of the book, the bit where you realize you have to get your hands (and more) dirty.

Mandarin drake

Wildfowl collections offer accessible bird subjects for practicing your technique. But be aware that many of the birds may be "pinioned" (some primary feathers removed to prevent them flying off). This handsome mandarin, a feral breeding species in Britain, was actually photographed on a river bank near my home, but the pinioned wing betrays its recent captivity. Observe the absence of a protruding wing tip on the near side.

Camera: *Nikon F5*
Lens: *AF-S 500mm f4*
Film: *Fujichrome Sensia 100*

(previous pages) **Black skimmers** *This post-roost flock in flight was photographed at approximately $^1/_{15}$ sec.*

GETTING CLOSE TO BIRDS

The great mystique about bird photography seems to be, how on earth can you get close enough to wild birds to take any worthwhile photographs? First outings with a telephoto tend to reinforce this impression for most people, and the need for specialist field skills and boundless patience quickly becomes apparent as birds disappear into the undergrowth. I don't wish to dismiss these difficulties too lightly, and indeed all bird photographers, however experienced they may be, continually face frustrations, near misses, and being told, "you should have been here yesterday" – but let's face it, if it was easy it wouldn't be that much fun. Besides, there are a number of techniques that we can learn to improve our chances.

Getting started

Assuming that you are now equipped to a reasonable level as has been described in earlier chapters, you will want to find some birds you can photograph relatively easily to get used to your camera and fire your interest. At this stage, it's not a bad idea to visit a park lake, or a wildfowl or other captive bird collection, where you have guaranteed subjects at close range. Other locations for more approachable subjects might be harbours, picnic sites, or gardens where birds are used to visiting bird tables and feeders and are habituated to people. Practice framing up on moving birds, experimenting with different lenses and camera positions, and generally familiarizing yourself with all the camera controls. If your equipment is totally new to

you, I would say it's even worth practising for a while without any film loaded until you feel more confident. But you'll have to expose film to determine whether you have mastered such crucial things as exposure control and critical focusing. Start with a faster film – say, ISO200 or 400 – and progress to slower, finer-grained emulsions as your technique improves.

When you have your first processed results, the chances are you'll be disappointed at the low proportion of good shots. Toss the rejects and show other people only the better ones. This is basically the same editorial process as

used by professionals, and it's neither cheating nor wasteful, just a necessary part of your development as a bird photographer. Being hard on yourself now will lead to more rapid progress, and you will get better.

I strongly suggest teaming up with a friend with similar interests so that you can fuel each other's enthusiasm and share in the practical aspects, particularly early on. The mutual support will accelerate your progress and help to see you through some of the inevitable frustrations. You could also benefit from belonging to a camera club, especially if other members are interested in birds and wildlife photography. Without doubt you should join the BirdLife International partner organization in your country, and learn as much as possible about the birds you would like to photograph, their habitat requirements and where you might go to find them. Develop a network of birdwatching friends, perhaps through a local bird club, and ask them to alert you to any good photographic opportunities (though nonphotographers tend to underestimate the distance of birds out in the open by a factor of about ten, in my experience).

Great bittern

Although bitterns tend to skulk in reed beds, they do emerge to feed in open water from time to time. This one was photographed from a public birdwatching hide at Lee Valley Country Park, Hertfordshire, U.K.

Camera: *Nikon F5*
Lens: *AF-S 500mm f4*
Film: *Fujichrome Sensia 100*

Gannet breeding colony at Bass Rock, Scotland

A trip to a seabird colony in summer is always a feast day for a bird photographer. Your greatest problem is likely to be the weather; if winds are unfavorable, boats may not be able to land safely at island sites such as the Bass Rock in Scotland's Firth of Forth.
Camera: *Nikon F4S*
Lens: *28mm f2.8*
Film: *Kodachrome 64*

Nature reserves with public observation hides frequently afford good photographic opportunities, particularly at wetland sites, and membership of a bird organization will give you free access to many of these. You do need to remember, though, that these are not primarily designed with photographers in mind, and you will have to be tolerant and considerate of other visitors, not least when movement over wooden floors makes your camera wobble. Perhaps you just need to get in earlier in the day to avoid the heavier visitor pressure. If you think the windows are too low or too narrow, or there is some annoying vegetation obstructing the view, by all means mention it to one of the reserve staff; if you do this politely, you might find some remedial action is taken. Many of my own favorite photographs have been taken from public hides such as these, usually just resting a beanbag on the window ledge.

Treat yourself to a visit to a seabird colony in the breeding season, and you will be thrilled at the approachability and sheer numbers of the birds and the chance to take lots of photographs in one session. This sort of experience can make up for a few disappointments and really lift your spirits. There are also a growing number of specialist holidays for wildlife photographers, and workshops with experienced professionals as tutors. Such holidays tend to go to destinations with reliable, good light and big, tame birds, but of course nothing is guaranteed. Tours such as these are not cheap, but are likely to suit people with limited holiday and leisure time.

Finding birds to photograph

As you gain in skill and confidence, you should be seeking out your own subjects rather than relying on organized activities. Inexperienced bird photographers often seem to believe that you have to be "in the know" about the best locations, but this is really missing the point. True, you have to know enough about a particular bird to predict where it is likely to be found and in what season, and this is an important part of your background research and developing field skills. There are a few "honeypot" sites for certain species that are regurgitated in various publications, but you shouldn't expect others to do the work for you all the time, or you'll never really mature as a bird photographer. There are potential subjects and latent photographs all around you, wherever you live, and your challenge is to be able to visualize them.

An closer inspection of the published photographic record will soon reveal that many bird species and their behavioral activities are under-represented. Where are all the photographs of the commonplace, such as house sparrows and starlings; the small and secretive, like willow warblers and chiffchaffs; the fast fliers, like swifts and swallows? Not to mention icons such as a song thrush at its "anvil" or a skylark in song flight – behavior we are all familiar with, but still largely unphotographed. I agree that some of these are particularly challenging subjects, but the difficulty does not lie in the bird's scarcity, or an inability to locate it. As a sometime picture researcher and photo library editor, I can testify that it is very difficult indeed to find top-quality photographs of garden birds at feeders, bird tables and nest boxes. Such subjects are neither hard to find nor difficult to approach, but many photographers look instead for subjects that they imagine are more exciting or desirable. But commoner birds can be equally beautiful and at least as interesting as the more unusual ones, and there is certainly a market for the photographs.

Planning an assignment is a great way to focus the mind, whether it be for a camera-club project, national competition or simply a self-set goal. Perhaps it is your lifetime ambition to photograph the King of Saxony bird of paradise, or a similarly rare and exotic bird, in which case you probably know more than I about how to get on with it. If you are not quite so dedicated or single-minded, choose a bird to which you might have ready access, something you should have the opportunity to do better than others. If you live near the coast you might specialize in shore birds. You could begin by looking at

what other photographers have achieved with the same subject, and think about how you might do it differently – or better! Read the published references, and learn all about your chosen bird's habitat and its food preferences, distribution and migration, social patterns and behavior, and its breeding ecology. You may also need to do some local research: it sounds obvious, but it really is no use turning up expecting to photograph a wader roost only to find it's low tide. Speak to some appropriate experts if you possibly can, whether these be academic researchers, farmers, gamekeepers or conservation managers, and pick their brains in order to gain further insights. Think more about what it is that makes the species attractive or interesting, and the behavior or posture you would like to portray. You should begin to form a mental picture of how you would like your photographs to look, right down to details such as background and season, and then set about aiming to achieve it for real. Quite possibly you will need to spend more time conducting your background research than you actually spend on the photography, but it is certainly not wasted time – good preparation always pays off.

Explore possibilities of access at various likely sites, and secure permission from landowners to set up hides, if necessary. This might be more difficult than you would first imagine, and it helps if you can show some credentials that testify to your being a responsible and trustworthy photographer – some work you have done previously, perhaps, or a letter of introduction from another landowner. There is often a presumption against portable photography

Robin in sub-song
Don't overlook photo opportunities close to home, where some types of bird may have become habituated to people. No hide or special preparation was needed for this portrait of a robin in my garden.
Camera: *Nikon F5*
Lens: *AF-S 500mm f4 plus 1.4x teleconverter*
Film: *Fujichrome Sensia 100 uprated to EI200*
Lighting: *Fill flash from SB-26 Speedlight*

hides being allowed on nature reserves, but it may be at the discretion of the site manager. Your chances will be much improved if you are known as a local supporter, the more so if you have given your time and help as a voluntary warden or helper. What else can you give back? The offer of duplicate or spare slides for staff to use in their lectures, or a print for the information center display probably wouldn't go unappreciated. And if you make the offer, be sure to follow it up. Next time ought to be easier.

The concept of the "home patch" is just as valid to a photographer as it is to a birdwatcher. Regular visits to known areas force them to yield up their secrets. I find that I am rewarded more often in locations that are familiar to me, and to which I have frequently returned, and somehow it is more fulfilling when you have taken the trouble to get to know a place and its birds. Furthermore, whatever your subject, and no matter how many times you have photographed it, you will never believe you have made the best possible photograph – there is always better to be had.

The photographer's hide

A photographer's hide (or "blind") is a device for concealing the photographer and getting closer to a bird than you could without it. Hides work, not because birds can't see them, but because they don't associate them with people, and so perceive no threat. To maintain that trust and lack of suspicion, you must observe a few simple procedures and disciplines (more on this below). Hides are set up at locations where there is a better-than-average chance of a bird returning, whether for food, water or a favorite perch or a communal roost. Predicting these places and being there at the right time is the difficult part, but we'll look at that, too.

The main requirements for a hide are that it should be rigid (not flapping or moving about), opaque, and dark inside. There needs to be a way in and out, an opening for the camera lens, and at least one viewing window. Beyond this, it

Wildlife photographer's dome hide
This model from Wildlife Watching Supplies fulfils most of my requirements, and is very light and compact for traveling.

can be any size and shape you like, and made of almost any material.

The traditional portable hide is a canvas or fabric structure on a wooden or metal frame. It is usually about 1.5m (5ft) high, with a base about 1m (3ft) square – just large enough to contain photographer, tripod and equipment. There are commercially available models like the Jamie Wood "Fensman," but many photographers make their own, tailored to their personal requirements and preferences. A modern variation is the dome hide, with flexible poles, such as the LL Rue "Ultimate" blind and Wildlife Watching Supplies dome hide. These are lighter, more compact and usually quicker to erect, so they are better suited to traveling, though they are not quite so robust for withstanding the elements over longer periods. Small tents and hooped sleeping bags can also be pressed into service as hides, and are great for low viewpoints, but there's a limit to how long you can lie on your stomach propped up on your elbows. Bag hides that are designed simply to throw over the photographer and camera on tripod are quite hopeless, because your shape and every movement are visible.

Lens openings need to be at a comfortable height when you are seated, and disguised somehow. A conical lens port can be sewn into one of the hide panels, with a drawstring for fastening tight around the lens barrel. These are good for concealing your hands and keeping out light, but when it's windy the movement of the hide material is transmitted to the lens so camera shake can be a problem. A better solution is the combined viewing window and lens opening, making use of two or more loose flaps of gauze or mesh material, so you can see out but the birds can't see in. I opt for a removable fabric panel making a rectangular window, which I then cover liberally with scrim netting that hangs loosely around the lens, and I find this gives me the best possible visibility with adequate screening.

There are a few other features you might pay attention to. Spiked poles driven into soft ground make for a very stable framework, especially with the addition of guy ropes; however, on a solid substrate you will need a

Niall Benvie
Eider drake, Montrose, Scotland

Niall Benvie is a hardy Scot who appears not to mind the cold, and regularly takes to the water with his favorite, home-made floating hide. I asked him to account for his preference:

" *Of the different species of waterfowl I have photographed from my amphibious hide, eiders have proved to be the most trusting. Once the hide is beached, as the tide ebbs, it is sometimes possible to stalk the ducks by edging forwards a few centimeters at a time. Some confiding birds have allowed me to approach as close as 5m (16ft). I think the amphibious hide is generally more successful than a fixed terrestrial one because it appears to the birds from the water; many species appear to associate a human threat only with the land.*

As far as stability is concerned, the hide works best when it is grounded but, given enough light and fast film, it is feasible to shoot from the open water. The trick is always to keep your feet on the bottom of the estuary or lake. Not only is this type of hide mobile, allowing the photographer to advance, withdraw, and move on to another group of birds, but it also offers an intimate, low-angle perspective on the subject. My current model allows me to have the lens just 15cm (6in) above water level, supported by a beanbag resting on the hide frame. An angle finder means that I do not risk flooding my chest waders as I look through the camera, and autofocus keeps the image sharp while I concentrate on panning the hide to follow the birds. This is the last word in "fluid action."

For this shot I used a Nikon F5 and Nikkor 500mm f4 AF-S lens, Fujichrome Sensia 100 film uprated to EI200, with an exposure of $^1/_{1,000}$ sec. at f5.6. During courtship in March, eiders swim all around my hide, often approaching too close to focus. The speed of this one's approach can be gauged by the bow-wave. "

---

self-supporting structure. Flaps or pockets at the base of the walls can be usefully employed for weighting down with rocks to give extra stability. Flat-topped hides are better with roof support members, so that accumulating rain-water can run off rather than drip through. Interior pockets are most useful for stowing accessories, keeping them handy, off the ground and out of the dirt.

Semi-permanent hides for longer-term projects can be made from marine plywood or glass fiber, while improvised hides might be built from local materials, such as rocks or fallen branches, perhaps with a sheet of plastic and a turfed roof for weather-proofing. I have even known photographers who have made hides out of carved blocks of snow, like an igloo. For working at height, scaffold towers might need to be bought or hired, with a suitable platform for accommodating your hide, but ensure you observe safety guidelines. Further refinements and specialisms include amphibious or floating hides, which are mainly used for ducks and waterfowl. I like the North American model that is disguised as a muskrat lodge; this is one for the intrepid, involving a semi-submerged operator propelling the structure through the water with fins. A hybrid hide I once encountered on an estuary floated serenely through high water and then grounded so that it was stable at low tide, and featured an amazing revolving turret like a military tank. So your imagination is the only limit.

(previous pages)
Corncrake in iris bed
This corncrake was photographed from a car window in the Hebrides.

Hide camouflage
Made from locally available, natural materials, this hide (below left) blends with the surrounding topography. The traditional canvas hide (below right) employs camouflage netting and leaf screen to disguise its cuboid shape.

Hide procedures

Before installing a hide, it is imperative that you obtain permission from the landowner or their agent. Even in the most remote location, don't presume that nobody will notice you. You should also consult other interested parties before going ahead – the farm manager, shooting tenant, grazier, or anybody else who might come across you and wonder what's going on. Many national parks and nature reserves around the world forbid the use of photographic hides, so before visiting make sure you are aware of the park regulations with regard to photography.

In most countries there are statutory laws governing photography of wild birds at the nest. Disturbance is strongly discouraged, and you may need to obtain a license to photograph some species. Erecting a hide near the nest would certainly count as intentional disturbance. Incidentally, possession of a license confers no right of entry, so you must still obtain the landowner's permission. Different systems apply in different parts of the world, and in some countries all nest photography is against the law. You should assume that there are regulations in force unless you know differently. Unfortunately there is no central register where you can investigate the various international legal requirements, but the BirdLife International partner organization in the relevant

country ought to be able to enlighten you.

To ensure the birds' welfare and improve your own chances of success when using hides, follow best practice at all times and err on the side of caution. The guiding principle is that the welfare of the bird is more important than the photograph.

Hides should be sited so as to be away from the attention of casual observers, as far as possible. Use depressions in the ground and topographical features, such as boulders and fallen branches, as natural cover. Digging down might be an option to keep a low profile, but be mindful that heavy rain could flood you out. Camouflage with nets and leaf screen, or local vegetation, such as reed stems, heather or foliage, to break up the outline of the hide, particularly at sensitive locations where you don't want to attract people's attention.

Work out your hide position by framing up with your preferred telephoto on the likely bird position, and if you have difficulty imagining the relative size of the bird, refer to a field guide for its dimensions and place a similar-sized object *in situ* so as to determine range. Consider where the light will be coming from at the times you expect to use the hide. It is best to introduce a hide in stages, beginning by erecting it some way off and moving up gradually to the final working distance. Alternatively, start with the hide in a heap on the ground and slowly build it up. To do this

responsibly might take as little as a few hours with garden birds at a feeder, or a couple of weeks with a bird of prey at the nest. Check after each movement that the birds have accepted the hide by watching from a distance, and if there is any suspicion that the birds are being prevented from going about their normal behavior because of the hide, move it back a stage or withdraw altogether. Only when you are positive that the hide is tolerated should you consider leaving it unattended. Secure against the elements, camouflage as above, and introduce a dummy lens for the birds to get used to before you commence photography. A black plastic plant pot is a good imitation of a lens hood, and cheaper to lose. If you think the birds might be especially sensitive, you could line the inside base with a reflective material such as aluminum foil to look more like a glass lens.

You must be sure that the birds you are targeting don't associate you with the hide, but it is difficult to be absolutely confident that you are not being observed entering and leaving. For this reason, it's customary to use an accomplice as a "walk-away." Approach the hide together. Your accomplice should remain close by until you are properly installed with all of your equipment. He or she then looks around and checks that you are completely invisible from outside, particularly when your hands are on the lens and your face is up close to the window. You may need to double up the scrim, or wear gloves and balaclava to cover up pale skin. Certainly avoid having any window or door opening letting in light behind you, otherwise your silhouette will be obvious. When all looks good, your accomplice can leave you to it. The idea is that the birds see the human disturbance arrive and disappear, and they return to their normal business. It does work, although photographers' folklore holds that with more intelligent birds like ravens you need to use several people as walk-aways. At the end of your session, the disturbance again arises away from the hide when your accomplice returns to collect you. Arrange to meet at an agreed time, and leave together as quickly and quietly as you can. If you can possibly coordinate it so that you are collected from the hide when no birds are around, so much the better. You can signal when the coast is clear by poking a handkerchief out of a side window, or maintain communication with a cell phone or walkie-talkie. Remember to replace the dummy lens when you leave.

So how long should you stay in the hide? In short, as long as you can bear it. Usually my minimum spell in a hide would be about six hours, but it depends on the species of bird and the situation. Two or three hours might be appropriate for a drinking pool or garden bird feeder, with different birds coming and going

A recessed hide
Situated at a bird of prey feeding station, this hide was partly dug into the ground and camouflaged with net, leaf screen and dead bracken to make it as inconspicuous as possible. Note the bottle that is used as a dummy lens in between photography sessions.

Swallow

A completely fortuitous accident resulted in this photograph. My hide was set up for a larger subject at greater range when this swallow landed just in front.

Camera: *Nikon F3*

Lens: *300mm f2.8 plus 2x teleconverter*

Film: *Kodachrome 64*

(opposite) **Great bustard male courtship display**

Photographs like this can be achieved only through careful and sustained hide work (see pp.126–7).

Camera: *Nikon F4S*

Lens: *500mm f4*

Film: *Fujichrome Provia 100*

all the time, but for more sensitive subjects, such as birds of prey or grazing geese, it would be more like twelve hours, and could be from dawn until dusk.

You want to avoid repeated disturbance at all costs, and it would be bad form to keep entering and leaving the hide, or have an accomplice attempt to flush birds on to a choice perch, make them fly, or otherwise harass them. Apart from being unethical, it's unlikely to produce the results that you want.

Settle into the hide quietly, try to avoid making any sudden movements of lenses, and on no account poke hands outside the hide. Do not allow the lens to protrude too far – a camouflage sleeve, tape or cover helps to make it less obvious. When birds first return within range, try to contain your excitement; it is usually best to give them a chance to settle and not just hit the motordrive. Leave the lens pre-framed and focused on a likely perch or resting position, make only minor movements at first and keep them slow and smooth. Perhaps try a single frame initially to test the birds' reaction to the noise of the shutter and film advance, and you'll begin to see just how much they will tolerate. As they become more confident you can take greater liberties, but this seldom means being able to swing the lens around indiscriminately; neither should you change lenses while birds are present. To attract a bird's attention and make it look up, you could try whistling softly, but I wouldn't do much more than that. Don't be lulled into a false sense of security if birds seem to ignore the hide and camera completely; if you overstep the mark and flush a bird, it is most unlikely that you'll be able to retrieve the situation.

When you withdraw your hide at the conclusion of photography, remove all trash from the site and make good, replacing turfs or anything else you might have disturbed. It should look as if you were never there.

The above describes a cautious and responsible approach to hide work, and it's the way I always try to work until I know a particular bird well enough to be sure I can

afford to relax a little or vary the routine. In some situations it might be possible to enter and leave the hide under the cover of darkness without the need for an accomplice – for example at a field used by grazing geese, which go to roost elsewhere at dusk. You have to use your common sense as to where shortcuts can be made without disturbing the birds unreasonably or spoiling your own chances. For a high-tide roost of shore birds there is no harm in setting up your hide at low tide when there are no birds around, sitting out the tide and exiting after they have all dispersed to feed again; but you would still do better if they have time to get used to the hide first.

Comfort in the hide

Whether your working session is six or twelve hours, it's a long time to sit still and be quiet. Hide sessions can be arduous and often boring, but there's no merit in enduring hardship for the sake of it. Anyway, if you are cold and restless it's going to affect your work, for the worse. The more comfortable you are, the longer you can persevere and the better you can concentrate on your photography.

First of all, make sure you have a comfortable seat. It needs to be light and portable, quite compact and low to the ground. I prefer a canvas chair with rails rather than pointy legs, so it doesn't sink into soft ground so easily – there's nothing worse than tipping over on one corner all the time. A back rest is a huge benefit so that you can relax in between spells of photography. Fishing tackle shops usually offer a good selection of folding chairs, if you have trouble finding them elsewhere.

Inactivity causes you to feel the cold more than usual, so dress well for cold-weather sessions and wear extra layers. Thermal underwear is highly recommended, as well as hat and gloves. Handwarmers are a good idea, either the charcoal-burner type, or chemical packs. In hot weather you just have to strip off and hope you don't get any surprise callers.

Food and drink will sustain you, but remember that what goes in must come out. Large plastic bottles can be useful in this respect, and they can also double as a dummy lens (when empty!). If you're not too fussy, just

ensure you know which way is downhill and that the land drainage is good. For more serious calls of nature, I recommend you keep a plastic bag and some toilet tissue standing by for emergencies. Mercifully, I have never needed to resort to this.

If you are ambitious, planning sustained hide sessions with overnight stops, you really want a hide large enough in which to stretch out and lie down. Bring a sleeping bag and mat. For five-star accommodation, you could even consider a portable gas cooker and chemical toilet, but it would have to be a pretty serious photography project to warrant this trouble. Sometimes I use a hooped sleeping bag pitched next to my hide with a camouflage net covering both, so I can crawl unseen from sleeping bag to hide and vice versa.

It helps if you are happy with your own company in a confined space. Some photographers I have tried to introduce to hides during workshops couldn't stand more than half an hour cooped up in there on their own; if you think you might be of a similar disposition, perhaps you have to admit you might not be cut out for hide work. Other photographers I know read books, listen to a personal stereo and even smoke a pipe in their hide. Personally, I think all of these distractions are ill-advised as they inevitably disturb your concentration. There might be long periods of bird inactivity, but you have to be ready to respond very quickly when some action does eventually occur. With limited visibility, audio cues become very important. At a golden eagle eyrie I once photographed, not only could I hear when an adult bird approached but I could identify the female before I saw it, from the hum of its wing where a primary feather had molted.

It's a good idea to keep a log of bird activity observed from the hide. Such notes can be very helpful when planning future photography if you are trying to remember seasonal timing or frequency of feeding visits. You might also witness bird behavior that deserves to be reported to researchers or written up as a note to a journal – quite possibly few people will have ever seen the things you are privileged to observe from

your hide, so you can make a worthwhile contribution to the scientific record.

Other than a notebook and pencil and the usual camera accessories and consumables, there are a few other items you might find useful to have in a hide: a small flashlight for finding things in your bag or dropped on the floor, or checking more obscure camera settings; spare scrim for extra camouflage; safety pins for fastening scrim and emergency repairs; and a Swiss Army knife or Leatherman tool.

Photographing birds at the nest

It is a matter of historic convenience that until about the 1960s birds were almost always photographed at the nest. Large, heavy plate cameras with short focal length lenses, slow film emulsions and slow shutters dictated the technique. Birds would have to return to their nest to incubate their eggs and feed their young so, if you pitched up alongside, sooner or later you would obtain your photograph. Sometimes it was a risky business, leading to the desertion of nests when it was not carried out with sufficient care, but there were comparatively few bird photographers, and it was in an era when the fascination for nests and eggs was more widely tolerated. Nowadays, we have many more ways that we can go about our bird photography, and society tends to frown on what it sees as an unhealthy or misguided obsession with birds' nests. Moreover, editors are tired of seeing nest shots and want a change. Who can blame them, when nesting represents just a small part of a bird's life cycle and there are many more interesting types of behavior to photograph? On the whole, it's better to look for alternative subjects to photograph.

Nevertheless, I don't believe that nest photography should be either outlawed or censored – the breeding cycle is an important aspect of bird biology and there are occasions when it is perfectly appropriate to use nest photographs, in context, even for promoting conservation projects to a wider audience. Whether we are allowed to continue the practice in future depends largely upon whether responsible behavior is demonstrated by photographers.

Birds at the nest will almost always need to be photographed from a hide, with the exception perhaps of a few species of seabirds. This requires keen field skills, not least in finding suitable nests to photograph. Follow the hide procedures as detailed above, exercising particular caution and with a few additional considerations.

The location of nest sites should be kept secret, as far as possible. As well as being discreet with sensitive information, that will mean concealing your hide from the public gaze – camouflage as best you can, and don't leave it up longer than you need to. The rarer the bird, the more important this is. It is particularly important to introduce the hide in stages when working at nests, and assess the birds' reactions to it after each movement forwards. Be prepared to move the hide back, or withdraw it completely if they show signs of not accepting the disturbance. For instance, in species where both parents normally feed young, you should ensure that they are continuing to do so. Avoid working on the hide when it is unusually cold or hot, or during wet weather. It is safer to commence hide-building after chicks have hatched. Birds are most sensitive and easily disturbed when first prospecting nest sites, during nest-building, and about the time of egg-laying. Visits to and from the hide should be as few as necessary to complete the job, with changeovers kept as brief as possible. Again, avoid entering and leaving the hide during poor weather.

Keep the "gardening" of nest sites to an absolute minimum, so that only the most obstructive branches and foliage are gently tied back and then replaced after each photographic session. Opening up the nest makes it vulnerable to weather and predators, as well as inquisitive people, so the natural cover must be restored properly. Cutting back vegetation would therefore be very irresponsible. Sadly, it is still possible to see photographs of birds' nests where it is obvious that severe gardening has taken place, with

Hen harrier female feeding its young

No "gardening" was involved in this nest photograph of a specially protected bird. This was vital for the birds' welfare and ultimate nesting success, but in fact I think it also works better aesthetically – it seems more respectful of the subject, and in keeping with its ground-nesting habit. The foreground obstruction of heather is better for being well out of focus, and makes us feel as though we are being granted a privileged peek into the harrier's private life.

Camera: *Nikon F5*
Lens: *AF-S 500mm f4 lens*
Film: *Fujichrome Sensia 100*

Golden eagle female and chick
Photographing this wild golden eagle at the nest (top) remains my most demanding ever photo assignment. I used a scaffold hide (above) to get near to the nest.
Camera: *Nikon F4S*
Lens: *50–300mm f4.5*
Film: *Fujichrome Sensia 100*

foreground heather or reeds literally mowed to the ground. There can be no excuse for this.

Blocking of nest holes to make birds perch in the open, removing eggs and young from the nest for photography, or other such blatant interference could have a harmful effect on breeding success and should not be done under any circumstances. With colonial nesting birds, work only at the edges of the colony to avoid trampling nests and causing unnecessary disturbance.

Keep notes during your photography sessions and record the timing of all bird visits to the nest. This information can be used to convince yourself (and others, if necessary) that normal incubating, feeding and brooding behavior is continuing despite the presence of your hide. In the unfortunate event of a nest failure, it will at least be clear that you have taken every reasonable precaution.

Remember that a special photography license may be required to allow photographer disturbance of rarer birds at or near the nest. You will need to demonstrate to the appropriate agency that you have the necessary experience to work with nesting birds, and supply a reference. If you are lucky enough to obtain such a license, it should not be regarded as a *carte blanche* to do as you please and ignore the usual safe procedures. Rather, it is a privilege that carries additional responsibilities. At the end of the season you will be required to submit a return form detailing all your activities around the nest; failure to comply with any of the requirements of the license or any report of bad practice on your part would make it unlikely that you would receive another license.

If all of this sounds like a heavy burden of responsibility, I can only suggest that you steer clear of nest photography until you feel you have the necessary field experience. Certainly it would be best to avoid photographing birds at the nest as a first option. Ideally, you should learn from an experienced nest photographer.

Adapting to bird behavior
Different birds have different reactions to hides near the nest, and you should be ready to modify your approach in response. Even different individuals within the same species can vary in their behavior quite markedly, so

be prepared to ditch any preconceived notions. It's not necessarily the commoner birds that are more tolerant of hides and photographers; for example, familiar garden birds such as robins and song thrushes, or screech owls in North America, can readily desert nests and eggs if disturbed during incubation. Conversely, some rarer breeding birds such as the avocet and dotterel can appear quite tolerant. However, their confiding nature doesn't automatically mean that they are not experiencing stress, so make sure you exercise the usual care and respect.

Most birds of prey are very sensitive at the nest. It is customary to wait until after chicks have hatched before introducing a hide, and then it is still best to wait for downy chicks to start to feather so they are better able to control their body temperature. An alternative method for traditional eyries is to build a semi-permanent hide over the winter months, but work should be complete by February as nest-site prospecting gets under way very early with the larger birds of prey. And if they choose an alternative site, you have to try again another year!

The most difficult, suspicious bird I have ever photographed at the nest was a golden eagle in Scotland. After obtaining a Schedule 1 photography license and locating a suitable nest site, my hide and scaffold was built up over a period of two weeks, and well camouflaged. The adult eagles accepted each stage quite readily up to and including the addition of a dummy lens, but as soon as a real lens was substituted the birds became very touchy indeed. Even though the entire lens was contained within the hide itself, with a long tunnel of branches and foliage in front of it, I couldn't get them to accept a 300mm f2.8 lens – presumably because of its large object diameter. A 50–300mm f4.5 seemed to present a lesser threat, but I also found that I had to remove the front skylight filter, I assume because it was flat and more reflective than the curved front element of the lens. Still the eagles would not tolerate the slightest zooming action of the lens, even though the zoom mechanism was all internal, so any changes in focal length had to be made while the birds were absent. Strangely enough, they never seemed remotely concerned about the noise of the shutter and motordrive.

The smaller, weaker chick died very early on, as is usual with eagles. As the surviving chick grew larger, the visits of the parent birds became less and less frequent, so that there were days when I was in the hide for ten or twelve hours but saw adults at the eyrie for a total of only ten or twelve seconds as they dropped off food for the chick. This is quite normal behavior, but after all the effort I had put in to establishing the hide, and the long climb up to the crag each day, it was a little demoralizing. To end up with just a few static portraits of an adult eagle on the nest ledge seemed to be at odds with the glamorous reputation of the subject and my high expectations. It certainly made me appreciate how pioneers like Seton Gordon and Charles Palmar could have devoted their entire lives to obtaining a few remarkable images, without many of the advantages I had enjoyed. More to the point, if publishers ever ask me for photographs of golden eagles it's almost invariably a bird in flight they want to see.

Many of the photographs you see of adult birds carrying a bill full of insects or caterpillars are actually photographed only a short distance from the nest, as the birds return to feed their hungry chicks. This probably causes less disturbance than a hide that is set up to photograph the nest itself, as the photography can be conducted further away and without the need for nest gardening. You still need to proceed cautiously; use a hide and make sure your presence doesn't prevent chicks from being fed. Regular perches may be used on approach, and you can try introducing one of your own choice to see if it is accepted. Sometimes the birds like to look around from such a vantage point, to check that no predators are watching. Parent birds may also make use of perches as they leave the nest, possibly as they dispose of hatched egg shells or nestlings' fecal sacs.

Many ground-nesting birds in particular have young that are soon mobile and leave the nest within hours of hatching. These are dependent on their parents for some time

Skylark carrying food to its nestlings

Nest-approach perches are better alternatives to actual nest sites in most circumstances. Make sure that your presence doesn't prevent chicks from being fed.
Camera: *Nikon F5*
Lens: *AF-S 500mm f4 plus 1.4x teleconverter*
Film: *Fujichrome Sensia 100*

afterwards, whether for food or protection, so be vigilant. An agitated tern or wader might be bolder than usual and look like an ideal subject for photography, but think for a moment about why it is alarm-calling from a nearby fence post or above your head. You may be standing very close to its chicks.

Earlier in the spring, opportunities for photography may arise as birds seek out nest-building material. The soft mud at the edge of a puddle or garden pond could attract house martins or song thrushes; fallen twigs might be collected by rooks or pigeons; reed buntings like to line their nests with fluffy reedmace seed; long-tailed tits make use of soft feathers; hummingbirds use lichens and spiders' webs; great-crested fly-catchers collect snake skins; and goldfinches gather thistledown. Meeting these needs by creating a rich supply of raw materials might well pay dividends, and you can find many more favored nest materials for different species. It's a little more imaginative than nest photography, and makes for more interesting results.

Remote-control photography

There are occasions when it's easier or more desirable to get a small camera closer to a bird than a hide and its occupant, and fire it remotely from a distance. The most straightforward way of doing this is by means of an extended electrical shutter-release cable. Some camera manufacturers can supply these, for a price, but it is a simple matter to make your own. Take a standard shutter-release cable for your camera body, cut it in half, and solder opposite phono plugs to each end (say "male" to the camera socket end and "female" to the switch end, but it works just as well the opposite way round). For your extension lead, use a length of two-strand bell wire, and again fit opposite phono plugs to each end. The extension can be at least 50m (165ft) without creating too much resistance, in my experience. This extension is easily deployed when you need it, and the rest of the time you can use your shutter release at its normal length.

A neater solution is to use an infrared release, which has a transmitter and a receiver unit and can operate typically up to a range of

(right) **Arctic tern feeding young**
This image was photographed with a remote camera and a 30m (100ft) cable release.
Camera: *Nikon F3*
Lens: *28mm f2.8*
Film: *Kodachrome 64*
Exposure: *¹/125 sec. at f8*

about 100m (330ft), but requires a good "line of sight." Infrared releases usually have a choice of several channels (allowing you to operate more than one camera at a time), a test mode and confirmation light, and you can also select between single-frame and continuous film advance from the transmitter end. Radio releases can operate over still greater distances, even through a brick wall, but they tend to be enormously expensive and most countries require you to have a special license for their operation at specified radio frequencies.

The camera itself will need to be set up on a tripod, stand or bracket, or even on the ground. A soundproofed box, or "blimp," for the camera can be a great advantage in remote work as the bird will be so close. Make your own with plywood or similar, to accommodate your favorite camera body, and pack the spaces with foam rubber. You must incorporate a lens opening, shutter-release cable access, tripod fastening or adjustable feet, and a means of access to the camera viewfinder. Either install the camera through a removable back panel, or use a top-fitting lid and view through a waist-level finder or right-angle eyepiece attachment. A box will also offer some degree of weatherproofing and protection for your camera.

Most often, remote-control bird photography is undertaken with a fairly wide-angle lens (say, 24mm to 35mm range) and this does give an unusual perspective for a bird photograph. It's also easier to frame up and pre-focus for maximum depth of field with a wide-angle. Of course, you will have no control over framing, exposure or focus from your operating position, so all of these must be set in advance. Usually it's most dependable to set the metering mode to aperture priority automatic. I wouldn't use autofocus in these circumstances as you can't be really sure of the bird position when the shutter is fired, so the AF could easily lock on to the background by mistake.

Instead, use manual focus and set the lens to its hyperfocal distance. This is the distance setting for a particular aperture that gives maximum depth of field, right through to infinity. For instance, if you expect your subject range to be about 1m (3ft) using a 28mm lens, don't just focus the lens to 1m and hope for the best, as even at f16 your depth of field won't extend much beyond 2m (6ft). However, if you focus the lens to just under 2m, still at f16, your depth of field will extend from about 0.9m (just under 3ft) to infinity, easily keeping your subject in focus, as well as the rest of the scene. Since your subject will hopefully dominate the foreground it shouldn't be necessary to keep focus in front of that, but it is best to have the background sharp. Most wide-angle lenses have these depth of field scales inscribed on the lens barrel, so use them to your advantage for setting hyperfocal distance.

If you are not using a blimp, remember to close the eyepiece shutter before withdrawing, or cover the eyepiece with tape or something similar to prevent stray light affecting the automatic metering. Alternatively, use mirror lock-up in combination with a manual exposure setting; this is riskier with regard to exposure, but has the advantage of cutting down noise and the delay of shutter operation, which could be helpful with a very close, nervous subject. Perhaps disguise the camera with pegged-down scrim or netting, taking care not to cover the lens. Make sure you have a fresh roll of film loaded, set the film advance mode and fire a test shot to ensure everything is working before you leave.

Finding appropriate subjects for remote-control photography is not that easy, and it is a technique with a high built-in failure rate because of its inherent unpredictability. Ideally, you need to be able to pinpoint a spot to which a bird will return with some degree of accuracy. This might be a favorite feeding spot or a regular perch, but if the bird is even slightly suspicious of the camera it may not come back and may just use an alternative perch or food source. As with hides, begin with the camera at a comfortable distance and gradually move it up towards its final photography position. A dummy camera,

Yellowhammer male in summer plumage

Photographed using my vehicle as a hide, this yellowhammer was found down a local country lane in the early morning. A well-managed hedgerow provides a better wildlife habitat and more photogenic perches than a line of sterile fence posts.

Camera: *Nikon F5*

Lens: *AF-S 500mm f4 plus 1.4x teleconverter*

Film: *Fujichrome Sensia 100 uprated to EI200*

Exposure: *$^1/_{250}$ sec. at f5.6*

or your soundproofed box with the camera removed, can be left out over a period of days to allow the bird(s) to get accustomed to it. Some particularly tolerant ground-nesting birds, such as some species of waders and terns, can make suitable candidates for remote-control photography if approached with due care. Once again, move the camera up in stages and withdraw it if the incubating or brooding parent does not return and settle within a few minutes.

Viewing from a distance, it can be difficult to judge when the bird is in frame at the pre-focused range, and even more difficult to see when it is in a photogenic posture and in good light. Watch through binoculars to identify the optimum moment, and observe the bird's reaction when you take your first shot. Usually you can see a bird flinch slightly on the first occasion the shutter is fired, but it should soon calm down and accept the slight noise. Count off your frames, and don't be tempted to return to the camera to check it's operating properly or fiddle with the controls until you have used a whole roll or you decide to abandon photography for the day.

Using a vehicle as a hide

Photographing from a vehicle window may not be the most romantic idea, but it is often highly effective. A car makes a great mobile hide, and takes you closer to many birds than you could reach on foot. As with purpose-built portable hides, birds just don't seem to associate vehicles with people, though you may need to do a bit of discreet covering up to disguise the human form.

Park up by a likely perch or feeding spot, with your telephoto at the ready resting on a beanbag or car-window clamp. Most likely you will need at least a 600mm lens for this kind of work. Cover the window with scrim netting if you have the opportunity, and black out light from the window behind and sunroof above so your silhouette is not visible. Wait quietly for birds to return. It doesn't really need saying, but turn off the car engine to cut out noise and the risk of camera shake. If you spot a potential subject while driving slowly, you might get closer by turning off the engine a little in advance and coasting the last few meters.

Photographing birds from a car window
With your telephoto lens supported on a beanbag, you should be able to get sharp results at shutter speeds of $^1/_{250}$ sec. or even slower. When possible, screen yourself with scrim net and black out the sunroof and the passenger side window.

Juvenile little owl
This young owl was photographed from the car window not far away from the yellowhammer opposite. It was quite late in the evening by now, and I think there may be a message in here somewhere ...
Camera: Nikon F5
Lens: AF-S 500mm f4
Film: Fujichrome Sensia 100

Bar-tailed godwit in winter plumage

Stalking shorebirds is generally more successful in cold weather, when they are anxious to feed, and tourist beaches out of season are often good places to find them. Low winter light distinguishes an otherwise straightforward shot.
Camera: Nikon F5
Lens: AF-S 500mm f4 plus 1.4x teleconverter
Film: Fujichrome Sensia 100 uprated to EI200
Exposure: 1/160 sec. at f5.6

I have successfully photographed many species of birds from car windows in a whole variety of different habitats, from skulking corncrakes to waders in tidal creeks and singing corn buntings in hedgerows. Clearly you are limited in where you can go, and there are safety issues to consider, too – finding quiet country lanes with adequate roadside parking can be something of a challenge in developed areas, and you'll need to check your rear-view mirror constantly. Another disadvantage is that many of the birds you will be able to photograph are inevitably perched on boring fences or walls, or else out of sight behind them. Sometimes you can "enhance" a perch such as a fencepost by placing a rock on top of it and framing so that only part of the rock perch is visible; birds often take readily to these modified perches. Is that cheating? Does it matter if nothing is harmed or misrepresented? Don't get carried away with this car-oriented technique. It is not meant to be a lazy person's charter.

Stalking

The term "stalking" conjures up images of commandos in battle dress and face paints, or Native Americans with their ear to the ground listening for buffalo. Usually, when bird photographers talk about having "stalked" a bird, they mean they were lucky enough to have been able to walk up and photograph it without a hide. But for many birds in most parts of the world, this is going to be a difficult undertaking. It

requires patience and persistence.

Clearly you can't go about trying to stalk a bird with undue haste or noise. It is best to work alone, keep a low profile and try to avoid making a silhouette of yourself against the sky. Use the cover of bushes and rocks where available – even having these behind you is quite effective. In the latter stages of your approach, as you enter the bird's "comfort zone," you might need to crouch or crawl, a little at a time. It often helps to approach at an oblique angle, zigzagging forwards and not looking directly at the bird, or pointing your lens at it. Sudden movement or noise would be disastrous at this stage. Remember that birds prefer to take off into the wind, so they feel more comfortable if you don't block their escape route upwind. Quietly take a frame or two as you come within camera range and gauge the bird's response; if it doesn't appear too concerned you can advance a little further in the quest for a larger image. You may ultimately reject a great many of these early photographs, but you never know how close you're going to finish up, so take a few insurance shots along the way. More often than not you will try stalking a bird and end up with nothing; it is worth persisting until you find the bird that doesn't object to the camera.

You need to be pretty mobile for successful stalking. Abandon your backpack and carry only the bare essentials, perhaps in a photographer's vest. A monopod might be more useful than a tripod to give you the versatility and mobility required, but for ground birds you will do best to lie down. Resting on a beanbag or directly on the ground is the most solid possible lens support and gives a terrific low-angle view, provided that you can find a line of sight without any obstructions. Mostly you will need to use the longest lens you can wield when working out in the open, so image stabilization can be a considerable help.

On the other hand, I can think of circumstances where approachability was not the main issue, but rather keeping up with fast-moving birds flitting through the bush. In the Seychelles, I found that an 80–200mm zoom hand-held with fill flash allowed me the freedom and speed of reaction I needed to photograph some of the passerines. So you have to be adaptable.

Rather than chasing after a reluctant subject, lie in wait and let the bird move close to you. Sometimes you can successfully predict where a bird might return – for example, to a regular song perch or feeding spot. An advancing tide or the urgency to feed on a cold day might gradually push birds towards you. Make yourself as inconspicuous as possible and see if they will cooperate, but don't allow your presence to threaten their survival or breeding success. If you are sitting on a cliff top in summer and can't believe your luck when a peregrine repeatedly flies low overhead, calling loudly, it's because you are too close to its nest site! Keep aware of your actions and their potential consequences. Good fieldcraft is the most important ingredient, as ever.

Food

Birds respond to locally high concentrations of available food. In nature, this might be a swarm of emerging insects, a shoal of fish that is trapped behind a sandbar, or a crop of ripe berries. In the managed countryside, it could be gulls following the plow or herons congregating at a fish farm. You can think of lots of other examples. Use this knowledge and observation to plan photography assignments and possible hide locations.

Alternatively, you can create your own artificial supply of bird food; match the food with the birds you want to attract. You can even set up a feeding station for many different birds by providing a whole selection of foods in a natural-looking set within range of your hide. It may take some research and experimentation to work out the most effective food for a particular subject.

In a garden situation, sunflower seeds and peanuts seem to draw the widest range of species, but there are many other specialties. Robins and dunnocks find live mealworms irresistible, while goldfinches can be tempted by black thistle seed, and great spotted woodpeckers love beef suet. Grain works for sparrows and buntings. Windfall apples and pears are good for winter thrushes and starlings. In North America, chickadees love sunflower seeds and peanut bits, while orioles and tanagers take oranges and other fruit from feeders. Hummingbirds come in for hummer nectar (sugar solution)

Osprey with rainbow trout
Abnormally high concentrations of food, such as trout at a Highland fish farm, are bound to attract hungry visitors. Fortunately, the ospreys are welcomed by the owners here. This was the best result from several early-morning hide photography sessions, in pre-autofocus days.
Camera: *Nikon F3*
Lens: *300mm f2.8 manual focus plus 2x teleconverter*
Film: *Kodachrome 200*
Exposure: *^{1}/500 sec. at f5.6*

Laurie Campbell

Golden eagle on a dead stag,
Lochaber, Scotland

Influential nature photographer and author Laurie Campbell rarely works beyond his native Scotland, and is the most dogged and persistent fieldworker I have ever met. His summary of the circumstances leading up to this landmark photograph gives some indication of his determination:

66 *After almost three years of working with golden eagles, this picture represented a real milestone for me as it was from my first-ever close encounter with a wild golden eagle away from the nest. It is from a sequence that I shot over a week-long period, covering a bird that I had managed to tempt with bait. I was working on a collection of pictures to illustrate a book on these birds and had already spent two summers photographing these individuals near to the nest, so I already knew something of their movements around this particular glen. It seemed natural therefore, to continue to attempt to photograph them on the same territory over the winter. I began in the autumn by building an igloo-shaped hide from*

rocks. It overlooked a stretch of ground that I knew the birds hunted over and that received good light – even in midwinter. It was also reasonably accessible, and I could drive my camper van to within a kilometer of the site – an important consideration, given that I needed to transport heavy camera gear and deer carcasses for baiting.

By late December, the short days as well as the poor visibility caused by low cloud and snow forced the birds to look for quick and efficient ways of finding food. Once the eagles were coming to the bait regularly, to build their confidence it was really important for them not to see me anywhere near the hide. This meant that whenever I wished to use the hide I needed to both enter and leave under cover of darkness. My only problem then was remaining comfortable while waiting for the birds' daily visits. Not too difficult really given today's choice of outdoor clothing.

My equipment on this occasion was a Nikon F3 and 300mm f2.8 lens, using Kodachrome 200 film with an exposure of $^1/_{125}$ sec. at f4. 99

With typical modesty, Laurie neglects to mention that he was snowed into the glen for the duration of the week and unable to leave even if he had wanted to!

provided for them in a special feeder. There are many different types of foods you can try, and there are bound to be regional variations and preferences. You may even hear some photographers brag about their own "secret" recipes, but stick with the evidence of your own eyes. Plain old sliced bread can be a useful contingency, not just for ducks and seaside gulls – many is the time I have sacrificed my sandwiches for the sake of a photograph.

If you don't want to show artificial feeders in your photographs, then cache the food in crevices in a tree trunk or branch. Locate feeders near to attractive natural perches, or introduce your own, and photograph birds as they approach the feeder. You might not wish exotic food items such as peanuts to be visible in the bird's bill, so replace them with wild foods such as acorns, beech mast or hazel nuts when the birds have got used to coming to a particular spot.

With wild foods, if you can create a temporary glut, somehow this can be very effective at narrowing down birds' feeding options. Digging over an area of flower border or even just watering a small patch of lawn makes lots of invertebrates suddenly available to ground-feeding birds such as robins and thrushes. When there is a good crop of acorns in season, collect and store a load somewhere cool and dry, and then put them out again a couple of months later when the natural supply has become exhausted. Concentrate them in a small area near your hide, cover with dried leaves, and watch birds such as jays and wood pigeons soon discover them. With ripening fruits and berries, you can try covering just one bush with netting until all its neighbours have been picked clean, but be careful that this doesn't entrap eager birds.

If you have a large enough garden or access to suitable land, consider planting specifically for birds; native trees and shrubs provide valuable bird food. Ivy is favored by wood pigeons, mistle thrushes and wintering blackcaps, and makes a beautiful evergreen background, too. Sowing a patch of thistles, teasels or sunflowers will be sure to attract flocks of finches. Berry-bearing shrubs such as

cotoneaster, pyracantha and berberis are also worth planting to tempt birds into your garden.

Some birds of prey and crows can be lured down to feed at carrion, especially in hard weather, but carcasses of large mammals like sheep, goats or red deer might be difficult to obtain, especially as some countries have laws about the safe disposal of dead livestock. A road-kill victim, such as a rabbit, is probably the easiest sort of carrion to come by, but smaller prey like this should be staked down with tent pegs or similar so as to prevent foxes removing it in the night,

Crested tit in Scots pine
The peanut feeder is just out of frame, but the crested tit appears to be foraging in its natural habitat. Choose the bird's likely approach perches with care.
Camera: *Nikon F5*
Lens: *AF-S 500mm f4 plus 1.4x teleconverter*
Film: *Fujichrome Sensia 100 uprated to EI200*

or larger birds from dragging it away. Place a perch, like a fence post or boulder, nearby and birds may be persuaded to use this on their approach. Expect a baited site such as this to take some time to become established, and make sure you get your hide up well in advance of your proposed photography. Day-old chicks from poultry farms are commonly fed to birds of prey and owls, but again it's a lengthy process to establish regular feeding patterns for photography.

Dead fish can be used successfully to attract some fish-eating birds, and this can be spectacularly effective at sea. Some birdwatching pelagic, or open-sea, voyages rely on the use of "chum" to draw in seabirds like petrels and shearwaters – this is an evil-smelling brew of fermented fish offal and oil, mixed with popcorn to help it float. Apparently, tuna oil works very well indeed, and chopped shark's liver is another really choice ingredient if you can get it. The Procellariiformes (tubenoses: albatrosses, petrels and shearwaters) are able to detect certain chemicals over some kilometers, and quickly arrive on the scene from an apparently birdless ocean. It has been found that storm petrels in particular respond to dimethyl sulphide (DMS), which is a substance emitted by phytoplankton that attracts the zooplankton on which the storm petrels feed. Neat dimethyl sulphide is a very potent attractant and is sometimes used on these pelagic expeditions, although it would be cruel to use DMS alone and not reward the birds with some food.

These are just a few ideas of feeding projects that can be attempted, and are not meant to represent an exhaustive list. Of course, the feeding patterns of many birds don't lend themselves readily to photography. For instance most insectivorous birds, especially those that feed on the wing, will nearly always be out of camera reach. And whatever can you do about diving ducks?

The use of live prey to bait birds for photography raises several ethical questions. While most people wouldn't think twice about using the odd worm, or even a few small fish, anything larger or warm-blooded moves us into controversial territory. Few of us would wish to cause pain or suffering to a bird or mammal, and wouldn't dream of deliberately baiting with them. Indeed, there are cruelty laws that forbid this in most Western countries. However, by putting out food for small birds in our gardens we might inadvertently create a food source for sparrowhawks and other raptors. I guess the difference is that you're not restraining the potential prey, which have a fair chance of escape. Personally, I can't think of anything more exciting than being able to photograph a predator capture its prey in the wild. But when it comes to live bait, I think I'll stick to worms and fish.

Water

Just as birds need to feed, so they need fresh water for drinking and bathing to keep their feathers in good condition. Seek out regular watering holes – the more concentrated the water source, the better it will be for photography. It is best if there is a shallow beach or entry point, or some emerging branch or rock for birds to perch on. Areas where fresh water is an otherwise scarce resource will be the most productive. Freshwater outfalls at the coast are good for attracting birds, particularly those that can't utilize saltwater.

A near-dry Middle Eastern desert *wadi* might look unpromising, but for ten minutes at the same time every morning thousands of pin-tailed sandgrouse may converge from miles around to collect water in their breast feathers and then carry it back to their chicks. It's rarely as spectacular as this, but photographing at waterholes can be quite exciting as you never know what is going to appear next. On one trip to Spain, a friend and I found a tiny puddle

Redwing feeding on hawthorn berries

An early autumn migrant, tired and hungry after its journey, is keen to replenish energy reserves. Native berry-bearing shrubs can be planted in your garden to attract a wider range of bird visitors to photograph.
Camera: *Nikon F4S*
Lens: *500mm f4 plus 1.4x teleconverter*
Film: *Fujichrome Sensia 100*

in a farm track where a few rock sparrows were drinking following a recent rain shower. We introduced a hide, and over the following three days of dry weather we kept the puddle topped up from a water bottle and were rewarded with 24 different species coming to drink. As they ranged in size from serin to booted eagle, a high-ratio telephoto zoom would have been useful! Waterholes are good for attracting birds you might have difficulty getting close to by other methods. Seed-eating birds in particular need to drink quite frequently, and tree-top species such as redpolls and crossbills are easier to photograph when they come down to water than at any other time.

A dripping tap or sprinkler in the garden can be all it takes to bring down birds to drink, but a birdbath or garden pond is a better way to ensure regular visits. You can make your own pond quite easily with a plastic or butyl pond liner – keep it small and compact with

shallow edges, and line with sand or gravel to make it appear more natural. You will need to replenish the water often. Emergent perches make convenient stopping-off points, and help to separate birds from their background. Try to photograph birds on their way in, as they can look pretty scruffy and bedraggled when saturated after a good bathe. However, action shots of bathing birds with arcs of spray and water droplets can look very dramatic. Following a soaking, birds will usually rest up on a nearby perch to preen and dry.

A small sheet of plastic, about 1m (3ft) square, is a useful supplement to your field kit. It will enable you rapidly to improvise a drinking pool for photographic purposes almost anywhere you go.

Roosts

Roosts are safe locations where birds regularly return to rest or sleep, often in large flocks for security. Most species of birds go to roost at

Sparrowhawk harrying coal tit
Concentrations of small birds at garden feeders attract predators, which can become quite regular and predictable. I was just grateful for the opportunity to witness and photograph the chase. The coal tit escaped on this occasion, though I'm not sure if it was helped or hindered by the squirrel-proof basket.
Camera: *Nikon F4S*
Lens: *300mm f2.8 manual focus*
Film: *Fujichrome Provia 100 uprated to EI200*
Exposure: *$^1/_{500}$ sec. at f4*

Bob Glover
Oystercatcher bathing, Essex, England

Bob Glover is very much his own man, not easily tempted by foreign travel and technical gadgetry. Well known for his splendid photographs of waders on the East Anglian salt marshes, Bob is secure in his local knowledge and technique. Here he gives us an insight into how he prefers to work:

66 *I have been photographing birds along the Essex estuaries for the past 16 years, and I rarely travel outside the county to take photographs. Working a local patch so thoroughly brings with it a knowledge of bird behavior that pays off in the long term. It also helps in building relationships with landowners, who allow me to set up hides on private land.*

A fair proportion of my time has been devoted to capturing shots of waders and wildfowl bathing. Although they spend much of their time far out on intertidal mudflats, waders prefer fresh or brackish water for bathing. This might be an outfall on to the mudflats or a brackish pool inside the sea wall. Inland pools are easier to work, preferably with some shelter from the elements, since I use cloth hides and generally leave them up for several weeks at a time. I set my hides as low as possible, to reduce the birds' suspicions but also because I like very low profile photographs.

My photographic equipment hasn't changed much since I started bird photography and I still use the same manual focus 600mm f5.6 Nikkor lens. Until recently, I wouldn't have trusted the capability of autofocus in all situations. Autofocus also didn't used to work well with teleconverters, and in my estuary work I can rarely get by without one of these. For the oystercatcher photograph I would have been using the 600mm lens with a 1.4x teleconverter wide open at f8, and by pushing Fujichrome Sensia 100 film one stop would have just squeezed a shutter speed of ^{1}/500 sec. 99

dusk and depart again at dawn, but gulls and shore birds roost when high tides make their feeding grounds inaccessible. Nocturnal birds such as owls tend to roost during the daylight hours, and are often quite approachable then, if you can find them – sometimes owl roosts are given away by the cacophony of scolding blackbirds and robins that have detected the presence of a predator. Vast flocks of starlings roost in trees and, in urban areas, on the ledges of high buildings. In North America, blackbirds and American robins gather in large numbers at dusk. Geese congregate on open water, swallows and pied wagtails frequently choose reed beds, while wood pigeons and stock doves prefer dense woodland. Treecreepers sometimes nestle in the soft, ridged bark of wellingtonia trees, but can be very difficult to find by flashlight. Well-used roost sites of any kind of bird might be betrayed in daylight by droppings on the ground beneath the perches. All of these sites represent potential photo opportunities for the enterprising photographer, some more difficult than others.

If you are dealing with large flocks, it makes sense to attempt to portray the spectacle of the roost. Shore birds such as knot make an absolutely magnificent sight as they swirl around and turn in unison, often likened to a smoke cloud or amoeba, white one second, turning gray in an instant. This is just the pre-roost gathering and, if you do your homework on seasons and migrations, times of high-water spring tides, and favored roost locations, you might be lucky enough to get a hide up in the right place well in advance of the flock landing and settling. Many times you might wait out a whole tide cycle only to be disappointed at the total absence of birds. If by chance they do land close to your hide, even if not close enough for photography, you will have to sit it out until after they disperse at the end of the roost; it can be a long wait watching a dense flock of tens of thousands of birds all with their heads tucked under their wings. But after an hour or two, as they begin to get restless again, some birds might break away from the group to bathe and preen,

Corn bunting drinking
from a puddle
This was just one of 24 species that came to drink here over a three-day photography period. The puddle was refreshed each day from a water bottle.
Camera: Nikon F4S
Lens: 500mm f4 plus 1.4x teleconverter
Film: Fujichrome Velvia

Jan Töve

*Starlings going
to roost,
Lake Hornborga,
Sweden*

Like many Scandinavian
nature photographers,
Jan Töve makes the
most of the light in his
photography. He is just as
happy photographing
landscapes and wildflowers
as birds, working with
medium-format cameras
as well as 35mm, which he
often carries with him on
cross-country skis during
the winter months. Jan
describes his photographic
interpretation of this
starling roost:

66 *I took this
photograph at Lake
Hornborga in the southern
part of Sweden late one
evening in April. The
starlings had just left the
field where they had been
feeding. On their way to
their night-time roost in the
reeds that border the lake
they gathered in a tree, and
I saw the possibility of
taking a picture that told
the story of this behavior. It
looked like a flood of wings
streaming from the tree. To
capture that impression, I
used a slow shutter speed of
$1/8$ sec. on my Pentax 645
camera with a 200mm f4
lens. The film was
Fujichrome Velvia. And of
course I used a tripod.* 99

Long-eared owl at daytime roost
It was a surprise to be told that this normally elusive bird was roosting in a birch tree just a few meters outside my office, quite open and approachable. More often long-eared owls remain undiscovered in thicker cover.
Camera: *Nikon F4S*
Lens: *500mm f4*
Film: *Fujichrome Provia 100*

offering fresh photography opportunities. Occasionally, there may be a commotion as a passing predator disturbs the roost, and the whole lot suddenly takes flight. That certainly makes you sit up.

Working at dusk or dawn, light is going to be in short supply, so you might need to use shorter, faster lenses, and consider using faster films or uprating and push-processing. Making silhouettes of flight flocks against a sunset sky

can keep the shutter speed fast enough to retain sharp outlines. An alternative technique would be to use slower shutter speeds to show movement in the flock, and the pattern it creates, but with individual birds blurred. For this to be successful probably requires some experimentation, and it helps if you have an interesting sky of variable color and texture, or some other feature in the landscape, such as a silhouetted treeline or reflective water.

Leks and display grounds

Some species of birds, especially grouse and other game birds, have traditional display grounds known as leks, where the males congregate to compete with their rivals and seek the sexual favors of females. There are some waders that exhibit this complex breeding behavior, too, such as ruff and great snipe. The displays can be very elaborate with dramatic changes in plumage, and sometimes fighting between males, and the conclusion might be that successful males get to copulate with one or more females. This all makes for very exciting photography.

Lekking is a temporary, seasonal phenomenon, occurring in spring (in the temperate regions), sometimes lasting for just a few minutes over several consecutive days, in other species extending to several hours a day, week after week. Generally this activity occurs in the very early morning before dawn breaks, though unusually it can take place in the evening – in the great snipe, for example. The lek itself is usually a more or less fixed location to which the birds have a very close affinity. This makes it a fairly reliable location for photography, but also means that extra care must be taken not to disturb such a crucial event in the birds' breeding cycle. Hides should be introduced the night before for morning leks, and occupied during hours of darkness. This could mean camping out at more remote locations. The first males could arrive long before dawn in nearly complete darkness, and well before you have any realistic chance of photographing them. It is an agonizing wait watching these entrancing displays and strange postures through the gloom, and it can be frustrating to witness copulations in front of your hide when the meter reading indicates a 4-second exposure, wide open, but the whole event lasts less than a second! But as the season progresses and lekking behavior becomes more intense, it may continue longer into the daylight hours and give better opportunities. Only remove the hide after lekking behavior has finished and the birds have dispersed for the day. It's not a good idea to leave hides in place at leks for prolonged periods as you will only draw unwelcome attention to the site.

In the U.S., greater prairie chickens, sharp-

Black grouse males at lek

To be in position to photograph this bizarre but beautiful display meant sleeping on location in a hooped sleeping bag, pitched next to my hide, all under cover of a camouflage net. When woken by the bubbling calls of the black grouse males, or blackcock, still some hours before sunrise, I crawled from my sleeping bag into the hide. Eventually, it became light enough to work.
Camera: *Nikon F5*
Lens: *AF-S 500mm f4*
Film: *Fujichrome Sensia 100 uprated to EI200*

(opposite) **Robin singing**

*Robins are with us all year round
and hardly seem to stop singing.
No hide or tape lure was necessary
for this bold back garden resident.*
Camera: *Nikon F5*
Lens: *AF-S 500mm f4 plus
1.4x teleconverter*
Film: *Fujichrome Sensia 100*
Lighting: *SB-26 Speedlight*

Nightingale singing

*Normally unseen and most active
in hours of darkness, nightingales
can best be glimpsed in daylight
soon after they arrive in spring.
Here, I simply sat down with my
tripod and waited quietly for this
singing male to move into shot.*
Camera: *Nikon F5*
Lens: *AF-S 500mm f4 plus
1.4x teleconverter*
Film: *Ektachrome E100VS*

tailed grouse and wild turkey are all good
candidates for photographing lekking
behavior. In the U.K., regular leks exist only for
black grouse and capercaillie; both species are
in decline, and the few known leks come
under intense pressure from birdwatchers and
photographers alike. The best recommendation
would be to leave these well alone until
populations recover sufficiently, or to
photograph them elsewhere where they are
more common, for example in Scandinavia.
From time to time there are reports of rogue
male capercaillies that behave particularly
aggressively, as a consequence of a hormonal
imbalance. They are strongly territorial, display
throughout the day, and attack people and
cars as well as other male capercaillies. These
rogue birds are the most accessible photographic subjects – but definitely not
for the fainthearted.

Song perches

Many male birds sing from prominent spots in
spring, in order to announce to other males
that they are holding territory, and to attract
females with which to pair and breed. The
perches they use for singing are confined to
the relatively small area of the breeding
territory, and the same few perches tend to be
used repeatedly, with the territorial male
circulating between them. Song perches of
woodland birds are often quite high up and
therefore difficult to photograph, but you may
be lucky and find more accessible ones. Clearly
it's helpful if you are able to identify birds from
their song to enable you to locate them, and
there are useful recordings available on CD
and tape for reference.

Once you have identified a suitable song
perch, introduce a hide or set about stalking
on foot or from a vehicle. Don't delay too
long, as the males soon become silent as
nesting gets under way. Early morning is
usually the best time, though many birds sing
in the evening, too. If your bird goes quiet
temporarily, or moves off to a different perch,
don't chase after it but give it time as it may
well return to the same perch to sing after a
short absence.

Most likely you will need a long focal
length telephoto, possibly with teleconverter
or extension tube fitted for smaller song birds.

Fill flash will help with birds in shade or dappled light, or against strong backlight. It's common to see photographs of singing birds with the lower mandible blurred as it can vibrate at great speed, so keep your shutter speed fairly fast ($^1/_{250}$ sec. or faster), and take short bursts of photographs on the motordrive to try to capture the momentary pauses when the bill is wide open.

Migration routes

Spring and autumn migration are great times for bird photography. Large numbers of birds can concentrate in quite small areas, and there might well be chances to photograph birds you don't often see. Tired migrants freshly arrived from over the sea can be more approachable than usual, and while it is exciting to witness such a "fall," remember that these birds will have just lost a huge proportion of their body weight, consuming fat reserves over their long journey. They desperately need to feed and rest, and there is a very real risk of hounding them to death. Rarer vagrants blown well off their normal course tend to attract even more attention from birdwatchers, and it is significant that many of these celebrated rarities have ended up falling victim to birds of prey or domestic cats. So approach with sensitivity, and keep the birds' welfare in mind.

If you are attempting to photograph at a regular birding site, consider other people and don't try to approach closer than everybody else. Use the longest lenses you can muster, and stack teleconverters if necessary. Alternatively, try to return on a weekday after the excitement has died down a bit. But frankly, don't expect to produce any masterpieces at these busy locations.

There are some well-known migration hot spots, which often have bird observatories associated with them. Within the British Isles, the Isles of Scilly and Shetland, Cape Clear, Portland Bill and the north Norfolk coast are famous for their migrant birds. In North America, Cape May in New Jersey and Point Pelee in Ontario are renowned. Birds of prey in particular tend to follow migration routes that avoid long sea crossings, so the Straits of Gibraltar, the Bosphorous, Eilat in Israel, and Falsterbo in Sweden are terrific viewpoints for vast numbers of migrating raptors, though conditions need to be especially favorable to bring birds close enough for photography. The island of Lesvos in the Aegean Sea has been popular in recent years because of its high concentrations of spring migrants, often at close range.

There are also the wintering grounds, notably the wetland sites, which host great numbers of wildfowl. In the U.K., try Islay and Caerlaverock in Scotland for barnacle geese, the Ouse Washes in Cambridgeshire/Norfolk, and Slimbridge in Gloucestershire for Bewick's and whooper swans. In North America, good sites include Arkansas National Wildfowl Refuge (NWR) for whooping cranes and Red Rock Lakes in Montana for trumpeter swans. Other excellent wintering grounds include Bosque del Apache, New Mexico for snow geese and sandhill cranes, and Extremadura in Spain for common cranes. There are many others throughout the world. Most of these destinations feature regularly in the birdwatching magazines and have quite detailed birders' guides pointing out where to go and the best times.

At the more local level, watch for pre-migration gatherings of such birds as swallows and house martins on telegraph wires, or massing flocks of post-breeding lapwings. Certain weather patterns may give good indications of impending falls of migrant birds. For example, the north Norfolk coast in autumn is often good following a strong easterly blow and low cloud overnight, while in the Scillies and Cornwall westerly squalls are eagerly awaited in the hope that they might assist North American vagrants. In the U.S., warm fronts from the south bring migrants north in spring, while the opposite happens in the fall following cold fronts from northwest to southeast. Storms at sea can often lead to quite unlikely birds, such as divers (loons), auks, skuas (jaegars) and shearwaters, turning up at inland lakes and reservoirs, and this could be the best chance you ever have of seeing them at close quarters. Cold weather spells also account for movements of flocks of lapwings, golden plovers, fieldfares and redwings as they

retreat towards the warmer southwest. You should always be prepared to capitalize on these favorable conditions.

Decoys, models and tape lures

There are various props and lures that bird photographers might employ from time to time to aid them in their photography. I hesitate to include reference to some of them as they can be somewhat controversial, but conclude that it is better to discuss them in a responsible way rather than ignore them, or gloss over the subject.

One controversial example is the use of tape lures, which emulate rival males singing or the calls of receptive breeding females. Amplified tape loops or CDs are widely used by birders, particularly in North America, as they can make birds that are often difficult to see come out into the open. In effect, they are looking for an intruding bird. This is not a problem if the playback is of brief duration and the bird is then left alone, but persistent or repetitive playing of tapes amounts to unreasonable disturbance and could cause birds to invest too much time investigating the

"threat," and lead to ultimate breeding failure. There is clearly a temptation for photographers to overdo this in pursuit of an ever-better shot. If you try this technique, use it with discretion – doubly so if you are in a known breeding territory. Avoid using bird-call tapes or CDs altogether at well-known birding locations where others might be doing the same thing. And the use of tape lures near the nest of a protected bird would qualify as intentional disturbance within the meaning of the law, and you should therefore first obtain the appropriate photography license.

On the few occasions I have tried tape lures the results have been rather disappointing, with one of two possible outcomes. Either there is no visible response (although I do believe that it is more often effective in other parts of the world), or birds become very agitated and behave quite out of character, albeit closer than usual. So quite apart from the fact that I am obviously upsetting their normal behavior, it's not really the kind of photograph I want to take. The one species for which I know tapes do work astoundingly well is the cuckoo. Males arrive in spring on average

Winter flock of pink-footed geese
North Norfolk is well known for its wintering population of pink-footed geese, which like to feed on arable fields in the daytime, and roost on the mudflats of the Wash estuary at night.
Camera: *Nikon F4S*
Lens: *500mm f4*
Film: *Kodachrome 64*

Tony Hamblin
Goldcrest singing, Warwickshire, England

You don't see too many photographs of tiny birds like goldcrests, and to find one captured in full song in such perfect surroundings is quite exceptional. I asked Tony Hamblin how he did it:

❝ *This goldcrest sang high in a blue spruce tree 5m (16ft) from my front door all through one summer, so early on I erected a 4m (13ft) high scaffold and topped it with my hide. But although the goldcrest continued to sing, he now moved to the opposite side of the tree! The problem was solved when I made a tape of a goldcrest singing from a pre-recorded CD, and played it back through a loud speaker for brief periods, at moderate volume. This encouraged the goldcrest to sing well for me, in view of the camera, on and off for over an hour. I was able to take a number of photographs with my Canon EOS 1-N and 300mm f4L lens. The exposure was $^{1}/_{125}$ sec. at f8 on Fujichrome Sensia 100 film.*

Sadly, in the autumn I discovered the body of a goldcrest in a flowerpot under a window. Presumably it had died as a result of a collision with the window, and I guessed it to be the mate of the singing male that I had photographed. ❞

about two weeks before the females, and if you play the bubbling calls of the female within about a kilometer (half a mile) of a singing male, it will home in on the sound very quickly indeed, eager to find a mate. But it won't necessarily perch where you'd like it to.

Playing tapes is not so very different from hunters using duck calls to attract their quarry, and there are other specific sounds that work just as well. In the north and west of Scotland, it is well known that corncrakes can be attracted through imitating their rasping call by drawing a comb across the edge of a credit card. Some country people also claim to be able to pull in hunting short-eared owls by making a squeaking noise with pursed lips, which is supposed to sound like a rabbit in distress. Another birders' device is the practice of "pishing" – a softly repeated "psshhh, psshhh, psshhh" sound, which can flush out certain skulking birds like goldcrests, reed warblers and sedge warblers. Just why this should happen is somewhat obscure, but the best theory seems to be that it sounds like the alarm call of a bird reacting to a predator, so others come to join in the mobbing behavior. Again, pishing seems to work for a wider range of birds in North America than in Europe.

Rivals can also be falsified by means of model birds, and even reflections in mirrors. You may have seen birds attacking their own reflection in a car wing mirror or polished hub cap, mistaking it for a rival male. Robins are notoriously aggressive to intruders, and respond quite dramatically to a mirror placed in their territory, displaying back to the strong stimulus of the red breast. Quite crude models can also have a similar effect with a number of species of birds, if you can identify the crucial color or plumage feature that elicits the threat display. Models of ducks or geese grazing in a field might persuade other birds flying over to join them on the ground, instilling the confidence of the flock. Carved, painted decoys of ducks are traditionally used by wildfowlers to lure live birds down to open water in the same way.

The frontiers
There are various other more or less reliable locations for photographing birds relating to particular aspects of their behavior, but too numerous and diverse to detail here. Some of the more obvious ones include sunbathing spots and dust baths, and plucking posts where sparrowhawks and goshawks pluck their prey

before feeding it to their chicks. Some are less obvious or well known, such as the forest tracks where grouse or pheasants come to take grit, which aids in their digestive process. In the New World, one thinks of the "salt licks" where macaws come to ingest vital minerals, and the bizarre but beautiful bowers of the bowerbirds. All offer great opportunities for you and your camera. In the end, it will be down to your own powers of research, observation and field skills to locate and depict these natural wonders through your photography.

Beyond these relatively accessible sites, we have the bird subjects that are always going to be "out of reach" to some extent – those that are restricted by virtue of their geographical range, habitat or behavior. Future challenges will be to find ways of photographing such subjects as birds of prey away from the nest, seabirds at sea (rather than on land where they appear out of place and out of character), and high-flying insectivorous birds such as swifts, which spend almost their entire lives on the wing. We could well expect further technological advances to come to our aid. Smaller, lighter telephotos that have faster autofocus and even better image stabilization will make us more responsive and able to work with subjects at greater range. Digital cameras will provide the means to work at lower ambient light intensities, amongst other things. But there will always be a basic need for both ingenuity and field skills on the part of the photographer.

Some of our "frontiers" will be issues of style – so although it might be possible to achieve ever sharper, bolder images, we might still prefer to make sensitive studies with soft light and small, blurred subjects. Whatever the preferred style, it is hoped that these innovations will be used wisely and in a way that celebrates birds and their place in nature.

CAMERAS ON LOCATION

We've dealt with the theory, but what about when you're cold, wet, tired and hungry, and the bugs are biting, too? Real-life working conditions for wildlife photographers can be quite testing, so you need to go properly prepared. Some practical suggestions follow.

Organizing your field kit

Early decisions need to be taken about what to take out with you in the field. There is a temptation to try to carry everything you might possibly need to cover all eventualities, but this would be a mistake. It is better to limit yourself to what is easily manageable when

Swifts screaming display
The aptly named swift is not hard to find but quite a challenge to photograph. I wanted to portray the typical social behavior of the flock as the late evening sunlight glanced off the birds' wings. Hand-holding my 500mm f4 telephoto was the only way to keep up, and in continuous servo AF the waste proportion was high, but I managed to obtain a small number of sharp shots.
***Camera:** Nikon F5*
***Lens:** AF-S 500mm f4*
***Film:** Fujichrome Sensia 100 uprated to EI200*
***Exposure:** 1/1,250 sec. at f4*

Doug Allan

Guillemots diving under the ice cap,
Baffin Island, Canada

The underwater world certainly represents something of a physical frontier for all photographers. Here is a remarkable photograph from the very limits of human endurance, and illustrates the lengths to which some people will go to get a placing in the BG Wildlife Photographer of the Year competition (Winner, "Underwater" Section, 1996)! Doug Allan is a professional underwater film cameraman, and one of the few who also takes his own stills photographs. On this occasion he was working for a National Geographic TV special called *Arctic Kingdom – Life at the Edge*. Doug takes up the story:

❝❝ *The shot was taken in June in the Canadian Arctic at north Baffin Island, where I was filming at the "floe edge," that wonderful margin where the open sea meets the winter sea ice still frozen in the big bays and inlets. There's a magic*

window of opportunity for about two weeks when the ice edge is accessible and the water is gin clear, before the plankton bloom starts.

The guillemots were swimming in a couple of groups, about 50 birds in each, paddling into the ice edge before diving for two to three minutes in search of fish. I found them pretty wary to approach, even when I was only snorkelling, and most of the time there would be a minute or more between the first bird of the group and the last leaving the surface. However in this case they all suddenly went down together, and the shot manages to capture that starburst explosion effect of the synchronous dive. The clarity of the water and its surface stillness, and the looming presence of the ice lumps in the background rather than simply open water, also somehow enhance the drama of the moment.

The water temperature was –1.3˚C (29.6˚F), but with a dry suit I could stay in for up to 90 minutes before getting too chilled. I spent three hours in the water shooting movie and one roll of stills, using a Nikonos 5 camera with 20mm lens, available light, Kodachrome 200, $^1/_{250}$ sec. at f5.6. ❞❞

you are fresh and fit, and should still be just manageable when you are tired. You are more likely to be able to keep within sensible limits if your backpack isn't too large in the first place.

For a typical bird photography assignment on foot, I would expect to carry the following main items in my backpack:

- camera body and back-up
- 500mm telephoto
- one shorter telephoto or zoom
- 1.4x and 2x teleconverters
- standard lens or mid-range zoom
- wide-angle lens or short zoom
- one flash gun
- stock of films of various speeds
- spare batteries
- two shutter cable releases
- blower brush, lens cleaning cloth, chamois leather
- notebook and pencil
- plastic bags

I would also carry the following vital additions: a hefty tripod, which I normally carry in the hand or over the shoulder, and binoculars, worn around the neck.

Depending on circumstances, I might add or substitute some or all of the following:

- extension tube(s)
- flash extender and off-camera TTL flash cord
- macro lens
- additional lens filters
- scrim netting and lens sleeve
- waterproof covering
- food and drink
- pocket flashlight, penknife, safety pins
- toilet tissue
- small sheet of plastic to improvise a drinking pool
- beanbag
- monopod

A back-up camera body is useful when fitted with a different lens, or to load a different speed of film. If both bodies are the same model (a sensible move), do something to enable you to distinguish one from the other at a glance – I use a colored sticker on the pentaprism of one camera, and make that my "slow film" body. A back-up is also there if something goes wrong with the main camera, or you simply haven't got time or opportunity

to change batteries when they go down.

To maintain your state of readiness, have films and batteries unpacked in preparation for rapid reloading. Four 35mm film canisters fit neatly into a plastic slide box, which keeps them clean, and the canisters can be inverted and replaced once exposed so that you don't mix them up. Batteries can also be repackaged in appropriate quantities in zippable plastic bags so that you don't have to spend ages removing them from blister packs when called for. These simple preparations also help to cut down on unnecessary bulk.

When uprating films, so that I know which need push-processing by the lab, I mark rolls on removal from the camera with a permanent marker pen, or by scratching the casing with a key or penknife. If there is no time to do this immediately, I always put uprated films in the same coat or shirt pocket so I know to mark and separate them later.

Traveling

Traveling by car means that weight isn't too much of an issue, but security is. Try to avoid leaving any camera gear in an unattended vehicle, even out of sight in the trunk, and don't have telltale camera club stickers displayed in the window! Your insurance cover will probably be of higher value if your car has a factory-fitted alarm. The chances are that insurance will be invalidated if equipment is left in a vehicle overnight, or indeed at any time – check the small print on your policy.

Overseas trips call for stringent measures. Keep your kit down to an absolute minimum, and carry all cameras and lenses as hand luggage. You must also carry spare batteries as hand luggage, and preferably film, too. Airlines seem to be getting increasingly strict about weight allowances for hand luggage, so this can be quite tricky. So far, I have always been able to carry my Lowepro Photo Trekker on to the plane, and it does fit snugly into an overhead locker, but I suspect it might have been more difficult if I had been traveling with a party of similarly equipped photographers. As a back-up I wear a photographer's vest loaded with films and ready to accept cameras and lenses from my backpack if need be.

(previous pages) **Atlantic puffin in flight**
This was photographed with a hand-held, manual-focus 200mm macro lens. After practising on a few flight approaches to the breeding colony, I pre-focused the lens for the desired image size, and depressed the shutter button just before the bird came into sharp focus. Plenty of out-of-focus efforts were rejected in editing.

(opposite) **Female osprey on nest**
This osprey was photographed from a hide installed on a conveniently adjacent slope. I generally expect to put in a 12-hour shift when photographing birds of prey at the nest.
Camera: *Nikon F5*
Lens: *AF-S 500mm f4 plus 1.4x teleconverter*
Film: *Fujichrome Sensia 100*

Use zooms in place of prime lenses to keep the number down, and you may be able to use slower, more compact lenses if you are traveling to destinations where good light is guaranteed. Image-stabilized lenses mean smaller, lighter tripods can be considered.

Tripods and tripod heads should pack into hold baggage, well padded; carbon fiber helps keep down the overall weight. A lightweight portable hide can go in the hold too, if needed, and throw in a couple of empty beanbags ready to load with the cheapest available filling when you arrive at your destination. I used to be quite confident of packing spare film in my suitcase – even super-sensitive ISO1600 films that had passed through several airport security checks showed no ill effects, but recently upgraded X-ray equipment for hold baggage at certain airports means this can no longer be relied upon. Make every effort to carry films as hand baggage, as these scanners are still quite safe. You can try asking for a hand search, but it's at the discretion of the airline.

Allow me to make a suggestion about photographing birds in developing countries. If you come away with some good results, why not donate some duplicate slides or a selection of scanned images on CD for the local use of conservation groups such as BirdLife International? Good photographs are vital but all-too-often scarce resources, and such a contribution could make an enormous difference to the effectiveness of fledgling conservation programs. Just because photographs of these birds seem to be quite commonplace in Europe and America, it's very easy to assume that they are freely available worldwide, but so often that isn't the case.

Tough conditions

Usually, maintaining your equipment involves little more than dusting off the lens and an occasional spray of "canned air" with the camera back open. Gentle rain showers can be shrugged off, as long as you dry the gear thoroughly before packing it away. To wipe water droplets from the lens filter, use a small piece of chamois leather (incidentally, it's actually cow leather these days). For heavier or

persistent rain it makes sense to cover up, and a large plastic trash bag is ideal for this. Damp and condensation can penetrate deep, and I have found this to my cost when leaving lenses out over a clear, chilly night – as the sun warms everything up the next morning, a cloud of fog appears on internal lens elements and is very difficult to dispel.

The corrosive effects of saltwater spray are more serious still, and if you are working on a boat or a windy seashore you should take precautions against it. A quick and inexpensive remedy is to cut the corner off a plastic carrier bag, making a hole just large enough to slip over the lens barrel. Tape the small opening around the lens hood, and the longer part of the bag should cover the camera leaving ample access at the back to carry on working. Use chamois leather again to keep lenses clear. For amphibious landings with your camera gear, the ubiquitous plastic trash bag is useful, but if you do this kind of thing regularly investigate the heavy-duty plastic camera cases with O-rings for a perfect waterproof seal.

A cut-off carrier bag is quite effective against wind-blown sand, which is a real menace anywhere near cameras – be especially careful when changing films not to allow sand into the camera back, as the merest speck on the pressure plate can scratch roll after roll.

In the tropics, high humidity can be a hazard, and sometimes interferes with electrical functions. It is sensible to carry a back-up camera body. For extended visits you might want to consider an all-manual back-up, but for two or three weeks here and there I wouldn't worry too much, especially if you can retire to an air-conditioned hotel room at the end of the day. Working in rainforest, carry industrial-size packs of silica gel and place them in a sealed bag with your cameras overnight. The gel can be reactivated every few days by warming in an oven.

At low temperatures, cameras can become very sluggish or even pack up altogether. The use of lithium or Ni-MH batteries is usually recommended, and these should give you more films between battery changes anyway. Keep spare batteries somewhere warm, such as an inside pocket, and again make sure that

you have a back-up camera body available. Another effect of extreme cold is to make film leaders brittle and liable to snap, so reload carefully and keep your motordrive on a slow setting. If you have a metal tripod, cover the legs with foam pads to protect your hands; water-pipe insulation is good for this purpose. You will need to work the camera controls with your gloves on; inner glove liners are ideal for this and you can cover them with outer mitts when not shooting.

Handling long lenses

When you are working with long focal length lenses, camera shake is the main enemy and the commonest cause of out-of-focus photographs. It's tempting to believe that you can easily hand-hold a compact, lightweight lens like a 400mm f5.6, but actually the sheer mass of a larger, faster lens is likely to make that the more stable. There are a number of steps that can be taken to combat camera shake, apart from the obvious use of faster shutter speeds.

Firstly, use a substantial tripod and tripod head, and remember to leave the center column down. With stationary or relatively inactive subjects, once you have framed and focused, lock down the tripod head, use the camera in hands-free mode, and trigger the shutter via a cable release. With obliging

subjects at slower speeds, mirror lock-up can be a real lifesaver, since mirror vibration is the primary cause of camera shake at shutter speeds of around $1/15$ sec. In extreme circumstances, a tripod brace or monopod can be used as additional support for the camera body, but this doesn't leave you with much room for maneuver.

More often, you will want to keep your hands on the camera and your eye to the viewfinder to follow the action. In this case, grip tight, press your face to the camera back, hold your breath and gently squeeze the shutter button. Short sequences on the motordrive can improve your chances of getting at least one sharp shot.

For extra stability, you can place a beanbag on top of the lens over the centre of gravity, or you can suspend a heavy rock under the tripod, fastening with a scrim net or string bag – this is an especially useful technique when the tripod is on soft, spongy ground like heather moor. Ensure all fastenings are tight and secure; some telephotos have alternative tripod attachments, and I use the smaller, lower attachments on my Nikkor AF-S lenses as they seem less prone to vibration. A simple wooden wedge can also help to overcome lens wobble when using pan-and-tilt tripod heads.

The longer your effective focal length, the nearer that your shutter speed is to $1/15$ sec., and the windier the day, the more of these contingencies you are likely to need. Finally, of course, image-stabilized lenses can give you 2 or 3 extra stops to play with before camera shake becomes a problem – this must be the way forwards.

For safe handling when carrying your telephoto mounted on camera, always use the lens strap rather than the camera strap, as the latter would place too great a strain on the lens mount, possibly causing it to buckle or give way. Don't leave a camera unattended on a tripod, especially with a telephoto fitted: a sudden gust of wind catching a big lens hood can easily topple it over. Similarly, beware when you are changing camera bodies with a large lens mounted directly on the tripod – removing the camera body can unbalance the set-up, with disastrous consequences.

Fritz Pölking

Toco toucan, Pantanal, Brazil

There are few, if any, more experienced or better-traveled wildlife photographers than Fritz Pölking. I tried to find out if Fritz encountered any special difficulties with the climate on one of his South American expeditions:

66 *This toucan came every morning between seven and eleven o'clock to check the papaya trees, in the hope of finding a ripe fruit. If there was something ready he would stay on for a while, wrestling the fruit with his enormous bill and consuming the sweet flesh; otherwise, he just flew away and there would be nothing to photograph.*

I worked from a hide with a Nikon F5 and 500mm f4 AF lens and 1.4x teleconverter, on a tripod. The film is Fujichrome Sensia 100. This photograph is the best result from seven mornings' work. 99

When I persisted with my line of enquiry, Fritz replied simply, "No problems with heat and humidity – sorry!"

Chapter 4
CASE STUDIES

A series of case studies now follows, illustrating some varied photography assignments and projects from my own portfolio, and featuring a range of different subjects, methods and working conditions. These are the stories behind the pictures, if you like, from concept through execution. Most of these photographs were taken to support specific bird conservation initiatives.

The kingfisher
A classic "bait and perch" project

(previous pages) **Pre-roost gathering of knot**
Hidden in nearby sand dunes, I waited for the advancing spring tide to push this flock of knot towards me.

A female kingfisher
This kingfisher observes a potential predator overhead (above right) and on another occasion is seen poised to dive for fish (below). The hide-to-subject distance was dictated by a relatively open and well-lit location for the perch, and a suitable platform to accommodate the hide; ideally for such a small bird the perch would have been at about 5m (16ft), near to the minimum focusing distance of the lens.
Camera: Nikon F5
Lens: AF-S 500mm f4 lens
Film: Fujichrome Sensia 100 uprated to EI200

With its stunning plumage and secretive manner, it's hardly surprising that the kingfisher is such an alluring subject for photographers. Many photographers tend to assume that the best time to photograph a kingfisher is in the breeding season when the adults are feeding young, but this is not the only way. Apart from the fact that there are restrictions on photographing in the breeding season in many parts of the world, I think that autumn and winter actually offer better opportunities: the birds tend to prefer shady, wooded river courses, so there are fewer problems with extremes of light and shade when the leaves have fallen.

I got my chance to photograph kingfishers upon moving to a new house with a small stream running adjacent to the garden. Early sightings were comparatively few, usually of a bird in flight whizzing along the stream below the level of the bank, making its flight call. One of the first things I did was to place a branch low over the water, but just visible from the house, to encourage the birds to perch. They seemed to love the chance to fish a new stretch of water, and pretty soon became regular visitors. Then I introduced my hide at about 7m (23ft) from the perch, and simultaneously began to bait with fish. For this, I simply used a plastic storage box weighted with gravel and filled with river water, standing slightly out of the water surface near the perch. The fish were locally caught minnows and sticklebacks. (Incidentally, when baiting you should never import fish from another water course or introduce exotic – pet – species.) Finally, I substituted the branch with a reedmace stem in order to make a more attractive perch, appropriate for the habitat, and proportionate to the size of the bird.

The careful preparation paid off, and I was

(opposite) **The effect of light**
The warm autumn light really shows off the bird's metallic colors. The addition of a 1.4x teleconverter gave an effective focal length of 700mm, but with a shutter speed around $^1/_{60}$ sec. I was obliged to use mirror lock-up to prevent camera shake, which in turn called for manual focus and metering.
Camera: Nikon F5
Lens: AF-S 500mm f4 lens
Film: Fujichrome Sensia 100 uprated to EI200

able to take simple portraits on a few occasions before the birds moved on to fish another part of the river. Surprisingly frequently the kingfisher was happy to use my perch but chose to ignore the bait box and found its own fish in the stream, which suggested to me that I could probably have succeeded with the perch alone. But until I knew that, it seemed sensible to try everything I could think of to maximize my chances of success.

On reviewing the photographs, it is quite pronounced how the changing seasons and shifting light over just a few short weeks have had a big impact on the colors, background and overall mood. I was able to observe these qualities over the period of photography, but still underestimated their effect on film – even when you think you're taking large numbers of similar photographs, they can turn out quite differently.

Had the birds stayed around for longer I should have liked to vary the type of perch, perhaps by introducing an alder spray in the early spring or something to complement the colors of the kingfisher. Well, there's another project for the future …

The great bustard
Stake-out on the Spanish steppe

The location
Bustard feathers in this alfalfa crop (top) were a good indication of recent activity, possibly resulting from fighting between males. The hides (above) were dug in to present a low profile and camouflaged with straw bales and dead vegetation. A flower pot was installed as a dummy lens. The distant copse of umbrella pines was used as cover for my vehicle.

(right) *Female great bustards*
A "drove" of female great bustards is depicted feeding in alfalfa.
Camera: Nikon F4S
Lens: 500mm f4 plus 1.4x teleconverter
Film: Fujichrome Provia 100

The last European stronghold for this magnificent but threatened bird is the grassland steppe of western Spain. The bustard's majestic stature and plumage, together with its endangered status, mean that it's a frequently requested photograph in conservation publishing. I was somewhat surprised, therefore, to discover that there weren't too many photographs available of great bustards through the usual picture library sources. Usually this is a reliable indication of difficulty, so I knew that I couldn't just expect to turn up and "burn" film.

With this in mind, I set aside five weeks in the spring of 1995 to attempt this demanding assignment. I liaised with BirdLife International experts, and staff at the Sociedad Española de Ornitología (SEO), the BirdLife International partner organization in Spain, who put me in touch with local ornithologists and other photographers "in the know." They in turn advised me that it was necessary to get permission to photograph the bird from the regional Junta of Castilla y León. I also spoke to film cameramen who had experience of the species, and of course read everything that I could find on the subject. So it was with considerable assistance and after much preparation that I set about my task.

Arriving on location, I spent a few days with my new Spanish friends watching the birds and getting to know a little more about their behavior. In spring, the bustards roam around in same-sex droves, preferring to feed on cultivated vetch and alfalfa – normally away from roads, overhead power lines and active irrigation. It didn't take long to realize that these birds wouldn't be easily approachable by car, possibly because they are still (illegally) hunted as trophies and this is generally done from four-wheel-drive vehicles. Consequently I set about "digging in" three hides at some of the more promising sites, where we had either seen early display activity from a distance or found other encouraging signs such as the birds' gigantic droppings or lost feathers. Favorite sites seemed to be along the margins of "set-aside" fields bordering a cereal crop, and I was hopeful of the fallow fields bursting into flower as the spring progressed to provide a complementary background – a forlorn hope as it turned out, since the winter had

been too dry to provide such a spectacle.

My routine for the following weeks was to arrive at my chosen hide at least an hour before first light, deposit my camera gear and tripod, then park the vehicle under cover of trees about 1km (half a mile) away, returning to the hide on foot. If there was no sign of the birds by early afternoon, I might give up for the day. More often there would be some tantalizing bustard presence, too distant to photograph but close enough to make it impossible to leave without disturbing the birds, and I would be stuck there until after dark. Quite often I would glimpse displaying males on some distant rise, flashing like beacons as they turned and caught the sun. Although the birds favor traditional display grounds, these cover quite large areas, and days passed without any photography. The other birds were no more obliging; there would be the odd calandra lark or short-toed lark in the same field, or perhaps a passing lesser kestrel, but nothing to really get to grips with. Temperatures ranged from below zero at dawn, sometimes rising to 30°C (86°F) by midday, making conditions uncomfortable. There was lots of time to worry about what I might be doing wrong.

After a total of about 120 hours in the hide, a small group of female bustards arrived in my field one morning, casually feeding on young shoots and unconcerned about the hide. In close pursuit were a few males, the mature birds sporting fine moustaches and rich cinnamon-colored breasts, their tails cocked in semi-display. There were birds in camera range for about 20 minutes in all, and I was able to run off four or five rolls of film as they continued to feed and eye each other. Reassuringly, they still ignored the hide, apparently oblivious of my fevered activity.

Some time later, towards noon, the males returned and to my excitement one began to display very close to the hide. The light was quite fierce by then, but it was immaterial as they all promptly sat down and went to sleep for three hours! That was to be my final opportunity to photograph.

A male great bustard
Five weeks of fieldwork was rewarded with 20 minutes of photo opportunity, as this splendid male in its fine spring plumage strutted before my hide.
Camera: *Nikon F4S*
Lens: *500mm f4*
Film: *Fujichrome Provia 100*

The kestrel
An elevated position

Setting up the camera
This view of one of the west towers of Peterborough cathedral (above) shows my mesh screen in place at the top and the CCTV camera pointing down towards the kestrels' nest entrance. The Bronica SQ-Am in position (right), with Metz 45 CT4 flash gun fitted on a side bracket and all supported by a Benbo Mark 1 tripod. Note the tape player and the remote shutter-release cable.

One year, high above the historic vaulted ceilings of Peterborough cathedral, a pair of kestrels nested. Tall buildings frequently provide secure nest sites for birds of prey such as kestrels and peregrines, so this was not really unusual, but this particular year the Royal Society for the Protection of Birds (RSPB) had installed a CCTV camera looking down towards the nest to provide a public-viewing facility in the cathedral below. Publicity stills were required. The idea of photographing kestrels here appealed to me and I wanted to show something of the magnificent setting. As the cathedral is not too far from where I live, regular visits would present no special problem. However, photography would have to be conducted with even more sensitivity than usual because my every move would be in the public gaze, and I would be working on a protected, historic building where normal worship couldn't be disrupted or disturbed.

Having agreed terms of access with the cathedral's Dean and Chapter, I climbed the spiral stone staircase and clambered out on to a ledge near to where the birds had been seen landing with food. As kestrels normally nest in

holes, I wasn't too surprised to discover that the birds had exploited a tunnel in the stonework which was part of the roof drainage system, and the nest was completely hidden from view. There didn't seem to be any regularly used perch nearby, so it looked as though I would have to try for shots of the flight approach. The ledge was too small and unsafe to accommodate a hide, and afforded a poor angle of view – the camera really needed to be suspended over the edge looking inwards. Since there was no convenient viewing window from the adjacent stone tower, this assignment was developing into something of a challenge. The possibility of using a remote-controlled camera began to take shape in my mind.

I could hear the calls of chicks begging for food, so I knew the timing was right. Wasting no time, I returned the next day to begin to set up my remote camera. I decided to use a Bronica SQ-Am medium-format camera, for two main reasons. First, the larger film format would allow more room for framing a flying bird, and the 6 x 6cm film could be cut down to 35mm size if necessary. Second, because the site was in shade for much of the day, I wanted to use fill flash. At that time, the Nikon F3 (and all of its rivals) had a flash sync speed of only $1/60$ sec., but the Bronica's leaf shutter would allow flash sync at all speeds right up to $1/500$ sec. I framed up with the standard 80mm lens, leaving space for the anticipated line of approach, mounted the camera on a Benbo tripod, and fitted a single Metz 45 CT4 flash gun to provide the fill light – there was nowhere really to attach a second flash if I had wanted to. It was also impossible to rig a beam trigger because there were no fixing points for a transmitter and receiver. So it would have to be a hit-and-miss affair with a remote cable.

The remote cable was made from about 30m (100ft) of bell wire with a jack plug one end and a button switch the other. This was routed back from the camera, up the cathedral tower to a viewing position about 10m (33ft) above. From here I could look down on the kestrels flying in with pretty good all-round visibility, and hoped to see the birds with sufficient notice to fire the shutter.

Further preparations were necessary. I needed some screening to cover myself up, and sought the cooperation of a local tent maker who provided hides for me from time to time. Together we rigged up a screen of fine gauze netting, which had to be fastened with elasticated ropes to avoid any possibility of damage to the ancient masonry. It wasn't an ideal color, but was only required for a few days and seemed to be readily accepted by the birds. Finally, I had to do something to get the birds used to the terrible noise of the camera's motordrive – it was much louder than the contemporary 35mm motordrives, and was going to be operated at close range. For this purpose I recorded the sound of the camera on to a cassette tape, and played it back continuously over a few days and nights, using a tape player

left out alongside a dummy camera.

On the first day of photography, the camera was set up and pre-focused to the estimated range of the bird. A manual exposure was set for $^1/500$ sec. at f5.6–f8, using Fujichrome RDP 100 film uprated to EI200, and the camera mirror then locked up to cut down the shutter delay and keep the noise and vibration to a minimum. The flash gun was set to f4 on auto so that it would deliver $1^1/2$ stops less light than the ambient reading at a short flash duration.

Amazingly, my very first attempt resulted in the photograph you see here. Although I continued photography for a few days more, I never seemed to be able to replicate my early good fortune, and subsequent photographs had the bird out of focus, with its wing across the head, or partly or wholly out of frame.

Returning with prey

The male kestrel arrives with a nestling bird it has captured, to feed to its young. The fill-in flash and $^1/500$ sec. sync speed has been sufficient to arrest movement without too much "ghosting" and has also killed the worst of the shadow on the bird and the stonework. Fortunately, the ambient light did not fluctuate too much during my photography session and the pre-set exposure of f5.6–f8 held true.
Camera: *Bronica SQ-Am*
Lens: *80mm f2.8*
Film: *Fujichrome RDP100 uprated to EI200*
Lighting: *Metz 45 CT4*

129

The bald ibis
A globally threatened bird

A bald ibis feeding
This ibis was photographed from a vehicle as it fed among the shooting cereal crop. However it didn't seem to me that this was the best way to endear the bird to a wider public.
Camera: Nikon F4S
Lens: 500mm f4 plus 1.4x teleconverter
Film: Fujichrome Provia 100

(right) **Ibis in flight**
This image of a flock of bald ibis shows the Atlantic sea cliffs of the Souss-Massa National Park where they nest and roost.
Camera: Nikon F4S
Lens: 80-200mm f2.8
Film: Fujichrome Provia 100

The wild breeding population of the northern bald ibis totals no more than 250 birds, almost entirely confined to the Souss-Massa National Park in Morocco, so this is a bird on the very brink of extinction. There are a number in captivity, where they do breed quite well, but so far attempts at reintroduction into the wild have not been successful.

Plenty of photographs existed of bald ibis from the captive collections, but there were not too many of them in the wild, so this was my challenge. The Moroccan birds nest on the ledges of rugged Atlantic sea cliffs, and are quite inaccessible except to climbers with ropes, so nest shots were discounted. Instead I went to photograph them in the late winter, shortly before their breeding season commenced, at the invitation of the National Park managers and the BirdLife International bald ibis research team.

The bald ibis is a gregarious bird, with foraging flocks advancing through areas of semi-desert and sparsely cultivated land as they hunt for insects and small lizards on which to feed. They are reminiscent of a herd of sheep as they move forwards with their heads down, not easily diverted from their path. By anticipating the movement of the flock, and with the aid of a four-wheel-drive vehicle, I was able to get ahead of them on a few occasions and photograph a few individuals that passed close by, using a 500mm lens with 1.4x teleconverter resting on a beanbag. This wasn't too difficult given enough time, but I didn't want to keep harassing the birds in this way; in any case, it didn't really show them at their best. The harsh sunlight showed off the iridescent

plumage reasonably well, but the overall contrast of the black bird against the reflective sand was a bit of a problem. Many birds had their feathers soiled by the droppings of other birds from the night-time roost, and the nictitating membrane, which protects the eye from blowing sand, was often apparent in the photographs. Plus, you have to admit, they do look pretty ugly.

The flocks flying to roost at dusk seemed a much better prospect, although the low light conditions would present their own difficulties for photography. One evening I concealed myself among some rocks on a cliff top facing west towards the setting sun, and waited for the birds to arrive at their regular roost site. Using a 500mm manual-focus telephoto mounted on a tripod, and my Nikon F4S loaded with Fujichrome Provia 100 uprated to EI200, I began to photograph the assembling roost. Uncertain of where to land at first, and sometimes disturbed by sea anglers on the shore below, the birds circled over the sea a few times, giving me plenty of opportunities for flight shots. Their flight silhouettes made a much more evocative sight than the birds on the ground, with their distinctive curved bills and shaggy crests outlined against the sunset sky. There seemed to be something almost prehistoric about their appearance.

To begin with, shutter speeds of $1/500$ sec. were easily attainable with the lens at its widest aperture, and allowed me to run off a number of "safe" shots. Nevertheless, I wanted to make the most of this rare opportunity and take a range of different types of photographs, so I set a smaller aperture and tried panning at shutter speeds around $1/30$ sec., then $1/15$

sec. and $^1/_8$ sec. The greater depth of field meant that focusing wasn't quite so critical, and I could concentrate better on my panning action. As the sun set and light faded fast my options narrowed, and quite soon the lens was wide open even for the slowest workable shutter speeds. Using a second camera body I also tried a couple of rolls of Fujichrome Provia 1600 film pushed to EI3200 in desperation, and in due course even this was being exposed at $^1/_8$ sec. Eventually, the birds settled down for the night and I had to admit that photography was over.

Since I made these photographs, a mysterious mass mortality occurred in 1996, accounting for the deaths of more than 20 percent of the bald ibis population in the space of a week. Despite great efforts and many analyses to ascertain the cause, results have been inconclusive, but the most likely possibilities are an obscure virus or toxin. Fortunately however, a couple of good breeding seasons have resulted in the recovery of numbers to something like 220 birds. A great deal has been learned about the bird's biology in the interim, the appointment of local fishermen as wardens has mitigated the effects of casual disturbance, and the development of sustainable "ecotourism" in the park is now a high priority. Let's hope their future is assured.

Getting dark

This group of ibis were photographed long after sunset using fast film stock and a shutter speed of about $^1/_8$ sec. The graininess of the film and slow shutter speed imparts a feeling of bleakness.
Camera: Nikon F4S
Lens: 500mm f4
Film: Fujichrome Provia 1600 uprated to EI3200

A bird joining the roost at sunset
This shows the bald ibis in "prehistoric" silhouette.
Camera: Nikon F4S
Lens: 500mm f4
Film: Fujichrome Provia 100

The house sparrow
A stable residence

The house sparrow is a common bird in most parts of the world, usually associated with human habitation. It is also quite drab in appearance, so it is easy to take for granted and overlook as a potential subject for photography. Recently, concern has mounted in Britain that its numbers are in decline. Changes in farming practice are thought to be a contributory factor (although the birds are also declining in towns and cities for reasons as yet unknown), so it was heartening to be introduced to a farmer who was taking practical steps to improve the fortunes of house sparrows on his own farm.

Generally speaking, modern, efficient farming methods mean that little grain is spilt and left lying around fields and farmyard, hedges are less numerous than they once were, and outbuildings are maintained in a much better state of repair than formerly. As elsewhere, High Ash Farm in Norfolk previously supported great numbers of house sparrows, but witnessed a steady drop in numbers until there were only three birds remaining. The difference here is that the farmer was alert to the problem and prepared to do something about it. Addressing the birds' requirements for food, shelter and a place to nest, a few dense hedgerows were recreated around the buildings, and seed hoppers were provided. One other crucial step was taken: when re-roofing an old barn and riding stables, the farmer incorporated a total of 50 nest boxes underneath the pantiles. This worked incredibly well, and there was a slow but steady recovery in numbers of house sparrows. After eight years, there were 35 pairs nesting in these two buildings alone. Now, I understand, all of the nest boxes are occupied.

I came here in the spring when nest-building activity was at its peak, and indeed there was no shortage of house sparrows to photograph. There were possibilities for photography at or near the seed hoppers, or in the dry corner of a horse paddock where the sparrows frequently dust-bathed. But I was most attracted to the traditional pantiled roofs with their colorful tiles and encrusting lichens. To gain height and achieve a better vantage point, I was installed in a tractor bucket, which was then raised to roof level, and I crouched low with my 500mm lens and 1.4x teleconverter resting on a beanbag on the edge of the bucket. Some scrim netting thrown over my head completed the makeshift hide.

Nest-building must have been well advanced as there were relatively few comings and goings. However, I noticed that occasionally birds were arriving carrying downy feathers – preferred items for lining nests. During a break, I searched around the farmyard for any more loose feathers, but they were hard to find as the house sparrows must have collected most of them. I mentioned this to the farmer, and resumed my position in the tractor bucket. Still nothing much happened for a while, but then there was a sudden flurry of activity with house sparrows arriving from all points with feathers in their bills. This went on for 15 or 20 minutes, and I was able to take quite a few photographs. It turned out that, since our conversation, the farmer had gone to the tractor shed where he knew there was a pigeon roost in the rafters and swept out all of the discarded feathers from the floor below. Great to have such a perceptive accomplice!

Sparrows on the farm
A female house sparrow approaches her nest entrance with one of the feathers provided (opposite). This male sparrow (below) is shown pausing on the stable roof.
Camera: *Nikon F5*
Lens: *AF-S 500mm f4 plus 1.4x teleconverter*
Film: *Fujichrome Sensia 100*

The white-tailed eagle
Documenting a successful reintroduction

White-tailed eagle in action

A white-tailed eagle emerges from the morning mist (top). An adult eagle in fine plumage flies from its sea cliff eyrie (top middle). The eagle about to seize a fish, photographed at approximately ¹/₂₅₀ sec. (bottom middle). Success (bottom).

After a period of extinction as a British breeding bird due to human persecution, the magnificent white-tailed eagle (or sea eagle) flies wild and free in Scottish skies once again, thanks to an ambitious and dedicated program of reintroduction spanning 25 years. There are currently thought to be about 20 breeding pairs in Scotland, rearing about a dozen chicks a year, with numbers increasing all the time. There would be more if not for the malicious depredations of egg collectors.

My first serious association with these awesome birds came in 1985, when as the RSPB's staff photographer I was privileged to be able to witness the maiden flight of the first young reared in Scotland for some 70 years. Photography at the secret nest location was certainly not an option at that time, with so much at stake, but I returned to the area during the following winter, full of optimism, and set up a hide and feeding station down by the shore.

For ten cold days I watched and waited in the hide, photographing buzzards feasting on the rabbit carcass bait as a consolation prize. Since my range was predetermined for a much larger subject, my 400mm Nikkor ED telephoto began to feel pretty inadequate, so after several days I was tempted to switch to a 1,000mm mirror lens to improve the image size of the buzzards. Hard to believe now that I should have considered such an option with an f11 lens in that pre-Kodachrome 200 era, but it seemed the right decision at the time. So with my ISO64 film and an unremembered but agonizingly slow shutter speed, I had to make the best of the circumstances when a juvenile sea eagle eventually landed between me and the bait.

After all that effort the results were a bit of a disappointment, as the close-up head portrait at near enough minimum focus could easily be mistaken for a bird photographed in captivity. It was indeed the surviving juvenile fledged earlier that year, and I had at least made a passable shot for the historical record, but I felt a bit cheated. Not at all what I had in mind! He didn't stay down for more than a few moments, clearly uneasy about the hide, and after I'd taken a couple of frames he flew to a new perch beyond the bait before flying off for good. So all in all, I suppose I had about 5 minutes of photo opportunity for my ten days' work.

For some years afterwards I tried to stay alert to any new photographic opportunities that might present themselves, but without much success. There were a few occasions when I was able to accompany RSPB fieldworkers under license as they checked known nest sites for signs of breeding success at remote sea cliffs in the Western Highlands and Islands – this usually entailed long hikes of three or four hours carrying heavy equipment over the hills, occasionally rewarded with a glimpse of an adult taking off some distance below us. A 500mm telephoto with a 1.4x teleconverter sometimes sufficed, but there were never more than a few minutes for photography before we'd have to move on and leave the birds in peace.

Then, in the mid-1990s, I began to hear vague reports of a particular pair of white-tailed eagles that had become accustomed to feeding from the discarded by-catch of local fishing boats, which I also knew to be quite a common habit in the Norwegian fjords. Gradually the rumour became increasingly substantial, and in 1997 I arranged to follow it up with my RSPB Scotland colleagues, hardly daring to hope that this might be the big opportunity I had been waiting for.

Equipped with a photography license from Scottish Natural Heritage, and supervised at all times by an officer of the sea eagle project team, I set about getting to know the area and meeting the fishermen. I learned that commercial fishing for Dublin Bay prawns (or langoustines) was a fairly new enterprise in that part of Scotland, as the fishermen were trying to adapt to new market demands, and these were the people who were seeing most of the sea eagles.

It soon became clear that moving about by boat was an awful lot easier than going overland, not only in terms of personal comfort, but also because the eagles were so much more approachable from the sea, having become habituated to the creel boats, which operate close inshore. On one especially calm morning, we saw an adult bird sunning itself on a large boulder close to the shore, and we were able to come within about 40m (130ft) of him (until the water became too shallow) without disturbance. This was a phenomenal revelation. Standing on the open deck with my 700mm lens combination supported on a monopod, motordrive whirring and changing

films at will, it was hard to believe that this was a wild bird – the same bird that would fly off before you could come within a kilometer of it if you approached overland.

Nevertheless, there was still a lot of time spent waiting around as there are not so many fine, calm mornings in the west of Scotland, even in midsummer. Even when the weather was fair, the eagles didn't always oblige by flying to feed. Sometimes we could see that one or other parent had recently arrived at the eyrie with a freshly killed rabbit or fulmar, at other times they would chase after a great black-backed gull and force it to disgorge its fish some distance from the boat. After many early mornings and evenings, at last everything came together and we made our long-overdue rendezvous with a sea eagle on its feeding flight. It was a truly magnificent experience, and happily one that I have been able to repeat on a few occasions since.

The triumphant ascent
Sea eagles don't plunge into the water like ospreys, but just skim the water surface with their talons. This captured pollack will be quickly devoured by hungry chicks, once the adult has removed the head. The viewpoint was intentional, and worked for, to be able to show the eagle's tail and water spray against the light.
Camera: *Nikon F5*
Lens: *AF-S 500mm f4 with monopod*
Film: *Fujichrome Sensia 100 uprated to EI200*
Exposure: *$^1/_{1,000}$ sec. at f4*

The waders

Angles on a high-water roost

High tide

A purple sandpiper roosts on a breakwater (top). These knot and oystercatcher (above) were photographed from a public hide at Snettisham RSPB reserve in Norfolk.

Camera: *Nikon F5*

Lens: *AF-S 500mm f4 (for the sandpiper), 80–200mm f2.8 (for the knot and oystercatcher)*

Film: *Fujichrome Sensia 100 (uprated to EI200 for the sandpiper)*

The Wash estuary is an internationally important feeding ground for hundreds of thousands of wading birds in winter (it is a listed wetland under the Ramsar Convention, as well as a European Union designated Special Protection Area), and the massive flocks flying to roost at each high tide are really quite spectacular. For many years I have returned to a favorite stretch of the Norfolk coast to watch in wonder, and to try to capture something of the magic in my photographs.

It's always something of a dilemma deciding whether to commit to a hide and hope for some close-up encounters (at the risk of missing out entirely), or to stay out in the open with the freedom and mobility to follow the flocks to some extent, albeit at greater range. Both methods have their merits and drawbacks, and both have rewarded me in their different ways.

At one regular roost in an excavated shingle pit just above the high-water mark, I have often used a purpose-built photographic hide close to one of the main roosting islands, which is made of driftwood and half buried in shingle. Here, I know from experience that I have to get in the hide at least two and a half hours before high water to be in position before the birds start to arrive, and will likely have to stay for at least as long afterwards. As the best high-water spring tides tend to occur before eight o'clock in the morning, this is yet another of those projects that calls for an early start. It also means that it's often a struggle for light, especially in the depths of winter. The low angle is great for candid portraits of single birds, if you can separate them from the main mass, but not ideally suited for showing the sheer numbers of birds involved – you just can't get the depth of field you want through the flock. I have tried to work around this in a number of different ways.

One solution was to use a remote-controlled camera located rather hopefully on a favorite roosting island, leaving it in place for several days over an early autumn tide series in the hope that at least some birds would settle nearby. The 28mm wide-angle lens was pre-focused on a shallow stretch of water previously used for roosting, estimating where the sun would be at the time of exposure, and up-wind of where the birds should be, so they ought to be facing the camera. The camera was contained within a soundproof box, covered with pebbles, and left on aperture priority automatic mode at f8 – with ISO200 film, this should allow for shutter speeds of 1/250 sec. or perhaps faster, given reasonable light. I made some compensating adjustment, about plus 2/3 of a stop as I recall, to allow for the area of bright sky in frame. An extended cable release was routed back to the hide position, and then it was just a question of waiting. Not surprisingly, two or three tides passed without any birds coming anywhere near the camera, but I was equipped with another camera and telephoto in the hide so I was able to carry on photographing other things. Then, one morning, a small group of dunlin began to build up around the remote camera, and as more birds arrived they shuffled closer and closer. From my hide, it looked as though they were really packing in tight, so I waited for a few flying birds to fill the space at the top of the frame and took my first shots. There were a few more chances like this on the same tide as more birds joined the roost, but the group soon evaporated when a passing marsh harrier disturbed them all.

Another experiment involved the use of a Linhof Technikardan 5 x 4in camera. I wanted to use the camera movement properties of this monorail, large-format camera to make the plane of focus coincide with the receding flock of birds (the Scheimpflug Principle: subject, lens board and film planes must be parallel to each other or meet at a common point for optimum definition at a large aperture). By tilting the lens downwards and tilting the film back independently, I could see the focus plane shift until it was parallel with the ground. The depth of field would now extend above and below the resting flock, rather than front to back, so all the birds on the ground would be in focus. But the lenses normally available for these cameras are quite short, with relatively slow shutters; the longest I had was a 260mm Schneider Tele-arton, which is barely longer than the 150mm standard lens for the 5 x 4in film format. So I had a special back panel made for the Linhof incorporating a Nikon F mount, which replaced the ground-glass focusing screen and normal film holder. Now I could attach my Nikon 35mm camera body to the back, using its own focal plane shutter and restoring the moderate telephoto effect of the 260mm lens, while still being able to exploit the large-format camera movements. It meant measuring exposure manually using a handheld lightmeter, setting the aperture on the Schneider lens but the shutter speed on the Nikon, and bracketing like crazy to allow for bellows extension. But it worked!

Sometimes I have tried portable hides on the intertidal mudflats to get close to different species, such as curlew, gray plover and bar-tailed godwit. This demands exceptionally good local knowledge of tides and potentially dangerous creeks, and even then it's a very unpredictable affair; one day you are left stranded high and dry with the roosting birds a long way off, the next you get thoroughly

soaked. Variations to this technique involve mounting a hide onto an inflatable dinghy, or making a rigid, portable hide that you can pick up and carry with you as the tide laps around your feet. Either way it's a messy business, and bound to be time-consuming.

Often, a more straightforward approach has produced very worthwhile results. Some roosts I have been able to stalk by crawling through sand dunes and lying in wait overlooking a sandbar as the tide pushes the flocks closer and closer. The more populated beaches of the holiday resorts can be excellent for photography, as the birds tend to be habituated to people and allow a close approach. At high tide, I have often found small groups of sanderling and turnstone tucked up asleep on the beach, or using the breakwaters, and been able to crawl up within telephoto range, to the amusement of passersby. There are also several nature reserves along this coast with excellent public viewing hides which, if you time your visit right, give fantastic photo opportunities of wader roost flocks. Even standing on the shore at choice vantage points can give great views of large flocks of waders wheeling over the mudflats, and streaming low over your head as they fly into the roost. These venues tend to be well publicized, often with guided walks for those less familiar with the area.

Remote control
These summer-plumaged dunlin were photographed by means of a remote-controlled camera in aperture priority automatic metering mode. The wide-angle lens shows a somewhat unusual perspective, with a more spaced-out flock than was apparent from the hide.
Camera: *Nikon F3 with MD-4 motordrive*
Lens: *28mm f2.8*
Film: *Kodachrome 200*
Exposure: *Approximately 1/250 sec. at f8*

Camera movements
These knot and dunlin were photographed using the Linhof/Nikon hybrid with a 260mm Schneider Tele-arton lens. The Scheimpflug Principle accounts for the overall sharp focus through the flock.
Film: *Fujichrome Sensia 100*

The seabirds
A life on the ocean wave

Manx shearwater
Calm sea conditions and a small yacht allowed a reasonably close approach to this Manx shearwater southwest of Ireland.
Camera: *Nikon F4S*
Lens: *300mm f2.8 manual focus plus 1.4x teleconverter*
Film: *Kodachrome 200*

Photographing seabirds at their breeding colonies on land is certainly the easiest way, but doesn't seem to fairly represent their typical habitat and behavior – they're only ashore for a few weeks each year, and they still feed at sea even then. The alternatives are not straightforward or simple, however. Where do you start to look when you have a whole ocean to search? Suggestions follow based on a few of the sea trips I have made. If you are susceptible to seasickness you may as well forget it!

Some seabirds like kittiwakes and gannets are in the habit of following ships, so there can be opportunities to photograph them in flight from scheduled ferries. The Bay of Biscay ferry routes from Portsmouth to Bilbao and Plymouth to Santander in northern Spain have recently become very popular among birders and cetacean watchers in the late summer, offering good views of great and Cory's shearwaters and even a few little shearwaters, though you are a long way above the sea surface so photography conditions are far from ideal. The Irish Sea and Hebridean island passages can also afford reasonably close views of rafts of manx shearwaters, and these ferries tend to be smaller. The English Channel and North Sea are pretty barren in my experience, but no doubt there are many other profitable routes around the world. To be realistic, most of the time it's difficult to get a decent image size even using 500mm or 600mm lenses with teleconverters.

We have talked about the possibilities of baiting some kinds of seabirds, such as petrels and shearwaters, with "chum." There are organized pelagic trips for the benefit of birdwatchers, which reliably turn up great numbers and varieties of seabirds, and those off South Africa in particular are known to be excellent. But you will probably struggle to

move about the boat and get to a good position for photography on such trips, as they tend to pack in as many fare-paying passengers as possible. It is better by far to charter a yacht or game-fishing boat for the specific purpose of photography, and keep the numbers of passengers down to a minimum. This won't be cheap, and you might struggle to find a captain with the necessary experience and the flexibility to put to sea at a time that suits you and the weather.

Once I was lucky enough to be able to join a yacht sailing out of Baltimore in County Cork, Ireland, past Cape Clear and out to the edge of the Continental Shelf. Here we looked for commercial fishing vessels, which generally attract good numbers of birds when they are hauling nets, and tried to get close to them. Standing more or less at sea level meant that it was difficult to see anything too far away, but the fishing boats were detectable on the yacht's radar, and sometimes we were aware of the presence of fish shoals because of large flocks of gannets circling overhead and associated breaching dolphins. Fortunately the sea conditions were very calm, and this meant we could get quite close to manx shearwaters on the sea surface, which were reluctant to take flight. We tried using chum as well, but on this occasion it wasn't particularly effective – a few storm petrels came to investigate, but quite tentatively, and we concluded they must have been finding plenty of food elsewhere. The low position was good for photography, but of course small boats are not very stable so you feel every bit of swell. I was able to use a 300mm lens with 1.4x and 2x teleconverters, sometimes hand-held, sometimes supported on a monopod to relieve my wrists and arms. Obviously, tripods are totally worthless on a small boat.

On another occasion, I joined the Scottish Fisheries Protection Vessel *Sulisker* as she left Leith Docks, Edinburgh, on a ten-day voyage. I was mainly interested in the fishing activities of the Danish sand-eel trawlers operating around the mouth of the Firth of Forth, and wanted to obtain photographs. While the fishery is entirely legal, there are concerns about its effects on the food chain. Sand eels are the staple diet of

many seabirds, as well as other fish, and their commercial harvesting has been suspected as a possible cause of population crashes of arctic terns in the Orkney and Shetland Islands during the 1980s. Up to 20 trawlers were fishing here in the Firth of Forth this particular June, each capable of removing 800 or 900 metric tons of sand eels every few days. You can't help but wonder if this is really sustainable.

After only two hours' steaming, we reached the fishing fleet just as night fell, so photography was out of the question. Early next morning we could see several trawlers around us towing their nets in different directions, and we would follow them in turn. At intervals during the day, a crew of Fisheries Protection Officers would embark on their launch to board a trawler and investigate its catch. It was always "clean," meaning there were no appreciable numbers of any other fish species in the hold. I was able to board only one trawler as most of the time the sea swell was too high to risk passengers, so for the rest of the time I watched and photographed from the *Sulisker*. It would take several hours of towing before a trawler's nets were hauled to the surface, but this was the time to be alongside – as the bulging nets came to the surface, large flocks of plunge-diving gannets

would congregate around the trawler, pouncing on fish that spilled from the net. Scavenging great and arctic skuas joined in, sometimes chasing a gannet to make it regurgitate its meal. The ideal place to be taking photographs would have been from on board the trawler itself, as the gannets continued to feed very close in. As soon as the nets came too close to the ship, flocks of kittiwakes replaced the gannets, swooping on smaller fish and items that fell from the net right alongside the hull. For a few minutes the area was thick with seabirds, but they disappeared as quickly as they came once trawling resumed. I used both 500mm telephoto and 80–200mm zoom lenses on separate camera bodies, with the longer lens suported on a monopod.

I'm still trying to figure out a way to get close to winter-plumaged auks such as puffins and guillemots at sea. It seems as though you could spend the rest of your life afloat and not achieve it.

Plunging for fish

Gannets dive all around this Danish trawler as its nets are hauled to the surface.
Camera: *Nikon F5*
Lens: *80–200mm f2.8*
Film: *Fujichrome Provia 100*

Great shearwater

This was photographed from the Pride of Bilbao passenger ferry in the Bay of Biscay.
Camera: *Nikon F5*
Lens: *AF-S 500mm f4 plus 1.4x teleconverter*
Film: *Fujichrome Sensia 100 uprated to EI200*

The victims
Robins are a delicacy in Brescia

It has occasionally been my sad duty to report on some of the unpleasant things that happen to birds, as victims of natural disaster, environmental accident and, all too often, human persecution. Now it takes no particular skill or technique to photograph a dead or dying bird, or at least it's not usually a problem to get close to them. But it is distressing, and sometimes dangerous, so you have to be able to work without having to think too hard about what to do next. I'm not recommending this as a fun activity or even a rewarding photographic experience, but if you have the stomach for it you might help to publicize some of the atrocities that do occur, and work to bring about change.

Many Mediterranean countries are known to be death traps for migrant birds, which fall victim to guns, nets and various trapping devices in vast numbers. The illegal spring shooting of honey buzzards in Calabria is well documented, as is bird "liming" in Cyprus, and the shooting and netting of so many birds that happen to pass over Malta. There are many other examples. Some of these places I have visited in an attempt to make a photographic record, but with mixed results. To paraphrase a well-known saying: "If you've seen one dead bird, you've seen them all." To get close to some of the hunters would be to risk physical harm – there is a serious level of hostility to "conservationists" in many of these places. Going equipped with professional camera equipment in the company of known environmentalists would perhaps be asking for trouble. However, as a casual holidaymaker with no obvious political agenda who happens to be carrying a compact camera, you might more easily gain people's confidence.

The other way is to go by appointment, with armed police. One autumn I made a 24-hour visit to Brescia in the north of Italy and kept a rendezvous with a volunteer from the Lega Italiana Protezione Uccelli (LIPU), the Italian BirdLife partner, and some officers of the Corpo Forestale dello Stato (Forest Guard). Over a single morning we scoured a wooded hillside and recovered over 200 illegal *archetto* traps, which are set and baited with ripe berries for the specific purpose of trapping

robins. The *archetto* (or bow) serves as a spring device, which tightens a snare around the bird's legs when it lands on, and displaces, a loosely fitted perch. Six of these traps contained captured robins, some still just about alive, all with their legs broken. They were later put down in a humane way.

The robins are normally sold to local restaurants where they are served as a traditional delicacy. It has to be said that the trappers are mostly quite poor hill farmers who probably struggle to make a living. And it should also be pointed out that there is no evidence whatsoever that such trapping has any effect on the population or conservation status of the robin. Nevertheless, it seems desperately cruel and is definitely unlawful.

Obviously, there was no time to waste. It was important to take my shots quickly and let the LIPU and Corpo Forestale personnel get on with their job. Working with a 35–70mm zoom lens on a Nikon F4S and using a Speedlight SB-24 for fill flash, I simply did what was necessary. It wasn't too difficult to make a subject like this appear shocking. The photographs have not been widely published before, so I thought it was about time they were.

Confiscating traps
A Corpo Forestale officer gathers a number of illegal archetto *traps (top). Rows and rows of* archetti *were found baited with ripe berries (below), some containing recently captured robins.*

(opposite) ***A snared robin***
This robin was close to death when it was found.
Camera*: Nikon F4S*
Lens*: 35–70mm f2.8*
Film*: Kodachrome 64*
Lighting*: SB-24 Speedlight*

Chapter 5
POST-PRODUCTION

The creative process does not end with the pressing of the camera shutter. Much work remains to be done in the areas of quality control and administration, sorting the good images from the bad, and then setting about organizing and caring for them. This is before we can even begin to think of presenting our work to a wider audience.

(previous pages)
Screaming flock of swifts
This was photographed into the light with a hand-held 500mm telephoto, to evoke the mood of a summer evening.

Red kite in sleet shower
It's always worth taking a chance in interesting conditions like this, even if the light might seem inadequate. I got away with this shot, taken at the Gigrin Farm feeding station in mid-Wales, at a shutter speed of about $^1/_{160}$ sec., but several other frames taken at the same time were blurred and consequently rejected in editing.
Camera: *Nikon F5*
Lens: *AF-S 500mm f4*
Film: *Fujichrome Sensia 100 uprated to EI200*

PROCESSING AND EDITING

There is nothing that quite matches the bittersweet feelings of excitement and anxiety as you anticipate the return of your processed films from the lab. By now it's too late to rectify any (well, most) mistakes you may have made, but not too late to learn from them. And the wastebasket is still a powerful tool; you can be judged only by what you choose to show people.

I usually opt for non-process-paid films, and arrange for processing by a trusted, professional lab. I also prefer to collect and deliver films by hand rather than risk them in the mail, but much will depend on where you happen to live. As I don't expect to keep more than half of what I've shot, on average (though the shooting ratio varies enormously depending on the nature of the subject and how ambitious my treatment is), I ask the lab to return films cut and sleeved, but not mounted. There's less risk of damage to film this way, I can choose the kind of mounts I prefer and I don't have to pay for mounts I'm only going to throw away.

Transparency films are best viewed on a daylight-balanced light box, equipped with Philips color 950 fluorescent tubes (formerly GraphicA 47) or their equivalent. For critical assessment of sharpness, you should use a loupe (or "lupe"), which is a kind of hand lens specially designed for the purpose. Even the best of these is somewhat cheaper than most standard camera lenses, so go for top quality. My own favorite is the Schneider Kreuznach 4x Lupe, and this does seem to be the choice of most photographic editors, allowing you to view the full 24 x 36mm image area at the best possible resolution. Higher magnifications certainly show up any defects, but they are more difficult and less comfortable to use, especially over long editing sessions. Although you may wish to enjoy the impact of your slides projected large on to a screen, don't rely on this as a method of assessing sharpness, as projectors tend to flatter.

Be ruthless in the editing process, and reject any images that are poorly exposed, not sharp, or otherwise flawed. This is a difficult task when you have just made a large emotional and financial investment in the image-making process, but try not to kid yourself – if you can detect even the tiniest defect or hint of softness, imagine how it will be magnified in an enlarged print or reproduction. Imagine, too, how somebody more objective than you might view it – not kindly, probably. Sometimes the distance of time helps you to be less subjective and more dispassionate. I find that if I review work at a later date I am more inclined to be strict with it, although there is the danger of building up a backlog of editing work this way. It's a process that never ends – you need to go on editing and consigning yet more rejects to the bin every few months. Films get better, standards get higher (your own and others'), and you will be amazed and embarrassed at what you once thought was acceptable, five or ten years on.

Working with cut film strips inserted in clear-view sleeves, it is a simple matter to view all the images on one film side by side on the light box and mark up the sheets with a chinagraph pencil. I find this the quickest way to deal with a number of raw, unedited films at one time. View with frame numbers and manufacturers' film codes the right way round so that the film emulsion is facing downwards and images are in the correct orientation, and examine closely any potential "keepers" through the loupe. On the outer protective sleeve cross out the rejects or check off those you wish to keep with the chinagraph pencil. Cut the film strips carefully with sharp scissors, ideally while wearing cotton film-handling gloves, and finally separate out those frames that are destined for mounting.

There are various mounting presses on the market for different types of slide mount, with varying degrees of automation. I generally use Gepe metal mask, 2mm plastic mounts, which hold the film securely, pick up easily off the light box and don't jam in projectors. The gray surface should be on the bottom with the white surface uppermost. Gepe provides special plastic tweezers for picking up the film by the rebate sprocket holes and flexing to slot under lugs in the metal mask. The two halves of the mount simply lock together in the press through a system of interlocking ridges and furrows. Other designs of plastic mount are hinged or preglued, or designed for roller transport machines. Cardboard mounts are cheaper and easier to write on, but give fuzzy edges to your pictures and tend to fray and come apart.

With machine-mounted slides from the lab, you don't have the hassle of cutting and mounting film yourself, but beware the modern, ultra-thin mounts, which snarl up in many projectors. Frame-edge sensors in the mounting machine can be fooled sometimes if you have reloaded a partially exposed film, resulting in cuts occurring out of sequence (through the image instead of between frames).

Don't use glass slide mounts for your originals. They are prone to condensation spots, film sticking to glass or scorching, optical aberrations such as Newton's rings, and glass shattering in transit causing irreparable damage. The only thing they are good for is preventing slides from "popping" out of focus as they heat up when projected. So, fine for duplicates and computer-generated text slides (in which case use anti-Newton, or AN, glass mounts), but not for everyday use.

STORAGE AND CONSERVATION

Once mounted, your transparencies need to be filed and protected. There are various ring binders, box files and cabinets designed for the purpose, but the hanging files that store in standard office filing drawers are the most compact, universal system. These hanging files generally hold twenty-four 35mm mounted transparencies in pockets, and suspend from metal bars.

Ideal storage and archival conditions would be dry, dark and cool. A normal filing cabinet in a modern house or office would most likely qualify on the first two counts, but since "cool" is quite impractical for comfortable living, most of us compromise on that one. If you do live in a part of the world with very high humidity, you might be well advised to install a dehumidifier in the room to avoid the risk of fungus attacking your film. Otherwise there's no need to make any major modifications to your home. One thing to avoid is the vapor from volatile plastics and resins near your transparencies, so it's best to use storage files made of an inert material like polypropylene or polyester, rather than PVC, and store them in metal cabinets. Keep the drawers closed when not in use, and don't leave transparencies out in the light more than you need, to prevent colors from fading. Repeated projection will also lead to rapid deterioration of color pigments, so keep your best originals pristine, and project duplicates whenever possible.

I like to have the additional protection of 50mm square clear polyester slips (such as Secol "Tecs"), which help to keep out dust and guard against fingerprints when handling the transparencies. These slip over the mounted transparency before it is inserted in the hanging file – keep the open edges perpendicular to the file pocket opening for best protection and ease of insertion.

It shouldn't be necessary to clean your transparencies if you've been handling and storing them carefully until now, but if they have been in projector magazines or left out unprotected, they may require occasional dusting. Don't blow on transparencies to remove dust, as droplets of saliva will stain the

Sanderlings roosting
You might expect a better keep rate for shots of stationary subjects.
Camera: *Nikon F4S*
Lens: *500mm f4*
Film: *Kodachrome 64*

film. A clean blower brush (kept specially for slides) or anti-static brush will normally do the trick. Clean air duster in aerosol cans is a more powerful way to remove stubborn dust particles, but be careful always to use these in the upright position otherwise the propellant may be dispensed in liquid form, and this too causes stains on film. For more serious stains, surface marks or fingerprints, there are proprietary solvent cleaners on the market such as Aspec film cleaner from Pro-Co. Apply gently with a lint-free cotton cloth, or a cotton bud, and then polish clean. These solvents generally work on the residues of lacquer you sometimes find on transparencies returned by publishers after drum scanning. Of course they should clean them first, but they don't always oblige. On a few rare occasions, I have found residues that don't respond to the organic solvents available to me, but have been able to remove them by rewashing the film in water with a drop of Kodak Photo-Flo solution. Be very, very careful if you do this, as the film emulsion becomes soft and incredibly fragile, and the most innocuous contact can leave a nasty gash – definitely a last resort.

I've talked about the desirability of having duplicates in a number of circumstances. Duplicating transparencies inevitably leads to some loss of quality, but this may be hardly noticeable when the better copies are projected. Unfortunately the quality of duplicates is enormously variable, so what should you look out for? To begin with, I would strongly advise against the home copying outfits, which comprise little more than a bellows and daylight diffuser, intended for use with regular daylight-balanced transparency film. Results from such set-ups are always disappointing, exhibiting unacceptably high contrast and unwelcome color shifts. For a reasonable quality duplicate you should be using a tungsten light source with appropriate color filtration, batch-tested duplicating film stock such as Fujichrome CDUII, and a specialist 1:1 copying lens on a copystand or rostrum camera. With luck, this is what you will get from a lab advertising reproduction-quality duplicates, but even that isn't guaranteed, so check the results carefully,

comparing against the original for sharpness and a good color match. The best examples should make fine projection duplicates. For genuine reproduction-quality copies, you need high-resolution (A.C.T.) duplicates where the film to be copied is immersed in oil (minimizing light refraction) and then lit by collimated, stroboscopic illumination (separate red, green and blue light exposures) for maximum sharpness. This is the duplicating system preferred by most wildlife photo agencies, and it delivers copies almost indistinguishable from the original. It can even eradicate finer surface scratches and adjust for minor underexposure.

Some photographers (mainly professionals) like to have enlarged duplicates made of their prized shots, usually on 70mm film. While these can look impressive on the light box, they don't usually stand scrutiny under a loupe, because of the enlargement that has already taken place. Some editors and picture researchers understand this and allow for the fact, but all too often they don't, and reject the shot without asking further questions. Besides, a 70mm transparency is an unambiguous signal to the editor that they are looking at a duplicate, whereas a high-resolution 35mm duplicate could be taken for an original, so they might well be inclined to go with the latter. For this reason I tend to think of the 70mm duplicates as a waste of money, and prefer to supply high-resolution 35mm duplicates to clients where necessary.

ORGANIZING A PHOTOGRAPHIC COLLECTION

Sooner or later you will have to bring some sort of order and system to your collection of transparencies, or else you'll never find anything. There is no right or wrong way to do this, but you would be wise to establish some sort of filing discipline early on. If we're just talking about photographs of bird subjects for the moment, it would make sense to categorize them in the same order as the systematic list you would find in a field guide – it might take some getting used to if you're new to birding and bird photography, but at least all of the related species can then be found close together. Picture request lists often follow this taxonomic convention, too. Alphabetical order might seem logical but leads to all sorts of complications; you could use the convention of "warbler, willow" and "warbler, wood" in an attempt to keep related species close together, but then what would you do with "blackcap" and "chiffchaff" (also warblers)? On the other hand, you might prefer to file subjects geographically, in line with your various photographic expeditions. It's a matter of individual choice how you do it, but try to think through how your system will work when you have amassed thousands of transparencies. One hanging file might do for one species, or even one family at an early stage in your collection. As the file for each species grows, it's a good idea to subdivide, perhaps by sex, plumage, or behavior, so that each subject never has more than a few hanging files devoted to it. With hanging files in drawers, it is relatively easy to in-fill. Other filing systems might require major upheavals as the subject files multiply, so consider this at the outset.

Once you have a filing system up and running, it doesn't matter too much if you don't label all the individual transparencies straight away, but do file them in the appropriate subject areas so that at least you will know where to look. If you are well organized and neat minded, you might well want to caption and label all your new work at the time of editing. You will have more chance of remembering all the relevant details at this stage, and it's easier to run off many similar labels with slide-labeling software applications such as Cradoc Caption Writer. These computer labeling systems are great for printing out professional-looking slide labels, and make most efficient use of the small area of mount available to describe the image. Alternatively, use fine-tipped permanent markers (such as OHP pens) for writing on plastic slide mounts. Caption with both the colloquial and scientific name if you are likely to submit the slides to publishers or other users (the scientific name will be understood anywhere in the world and avoids conflicts between American-English and British-English bird names). Furthermore, if you

***Brent geese at Leigh-on-Sea**
Would you file this photograph under "brent goose," "brent geese" or possibly even "goose, brent"? On the other hand, might it be categorized by habitat or location? In which case, is it E for estuary, M for mudflats, S for saltmarsh, L for Leigh or T for Thames? If this bothers you, you might wish to consider keywording your collection.*
Camera: *Nikon F5*
Lens: *AF-S 500mm f4*

are sending out your slides it would also be a good idea to give each image a unique serial number to enable you to identify it in any communication. Don't forget to add a name and address label to identify yourself as the photographer – some people have these commercially printed in bulk.

Much as I aspire to be this well organized, I usually end up numbering and captioning transparencies only at the point when I send them out on loan. This does have the advantage that I don't waste time on labeling images that nobody ever asks to see. (They might even succumb to the next edit, making sure I never have to label them!) Then I just allocate a sequential number in the computer labeling program as each image comes to the top of the pile, regardless of subject category. At the end of each session, I save each update to my text database, and export the update to a report template, ready to print out as a delivery note. If I need to inquire about a specific transparency at a later date, I can easily search by number, subject name or any other criterion.

Remember that these search engines are entirely rational, so it pays to be consistent with your nomenclature if you expect to search your files this way. For example, you could resolve always to use the singular description "brent goose" in your naming system, since the search engine wouldn't understand that "brent geese" is actually the same thing. It's tempting to believe that a text database can provide you with the perfect cross-referencing system, allowing you to trawl across the species boundaries for attributes such as habitat, season, color, or even abstract concepts like "beauty" or "aggression." Such systems are incredibly time-consuming to set up and maintain, requiring you to establish lists of approved keywords and synonyms for efficient operation, as well as spending an age thinking about the caption for each new image. If you're only filing your own work, then I would suggest that your own memory is likely to be quicker, more reliable, and certainly more flexible.

As well as having duplicates made, you might also want to archive your best images as digital files. In this case, original transparencies and negatives will need to be scanned and the resulting files saved to a data disk such as CD or DVD-RAM (probably the two most stable storage media) because your computer hard disk will soon run out of storage space. The typical desktop flatbed scanner is not good enough for this task, even if it boasts a special "film adapter." You really need a dedicated film scanner such as the Nikon Coolscan, Polaroid Sprintscan, Minolta Dimage or similar if you want to scan transparencies to a reasonable quality. With a scanning resolution of 2,700 ppi (pixels per inch), my Nikon LS-2000 scanner delivers a maximum file size of about 25MB from a 35mm transparency, which is good enough for most printing and publishing purposes. The dynamic range of the scanner is also an important consideration, determining how well it renders tonal detail. A dynamic range of 3.5 or above and 36-bit sampling would indicate a good-quality film scanner, capable of recording subtle tonal differences, especially in the shadows. Investigate the scanner software before you buy – some applications are most unfriendly, and don't seem to be written with photographers in mind. Some offer automatic dust and scratch filtration, which spares you from long and arduous retouching sessions later. There are also bureaus that offer scanning services. Kodak Photo CD is the budget solution, but not renowned for its ability to handle film contrast. For the very best results, order a drum scan.

In theory, once you have a digital file you should be able to derive perfect, lossless copies ever after. However, sometimes files do become corrupted during transfer and the long-term stability of CDs has come into question, so it would be a sensible precaution to make back-up disks, and to keep backing up on a regular basis. Even if the medium remains perfectly stable, there may not be machines available to read CDs and DVD-RAMs in future, so you could find that you will have to copy all of these files on to some new medium eventually.

So now you have an archive of digital image files to worry about, too. As with slides in filing cabinets, a few CDs on the shelf holding perhaps 20 or 30 high-resolution images on each isn't too difficult to deal with. But as this collection grows you will need more than just a few scribbled titles on the cover sheet. An image database is the answer. To do this with high-resolution images would take too much space and be too slow, so an image database works with small, low-resolution image files or "thumbnails" instead. These can be stored right on your computer hard drive. There are a number of image database applications on the market, some of the better-known ones being Extensis Portfolio, Canto Cumulus, amd Image AXS. Use a **relational** database package so that when records require updating – say when a bird's scientific name is revised – you only have to do this once, not for each individual record. The image database should contain captions, unique image reference numbers and all other relevant text data, linked to the image, and include a reference to the location of the high-resolution file. It should be easily searchable, and allow you to sort the images by different criteria with the facility to display the thumbnail shortlist on a "light box." If you are already shooting on digital, you will need to establish a system like this pretty quickly. If not, then you had best start preparing for it.

PRESENTING AND PROMOTING YOUR WORK

You would be a rare photographer if you didn't want to show off your work a bit. Whether it's passing around a few prints to friends or mounting an exhibition at a prestigious gallery, we all like to share our photographs with others, and hope to receive some positive feedback. For many, the ultimate goal is to see their work published in print. Fortunately, there are more ways than ever before to disseminate photographic images.

The slide show is the traditional way to display transparencies to an audience, projecting the images on to a large screen in a darkened room. This format comes in for a lot of criticism and disparaging remarks these days, and indeed we can all think of tedious slide presentations we have had the misfortune to

attend. Still, it remains the best way to show a fine transparency in all its glory. Digital projection systems may have much greater impact when viewed on a computer monitor with some great fades and cuts, but they display to a fairly low resolution (typically 72ppi) and images appear pretty dim when projected large, so at present they are best suited to small gatherings of people. A thoughtful slide presentation of stunning bird images supported by an interesting and informative commentary takes some beating.

Bird clubs and camera clubs are always on the lookout for new speakers, and are often willing to pay a fee, so if you have the skills, you might find yourself in demand. It gets easier with practice. Maybe you could give free, illustrated lectures to local groups or schools initially, to gain confidence.

The Kodak Carousel (now Ektapro) is the workhorse of slide projectors, with its solid construction and universal, rotary slide tray. Leitz, Zeiss and Rollei also make good projectors with excellent lenses, but perhaps these are not quite so robust and dependable. Autofocus is a great asset on a projector so that you don't have to keep adjusting the focus control, especially when projecting slides in glassless mounts. An extended remote-control cord, or infrared handset will allow you to advance the slides without turning your back

Brown pelicans diving for fish
No post-production trick, digital composite or slide "sandwich" here – these pelicans really do synchronize their dives in this way. Since the left-hand bird is a bit tight to the edge of the frame, I might consider cropping a little from the right to balance it up in a presentation print.
Camera: Nikon F5
Lens: AF-S 300mm f2.8
Film: Fujichrome Sensia 100

on the audience. Normally a projector lens of about 150mm is appropriate for an average-sized hall, with a screen 2 to 3m (7 to 10ft) wide. Remember to take along spare projector bulbs, spare fuses and a power extension cord on all your lecture engagements.

When preparing slides for projection it is customary to "spot" the slide mounts, to aid loading in magazines. View the slide from the

Avocet in flight
Action shots are more likely to be in demand with magazine and picture library editors.
Camera: *Nikon F5*
Lens: *AF-S 500mm f4*
Film: *Fujichrome Sensia 100*

front with the image the right way round, and place the spot at the bottom left corner of the slide mount. This way, you know that if you hold the slide with the spot under your right thumb as you drop it into the slide tray, it will be loaded correctly. If you have a regular slide set for a particular talk, which doesn't vary, it's not a bad idea to have the whole lot duplicated and glass-mounted. The glass mounts will help to keep the slides in focus from edge to edge, but you must remember to dry out the slides before each presentation, or else distracting water marks appear as condensation between the glass warms up in front of the projector bulb. There are purpose-built drying cabinets for this, or you can just leave the slide tray on top of a low radiator for a couple of hours (remember we are talking about duplicates). On no account leave slide trays loaded with glass-mounted slides in a car on a cold night – it's asking for trouble with condensation. One other advantage of glass

mounts is that you can get various metal mask inserts of different aperture proportions (other than the standard 24 x 36mm), for critical reframing of images. These are useful for cropping out any distracting elements you wish you'd seen or been able to exclude when you took the photograph. Don't use these too often, or it will look as though you can't frame a photograph in camera.

Prints are a more convenient way of showing photographs, since you don't need any special equipment and can view them in normal light. To obtain the best conventional photographic prints from transparencies, order "reversal" prints, where the print is made directly from the slide without the use of an internegative. The best known of these is the Ilfochrome (formerly Cibachrome), and this is generally reckoned to be the most archivally safe form of color print, but there are other brands that are a good match, and often cheaper.

Fewer and fewer photographers have their own darkroom these days, and indeed it's probably not the time to be starting one up, unless you are passionate about silver halide prints and chemical toning. The digital print has come of age. There are various ways of printing out digital image files, commonly through laser, wax thermal and inkjet printers. The latter is the most widespread printing method in the home environment, and the modern inksets and premium papers can produce quite stunning quality prints from high-resolution scans, to rival the best Ilfochromes. Image-processing software such as Adobe Photoshop enbles you to make fine adjustments, so that in some ways you have more control over the finished print than you ever could over a conventional lab print. It is also more convenient, more economical, and involves much less risk to your original transparency. On the downside, inkjet prints are slow to output, and there is still a lot of doubt about their long-term stability, with some users experiencing color shifts and fading after just a few weeks. No doubt great research and development efforts are going into rectifying this, but I'm already sold on the virtues of inkjet prints. For the best of both worlds, send your own digital file to a bureau for them to output as a Kodak CRT or Kodak LED print, Cymbolic Science Lightjet, or Durst Lambda (for larger sizes) print, all of which utilize traditional photochemistry and should therefore last as long as conventional prints. Fuji Pictrographs are also very interesting, high-quality digital prints available through some bureaus, but they employ a unique type of chemistry that may not have the same archival stability.

For portfolios, the presentation of prints of any description can be much improved by dry-mounting them on card. Window mounts with mat cut-outs also do much to enhance a fine print. Framing under glass will further prolong print life, and it's always worth having this done professionally, especially if you plan to exhibit or sell. Galleries might be disinclined to take the risk with an "unknown" photographer, and in any case they would take a hefty commission on print sales, but there are countless restaurants, hotels, banks, libraries, visitor centers and so forth that might be pleased to host a display of your work for nothing, and allow you the opportunity to sell off the wall. If your photography and pricing structure do find a ready market, the craft fairs beckon!

There are other ways of achieving wider recognition for your work, not least through participating in photographic competitions. These might be organized by a local camera club or town show, promoted by a magazine (not only photographic magazines), or be internationally recognized events like the BG Wildlife Photographer of the Year. The BG competition is well established and influential, attracting thousands of amateur and professional photographers from all over the world, so it might not be the easiest place to make an impact. However, its touring exhibition and the published portfolio reach huge audiences, so it's got to be worth having a go. Many camera clubs are also active on the international competition scene. Don't overlook the smaller and more obscure competitions where you might have a more realistic hope of being a big fish in a small pond.

Commissioned assignments for wildlife photographers are a very rare phenomenon.

Nobody wants to pay by the day, as the risk of failure is simply too great. Instead, the publishing industry is served by specialist photo agencies (and increasingly by clip-art or copyright-free providers), who keep a wide range of stock photographs. The agents represent the work of a number of photographers, retaining a proportion of their best originals and selling reproduction rights for specified uses, for an agreed license fee. For this service the agent takes a commission, usually about 50 percent, and the photographer receives a sales statement at regular intervals. Most importantly, the photographer retains copyright and ownership of his or her work, and can recover it at any time, subject to the terms of the contract. It is the agents who have the established client base and network of contacts, a knowledge of market prices, and are generally in the best position to give a quick, professional service. Whether photographs are used in a book, on a T-shirt, or as part of a global advertising campaign, the agent will know how to supply and how much to ask. Therefore, bird photographers who aspire to selling their work to publishers generally look for an agency to take them on.

Agents' names can be found in books and magazines in the credits accompanying photographs; they usually follow the photographer's name but sometimes replace it altogether. Alternatively, ask their representative organizations BAPLA (British Association of Picture Libraries and Agencies), CEPIC (Co-ordination of European Picture Agencies Press and Stock) or PACA (Picture Agency Council of America) to supply you with a list of members. You may have to pay for a printed directory, so don't overlook the internet as a source of this information. It is a very competitive field and a bit of a buyer's market, so breaking into it is not a straightforward proposition. By and large, agencies will want photographers who can consistently supply good work in volume. As a guideline, the first submission is usually expected to be some hundreds of transparencies, which will be edited rigorously if accepted for consideration. Don't be surprised if you are told they don't have any openings for more bird photographers –

151

photographs of mammals are more often requested than those of birds, and pets are the most saleable subjects in the animal world. If you do get past this first hurdle and are invited to submit a portfolio, do ensure that the transparencies are neatly and accurately labeled, and well presented in see-through wallets. Nothing is more guaranteed to irritate a picture researcher or editor than a mass of loose slides in boxes. You will further enhance your chances if you show you can edit properly – don't be tempted to make up the numbers with a few "very nearly sharp" photographs as these will fool nobody and suggest that you can't tell the difference. Above all, keep trying. If you are convinced that your own photographs are at least as good as many you see in print, then somebody somewhere must want them, and be prepared to pay. Recently established agencies will be more inclined to take on new photographers. The copyright-free collections tend to be less selective, and usually offer only a one-time payment, which might make for poorer returns over the long term.

Although competition is increasing all the time, so are the number of outlets for published photography. In recent times the desktop publishing revolution has resulted in a proliferation of new magazines, club newsletters and company reports, all of which demand good-quality photographs even though they don't all expect to pay for them. There are also many new "pursuit" magazines targeted at particular hobbies, and these often welcome photographic contributions, with some making special provision for readers' portfolios and paying modest fees. If you can write well, you might try to present a complete package of article and pictures to maximize your chances of success. Again, good presentation is crucial to getting noticed. If you are sending original transparencies, check first that the intended client is happy to receive them (especially if you are dealing with a busy weekly publication or daily newspaper), as you might not get them back otherwise. You could of course submit good-quality duplicates. Sending a selection of scanned images with captions and any other accompanying text on CD is a good idea, but if you do this supply a hard copy of one or two photographs to tempt the editor to look a little deeper. Inkjet prints are good for this purpose. If they reject your proposal or don't even get around to looking at it, at least you haven't lost much in the process. Expect rejection and even lack of acknowledgment from time to time, but don't let this deter you – persistence pays off in the end, assuming your work is of a sufficiently high standard.

Once you are known to a particular publisher or editor, you might supply scanned photographs as e-mail attachments, but don't send these unsolicited as the large files can jam up some networks, and this is not likely to endear you to the company. Low-resolution previews can be saved to 72ppi (monitor resolution) and transmitted in the j-peg file format (minimum compression) to keep the file size down but maintain reasonable image quality. You can even supply high-resolution image files in this way if asked, but let your client stipulate just how files should be supplied to suit their requirements. Some are happy to work with straightforward RGB files, but high-quality publications are more likely to demand press-ready CMYK separations, and this demands some in-depth knowledge of color management, so don't bluff.

Electronic, online publishing is also an obvious growth area. Copyright does extend to photographs published on the World Wide Web, but can be more difficult to enforce. If somebody wants to use one of your photographs in their own web site or online publication, you are entitled to ask for a fee. And of course, you can create your own web site to display and promote your photography. This a great way of exhibiting a "virtual portfolio" of images to which you can refer interested parties and potential clients – but don't expect the world to beat a path to your door. While it is the perfect opportunity to self-publish, remember that there are an awful lot of people doing something similar. Web-authoring packages are readily available from a number of software houses, some of which include design templates for standard sites. Engaging a professional web designer is certain

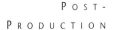

Atlantic puffin
*Birds with strong, easily
recognizable shapes like this
puffin tend to work quite well
in silhouette.*
Camera: *Nikon F4S*
Lens: *500mm f4*
Film: *Fujichrome Sensia 100*

to result in a more distinguished-looking site, for a price. Photographs need to open quickly, so file sizes are normally kept quite small – again, working to the monitor resolution of 72ppi, save as j-peg or gif file formats, and aim for final file sizes under about 50KB. This also makes your photographs more secure against copyright theft. Although they can easily be lifted and used on another web site, at this size they won't really be good enough to reproduce in print. For additional security, you can add visible and invisible watermarks to your photographs – the latter require that you subscribe to a "policing" service, so that for an annual fee the service provider will search for and notify you of any unauthorized uses of your photographs. Some invisible watermarks purport to be detectable even after they have been copied or printed. All of these systems can be overcome with sufficient determination – you can just hope to make an adequate deterrent.

In conclusion, just make sure that you don't let the 'office' interfere too much with your fieldwork, and remember what motivated you in the first place.

I wish you success, and hope that you will derive as much pleasure from photographing wild birds as I have.

Appendix I

The Nature Photographer's Code of Practice

These excellent guidelines were first drafted in the 1960s by the British nature photographer Derek Turner-Ettlinger, and were later adopted and revised by the Nature Group of the Royal Photographic Society, and endorsed by the Royal Society for the Protection of Birds and the British government's statutory conservation agencies. The principles apply anywhere in the world, and it is my pleasure (duty, no less) to reproduce the sections pertaining to bird photography in the hope of promoting their wider observance.

Introduction

There is one hard and fast rule, whose spirit must be observed at all times. The welfare of the subject is more important than the photograph.

This is not to say that photography should not be undertaken because of a slight risk to a common species. The amount of risk acceptable decreases with the scarceness of the species, and the photographer should do his utmost to minimize it.

Risk to the subject, in this context, means risk of physical damage, causing anxiety, consequential predation, or lessened reproductive success.

The Law as it affects nature photography must be observed. One should find out in advance any restrictions that apply. Apparently lax (or absence of) local legislation should not lead photographers to relax their own high standard.

General

The photographer should be familiar with the natural history of the subject; the more complex the life form and the rarer the species, the greater his knowledge must be. He should also be sufficiently familiar with other natural history subjects to be able to avoid damaging their interests accidentally. Photography of uncommon animals and plants by people who know nothing of the hazards to species and site is to be deplored.

For many subjects some "gardening" (i.e., interference with the surrounding vegetation) may be necessary to tidy the habitat, or move obscuring vegetation. This should be kept to a minimum to avoid exposing the subject to predators, people, or weather. Plants or branches should be tied back rather than cut

off, and the site should be restored to as natural a condition as possible after each photographic session. The photographer should always aim to leave no obvious sign of his visit. If the photograph of a rarity is to be published or exhibited, care should be taken that the site location is not accidentally given away. Sites of rarities should never deliberately be disclosed except for conservation purposes.

It is important for the good name of nature photography that its practitioners observe normal social courtesies. Permission should be obtained before working on private land and other naturalists should not be incommoded. Work at sites and colonies that are subjects of special study should be coordinated with the people concerned.

Photographs of dead, stuffed, homebred, captive, cultivated, or otherwise controlled specimens may be of genuine value but should never be passed off as wild and free. Users of such photographs (irrespective of the purpose it is thought that they will be used for) should always be informed, however unlikely it may seem that they care.

Birds at the nest

The terms of the Wildlife and Countryside Act must be observed and licenses obtained to photograph Schedule 1 species from the appropriate Statutory Nature Conservation Agency.

It is particularly important that photography of birds at the nest should be undertaken only by those with a good knowledge of bird breeding behavior. There are many otherwise competent photographers (and birdwatchers) who lack this qualification.

It is highly desirable that a scarce species should be photographed only in an area where it is relatively frequent. Many British rarities should, for preference, be photographed in countries overseas where they are commoner. Photographers working abroad should of course act with the same care as they would at home.

A hide should always be used when there is a reasonable doubt that birds would continue normal breeding behavior otherwise. No part of the occupant (e.g. hands adjusting lens-settings, or a silhouette through inadequate material) should be visible from the outside of the hide.

Hides should not be erected at a nest site

where the attention of the public or any predator is likely to be attracted. If there is any risk of this an assistant should be in the vicinity to shepherd away potential intruders. No hide should be left unattended in daylight in a place with common public access.

Tracks to and from any nest should be devious and inconspicuous. As far as possible they (like the 'gardening') should be restored to naturalness between sessions.

Though reported nest failures attributable to nest photography are few, a high proportion of those that occur are due to undue haste. The maximum possible time should elapse between consecutive stages of hide movement (or erection), introduction of lens or flash-gear, gardening and occupation. There are many species that need at least a week's preparation; this should be seen as the norm.

Each stage of preparation should be fully accepted by the bird (or both birds, where feeding or incubation is shared) before the next is initiated. If a stage is refused by the birds (which should be evident from their behavior to a competent bird photographer) the procedure should be reversed at least one stage; if refusal is repeated the attempt at photography should be abandoned.

In some conditions it may be necessary to use a marker in the locality of the nest hole to indicate its occupancy. This type of disturbance should be kept to a minimum.

The period of disturbance caused by each stage should be kept to a minimum. It is undesirable to initiate a stage in late evening, when the birds' activities are becoming less frequent.

Remote-control work where acceptance cannot be checked is rarely satisfactory. Where it involves resetting a shutter, or moving film on manually between exposures it is even less likely to be acceptable because of the frequency of disturbance.

While the best photographs are often obtained about the time of hatch, this is not the time to start erecting a hide – nor when eggs are fresh. It is better to wait till parents' reactions to the situation are firmly established.

There are few species for which a "putter-in" and "getter-out" are not necessary. Two or more may be needed for some species.

The birds' first visits to the nest after the hide is occupied are best used for checking routes and behavior rather than for exposures. The quieter the shutter the less the chance of birds objecting to it. The longer the focal length of the lens used the more distant the hide can be and the less risk of the birds not accepting it.

Changes of photographer in the hide (or any other disturbance) should be kept to a minimum, and should not take place during bad weather (rain or exceptionally hot sun).

Nestlings should never be removed from the nest for posed photography; when they are photographed in situ care should be taken not to cause an "explosion" of young from the nest. It is never permissible to artificially restrict the free movement of the young.

The trapping of breeding birds for studio-type photography is totally unacceptable in any circumstances.

The use of playback tape (to stimulate territorial reactions) and the use of stuffed predators (to stimulate alarm reactions) may need caution in the breeding season, and should not be undertaken near the nest. Additionally the use of bait or song tapes to attract birds to the camera, even though this is away from the nest, should not be undertaken in an occupied breeding territory.

Birds away from the nest

Predators should not be baited from a hide in an area where hides may later be used for photography of birds at the nest. Wait and see photography should not be undertaken in an area where a hide may show irresponsible shooters and trappers that targets exist; this is particularly important overseas. The capture of even nonbreeding birds for photography under controlled conditions is not an acceptable or legal practice. Incidental photography of birds taken under license for some valid scientific purpose is acceptable provided it causes minimal delay in the bird's release. If any extra delay is involved it would need to be covered by the terms of the license.

Published by The Nature Group of The Royal Photographic Society, The Octagon, Milsom Street, Bath BA1 1DN. Tel: 01225 462841.

Appendix II

Principles of Ethical Field Practices

NANPA (North American Nature Photography Association) believes that following these practices promotes the well-being of the location, subject and photographer. Every place, plant, and animal, whether above or below water, is unique, and cumulative impacts occur over time. Therefore, one must always exercise good individual judgment. It is NANPA's belief that these principles will encourage all who participate in the enjoyment of nature to do so in a way that best promotes good stewardship of the resource.

Environmental: knowledge of subject and place

- Learn patterns of animal behavior – know when not to interfere with animals' life cycles.

- Respect the routine needs of animals – remember that others will attempt to photograph them, too.

- Use appropriate lenses to photograph wild animals – if an animal shows stress, move back and use a longer lens.

- Acquaint yourself with the fragility of the ecosystem – stay on trails that are intended to lessen impact.

Social: knowledge of rules and laws

- When appropriate, inform managers or other authorities of your presence and purpose – help minimize cumulative impacts and maintain safety.

- Learn the rules and laws of the location – if minimum distances exist for approaching wildlife, follow them.

- In the absence of management authority, use good judgement – treat the wildlife, plants and places as if you were their guest.

- Prepare yourself and your equipment for unexpected events – avoid exposing yourself and others to preventable mishaps.

Individual: expertise and responsibilities

- Treat others courteously – ask before joining others already shooting in an area.

- Tactfully inform others if you observe them engaging in inappropriate or harmful behavior – many people unknowingly endanger themselves and animals.

- Report inappropriate behavior to proper authorities – don't argue with those who don't care; report them.

- Be a good role model, both as a photographer and a citizen – educate others by your actions; enhance their understanding.

©NANPA (North American Nature Photography Association)

Organizations

American Birding Association
P.O. Box 6599
Colorado Springs, CO 80934
ph: (719) 578-9703
fax: (719) 578-1480
www.americanbirding.org

Cornell Lab of Ornithology
159 Sapsucker Woods Road
Ithaca, NY 14850
ph: (800) 843-BIRD
e-mail: cornellbirds@cornell.edu
birds.cornell.edu

National Audubon Society
700 Broadway
New York, NY 10003
ph: (212) 979-3000
fax: (212) 979-3188
www.audubon.org

National Wildlife Federation
11100 Wildlife Center Drive
Reston, VA 20190-5362
ph: (703) 438-6000
www.nwf.org

North American Nature Photography Association
(NANPA)
10200 West 44th Avenue,
Suite 304
Wheat Ridge, CO 80033-2840
ph: (303) 422-8527
fax: (303) 422-8894
www.nanpa.org

Sierra Club
85 Second Street, 2nd floor
San Francisco, CA 94105-3441
ph: (415) 977-5500
fax: (415) 977-5799
www.sierraclub.org

Useful Publications

Magazines

Birder's World
Kalmbach Publishing Co.
21027 Crossroads Circle
P.O. Box 1612
Waukesha, WI 53187-1612
ph: (262) 796-8776
fax: (262) 798-6468
www.birdersworld.com

Bird Watcher's Digest
P.O. Box 110
Marietta, OH 45750
ph: (800) 879-2473
e-mail: ReadBWD@aol.com
www.petersononline.com/birds/
bwd

Living Bird
Cornell Lab of Ornithology
159 Sapsucker Woods Road
Ithaca, NY 14850
ph: (800) 843-BIRD

National Wildlife
National Wildlife Federation
11100 Wildlife Center Drive
Reston, VA 20190-5362
www.nwf.org/natlwild/

Outdoor Photographer
Werner Publishing Corporation
12121 Wilshire Blvd., 12th floor
Los Angeles, CA 90025-1176
ph: (310) 820-1500
fax: (310) 826-5008
www.outdoorphotographer.com

WildBird
3 Burroughs
Irvine, CA 92618
ph: (949) 855-8822
fax: 949-855-3045

Books

The Art of Bird Photography
by Arthur Morris
(Amphoto Books, 1998)
Thoroughly addresses all aspects
of bird photography, including
environmental/conservation
concerns and proper conduct
for photographers while in the
field. Stunning photographs
and extensive resources,
including listings of bird
photography hot spots
throughout the United States.

Birds (The Field Guide to
Photographing series)
by Allen Rokach and Anne
Millman
(Amphoto Books, 1995)
Includes information on nest
and bird-feeder photography.

Nature Photography Hotspots
by Tim Fitzharris
(Firefly Books, 1997)
Lists hotspots worldwide and
offers information on prevalent
species and best seasons at
each one. Substantial bird
information. Covers sites in
Belize, Canada, Honduras,
Kenya, Mexico, Zimbabwe, and
the United States (including
Alaska).

**The New Complete Guide to
Wildlife Photography**
by Joe McDonald
(Amphoto Books, 1998)
Covers a wide variety of
subjects and all equipment and
techniques extensively.

Bibliography

Benvie, N. *The Art of Nature Photography*, David & Charles, 2000

Campbell, L. *The RSPB Guide to Bird and Nature Photography*, David & Charles, 1990

Cramp, S. et al (eds.) *The Birds of the Western Palearctic*, vols I–IX, Oxford University Press, 1977–1994

Hill, M. and Langsbury, G. *A Field Guide to Photographing Birds in Britain and Western Europe*, Collins, 1987

Langford, M.J. *Basic Photography*, Focal Press, 1965; 5th edition, 1986

Langford, M.J. *Advanced Photography*, Focal Press, 1969; 4th edition, 1980

McDonald, J. *The New Complete Guide to Wildlife Photography*, Amphoto Books, 1992; revised 1998

Morris, A. *The Art of Bird Photography*, Amphoto Books, 1998

Pölking, F. *The Art of Wildlife Photography*, Fountain Press, 1995

Scott, S. (ed.) *Field Guide to the Birds of North America*, National Geographic Society, 1983; 2nd edition, 1987

Shaw, J. *The Nature Photographer's Complete Guide to Professional Field Techniques*, Amphoto Books, 1984

Stroebel, L. *View Camera Technique*, Focal Press, 1967; 4th edition, 1980

Acknowledgments

First and foremost, thanks to my parents for their patience and understanding, and the gift of opportunity.

Per Axel Åkerlund, naturalist, photographer and family friend, inspired me in my youth.

John Horsfall kept me going on those long bike rides to the coast, when all was fresh and there to be learned. We're still learning.

The late Bobby Tulloch was a great companion during my time in Shetland, and I recall our shared photographic excursions with fondness and gratitude.

Sincere thanks to the Royal Society for the Protection of Birds, not just for the hugely important work they do for birds and biodiversity, but also for appointing me to the best "job" in Britain. Nicholas Hammond had faith in me when it counted. I am especially indebted to the many RSPB reserves and conservation staff and their families, too numerous to name, who gave their hospitality, time, knowledge and enthusiasm so willingly over the years. Paul Fisher and Colin Crooke deserve a special mention for their friendship and support, which has always extended well beyond the call of duty. Andy Simpson helped me at a difficult time.

Many, many people have assisted on my various photographic assignments, notably: Gabriel Sierra and Carlos Sanchez, and the Sociedad Española de Ornitología in Spain; Chris Bowden and Mohammed Ribi in Morocco; Steve and Paula Parr in the Seychelles; Signor Perluigi Candela and the Lega Italiana Protezione Uccelli in Italy; Chris Skinner in Norfolk; Tony Cross, Eithel Powell, and Chris Powell in Wales; and Peter Urquhart, Justin Grant, and the Scottish Fisheries Protection Association in Scotland. Thank you all, and to those I have undoubtedly overlooked.

Ian McCarthy and Kirk Mottishead made absolutely brilliant photographic models, and Phil Cottier obliged by taking my portrait for the dustjacket.

Freya Dangerfield, Diana Dummett, Sarah Hoggett and Anna Watson at David & Charles managed to keep me on track, and transformed my efforts into this beautiful book.

I should also like to acknowledge the invaluable contributions of the guest photographers, and express my gratitude for their confidence in this project. Apologies to the many other excellent photographers it wasn't possible to include on this occasion.

John Horsfall, Mike Lane, Bill Thompson III, Roger Tidman and Robin Wynde kindly made helpful comments on the manuscript, and probably saved me some embarrassment. But perhaps not all .... Of course, I accept full responsibility for any factual errors and all opinions expressed.

Finally, none of this would have been possible without the love and support of my wife, Pat, and daughters, Hannah and Alice. I took an outrageous risk with their futures by leaving a perfectly good job and regular salary to pursue a dream. To them, I shall be forever grateful.

Index